The Shifting Grounds of Race

POLITICS AND SOCIETY IN
TWENTIETH-CENTURY AMERICA

SERIES EDITORS

William Chafe, Gary Gerstle, Linda Gordon,
and Julian Zelizer

A list of titles in this series appears at the back of the book

The Shifting Grounds of Race

BLACK AND JAPANESE AMERICANS IN THE
MAKING OF MULTIETHNIC LOS ANGELES

Scott Kurashige

PRINCETON UNIVERSITY PRESS   PRINCETON AND OXFORD

Copyright © 2008 by Princeton University Press

Published by Princeton University Press, 41 William Street, Princeton, New Jersey 08540

In the United Kingdom: Princeton University Press, 3 Market Place, Woodstock, Oxfordshire OX20 1SY

All Rights Reserved

ISBN-13: 978-0-691-12639-5

Library of Congress Control Number: 2007933665

British Library Cataloging-in-Publication Data is available

This book has been composed in Sabon

Printed on acid-free paper ∞

press.princeton.edu

Printed in the United States of America

10 9 8 7 6 5 4 3 2 1

*For my grandmothers, Yasashi Ichikawa
and Kikue Kurashige*

Contents

Illustrations

Tables

The Shifting Grounds of Race

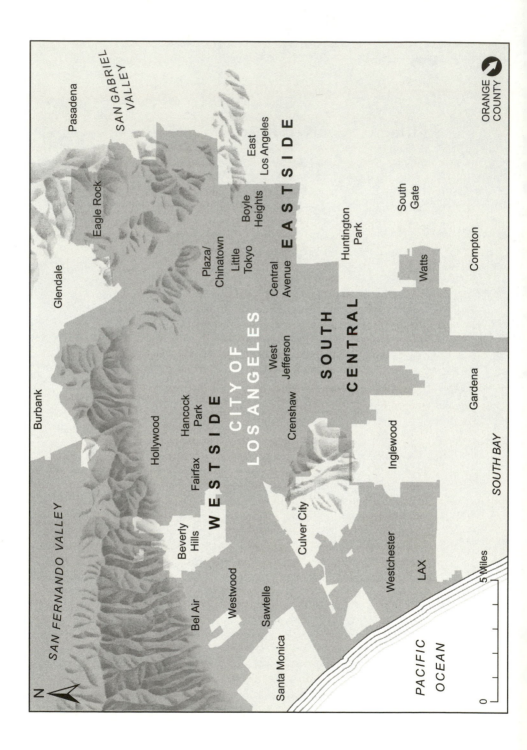

Introduction

IN THE MIDDLE OF 1943, Arthur Miley, an aide to Los Angeles County supervisor John Anson Ford, declared, "From all I heard it appears that Little Tokyo is going to be one big headache." Conditions of squalor in the congested, segregated neighborhood in downtown Los Angeles alarmed public officials, social workers, and ethnic community leaders. Large families routinely occupied storefronts, warehouses, and churches never intended for human habitation. With others living in shacks, garages, and sheds, Miley warned that "permanent occupancy" in such facilities "would lead to juvenile and moral delinquency." Inspectors from the city health department discovered one family living in an apartment so small that a set of twins was forced to sleep in dresser drawers. They later found a family of nine inhabiting one room with a five-foot ceiling and no windows. Fears of a public health catastrophe mounted. The chair of the Little Tokyo Committee of the Council of Social Agencies reported, "Garbage is scattered about and the rats are taking over." Los Angeles mayor Fletcher Bowron vowed to eliminate the neighborhood's "deplorable overcrowding of as many as 16 adults and children in one room and extremely serious disease hazards." Demanding more than "patchwork remedies," the Communist Party's local branch called for "the adoption and enforcement of a public policy" that would "make 'Little Tokyos' impossible." Arthur Miley concluded that officials needed to take action "immediately on a large scale" or risk subjecting the city "to disease, epidemics, race riots and a general breaking down of the home front in this area." But while public officials employed racially loaded language to characterize Little Tokyo, its residents at this time were not Japanese. Following the removal of Japanese Americans from Los Angeles during the early months of World War II, the ethnic enclave had shifted from being the center of the "Japanese problem" to serving as ground zero for the "Negro problem." In May 1944, the *Los Angeles Times* declared that both residential and commercial structures formerly occupied by Japanese Americans were "now overflowing with thousands of Negro families from the Deep South."[1]

The wartime transformation of Little Tokyo into a community that African American entrepreneurs and community leaders dubbed Bronzeville most literally exemplifies the intersection of Black and Japanese American histories in twentieth-century Los Angeles. That African Americans would reside in a space previously carved out by Japanese Americans was no coincidence. Because the city's white elites were preoccupied with building a business-friendly "open shop" town by subduing white labor unions, both Black and Japanese American pioneers arriving before the First World War had initially seen Los Angeles as a site of relative freedom and opportunity. As they simultaneously faced exclusion from segregated white neighborhoods, members of both groups lived in the same geographic niches during the first half of the twentieth century. Although the federal government allowed interned Japanese Americans to return to the West Coast in 1945, the sharp wartime rise in the Black population had overextended these small pockets of unrestricted housing. As the war neared its end, the question of how Little Tokyo's recent arrivals would get along with the district's prewar inhabitants thus became a major source of debate. Prominent white politicians and media outlets predicted violent turf battles between Black and Japanese Americans would erupt. Black and Japanese American activists, by contrast, envisioned a new level of interethnic political cooperation developing from heightened interaction between their communities. Those with only a conventional understanding of "race relations"—characterized by the bilateral interaction between a white majority and a Black minority—were ill-prepared to respond to these developments.

Three issues at the fore of the Little Tokyo/Bronzeville story—the omnipotence of white racism, the specter of interethnic conflict, and the promise of interethnic coalitions—resonate throughout this book. In the pages that follow, I will demonstrate how and why Black and Japanese American communities came to occupy overlapping positions within the racial politics and geography of twentieth-century Los Angeles.

To provide an overarching framework for this investigation, I trace the contours of the city's multiracial hierarchy as it changed from the "white city" of the early twentieth century to the "world city" of the more recent past. Charting the rise of segregation, I posit that racism lay at the core of the 1920s real estate boom that made Los Angeles a major metropolis with a population surpassing 1 million. Although popular conceptions associate suburbanization with post–World War II American culture, the Southland's decentralization took off three decades before the fifties sitcom *Leave It to Beaver* began filming in the San Fernando Valley. Unlike the old downtown elite, who championed industrial Los Angeles as the "Chicago of the West," a rising bloc of developers and realtors drew on an idealized vision of the suburban neighborhood to market Southern California, especially the "Westside," as a site for the preservation and renewal of whiteness. Viewing World War II as a turning point, I highlight the distinct but equally critical roles Black and Japanese Americans played in the rise and fall of integration. The war brought a new sense of unity and difference. As whites and Blacks came together around the notion of "interracial progress," they did so primarily because anti-Japanese mobilization had created a heightened basis for national unity. Nevertheless, the postwar movement for integration brought about a reversal of Black and Japanese American fortunes. Whites increasingly exhibited either a passive or active acceptance of Japanese Americans but took greater measures to distance themselves both socially and geographically from Black (and Mexican) Americans. The ideological characterization of Japanese Americans as a "model minority" to be integrated served to stigmatize the others as "problem" minorities to be contained. But to the degree any postwar consensus existed, it was torn apart by the Watts Rebellion, signaling the demise of both integration and white hegemony. The book closes in the aftermath of Watts and at the dawn of the multicultural era, as African American mayor Tom Bradley and grassroots activists advanced and competing visions of Los Angeles as a multiethnic city within a global community.

This explication of urban political conditions provides context for closer scrutiny of the debates and struggles that took place within and between Black and Japanese American communities. The historical significance of these communities during this period is considerable. Los Angeles housed what were by far the largest concentrations of African Americans and Japanese Americans on the West Coast. Furthermore, while Blacks were of course the nation's largest nonwhite minority, Japanese Americans comprised the bulk of all Asians living in the United States. Ultimately, however, the presence of these two groups transcended numbers. At distinct historic junctures, the city's Black and Japanese American communities respectively served both as central targets of white supremacists and as models of racial progress.

My study couples two interconnected levels of analysis. At the most immediate level, this book is an account of how Black and Japanese Americans battled for housing, jobs, and political representation in Los Angeles as members of distinct ethnoracial groups. Drawing connections between seminal "Japanese" events like World War II internment and "Black" events like the civil rights movement, I compare and contrast the socioeconomic status and political standing of African Americans, Japanese Americans, and whites over the course of much of the twentieth century. My research further reveals how Black and Japanese Americans responded to instances of interethnic competition, as well as the degree to which they embraced opportunities for cooperation within oppositional social movements. As the narrative unfolds, it explains why Black and

Japanese Americans faced common forms of racial discrimination prior to World War II but were subsequently thrust onto different historical paths.

On a second and broader level, this book is a case study of how race functions in a multiethnic context. By highlighting the triangular nature of relations between African Americans, Japanese Americans, and whites, my study provides multiple vantage points from which we may contemplate how diverse residents of Los Angeles saw their place within a multiracial order. Exploring the range of meanings these residents attached to both segregated and integrated communities, it offers a sense of how the multiethnic city was experienced on the ground. But it also shows how the ground itself shifted over the course of the twentieth century. What I mean by this is that the book's central categories of analysis—"African American," "Japanese American," and "white"— were historically contingent constructs. Racial definitions varied over time and space in conjunction with demographic, economic, and political changes that resituated Los Angeles within a regional, national, and global order. Most obviously, a host of terms have been employed to identify these groups, many of which are now anachronistic and some of which have always been pejorative—"Negro," "Black," "colored," "Japanese," "Oriental," "Caucasian," as well as a host of vulgar epithets.

While racialized struggles over resources altered the status of groups and their relationship to power, they perhaps less obviously changed the rules by which racial politics operated. Beyond charting material relations between Black, Japanese, and white Americans, my research uncovers the ideological bases of these triangular relations. White elites played Black and Japanese Americans off against each other to solidify white hegemony. In turn, Black and Japanese Americans remained highly conscious of each other's image and status as they negotiated and renegotiated their position within a multiracial social order. Differences in racialization became a basis for an opportunistic form of triangulation. By actively distancing themselves from the other group or passively accepting the distance created by white denigration of the other group, both Black and Japanese Americans were at times able to promote a sense of national belonging and greater white acceptance. Yet, if triangulation represented a form of capitulation to a hegemonic multiracial discourse, progressive activists of all races repeatedly sought to develop a counterhegemonic vision of multiracial solidarity.[2]

As much as this book is about *what* transpired in the past, it is equally concerned with *how* we think about the politics of race. Moving in step with the multiethnic rhythms of life and politics in Los Angeles requires interrogating and in some cases abandoning commonly held assumptions drawn from histories written in black and white. For the remainder of this introduction, I argue that putting Black/Japanese American relations at the center of the history of race, politics, and urban space complicates what we have come to know as the "urban crisis," thereby challenging us to better come to terms with the origins of the "world city."

BEYOND THE BIRACIAL CITY

A focus on multiethnic Los Angeles history from the perspective of Black and Japanese Americans offers new ways of seeing and new modes of interpreting what historian Thomas Sugrue has called "the origins of the urban crisis." Part of my story can be explained by the national patterns of urban segregation and inequality outlined by Sugrue in his influential 1996 book and expanded on by others in his wake. The Great Migration brought southern Blacks seeking political freedom and economic opportunity to the cities of the North and West, especially as the demand for their labor soared and Executive Order 8802 provided a measure to combat employment discrimination during World War II. Although a wave of European immigrants had used industrial employment as a first step toward social assimilation and economic security, racism and deindustrialization ultimately denied African Americans the same form of advancement. Whites viewed workers of color as competitors for their jobs, and they feared that integration would destroy their property values and deteriorate their children's schools. They deployed legal mechanisms, political pressure, grassroots mobilization, and racist violence to defend white privilege. Furthermore, postwar development, which was a joint product of private enterprise and public policy, magnified the scale of Black/white segregation and inequality. While new housing and employment opportunities concentrated in predominantly white suburbs, urban renewal efforts ravaged low-income residents and communities of color. Lastly, Cold War conservatism further dampened the prospects of urban Blacks by undermining the redistributive aspects of New Deal reform and repressing social democratic movements that advanced the principles of multiracial unity and "civil rights unionism."[3]

At its core, the urban crisis narrative is an account of the failure of racial integration—a social movement and historical process whose fate has been inextricably bound to the construction of American national identity. First propelled by the optimistic liberal nationalism of World War II, the concept of racial integration prompted a heated public debate about national character. Social scientist Gunnar Myrdal's assertion that the "Negro problem" was a "moral issue" striking at "the heart of the American" served as the opening salvo. Published in 1944, Myrdal's monumental book, *An American Dilemma: The Negro Problem and Modern Democracy*, argued that racism was the central defect of a nation built on the principles of liberty, democracy, and equality. He was convinced, however, that Americans—by which he essentially meant white Americans—were inherently moral and rational beings, who would resolve the glaring contradiction preventing their nation from attaining its highest ideals. What followed in actuality was a quarter century of sharp conflict proving that integration was a difficult if not impossible goal to achieve. Epitomizing the pessimism of the late 1960s was the "basic conclusion" of the Kerner Commission. Charged by the federal government to investigate social conditions in the aftermath of the wave of urban rebellions, the blue-ribbon panel proclaimed, "Our nation is moving toward two societies, one black, one white—separate and unequal." The urban crisis narrative reflects the cumulative effort of an entire generation of scholars and political commentators to comprehend why things went so terribly wrong.[4]

While the urban crisis scholarship has enriched our understanding of the structural bases of poverty and racial oppression, it has yet to transcend the binary logic that has most informed scholarly and popular discourse on race in the United States. For example, the analysis Sugrue presents in *The Origins of the Urban Crisis* revolves around "the color line between black and white," which he characterizes as "America's most salient social division." To be certain, my narrative recognizes that Black/white relations have played a critical role in the shaping of American politics. Like other major metropolitan areas, Los Angeles developed a predominantly Black ghetto that became socially and economically isolated from the more prosperous and predominantly white suburbs. As frustration and anger mounted, mainstream politics did little to redress inner-city problems. Erupting in 1965, the Watts Rebellion marked one of the first major uprisings of the decade anywhere in the United States. Yet, in spite of these parallels, the established narrative stressing failure, repression, and decline cannot properly explain the history of racial politics in multiethnic Los Angeles. I maintain that it is impossible to grasp the predicament of African Americans or envision viable forms of African American political struggle without taking into account the many concerns that arise from multiracial dynamics. In Los Angeles, Black/white relations were neither autonomous nor so demonstrable as to make all other racial and ethnic relations residual. For instance, both anti-Black and anti-Japanese rhetoric and tactics proved integral to the architecture of segregation. To lure white migrants, suburban champions devised racial restrictive covenants to "protect" residential subdivisions from "invasions" by Black and Japanese Americans largely confined to the working-class Eastside neighborhoods like Little Tokyo and the Central Avenue district. What must also be stressed is that the communities Black and Japanese Americans created were never defined solely by their exclusion

from white suburbia but rather through an array of interethnic and multiethnic relationships.[5]

It is my contention that the urban crisis has spawned an equally menac-
ing epistemological crisis. Viewing integration as an aborted process, we
have become transfixed with changes that did not occur at the expense of
fully comprehending those that actually did. We need to complement our
intricate knowledge of what was lost in the past with an awareness of
what has created the new problems and possibilities we are now facing.
My account is premised on the notion that the origins of the urban crisis
overlapped with the origins of the economically vibrant and multicultural
"world city" in postwar Los Angeles. To understand how these two seemingly opposing tendencies could be intertwined, we need to raise new
questions about the history of segregation and integration: How and why
did African Americans and the "Negro problem" become materially and
ideologically linked to the "urban crisis"? How and why did Japanese
Americans and the "model minority" become materially and ideologically
linked to the rise of the "world city"? I submit that these were mutually
constitutive processes that are best understood when situated within a
multiracial context that recognizes the interconnection of local, national,
and transnational dynamics.

FROM WHITE CITY TO WORLD CITY

Los Angeles has served as a major testing ground of American race relations owing to its proximity to both the Mexican border and, as my account especially recognizes, the Pacific Ocean. Writer Carey McWilliams
remarked that the nation's imperial expansion turned the Pacific into an
"American highway." Consequently, a transpacific imaginary always factored into the construction of the West Coast's multiracial relations during the twentieth century. It loomed especially large in the minds of the
city's leading figures. Heir to the fortune of the Southern Pacific railroad,
Henry Huntington became one of the region's wealthiest men and most
extensive landholders of the early twentieth century. "Los Angeles is destined to become the most important city in this country, if not the world,"
proclaimed Huntington in 1912. "It can extend in any direction as far as
you like; its front door opens on the Pacific, the ocean of the future. The
Atlantic is the ocean of the past. Europe can supply her own wants; we
shall supply the wants of Asia." The city's first African American mayor,
Tom Bradley, entered office six decades later with nearly an identical vision. "It was something that was just so clear to me that I never questioned
it," he recalled, "the development of this city as a gateway to the Pacific
Rim." Bradley, of course, was in a much better position to actualize this

vision, for the advance of globalization had put a new premium on the importance of "world cities" as a nexus of international trade.[6]

A large body of scholars has devoted the past two decades to understanding Los Angeles as a "world city." Many assert that the former "exception" is now the model of urbanism for the "post-Fordist" era of globalization. While researchers have traced the origins of the city's decentralized spatial form and its "flexible" regime of accumulation, racial politics has especially come to the fore of scholarly attention. Most notably, *City of Quartz* by Mike Davis demonstrated the centrality of race and class to the operation of power in twentieth-century Los Angeles. Davis's groundbreaking work sparked a flurry of regional studies that have tended to focus on explaining the post-1848 ascendance of the "white city" or the post-1965 immigration reshaping the "world city." But there remains a chronological and intellectual void waiting to be filled. How did a city governed by white supremacy become a center of multiculturalism? The city's postwar reorientation complicates the traditional view of the mid–twentieth century as a time when a lull in immigration heightened the assimilation of ethnic groups and aided the consolidation of a national consensus. My contention is that many of the new dynamics that would later characterize multiculturalism were initiated in this same period. In order to situate itself as the "capital of the Pacific Rim," Los Angeles had to develop a self-awareness of its multiracial diversity and an interconnection to the peoples and cultures of the global community. While Los Angeles did not exercise a full commitment to racial equality, its qualified embrace of multiculturalism was a prerequisite for its emergence as a "world city."[7]

Drawing attention to this overlooked historical evolution of multiracial relations in Los Angeles, I devote careful attention to the factors that caused the historical trajectories of Black and Japanese Americans to converge and diverge. The book is roughly divided into three chronological sections. Chapters 1 through 3 examine *two overlapping processes of exclusion* during the interwar era that created experiences with racism common to both groups but situated them as leaders of distinct spheres of struggle. Revolving around World War II, chapters 4 through 7 detail how the *total exclusion of Japanese Americans* and *the integration of African Americans* alongside other non-Japanese minorities drove a wedge between the two groups while creating a paradigm shift in racial politics. Addressing the postwar aftermath of this shift, chapters 8 through 11 focus on the *two overlapping processes of integration* that set the two groups apart and ultimately gave rise to multiculturalism.

For African Americans from the Jim Crow South, moving west was a common strategy of survival and advancement, especially when job opportunities opened during World War II. What they encountered in

Los Angeles, however, were new ideas and technologies to propagate segregation and inequality in their new surroundings. Challenges to white racism led not to its elimination but its evolution into more socially acceptable forms over the course of the twentieth century. In the early 1900s, prominent civic leaders openly espoused white supremacist beliefs, and advocates of Klan-type violence and intimidation called the city home. Yet, as the promotion of segregation and white privilege became increasingly attached to suburbanization, whites sought primarily to avoid people of color rather than engage them in direct conflict. They rarely concealed the racial prejudice behind their motives before World War II, but postwar civil rights measures forced them to make significant adjustments. Denying their involvement in a racist system, postwar culprits of segregation instituted a "more insidious" form of Jim Crow couched in the ostensibly race-neutral concept of "individual rights." By the 1970s, with the movement for integration having been undermined, Black/white polarization reached an extreme stage that sociologists call "hypersegregation." To be certain, some moderate achievements of integrationism left their mark on Black Los Angeles. The most blatant forms of overt racism had been eliminated, and a new African American professional class had risen. But the new sense of belonging and mobility that minority professionals experienced stood in stark contrast to the devastation of inner-city neighborhoods. The decoupling of integration from social democratic reform especially hurt urban African American workers, whose fortunes were tied to the dwindling prospects of the Fordist economy.[8]

Japanese Americans experienced the swiftest and most dramatic transition from segregation to integration. As "aliens ineligible to citizenship," pre–World War II Japanese immigrants were political pariahs oppressed by racism and forced to make all sorts of accommodations just to maintain a stake in America. With the onset of war, the dehumanization of the Japanese "race" built on a legacy of exclusion and demagoguery to fuel the demand for Japanese American internment. And yet, scarcely two decades removed from the camps, Japanese Americans would emerge as the only "successful" model of racial integration. Whereas racial essentialism had previously tied ethnic Japanese to the transpacific "Yellow Peril" discourse, the postwar era and the American occupation of Japan linked them to transpacific integration. Driven by liberal tolerance and imperial arrogance, American elites sought to integrate the non-Communist Third World into its sphere (the "free world") and promote the heightened level of international trade we now associate with "globalization." A necessarily multiracial discourse became a constitutive element of American efforts to achieve and maintain global hegemony. Consequently, the assimilation of the American-born Nisei into many neighborhoods and professions previously restricted to whites carried special political significance to the city and the nation. Demonstrating the malleability of race relations, "successful" Japanese American integration ostensibly proved that the spread of American values could transcend the supposed racial divide between "Caucasians" and "Orientals."[9]

Far from mutually exclusive, these Black and Japanese American trajectories were mutually determining over the course of a period stretching a quarter century before and after the Bronzeville/Little Tokyo encounter of the mid-1940s. During the interwar era, Black and Japanese Americans were roughly equal targets of degradation by whites. However, as variations by race and nationality differentiated the responses of Black and Japanese Americans to both housing and employment discrimination, members of each group looked to their counterparts in the other group for models of racial progress. There were, for instance, ways in which the national origins and ethnic heritage of Japanese Americans provided relative advantages. Before internment, Japanese immigrants possessed a common homeland that provided them with a psychic boost of nationalist pride and a basis for cooperative enterprises. In fact, Black organizers, who espoused self-help and economic nationalism, marveled at the ability of local Japanese entrepreneurs to capture segments of the city's expanding consumer market. At the same time, the Black community's greater legal standing and prowess made it better positioned to press for full citizenship rights. Seeking "better" housing, Japanese immigrants followed African Americans into Westside neighborhoods where Black homeowners and activists had begun to break down racial restrictions. Complementing previous research on multiethnic solidarity in the Eastside, my account recovers a neglected history of Black and Japanese American solidarity in the Westside, ranging from West Jefferson as early as the 1920s to postwar Crenshaw as late as the 1970s and beyond.[10]

But we should not assume that overlapping histories point only toward interethnic coalitions and affiliation. They can also explain divergences in Black and Japanese American trajectories, thereby serving to demystify interethnic tensions. During World War II, national imperatives to defeat a transpacific enemy shaped the city's multiracial politics. The expansion of war-related jobs and the push for civic unity created the conditions for racial harmony—but only for those who escaped detainment behind barbed wire. As "national security" measures stripped Japanese Americans of citizenship and constitutional rights, they created space for African Americans to assert their "Americanness." Framing its militant activism as the highest form of patriotism, the Black community mobilized to demand its fair share of wartime economic growth and to push for a voice in local governance. African Americans united with labor activists to build an alliance of the dispossessed that some contemporary observers perceived to be an unstoppable force for progressive social change. But as Black segregation, poverty, and militancy intensified during the postwar era, Japanese Americans were invoked as a "model minority" whose achievement surpassed even that of whites. Tacit acceptance of Japanese Americans allowed whites to act in a manner consistent with modernist narratives of integration, to see themselves as tolerant people with rational rather than prejudiced reasons for opposing Black political demands. If Japanese Americans could attain middle-class status after being interned—so went the "model minority" argument—then Blacks had only themselves to blame if they did not follow suit. The creation of this "success story," however, was largely an ideological construction, for it disregarded the lingering damage the internment had inflicted, and it erased from history those members of the Japanese American community who failed to achieve upward mobility. Its purpose was to buttress the claim that America was a progressive, egalitarian nation and to blunt the arguments of both domestic and foreign critics who claimed otherwise.

Many of the key roots of the "world city" run directly through these mutually determining trajectories of Black and Japanese American history. As US Cold War strategy prioritized alliances with Japan and other Asian governments, Los Angeles increasingly tied its economic and cultural life to the Pacific Rim. Moving toward a celebration of ethnic diversity, the city proved that the changes brought about by imperial entanglements were not unidirectional. Still, the "world city" was a product of local as well as global conditions, taking a particular form in Los Angeles due to the configuration of urban politics symbolized by Mayor Tom Bradley's ascension. More than a reflection of elite motives and behavior, the "world city" also resulted from grassroots challenges to racial discrimination and exclusion. Bradley launched his career through neighborhood organizing efforts in Crenshaw, the multiethnic district that became the central focus of postwar Black and Japanese American efforts to integrate the Westside. The mayor's dominant representation of the "world city" reflected the moderate achievements of integrationists, who helped create a diverse community in Crenshaw and then sought to replicate this diversity by practicing affirmative action to change the face of municipal government. Meanwhile, young radicals in Crenshaw produced oppositional forms of multiculturalism under the rubric of "Third World" liberation. Both the moderates and the radicals could cite the polyethnic culture of a Crenshaw institution like the Holiday Bowl as inspiration.

Although a full analysis of post-1965 Los Angeles lies beyond the scope of the book, the research on which this history is based is unquestionably a product of this multicultural era. As a critique of the notion of history as a grand narrative privileging the dominant elements in society, multiculturalism has made us more receptive to hearing voices on the margins and to seeing history from diverse perspectives. What it has not done is provide a framework for understanding the many intersections of the ethnic narratives it has produced. Through a detailed study of the triangular relations between African Americans, Japanese Americans, and whites, I attempt to show how the fragments of interethnic history accessible through existing sources can be pieced together. This I take as the primary challenge to comparative ethnic studies scholarship ready to move from documenting the oppression and resistance of minorities to locating the emergence of a nonwhite majority. In this way, we might see the future in the past. As the well-traveled writer and activist Carey McWilliams argued in the mid-1940s, Los Angeles stood at the forefront of the nation's "racial frontier" because of what he labeled its "quadrilateral" pattern of interaction between white, Black, Asian, and Mexican Americans. This uniquely West Coast configuration provided the nation with "one more chance, perhaps a last chance, to establish the principle of racial equality." Those observing the city were thus blessed with "a ringside seat in the great theatre of the future." That future has arrived. Multiethnic Los Angeles is no longer exceptional; it is a symbol of twenty-first-century American culture.[11]

CHAPTER 1

Constructing the Segregated City

"PEOPLE ARE COMING here by the thousands now. All of them must have homes." So declared a December 1912 advertisement from Pacific Home Builders, the self-proclaimed "largest owner of Home Building property" in Los Angeles. Firm in the conviction that Los Angeles was emerging as the leading port city of the new Pacific era, the company urged investors to reap the fortunes destined to arise from the "fastest growing and most prosperous city in the world." Vast improvements to San Pedro harbor, creating "the safest seaport in the world," had been completed just in time for the opening of the Panama Canal. Los Angeles was best positioned to capitalize on the rising trade from "new lines of American, Japanese and Chinese ships" because it was closer to the canal than San Francisco and possessed a "perfect climate." In this same era, the *Los Angeles Times* also envisioned the city poised to become the center of a new American empire tied to the Pacific. Thousands of migrants begat eventual millions drawn to Southern California's sunny shores. As historian Natalia Molina has argued, whether the newcomers sought invigorated health or commercial wealth, they generally "believed that the promotion of the white race in the West, California, and Los Angeles in particular was central to the city's development." As an August 1909 editorial of the *Times* declared, "A day will come when this Coast shall be another Aryan pyramid. It will overtop itself, break and sweep on to Cathay."[1]

Both the advertisement of the Pacific Home Builders and the *Times*'s white supremacist vision of manifest destiny exemplify Los Angeles boosters' efforts to craft a distinctive brand of growth for the nation. America experienced a new nationalist fervor at the turn of the twentieth century. As technological advances fueled industrial growth, the nation flexed its new might by capturing Spain's former colonies and other possessions in the Pacific. Millions of immigrants were recruited to provide cheap labor to fuel the economic expansion while nonwhite peoples were put under American authority abroad. As a result, the nation faced a racial crisis. What took shape during the second and third decades of the twentieth century was a process of racialization and Americanization. New policies and cultural pressures compelled southern and eastern European immigrants to conform to standards of "native-born" white Americans. At the same time, the US government curtailed further immigration and precluded nonwhites from full citizenship in the white nation. In this context, developers, realtors, and residents of Los Angeles coalesced around the notion that their city offered the ideal location for white settlement. Combined with sun and narratives of a romanticized past, discount railroad fares had drawn an endless wave of white migration beginning with the boom of the 1880s. In 1870, the City of Angels was home to but 5,728 mortal souls and claimed less than 4 percent of San Francisco's population. By 1900, its population had reached 100,000, and it would surpass 500,000 before 1920. No major city in America kept pace with the scale of growth in Los Angeles between the end of Reconstruction and the start of the Great Depression. "For centuries, the Anglo-Saxon race has been marching westward," declared the official publication of the Los Angeles Chamber of Commerce in November 1924. "The apex of this movement is Los Angeles County."[2]

The development of Los Angeles between the First and Second World Wars reflected the paradox of an America that boasted of bringing forth a prosperous modern world marked by global commerce and intercultural exchange while it simultaneously retreated into a defensive sense of place and belonging defined by narrow nationalism and racial purity. Driven by a process of suburbanization, the Southland's geographic and demographic expansion of the 1920s (in absolute terms) dwarfed that of every prior decade, creating the sprawling pattern of settlement that became the trademark of Los Angeles. The city's population more than doubled to 1.2 million, while the rest of Los Angeles County harbored an additional 1 million residents. To a large degree, this decentralization was part of a national trend of metropolitan regions pushing their boundaries outward. What distinguished Southern California, however, was that suburban development quickly began to eclipse the city's modest downtown and thus define the entire region. Following an overview of the city's racial politics pre–World War I, this chapter details how white boosters constructed the suburban ideal and the segregated city during the interwar period. In suburbia, white residents discovered a place where they could experience the benefits and conveniences of modern America without suffering the costs of industrialization. As they confronted the troubling presence of nonwhite "others," proponents of suburban expansion created a new cultural geography predicated on the heightened distinction between the Westside and the Eastside. Through the deployment of restrictive covenants, Westside property interests "protected" white neighborhoods from perceived nuisances they associated with the Eastside. Exerting both economic and cultural leadership, developers and realtors sought to control not only the trade in bricks and mortar but also the trade in images of race, neighborhood, and community. Through membership in racially exclusive homeowners' associations, white residents provided a grassroots basis for their vision. They were materially and psychologically tied to the investments of the city's elites and their plans for maintaining order and prosperity. Collectively, white realty interests and residents defined spatial patterns that would shape Southern California for the next half century.

THE NEW FRONTIER

On the evening of October 24, 1871, word spread throughout Los Angeles that the city's Chinese residents had run rampant and needed to be taught a lesson. Reportedly, a clash between rival tongs vying for possession of a woman had led to an outbreak of gunfire in the Chinese quarter formally known as Calle de los Negros but popularly referred to by the racist moniker "Nigger Alley." Two police officers had been killed after chasing a group of Chinese men into the Coronel Building. Surrounding the structure, a white mob chanted, "Hang them! Burn them out!" A deputy called for the crowd to stay back and for the Chinese to surrender. But the first Chinese man to emerge was riddled with bullets, and so was the next. A third murder demonstrated the ferocious persistence of the assailants. The Chinese victim was beaten by the mob, taken by a policeman, and then recaptured by the mob. He was strung up on a cord, which broke, then hung again and killed. It was now open season on all Chinese. One group fetched a fire hose to "wash them out" while others ascended the Coronel Building, hacked through its roof with axes, and fired bullets from above. Meanwhile, rioters looted the rooms and dragged Chinese men into the street. Others went door-to-door down "Nigger Alley" rounding up every Chinese they could find, including a fourteen-year-old boy. Over five hours, an estimated five hundred persons engaged in mass rioting and lynched eighteen to twenty-two or more Chinese residents.[3]

Capping off a chaotic period of frontier justice following the 1848 American conquest of Mexican California, the Chinese Massacre of 1871 sent the city's leadership on a quest to secure law and order. To be certain, Anglos had established themselves as the dominant race in Alta California by then. The region's indigenous population had been beset by European diseases, coerced to labor on Spanish colonial missions, and subjected to debt peonage on the Mexican-era ranchos of Californio elites. In the post-1848 period, Anglo militias pushed the decimated ranks of Indians into the remote corners of the state. Cast by whites as a vanishing race, few native inhabitants remained in Los Angeles. Chinese immigrants ranked just above Indians in the racial hierarchy. Most whites denied their humanity, but some coveted them as a menial labor source. One more step higher, Mexicans were stripped of artisan positions they had held in the rancho economy and relegated to low-skilled work. Still, they retained a pretense of claims to American citizenship rights under the Treaty of Guadalupe Hidalgo. As a class, the Californios fell furthest, losing their land and fortunes to Anglos under the American system of law and trade and eventually losing their history, as well. By the end of the nineteenth century, Anglos wanting to provide a sense of place and depth to the city's marketing efforts would declare themselves the rightful heirs to the Spanish colonial past. As historian Kevin Starr has noted, journalist Charles Fletcher Lummis's promotion of Los Angeles as "the new Eden of the Saxon homeseeker" relied on Spanish mythology to craft "an image, a brand name, to promote sales." Such boosterism whitewashed the Mexican-American War to portray the conquest as a victimless process. "No hand was raised against" the Spanish-Mexican culture, booster Joseph P. Widney's account surmised. It had "simply faded away." In truth, a handful of storied Mexicans were incorporated into a multiethnic ruling class alongside American-born Anglos and Jewish, French Canadian, British, and German immigrants. Racialized as "Europeans," they were largely ceremonial members of a new white majority that coalesced during the 1860s. Perched atop the racial hierarchy, Anglo business elites were nonetheless dissatisfied with the state of the city. The struggle for power in Los Angeles continued in the war's violent aftermath, creating a social climate in which too many conflicts were settled by brute force. The city's murder rate led the nation during the 1850s. Legal executions were common but so was lynching. No sum of money seemed large enough to attract a decent sheriff, and those who signed on often quit before tackling a serious assignment.[4]

By the 1880s, a new governing class headed by local capitalists had put to rest the specter of mob rule in Los Angeles. Seeking to enhance the prospects for investment, it fostered what political scientist Steven P. Erie has called a "statist growth regime." In particular, it moved to overturn what it deemed the colonial rule of the Southern Pacific railroad, which connected Los Angeles to national trade and migration routes but expressed little interest in developing the city into anything more than a tourist destination. Headed by Harrison Gray Otis of the *Los Angeles Times*, the new regime prioritized transforming the "cow town" into an industrial metropolis. It helped to initiate an extended period of demographic and economic expansion that was marked by a stunning series of publicly subsidized capital improvements. Trade grew exponentially at the Port of Los Angeles in San Pedro, which in turn was connected to new railroad lines that were incorporated into the city through a wave of annexations. In the early twentieth century, the discovery of oil fueled further industrial expansion, while the 1913 construction of the aqueduct boosted land values and sustained mass population growth.[5]

How the city's residents defined their quest for freedom during this early period of growth varied by race and class. Booster-employers like Otis believed that "industrial freedom" as represented by the "open" (nonunion) shop was the key to the city's development. In this regard, they viewed the predominantly white ranks of organized labor as their primary antagonist. With the *Times* serving as its "ideological spokesman," the open shop movement united business interests within the Merchants and Manufacturers Association to limit the impact of union organizing. With battle lines firmly entrenched by the turn of the twentieth century, the conflict reached a boiling point between 1905 and 1911. The fervor created by the alleged bombing of the Times building on October 1, 1910, carried over into the following year's election, when Socialist Job Harriman delivered a strong bid for mayor. However, labor allies John and James McNamara, under duress of detainment, confessed to the bombing, derailing the Socialist candidacy. Antiunion conditions would hold secure until late in the Depression. A pamphlet published by the Los Angeles Chamber of Commerce in the late 1920s crowned the city the "pioneer" of the "open shop," claiming it had attracted 5,800 local factories.[6]

While the mark it left on class relations was unmistakable, the capitalist regime's search for order and stability had equally profound effects on the city's race relations. Just as the new regime condemned what it saw as the violent actions of labor militants, it further declared the violent strains of white supremacy anathema to good business. Indeed, the proto-booster Robert M. Widney prided himself the man most responsible for ending the Chinese Massacre and parlayed that reputation into a long and successful career as a leading economic and political figure in Los Angeles. While they rarely confronted mob violence directly, business elites in Widney's wake cursed the mob mentality driving racist exclusion movements. In general, the city's capitalists were Republicans, whose rejection of staunch segregation and qualified embrace of racial tolerance was tied to both their moral beliefs and their class interests. In practice, the freedom they most upheld was their latitude as employers to draw diverse races into the labor pool. Upholding law and order thus meant restricting the actions of pro-union workers and securing a degree of freedom of mobility for nonwhites. Indeed, African Americans found representation on the city's police force at the dawn of the twentieth century. Henry Huntington's actions in response to a 1903 strike on his Pacific Electric railroad demonstrated how employers deployed Black and Japanese American migrants as allies of the open shop. The railroad baron undercut fourteen hundred Mexican American strikers affiliated with the American Federation of Labor (AFL) by luring an equal number of Blacks, mainly from Texas, plus several hundred Japanese to work as replacements.[7]

Although white workers cursed the open shop, it was a blessing of sorts for Black and Japanese Americans. The defeat of Reconstruction and the repudiation of African American citizenship had introduced a new period of racist violence and oppression throughout the North and South. During this nadir of postemancipation Black history, Los Angeles emerged as a place of relative freedom and opportunity. In 1913, W.E.B. Du Bois commented that the "open shop" was one of the principal reasons African Americans chose to migrate to Los Angeles over the San Francisco–Oakland area, where "the white trade unions . . . held the Negro out and down." The politically powerful and racially exclusive trade unions of Northern California had a more deleterious impact on the lives of Asian immigrants. Following its successful campaign for Chinese exclusion, white labor turned its hostility toward the Issei, or Japanese immigrants. The San Francisco School Board's drive to place Japanese students in segregated schools sparked an international incident, ultimately moving President Theodore Roosevelt to negotiate the immigration restrictions of the 1908 Gentlemen's Agreement. By contrast, around the same time, Los Angeles school superintendent E. C. Moore characterized Japanese students as "quiet, well behaved pupils, who set a good example to the others." Moore concluded there was "no Japanese question here." Further distressed by the great 1906 earthquake, many Issei left San Francisco for a Southern California region they judged to be more racially tolerant. From one hundred residents in the mid-1890s, the Los Angeles Japanese population grew to surpass ten thousand within two decades. Almost as many Japanese could be found scattered throughout the rest of Los Angeles County. "Let's go to Los Angeles" went a popular Issei refrain of the time. "Everything is wonderful there." By the end of World War I, the region housed the largest Japanese American community in the continental United States.[8]

Ultimately, the open shop influenced the city's multiracial social climate more than its hiring patterns. Industrial production in Progressive Era Los Angeles was largely craft-oriented and did not require the large pools of unskilled labor demanded by plants in other urban areas. Moreover, the city's Black and Japanese American leaders expressed little interest in attracting uneducated and unskilled workers, for they saw an opportunity to define their communities by standards of bourgeois respectability. In this way, they believed it was possible to maintain good relations with white elites and uplift the members of their own race. African American migrants to the city comprised a small and selective grouping. When compared to major destinations of the Great Migration, Black Los Angeles had an overrepresentation of those who were well educated and from urban areas, primarily New Orleans, Atlanta, and multiple cities in Texas. More than a few Black pioneers made large fortunes through investments that skyrocketed owing to real estate booms, and several sat on the Los Angeles Chamber of Commerce by the early twentieth century. On the heels of a well-publicized visit to promote the recently organized National Association for the Advancement of Colored People (NAACP), a highly impressed W.E.B. Du Bois devoted most of the August 1913 issue of *The Crisis* to Los Angeles. Over two thousand people, including some Japanese Americans, had come to hear the distinguished scholar. He stayed in the homes of the city's Black leaders, met with community organizations, and visited local small businesses before touring other parts of the state. The cover featured a full-page picture of Mr. and Mrs. William Foster sprawled out underneath a large palm tree on the front lawn of their grand dwelling. The image reinforced Du Bois's declaration that African Americans in Los Angeles were "without doubt the most beautifully housed group of colored people in the United States." Statistics supported his statement. While African American housing opportunities were not unbounded, they were far less confined before the 1920s. The rate of Black homeownership in Los Angeles reached a nationwide high of 36.1 percent in 1910. Leading realtors, such as Noah Thompson, frequently cited Du Bois's comments to push their own brand of boosterism as they promoted the city's racial tolerance, economic growth, and above all availability of housing to attract new business and migrants. Not to be undersold was the "sunny southland." Countering Anglo ethnology, Black booster E. H. Rydall claimed the regional climate as "distinctly African."[9]

While African Americans were trekking across land toward the Pacific, intellectuals in Meiji Japan were eyeing the American West as the overseas frontier of Japanese expansion. Although this idea bolstered Japanese state support for migration, the immigrants themselves saw America more as a generic frontier of opportunity. The first large wave was sent as contract laborers to Hawaii, where late-nineteenth-century demand for sugar plantation labor coincided with the exclusion of Chinese immigrants. Many subsequently left for the West Coast, where they were joined around the turn of the twentieth century by a new stream directly from Japan. The Issei were mostly peasants whose livelihoods had been undermined by Meiji industrialization and commercialization, yet they did not comprise the poorest of the poor. They rather more closely resembled a fallen middle class. As such, they embraced an ideology that historian Eiichiro Azuma has characterized as "success and striving." As with Black Los Angeles, entrepreneurs guided the formation of the local Japanese community. Although it began with a sailor setting up a restaurant during the 1880s, the community took particular shape during the first decade of the twentieth century. The *Rafu Shimpo* (*Los Angeles Japanese Daily News*) newspaper was created in 1903, and it soon catered to several thousand migrants from San Francisco. Among the new arrivals was Gentaro Isoygaya, who launched the city's first sushi restaurant.[10]

For a time, it seemed as if both communities were successfully negotiating the "race" problem. Indeed, the *Los Angeles Times* proclaimed in 1909, "If the negroes of Los Angeles and Southern California can be taken as examples of the race, it would seem from their own showing of indisputable facts that the 'negro problem' is a thing that has no existence." Like other Republicans, the *Times* management rejected slavery and its legacy among the Dixiecrats, whom it chastised for practicing "absurd, illogical, unreasonable and unjust discrimination." Generally endorsing notions of racial uplift that did not challenge the structural bases of free market capitalism, the *Times* described African Americans as "good, God-fearing law abiding men and women." Their churches maintained "highly organized bodies of Christian worshipers," while "not a few" of their homes represented the pinnacle of "elegance and luxury." Adults were industrious, entrepreneurial, and cultured. Children were studious and "often outstrip[ped] their white companions in ability." Black leaders took pride in such characterization, and while not similarly praised, Asians could take some solace from the *Times* critique of the "Yellow Peril bogie man." A 1906 editorial remarked, "Chinese and Japanese laborers are a blessing rather than a menace." While less than "ideal citizens," they were "industrious and serviceable menials" who were at least as "desirable" as the "scum and offal from Europe landing on the Atlantic Coast." The anti-Asian campaign was the product of "labor agitators," whose influence over the West Coast was a "detriment to the people and the prosperity of nearly all classes of business."[11]

In the multiethnic city, triangulation further informed the construction of racial identity and social position. Social scientist Charles S. Johnson wrote, "The focusing of racial interest upon the Oriental has in large measure overlooked the Negro, and the city accordingly, has been regarded by them, from a distance, as desirable and likely to yield for them important opportunities for living and earning a living." Echoing this view, African American author Arna Bontemps noted that "Los Angeles in legend became 'Paradise West' to Negroes still languishing in the Egyptland of the South, and not without some justification." In his view, the adjustment of Black migrants to Los Angeles was "perhaps better than that of any other group of equal size in any other American city." Bontemps reasoned, "Perhaps the Japanese and Mexicans are to be thanked. They drew off much of the racial hostility which otherwise might have been concentrated on the Negroes." Some Black leaders linked anti-Asian measures to their own advancement. James M. Alexander led the Afro-American Council, the community's most significant civil rights organization at the turn of the century. According to historian Douglas Flamming, Alexander launched an "America for Americans" campaign. Championing the role of African Americans in the imperial seizure of the Philippines and Cuba, he condemned the fact that Black Los Angeles was losing jobs to "Asiatic emigrants who contribute but little to the advancement of the country." Meanwhile, Japanese immigrant leaders instructed their brethren not to replicate the clannish and uncouth behavior they attributed to Chinese immigrants. In their rather chauvinistic opinion, Issei believed the Chinese had brought white hostility on themselves through their willingness to work as coolies and their failure to adapt to Western norms. As historian Yuji Ichioka has written, they saw themselves as representatives of a progressive, modern nation, while the Chinese reflected "a stagnant and decaying Asia from which Japan had already parted company."[12]

Ultimately, as marginalized minority groups, Black and Japanese Americans could control their public identity only within narrow parameters proscribed by the dominant culture. As such, their efforts often proved insufficient in the face of rising white antagonism. A scene reminiscent of the 1871 Chinese Massacre signaled the turning point. On February 8, 1915, a new sense of racial destiny developed as a troop of white-robed clansmen rode on horseback through the heart of downtown Los Angeles. Although the procession invoked the specter of white supremacy and mob violence, no lives were lost on this occasion. The robed riders were actors engaged in a publicity stunt for the premiere of D. W. Griffith's *The Clansman*, later to become known by its original subtitle, *The Birth of a Nation*. The thousands gathering on this evening included the city's leading figures. Griffith overcame the lobbying efforts of local Black activists seeking to ban the film, and his audience applauded him. California governor Hiram Johnson, a Progressive Republican, judged *The Clansman* "a very wonderful moving picture." Praising the dramatic sight of the Ku Klux Klan riding on horseback, *Los Angeles Times* reviewer Henry Christeen Warnack called it "the greatest picture in the world."[13]

Whereas the crowd of 1871 unleashed a violent form of repression, the crowd of 1915 demonstrated the power of white supremacist ideology. *The Birth of a Nation* became the biggest blockbuster film of its time, generating over $60 million at the box office through just its first run. On a national level, Griffith's film helped consolidate the bonds of whiteness by creating in both the North and South what he called a common "feeling of abhorrence in white people, especially white women, against colored men." Its heroic portrayal of "the Clansmen" contributed in no small measure to a resurgence of the KKK not only in the South but notably in the rural and urban North and West, too. Locally, *Birth* symbolized a new economy of racism in Los Angeles. The movie literally boosted Hollywood to the head

Fig. 1.1. "Japs keep moving." White residents protest settlement by Japanese immigrants in Hollywood during the early 1920s. National Archives photo. Courtesy of the National Japanese American Historical Society.

of the film industry, which in turn propelled economic growth in Los Angeles. But it also unleashed the mass-marketing power of white supremacist ideology. Racist imagery would prove even more central to the real estate industry, whose fortunes were arguably tied to cultural representations as much as those of movie moguls were. In the suburbs, life would imitate art. In his fictional quest for Southern redemption, Griffith staged Civil War battles in the San Fernando Valley and filmed the Klan's climactic ride "to save a nation" (his characterization) crossing the border from Los Angeles to Orange County. Over the ensuing decades, these formerly rural settings would come to take on new relevance as the actual sites of twentieth-century battles for white power in suburbia.[14]

Hollywood itself became contested residential territory. The Japanese Association had its own standoff with Cecil B. DeMille in 1915 over the "Yellow Peril" story line of *The Cheat*, in which an Issei merchant sexually assails a married white woman. But white residents clamored louder when a small grouping of Japanese immigrants moved into Hollywood.

Many of the Issei were servants and gardeners looking for housing near the studios and homes of film moguls where they toiled. In 1923, the Hollywood Protective Association formed to "Keep Hollywood white" and drive out the "yellow menace." One representative, Mrs. B. G. Miller, posed for a large picture in the *Los Angeles Examiner*'s May 18, 1923, edition by pointing to a banner spanning the front of her house reading "JAPS KEEP MOVING—this is a white man's neighborhood." The exclusion committee mobilized hundreds of residents through mass meetings. When a lone white dissenter voiced reservations about the campaign, he was driven from one such meeting by cries of "White Jap" and "Lynch him." Through door-to-door outreach, agitators further inflamed white opinion. One flyer condemned an Issei proposal for a Presbyterian church in a white neighborhood:

> JAPS
> You came to care for lawns,
> we stood for it
> You came to work in truck gardens,
> we stood for it
> You sent your children to public schools,
> we stood for it
> You moved a few families in our midst
> we stood for it
> You proposed to build a church in our neighborhood
> BUT
> We DIDN'T and WE WON'T STAND FOR IT
> You impose more on us each day
> until you have gone your limit
> WE DON'T WANT YOU WITH US
> SO GET BUSY, JAPS, AND
> GET OUT OF HOLLYWOOD

The message was crystal clear. Like the "Negro," the "Japs" were welcome in Southern California so long as they confined themselves to the proper social and geographical place defined by whites.[15]

The resurgence of racism in the years surrounding World War I introduced significant alterations to the social landscape. Postwar anti-Black riots broke out in urban areas throughout the nation, sparked by resentful whites viewing Black migrants from the South as unwanted competitors for jobs and housing. Although there were no major race riots in Los Angeles during the interwar period, the Klan surged in the early 1920s. Its organized public presence may have been brief, but the Klan's white supremacist ideology flourished in dozens of local organizations that committed acts of violence and intimidation toward Black and Japanese Americans. Because of their strong grassroots base, white supremacists held political sway, as well. Government officials and police officers joined the Klan, as did future mayor John Porter, who was elected in 1929.[16]

With the Japanese American fertility rate soaring and post–World War I relations between the United States and Japan chilling, racism fused with jingoism in a perverse instance of the maxim "think globally, act locally." As a result, the strongest anti-Japanese movement Los Angeles had ever witnessed emerged. In 1920, it focused on the passage of Proposition One, a California constitutional amendment designed to expand the Alien Land Law and a measure its proponents hoped would lay political groundwork for a ban on Japanese immigration. The election demonstrated widespread support for the anti-Japanese campaign, as Proposition One passed by a three-to-one margin in Los Angeles County. Although the *Los Angeles Times* recommended a "no" vote on the amendment, which it considered a product of labor demagogues, its editorial reversal was telling. No longer would it dismiss cries of "Yellow Peril" as "a tempest in a teapot," as it had just one decade prior. In blunt language, the *Times* warned that looming Issei "control of California farm lands" was "endangering white supremacy in California and threaten[ing] to overwhelm the Caucasian race." Judging the task too important to be "left to those who have nothing but race or class hatred to bring to the settlement," the leading newspaper called on responsible parties to direct the anti-Japanese campaign. Answering the call, prominent members of white society led the Anti-Asiatic Association in the 1920s. They included a former state senator from Massachusetts; the head of the Ohio State Society, one of the many popular social organizations established by midwestern transplants; and the California commander of the American Legion, Buron Fitts. With the help of ties to prominent Japanese exclusionists, Fitts would later become lieutenant governor and Los Angeles County district attorney. Groups like the Anti-Asiatic Association helped to popularize the notion that Japanese Americans were racially suspicious and unassimilable—ideas that would increasingly shape public policy leading to the World War II internment. It was real estate interests, however, who best developed "responsible" methods to inscribe white prejudices into the city's residential landscape.[17]

Suburban Racism

The downtown industrial elite had sought to transform Los Angeles into a "West Coast Chicago," but a new brand of suburban boosterism took root in the aftermath of World War I. Alarmed at what they perceived to be the physical and social decay of urban industrial centers, these suburban interests developed a vast industry of their own by catering to white repulsion from the "big city" as dirty, congested, dangerous, vice-ridden, and populated by immigrants and people of color. The sentiment itself was not a new one, for idealized visions of suburbia had arisen during the nineteenth-century rise of big cities. As Kenneth Jackson has pointed out, "The dream of a detached house in a safe, quiet, and peaceful place has been an important part of the Anglo-American past." Los Angeles, however, generally lacked a walking-city tradition and was therefore positioned to make decentralized and low-density settlement its predominant spatial pattern. In large measure, the early 1920s boom gave birth to the sprawling metropolis as 1,400 new subdivisions burst onto the local scene in just two years. By the end of the decade, 3,200 new housing tracts and 250,000 homes, nearly all of which were single-family dwellings, had risen in the city. The boosters contrasted the new development of Los Angeles with the immigrant ghettos and slaughterhouses of Chicago and its industrialized counterparts. By 1940, more than half of Los Angeles residents lived in single-family housing, whereas fewer than one in six did so in Chicago. Color was of course a central marker of difference. Between 1910 and 1930, Chicago's Black population expanded fivefold to reach nearly a quarter million persons. As white Chicago reacted with "fear" and "disdain" to the new arrivals, Los Angeles boosters turned increasingly to sunny weather, picturesque landscapes, and homogeneous white neighborhoods to attract migrants from the Midwest. "WHY IS EVERYONE talking Eagle Rock?" asked one neighborhood's aggressive marketing campaign of the 1920s. "As you journey about Eagle Rock," it continued, "enjoying immeasurably the ideal climate that is ours, you will observe that the residents of Eagle Rock are all of the *white* race." Expecting to triple its population to thirty thousand persons, the neighborhood's association "*insured* the future beauty of our Homes and the character of our associates by Building and Race restrictions."[18]

Unlike earlier boosters' efforts, the pastoral imagery the suburban boosters presented was not an inducement to take up farming. Their targets, instead, were the small-town midwesterners looking to leave rural life behind. Many of the early transplants were retirees whose economic success led them to search not for greener pastures but the green lawns of sparkling new subdivisions. The parochial charm of suburban Los Angeles offered a middle ground between the drudgery of agriculture and the vices of urban centers like Chicago. Boosterist outreach often began with marketing by the All-Year Club, which profusely produced publicly subsidized measures to attract tourism. Hundreds of thousands of tourists enjoyed extended stays in Southern California and returned to paint sunny pictures of the region in towns throughout the Midwest. Though the greatest share of migrants were born in Illinois, many came by way of Iowa. By the end of the 1920s migration boom, three out of every four white American-born residents of Los Angeles were from places outside California, and a half million belonged to midwestern state societies. Many of these "folks" shared the faith of men like Charles Edward Locke, the pastor of First Methodist Church. Locke was a conservative who advocated prohibition and Americanization, deemed Bolshevism "a reversion to the era of the caveman," and called for the Bible to be taught in public schools. He especially espoused the virtues of domesticity. A stern opponent of prostitution, he blamed its proliferation on "respectable" married women, who created a culture of licentiousness by dressing immodestly and socializing too extravagantly. Even his solution to the Japanese problem turned on domestic ideals. Whites needed to counter the rising yellow population by creating "more California homes—more California babies." Finally, Locke disowned the most virulent forms of racial hatred while upholding segregation. He invited African Americans to attend his yearly sermon commemorating the Emancipation Proclamation but forced the hundreds who came to sit in a separate section from whites.[19]

Over the course of the interwar era, the influx of younger, upwardly mobile white migrants came to outpace that of retirees. Fearing the consequences of industrialization but cherishing the wealth it created, the new suburbanites moved to contain rather than eliminate industry. As a result, they sought to distinguish the Westside of Los Angeles as the protected space for low-density housing, while relegating factories and workers' homes to the Eastside. Los Angeles was one of the first cities to adopt zoning ordinances to define the character of neighborhoods. Residents and promoters of single-family homes acted to "protect" their districts from perceived "nuisances," such as factories, apartment complexes, and unwanted institutions. The exclusivity of a zoning district was generally tied to its class character. The most restricted zoning favored wealthy neighborhoods like Hancock Park, whose opening advertisements proclaimed the subdivision "a residential district of such superior quality and so highly restricted, that it would soon become the natural selection of those families recognized as leaders in the community." At the opposite end of the spectrum, the city's industrial zones to the south and east of downtown were unrestricted. In between, both socially and geographically, lay middle-class and working-class residential zones. Class-biased zoning indirectly promoted racial segregation because neighborhoods designated to include only luxury homes drew residents from the ranks of the overwhelmingly white upper crust of the city. However, the Supreme Court's *Buchanan v. Warley* decision (1917) struck down "racial zoning ordinances." Enacted by local governments like that of San Francisco in the era of Chinese exclusion and by southern cities under Jim Crow, these explicit demarcations of where different racial groups could and could not reside were thus not at the disposal of real estate interests in the 1920s.[20]

Racial restrictive covenants prohibiting nonwhites from inhabiting houses provided the crucial instrument to advance residential segregation during the interwar period. Designed to evade the Fourteenth Amendment, restrictive covenants, unlike racial zoning, were attached to specific privately owned properties and deemed to be the actions of individuals rather than the state. To be certain, restrictive covenants in practice regulated many property-related matters including function, size, and decor. But as prohibitions on nonwhite residency or ownership became the most notorious use to which they were applied, the term "restrictive covenants" in common parlance came to signify racial restrictive covenants. Various racial restrictions on use and ownership had been attached to properties in California since the late nineteenth century, and Los Angeles developers began openly advertising racially exclusive housing tracts no later than 1905 or 1906. In the years following World War I, however, racial restrictive covenants spread throughout the city, leading one African American resident to characterize them as "invisible walls of steel." Sociologist Robert E. Park wrote in 1926 that "in spite of every effort to conciliate American public opinion," Japanese Americans were finding themselves pushed "into the same sort of racial ghetto in which the Chinese before them had found refuge." This form of racism by contract fulfilled suburban desire for racially homogeneous neighborhoods and the material benefits of white supremacy. At the same time, the ostensibly "nonviolent" methods deployed in pursuit of segregation allowed these white homeowners to distance themselves from the dominative forms of racism characteristic of the Jim Crow South and the harsh varieties of racial conflict they associated with urban industrial centers. Suburban whites could thus pretend that they were not contributors to the "race" problem in America.[21]

Privileging property rights over human rights, the 1919 *Title Guarantee and Trust Company v. Garrott* case provided the legal rationale for the usage of racial restrictive covenants. This was somewhat ironic given that civil rights advocates received the operative decision as a major victory. In 1915, African American police officer Homer L. Garrott purchased a Southwest Los Angeles home from a white widow, whom the title company cited for violating a deed agreement not to "sell any portion of said premises to any person of African, Chinese or Japanese descent." Under its established terms, the company sought forfeiture of the house and repossession. Garrott prevailed in both superior court and the court of appeals. But whereas the lower court recognized Garrott's right to purchase the house and equal protection under the Constitution, the appeals court recognized only the right of white owners to dispense with their property as they chose. The Fourteenth Amendment, it opined, prohibited the state only from granting "rights to one which, under similar circumstances, it denies to another." Thus, the state had no obligation to preclude the "individual invasion" of an African American's "individual rights" so long as it did not prohibit similar offenses "directed against Hindus, Cingalese, and Maoris, or any other class of persons except negroes." In essence, the court interpreted the Fourteenth Amendment to mean that all persons had the right to be discriminated against equally! Garrott prevailed only because the appeals court agreed with the lower court's invocation of medieval common law upholding the seller's rights with the same logic Parliament had used to free land tenure from feudal kingdoms. "Ever since the statute *quia emptores*," it declared, "the tying up of real property has been regarded as an evil that is incompatible with the free and liberal circulation of property as one of the inherent rights of a free people." In the immediate instance, this meant that the court could not enforce the title company's restraint on the white seller's "alienation" of her property. But the long-run consequences were more devastating for civil rights advocates. If the court recognized the seller's individual property rights as absolute, then it could not infringe on the rights of whites to *refuse* to sell to people of color. White homeowners and realtors would cling to this legal argument for the next five decades. Even after the courts rejected it, they maintained it as a moral stance.[22]

So long as court decisions in restrictive covenant cases rested on the primacy of property rights over civil rights and individualism over social justice, racist measures derived from "private action" could be designed in a manner that insulated them from constitutional challenges. Five months after the *Garrott* decision, the California Supreme Court validated racist restrictions barring occupancy by non-Caucasians in *Los Angeles Investment Company v. Gary*. While people of color were thus free to purchase homes from willing white sellers, they could be barred by covenants from living in their own domiciles. The longtime Los Angeles civil rights attorney Loren Miller noted, "The courts ordered an offending Negro's ouster with no thought and no responsibility for his housing, even where it was apparent that no shelter was available for his use. If he refused to move in response to an injunction, he was in contempt of court and was jailed."[23]

The *Gary* case was perfectly timed to allow for the use of racial covenants to spread throughout the region during the realty boom of the 1920s. For instance, the Janss Investment Company, creator of Westwood and one of the region's largest developers, covered thousands of homes and lots with the following restrictions: "No part of said real property shall ever be leased, rented, sold or conveyed to any person who is not of the white or Caucasian race, nor be used or occupied by any person who is not of the white or the Caucasian race whether grantee hereunder or any other person." The courts repeatedly emphasized the validity of racial covenants barring nonwhite occupancy. In 1925, the California Supreme Court sided with Janss in a lawsuit the company filed to prevent an African American family from residing in a Janss home originally purchased by a white man. The *Gary* opinion, declared the court, had become "settled law in this state and accordingly followed by subdividers of property and by purchasers of town lots and the owners of real property in general." One year later, the federal high court's *Buckley v. Corrigan* decision ensured that the racial segregation tactics deployed in California would be shared with the rest of the nation. The National Association of Real Estate Boards created careful guidelines instructing its affiliates how to promote segregation in a manner that was consistent with the law. Moreover, the federal government boosted this effort in the 1930s, when the Home Owners' Loan Corporation and the Federal Housing Administration structured race restrictions into the standard housing and mortgage practices they instituted.[24]

THE WESTSIDE

In early 1928, the *Los Angeles Times* sponsored its first Home Beautiful exhibit to stimulate public interest in both residential real estate and domestic furnishings. Not surprisingly, all six houses it chose to display were located in the Westside. Sponsors deemed the exhibit a smashing success. Crowds flocked to mansions in Beverly Hills, Hollywood, and Los Feliz. Nestled in the foothills of the Santa Monica Mountains, these districts connoted the new marker of residential exclusivity enabled by expanding car ownership. Previously, the city's rich and powerful had sited their imposing homes on choice locations near downtown and adjacent streetcar lines. In the 1920s, they moved above and away from the masses, often uprooting those who had been relegated to formerly undesirable highlands. African Americans operating small ranches and chicken farms in Bel Air and Beverly Hills were displaced to make way for hillside mansions with sweeping panoramic views. By themselves, however, the mansions of Bel Air and Beverly Hills were incapable of producing the geography of the Westside and establishing Los Angeles as the capital of suburbanization. Gawkers might dream of living in them, but they ultimately needed to find a home within their means. Recognizing this, the Home Beautiful sponsors sought to expand the suburban ideal to middle-class consumers by including two model homes from the Westside's vast flatlands, where roughly half of all homes were owner occupied by 1930.[25]

Priced below $10,000, these relatively accessible homes were part of the new 230-acre Leimert Park subdivision in Southwest Los Angeles. Launched in the spring of 1927, Leimert Park exemplified how the lower-lying sections of the Westside became the preserve of the city's rising white middle class. A self-proclaimed pioneer in "the creative development of restricted residential parks," its namesake founder, Walter Leimert, was part of a new breed of large-scale developers who in rapid fashion transformed thousands of acres of open land into idyllic neighborhoods. After nearly two decades of doing business in the Oakland area, he had recently shifted his tack to the bustling Southland market. Considering Leimert Park the greatest venture of his career, the developer lent his name to a subdivision for the first time. Marked by the high standard of its initial improvements, it featured extrawide and concrete-paved parkways with grassy medians, meticulous landscaping with hundreds of trees and other plantings, and modern electric lighting with stylish fixtures. Nearly one thousand structures were established in the decade following its opening.[26]

Integral to the city's interwar expansion, new developments like Leimert Park demonstrated the Westside's appeal to white homeowners. Leimert's marketing narrative provides an indication of what made them attractive. Providing access to "FIVE MAJOR TRAFFIC BOULEVARDS," Leimert Park was strategically located within a sprawling city in the midst of a car-induced cultural transformation. But while it was just a short car trip away from downtown, it provided sanctuary from the travails of urban life. Far from a congested inner-city neighborhood, the subdivision was "a park with concrete streets." Using the Home Beautiful exhibit to showcase his entire community, Leimert sought to convince buyers that they could be immersed in the same culture as the wealthy for one-fourth of the cost. Appealing to the myth of the Spanish past, Leimert offered a "modern adaptation of the Early Monterey homes" that was "reminiscent of Early California in its most romantic days." Barker Bros. provided complementary Monterey-style furnishings for the entire house, inclusive of wall hangings and dishes, which could be had for a retail price of just $495. To feed domestic consumerism, marketing agents demonstrated "the ultra modern conveniences of the kitchens and the heating systems" to women. Male breadwinners were urged to envision themselves lounging in front of "the big fireplaces" or relaxing on the "patios." Leimert was so impressed with the response that he launched his own Small Homes Exhibition the following year, claiming that 250,000 visited his namesake subdivision for the event. In this sense, Los Angeles residents garnered new ideas about planning and design from places like Leimert Park regardless of where they ultimately settled.[27]

Fig. 1.2. Leimert Park development. New suburban apartments reflect the "mission" or "Spanish" style popular during the 1920s. Most residences in the subdivision were single-family homes. Security Pacific Collection/Los Angeles Public Library.

While they collectively defined the suburbanization of the city, the several thousand new subdivisions laid out during the 1920s were far from identical. Many and perhaps the majority were the product of a speculation frenzy that left the region with thousands of vacant lots as the bubble deflated. Leimert Park represented one of a series of efforts by large-scale developers to consolidate and rationalize the real estate industry in conjunction with financial institutions and title insurance companies. Planning to meet the needs of entire communities, Leimert incorporated parks, schools, and retail outlets within his subdivisions and contributed toward the improvement of public spaces when necessary. While they certainly hoped to augment their market share and capitalize on economies of scale, developers of massive subdivisions also sought to establish uniform housing standards, as well as both social and economic stability. Leimert recognized that a builder's reputation was shaped not only by what he constructed but also by how well it stood the test of time. Maintaining high standards was the purpose of his "Community Association Plan of protective restrictions." He required all purchasers of property to join a common dues-collecting homeowners' association, whose funds supported the upkeep of public areas. Residents were also contractually bound by the terms of their deed and association membership to uphold communitywide standards. Historian Greg Hise has remarked that Leimert Park "set a pattern that, with modifications, formed a basis for community projects in the immediate pre–World War II period and into the postwar era."[28]

While multiple factors thus shaped the perceived character of neighborhoods, racial politics were ultimately at the core of any effort to offer white homeowners a sense of economic security and social stability. In their quest to maintain community standards, the new and massive subdivisions proved to be the greatest progenitors of residential segregation. Although whites in older sections of Los Angeles fought to keep nonwhites from inhabiting their neighborhoods, they often faced severe difficulties obtaining unanimous consent for race restrictions. To cover an existing neighborhood with a restrictive covenant required securing the approval of every property owner in the area on a house-by-house basis. Not only did this require a high degree of unity; it also necessitated a tremendous level of organization and technical proficiency in the vagaries of contract law. By contrast, developers of new subdivisions could incorporate restrictions directly into the deed of every lot. In this manner, homes across the newly developed Westside were put under the rule of exclusionary deed restrictions. Tens of thousands of white residents in Los Angeles took possession of new homes during the interwar period that were covered by restrictive covenants barring residency by nonwhites. Regardless of their own beliefs, they were required to uphold racial segregation.

Owners of new suburban homes generally found restrictions to be far more desirable than onerous. Not only did they not object; they actively sought out communities that were defined by their contractual obligations. While public spaces in the city were sometimes segregated, what most concerned suburban whites was the character of their neighborhoods. To be certain, in moments of heated white agitation, the city had barred Japanese residents from the public golf courses and tennis courts and restricted Black access to public swimming pools to Thursdays preceding water changes. But these affronts were challenged by civil rights activists and sometimes overturned by court order or political directive. Residential restrictions proved far more ubiquitous. In the eyes of their inhabitants, planned subdivisions provided a sense of order in a chaotic world. While almost every subdivision in the Southwest that preceded Leimert Park had been restricted to whites and openly advertised this fact, Leimert boasted of offering "the most comprehensive restrictions of any district in Los Angeles." He further promised that his plan of restrictions was "the ONLY ONE whereby BEAUTY, DISTINCTION and ORDER [could] be maintained PERMANENTLY." Residents willingly submitted to mandatory membership in the Leimert Park Community Homes Association, and they steadfastly upheld the restrictions obligated by their deed agreements. A decade after the subdivision opened, Leimert reported near universal compliance with the homeowners' association requirements. For instance, the delinquency rate with dues payments stood at only 0.01 percent. While Leimert was undoubtedly in the vanguard of segregated development, the restrictions he upheld were far more common than he let on. Thousands of white residents in the region were joining similar associations tied to other large projects.[29]

Indeed, Leimert and his cohort contributed to regional and national trends in residential segregation. Concerned that the task of maintaining order required all elements of the realty industry to abide by their standards, they became actively involved in regional and national organizations. Realty boards acting like guilds guarded access to the industry and overtly restricted membership to whites. The Los Angeles board issued a directive "that Realtors should not sell property to other than Caucasian in territories occupied by them." It further identified "Deed and Restrictive Covenant Restrictions" as "the only way" to control the "color question." The statewide body especially commended the Southwest Los Angeles Realty Board for its leadership in the drive for segregation as exemplified by the work of its "Race Restrictions Committee," which tutored white residents in the creation and operation of restrictive covenants.[30]

Although developers like Leimert saw themselves as "community builders," the cohesion they created was largely negative in character. Members of the community were encouraged to respect their neighbors . . . or be sued by them! Residents were thus bound to each other by contractual obligations and a shared sense of fear and prejudice. Such anxiety intensified in neighborhoods closer to the inner-city concentrations of people of color. In the late 1920s, University of Southern California (USC) researcher Bessie McClenahan remarked that white middle-class residents of an older suburb in the near Westside were "like branches or tree trunks caught in a swirling river current which find lodgment here and there against the river bank, only to be caught up again and hurried to another resting place." These white suburbanites were always on the lookout for a newer subdivision offering greater physical distance from the threat of nonwhite "invasion" and the latest standards in "protection." Monetary interests in the form of property values— inevitably linked to fear and prejudice—provided the ultimate basis for white neighborhood solidarity. Upton Sinclair once declared the city's residents had "no organized connection with one another," for the average individual desired only "to live his own life and to be protected in his own little privileges." Los Angeles was a "smug and self-satisfied" place where "the sacredness of property" was "the first and last article of its creed." In fact, suburban whites spent a high percentage of their income on their homes and expected them to be profitable investments. Realty interests fed both expectations of profitability and fears of loss. Announcing the opening of his eponymous subdivision, Leimert declared that purchasers of lots were assured "quick and certain profits." Promoting his association plan, he stated, "Detrimental changes in neighborhoods, through expiring short-term restrictions, which have robbed investors in Los Angeles and other cities of millions of dollars, can NEVER occur in Leimert Park." Ultimately, homeowners of every neighborhood in the city became highly concerned about property values, often to the point of obsession. Nearly inseparable from racist ideology, the "property values" argument was driven by circular logic, since it was primarily white prejudice that ostensibly rendered neighborhoods where the color line had been breached less marketable.[31]

State action facilitated the flight to newer suburbs. As much as white developers and residents espoused the virtues of private property, suburban development could not have occurred as it did without substantial public investment. This was especially apparent in the transformation of Leimert Park into the center of the new Crenshaw district. While Leimert boasted of providing $500,000 worth of public improvements on top of helping to build Audubon Junior High, the city subsidized his subdivision to a far greater degree. Public funding supplied $750,000 just to pave Angeles Mesa Drive and widen it to eight lanes. This served as the district's central and namesake thruway, following its rechristening as Crenshaw Boulevard in June 1930. Moreover, an important reason why the land Leimert had purchased from Clara Baldwin Stocker in the mid-1920s had not been developed was because it was prone to flooding. In conjunction with the opening of Leimert Park, the city addressed this major concern by launching underground construction of a massive twenty-eight-foot-wide storm drain beginning at Slauson Avenue and emptying into Ballona Creek. As realty interests converted profits into political influence, it seemed that nothing took precedence over subsidies for sprawl-oriented, car-friendly development. In the midst of the Depression, the public paid for the extension of Santa Barbara Boulevard with "allocations from the city's unemployment relief funds."[32]

Leimert Park was a symbol of white privilege during the interwar era—a time when racial animus accumulated and patterns of racial oppression consolidated in Los Angeles. Tied to the city's explosive economic growth and expansion of settlement, the Westside suburban ideal fed on notions of attraction and repulsion. As Los Angeles opened new horizons for white America, a kind of closing of a frontier occurred for Black and

Japanese Americans. The relative level of tolerance that had previously characterized the city began to fade. The more racial segregation shaped the reality of life, the more Black and Japanese Americans were correspondingly forced to adjust their survival strategies. And with racist measures like restrictive covenants solidly closing off most residential areas and overt white hostility marking much of what remained, they would have to fight house by house and block by block to expand their living opportunities.

CHAPTER 2

Home Improvement

"SENSIBLE BUILDING RESTRICTIONS prevent any shacks being built on this tract," declared Wilbur C. Gordon as he promoted a 213-acre "high-class Boulevard Sub-Division." Launching his ambitious project in December 1925, he purchased "a barley field" just outside the southwestern city limits of Los Angeles. Aiming to capitalize on the region's seemingly endless desire for new suburban housing, the doctor-turned-real-estate-developer vowed the eponymous Gordon Manor would become "a real place where trees and shrubs and flowers abound, where rolling grassy lawns prevail and every home would be a thing of beauty." Gordon was identical to Walter Leimert and other Westside developers in 1920s Los Angeles save one crucial feature—he was Black. With housing serving as perhaps the most prominent status symbol in the city, Gordon called on African Americans to create their "own Wilshire or Hollywood" through the development of what he deemed "positively the best and most desirable subdivision ever offered our group." In many ways, his project accommodated the decade's new racial order in that it made no attempt to challenge race restrictions explicitly and sought to build housing only for members of his race. A proponent of racial uplift, Gordon deployed class-based building restrictions in hopes of establishing a model community that would provide moral and physical evidence of racial progress. Working cooperatively with white financiers, he selected a relatively remote site that had never appealed to white residential developers.[1]

Despite such precaution, the proposed Gordon Manor alarmed powerful white real estate interests, whose repulsion from African Americans conveniently coincided with a belief that a regional park was critical to the development of the South Bay region. On April 12, 1926, they pushed a resolution through the Los Angeles County Board of Supervisors to take Gordon's property through eminent domain. The park proponents claimed an additional one hundred acres of agricultural land in response to a petition drive by white residents demanding "the removal of the Japanese tenants." With funds raised by the sale of public bonds under the recently approved Mattoon Act, the Board of Supervisors established Alondra Park by paying cash settlements to Gordon and a bank that had leased the farming land. However, when asked to pay the assessments needed to develop the park, nearby residents and municipalities balked.

They were satisfied with a weed patch devoid of Black homeowners and Japanese tenant farmers. Until the postwar era, it thus sat unimproved, much like the land surrounding a nearby drainage channel that was officially referred to as "Nigger Slough." The city's Black newspaper, the *California Eagle*, blasted the county supervisors for bowing to the wishes of "the Ku Klux Klan and Southern Crackers." Gordon called the move "THE BIGGEST SLAP IN THE FACE yet recorded in the history of California." County supervisor John Anson Ford would later remark that Alondra Park had been "conceived in sin and born in iniquity."[2]

The Gordon Manor debacle demonstrated the high degree to which white suburban interests believed their economic and social well-being required excluding people of color. As middle-class whites reserved as much of the Westside as possible for themselves, most Black and Japanese Americans before World War II lived on the Eastside, where the city's working-class neighborhoods and industrial zones were concentrated. The Central Avenue district and Little Tokyo, respective centers of Black and Japanese American social life, were adjacent Eastside communities. Neither was totally segregated; both were, in fact, multiethnic. But sites of "open" residency like this became hemmed in by race restrictions and white hostility.

The quest for housing "improvement" took place within this interwar-era context. Black and Japanese American elites sought to improve their housing options and thereby uplift their races through better living standards. But as the architects of racial oppression in Los Angeles accentuated the relative vulnerabilities of racial/national minorities, the two groups' experiences with racism, while overlapping, were not identical. Generally restricted to the same residential areas as African Americans, Japanese immigrants resented discrimination as much as or more than Blacks did. Yet their status as "aliens ineligible to citizenship" deprived them of even the latter's imperfect avenues of recourse. As foreign nationals, they were forced to rely on Japanese consular officials whose own interests lay in avoiding rather than confronting racial conflict at the local level. After being subjected to violent attacks and witnessing the complicity of law enforcement, Issei leaders ultimately recognized that racist structures affected all communities of color. Consequently, they looked to African Americans for leadership on the housing front. Denied access to new subdivisions, elite Black homeowners formed their own improvement associations to beautify their surroundings and enhance their moral environment. At the same time, civil rights lawyers employed carefully plotted strategies to break down restrictive covenants within existing white neighborhoods. Although housing struggles spanned the Eastside and Westside, the latter's West Jefferson became the interwar-era prize of the Black community's upper crust. Since Japanese American elites shared

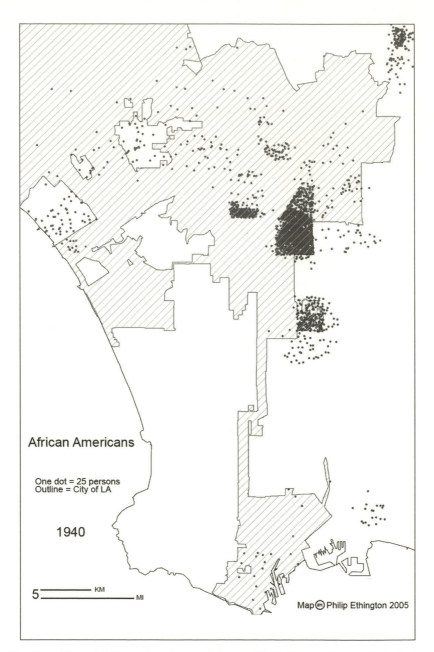

Fig. 2.1. Map of African American residences, 1940. Largest African American cluster represents the Central Avenue district. Smaller clusters represent West Jefferson (to the west) and Watts (to the south). Philip J. Ethington, Anne Marie Kooistra, Edward DeYoung, John P. Wilson, Dowell Myers, and Sungho Ryu, *Los Angeles County Union Census Tract Data Series, 1940–2000*, Created with the support of the John Randolph and Dora Haynes Foundation (Los Angeles: University of Southern California, 2000–2006).

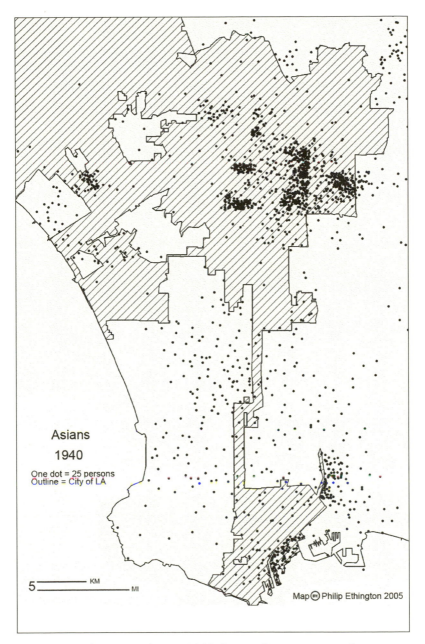

Asians
1940

One dot = 25 persons
Outline = City of LA

5 ———— KM
———— MI

Map ⓒ Philip Ethington 2005

Fig. 2.2. Map of Asian residences, 1940. Larger clusters represent Japanese communities in Little Tokyo/Central Avenue (center of map) and Boyle Heights (to the east). Smaller clusters of Japanese can be seen in the Westside; truck farmers occupy outlying areas. This map actually represents those racial or ethnic groups the census designated as "other." Japanese comprised the majority of this category, which also included other Asians and American Indians. Ethington et al., *Los Angeles Census Tract Data*.

that group's goals and values, they too sought access to neighborhoods that were first "opened" by Blacks. Herein lay the principal basis of a common Westside struggle that fused the racial uplift strategies of both groups.

THE EASTSIDE

Black and Japanese American settlement patterns overlapped considerably within the relatively unrestricted sections of the Eastside. The adjacent Little Tokyo and Central Avenue districts both emerged from older, transient sections of town with a history of providing low-rent accommodations for migrant laborers. Not coincidentally, both were also situated near the city's "red-light" district. Civic leaders fretted constantly about the Eastside. In 1906, the city created the Housing Commission largely out of desire to remove Eastside slums that visiting social reformer Jacob Riis called as bad as any he had ever seen. Race mixing, vice, and industrial pollution—all were feared by suburban whites, yet they were generally content to see those aspects of urban life contained within Eastside pockets. As restrictions barred African Americans from most of the city, Black culture and community life in Los Angeles became nearly synonymous with the Central Avenue district. At the northern and oldest section of the district sat long-established Black institutions like the *California Eagle* newspaper, as well as the First African Methodist Episcopal Church (known by its grand structure at the intersection of "Eighth and Towne") and Second Baptist Church. A half mile west of Central Avenue, however, stood white neighborhoods that would prove impenetrable until the postwar era. The strengthening of segregation created a distinct African American consumer market, while pushing community expansion southward. Characterized by historian Lonnie Bunch "as a miniature Harlem," the district featured jazz clubs and other nightlife hot spots that stretched down Central Avenue twenty blocks south of downtown toward the famed Dunbar Hotel. Still, it is important to recognize that African Americans were at most a plurality of the residents of the district, which had earlier served as a central place of embankment for Jewish migrants and continued to attract European, as well as Mexican and Asian, immigrants. Far from one-dimensional, the Eastside was rather a rich and diverse place.[3]

After redevelopment displaced the residents and businesses from prior Japanese concentrations on West Fourth and Sixth streets, Little Tokyo emerged in the East First Street area during the late 1910s. Previously known as "Five Points" according to scholar Mark Wild, this area was historically a mixed-usage, multiethnic, working-class neighborhood. Pioneering Black-owned businesses were once concentrated here. In the early 1900s, Jewish merchants predominated on East First, but friction developed as Japanese moved in. Claiming their brethren were mistreated, Japanese community leaders staged a boycott of Jewish-owned stores in 1907 and urged the Issei to buy only from their fellow countrymen—testimony to the long history of interethnic customer-merchant conflict and corresponding exploitation of the issue by ethnic business owners. Around the same time, the Afro-American Council lobbied for civil rights legislation in part because it claimed some Issei restaurants refused "colored trade." The *Los Angeles Times* commented, "The little brown Jap serves notice that the negro is no brother of his." Quite often, the mainstream press discussed the activities of this diverse section of town as if they were circus events. A December 1911 altercation between a German, an African American, and a group of Japanese was derided as a "war of nations" by the *Times*. Even after it became the center of the Japanese community, the Little Tokyo area retained its multiethnic character. As late as 1927, for instance, one-third of its thirty hotels and boardinghouses catered solely to whites.[4]

Demonstrating the interdependence of town and country among the Issei, Little Tokyo functioned as a social center for all and a business hub for Japanese Americans in agriculture and fishing. Centrally located between farming areas such as the South Bay/Moneta Valley, San Fernando Valley, and the San Gabriel Valley, Little Tokyo businesses supplied most of the services and supplies that farmers required. Rural residents also traveled downtown on weekends and holidays for cultural and religious activities, as well as for access to imported goods and ethnic fare. New migrants and seasonal workers particularly clustered around Little Tokyo's inexpensive boardinghouses, restaurants, and recreational outlets (such as pool halls, bars, and brothels) catering to the bachelor society. From here, employment agencies, which often served double duty as hotels and boardinghouses (and, in some cases, triple duty as churches), placed day laborers into jobs around the city and seasonal employment on the farms. In the off-season, the "floating" population swelled the Japanese ranks of the city by as much as 50 percent, as East First establishments reabsorbed most of the agricultural workforce.[5]

As the southern boundary of Little Tokyo blurred with the northern boundary of the Central Avenue district, commercial and interpersonal traffic were frequently exchanged between the two communities. Japanese churches of different faiths and denominations were centered in Little Tokyo, where a handful of Blacks and a significant number of whites could be found celebrating Hanamatsuri, the Japanese day of worship marking the birth of the Buddha. At the same time, Japanese Americans lived in the Central Avenue district because it offered unrestricted housing and close proximity to the wholesale produce and flower markets where many toiled. Sports and youth clubs brought Black and Japanese Americans into frequent contact. And while the image of whites slumming in Harlem establishments of the Jazz Age is ubiquitous, jazz culture in Los Angeles emerged from a multiracial context as diverse ethnic groups came of age with knowledge of each other's social and cultural worlds. Florence "Tiny" Brantley, for instance, played piano for a choir of Black and Japanese Americans, while drummer Hideo ("Little Krupa") Kawano performed regularly in Central Avenue hot spots like the Club Alabam with African American Johnny Otis and Mexican American Don Tosti.[6]

Outside these concentrations, there were pockets of unrestricted housing in suburban areas that had been settled by mixes of Blacks, Asians, and Mexicans prior to the 1920s. These included West Jefferson, Uptown/Pico Heights, Virgil/Madison, and Temple Street in the near Westside, as well as Sawtelle in the far west, Watts to the south, and Pacoima in the San Fernando Valley. Standing somewhat apart from all prewar neighborhoods, however, was Boyle Heights, which offered the best selection of single-family housing untouched by restrictive covenants anywhere in the city. Just east of Little Tokyo and across the river, the district housed the largest community of Jews during the interwar period. Mexican Americans moved to Boyle Heights as a wave of immigration provoked by the Mexican Revolution created a housing crunch in the historic Plaza district and other downtown neighborhoods were uprooted by industry. Their racial status before the law was somewhat ambiguous with regard to housing discrimination. While in some cases restrictive covenants explicitly excluded occupancy by "Mexicans," in other cases Mexicans were judged fit to occupy housing restricted to "Caucasians." Regardless, however, of the specific impact of restrictive covenants, social forces promoted segregation of Mexicans from whites. Thus, the initial suburban migration of Mexicans to Boyle Heights ultimately began a process that would later lead to the creation of the East Los Angeles barrio. During the 1910s, Japanese Americans first moved to the Evergreen section of Boyle Heights, where they were joined by a small cluster of African Americans. While the Central Avenue district expanded south, Little Tokyo with scarce room to grow became less and less attractive to families. Merchants comprised the first wave of Issei migrating to Boyle Heights homes that were only a short streetcar ride from Little Tokyo. By the outbreak of World War II, the majority of Japanese American wholesale produce workers lived there, as well. Increasingly, only the aging Issei bachelors still considered Little Tokyo a primary residential option.[7]

But with most of the Eastside restricted, few Black or Japanese Americans lived beyond Boyle Heights (see map opposite page 1). Directly to the east lay unincorporated Belvedere, which stubbornly opened up to Mexicans but repelled most Issei. Northeast of downtown, Eagle Rock was part of a collection of largely all-white and middle-class areas stretching toward posh suburbs like San Marino and Arcadia. A trickling of Japanese residents, or even a single family, moving into a northeastern neighborhood was sufficient to trigger cries of "invasion" by alarmed whites. In Rose Hill, at the north end of Lincoln Heights, exclusionists hoisted a large banner on Huntington Drive reading "Japs: Don't let the sun set on you here. KEEP MOVING." During 1921 and 1922, those exclusionists received resolutions of support from homeowners' associations across the city and sympathetic front-page coverage from the *Los Angeles Record*, the "pro-labor" daily that advocated a total ban on Japanese immigration. The newspaper warned that the city's Issei residents were "furtive brown invaders" seeking "to penetrate American civilization, and overthrow it." Other sections of the Eastside were the principal sites of residence for white workers, who generally lived near sources of industrial employment. Beyond the city's boundary in the southeastern section of Los Angeles County, "Black Gold Suburbs" like Bell, South Gate, Lynwood, and Maywood—all incorporated between 1917 and 1930—arose in concert with the development of the petroleum industry. As Becky M. Nicolaides has written, white workers who experienced less and less autonomy on the job asserted their independence through homeownership. Primarily "native-born" whites from the Great Plains, working-class migrants coveted the cheap and plentiful land, low taxes, and loose building and land-use regulations that these industrial suburbs offered in order to craft "semiproletarian" households combining wage labor with self-reliance. The small-town political climate of the suburbs also provided white workers with greater clout and authority to monopolize the jobs and homes in these areas. For instance, the Oil Workers International Union restricted membership to whites, while a Maywood subdivision advertised "race restrictions insuring a white American community." In 1930, Blacks represented only 1,766 of 650,219 total persons living in the "Black Gold Suburbs."[8]

The most highly contested section of the Eastside lay inside Los Angeles proper and between Black concentrations in the Central Avenue district and Watts. Although these areas lying west of the industrial corridor would later come to be known as the South Central Los Angeles ghetto, they were predominantly white during the interwar period. White workers flocked to new subdivisions in the southern section of the city, as builders met the needs of employers by churning out tracts and tracts of housing. New construction technologies, extension of utilities, and increased levels of financing all combined to make housing affordable. White workers simultaneously emulated and resented elite whites. Thus, on the one hand, racial exclusivity became a critical marker of working-class residential status. The Goodyear Park subdivision, for instance, was established in the early 1920s in conjunction with the Goodyear plant, considered a milestone in the city's industrialization and maturation. Catering to white workers expected to have first dibs on factory jobs, its developer declared, "Central Ave. and vicinity south of Santa Barbara Ave. is populated with high-class Caucasian people, and we wish to maintain this standard. GOODYEAR PARK IS PERPETUALLY RESTRICTED." On the other hand, working-class whites shut out from elite white neighborhoods by class-biased zoning and market forces often saw themselves as situated on the front lines in the fight against a nonwhite "invasion." With an avalanche of new construction, older neighborhoods became comparatively less desirable and marketable to whites. To Black and Japanese Americans, these places represented an opportunity to expand on limited housing options. Without recourse to bourgeois mechanisms, especially "protective" zoning and the uniform deed restrictions employed by new subdivisions, working-class whites often became anxious and belligerent. As one social critic observed, "If it is race which determines the adversaries, it is class which determines the weapons."[9]

White residents in the South Park district raised alarm that they stood in the path of the Central Avenue district's southward expansion during the 1920s. The South Park Improvement Association was well organized. It claimed twenty-six hundred members in 1920, when it launched a campaign to drive Issei merchants out of the area because they were "a menace to our white citizens' business interests." A new furor began when African Americans began to settle in South Park at middecade. Like weekly papers in most white neighborhoods, the *South Park Bulletin* served as the central propaganda organ for racist agitators. Resident James A. Bangle advised his neighbors to remember the lessons they had learned from dealing with "the Japs" who had "invaded California." Warning that miscegenation would bring the demise of the white race, he now called for deploying "Southern states' methods" to handle African Americans. While the use of harsh rhetoric, threats, and violence often symbolized the frightening resolve of racist agitators, they were frequently signs of frustration and desperation from homeowners lacking the exclusionary resources of white elites. Prejudice was widespread among white homeowners, and most desired to live in racially homogeneous surroundings. But to what lengths were they willing to go to fend off an "invasion" of Blacks or Japanese? Many "soft" white racists could tolerate a handful of nonwhite neighbors, so long as they kept their houses in order and did not interfere with white social life. But in a rapidly expanding city, whites with even moderate incomes had ample housing options. Both the fear of a nonwhite "invasion" and the anxiety caused by racist agitation itself caused white panic selling, hastening the racial transition of neighborhoods. In South Park, white homeowners filed lawsuits against Black residents for violating racial covenants, but they were ultimately defeated by the actions of fleeing whites. The court denied enforcement of the covenants, on the grounds that the already accomplished transition of the neighborhood negated their original intent.[10]

To shape the racial composition of their children's schools, white residents made concerted efforts to police the boundaries governing neighborhood school attendance. State law from the nineteenth century permitted segregation of Mexican, Indian, and Chinese students, and the state legislature acting under pressure of exclusionists added Japanese Americans to this ignoble list in 1921. Black political clout, however, was sufficient to fend off modest legislative attempts to permit segregation of African American students, and Los Angeles never used its license to formally segregate Japanese students. Color lines were thus established through local actions. In response to white complaints, the Los Angeles school board regularly gerrymandered school attendance boundaries and instituted other arbitrary measures to maintain segregation. White South Park residents were alarmed by the rising Black population of Jefferson High School, where their children and most of the Central Avenue district's students were channeled. Demanding their "equal right" to segregated schooling, whites were granted special permission to transfer to all-white Fremont High to the south. The Fremont Improvement Association, however, now worried that "the encroachment of the Negro and Mongolian races" jeopardized the racial homogeneity of that school. Its leaders called on white residents to "preserve the schools and district for our own race" by halting the southern line of Black residential expansion at Slauson Avenue. In situations like this, racist organizers had a relatively easier time keeping a neighborhood homogeneous than stopping a transition in progress. Fremont High remained predominantly white through the interwar era, although slogans such as "Keep West Slauson White" and "No Niggers at Fremont" continued to fuel racist organizing in the area during the 1940s.[11]

With much of the city blanketed by race restrictions and the expansion of the Central Avenue district slowed by white hostility, living conditions on the Eastside became increasingly congested. While exclusionary immigration laws limited the growth of the Japanese American community, the African American population quadrupled during the interwar period owing especially to migration from the South. By 1940, 70 percent of the city's 63,774 Black residents occupied the Central Avenue district. The typical African American denizen of Los Angeles lived in a census tract that was 79 percent nonwhite and housed a percentage of Black residents eighteen times greater than their share of the general population. "Doubling up" became a key survival strategy, and African Americans were almost twice as likely to have boarders than whites in 1930. The Depression intensified the city's general housing crisis, as new construction halted and Dust Bowl migrants streamed into the region from even harder-hit parts of the country. In 1937 the city's health department noted that impoverished families lived in ramshackle housing on small, cheap, and unimproved lots sold by "unscrupulous land sub-dividers" to desperate households. As bad as things were, according to its report, "conditions with reference to colored people [were] bound to become worse." Describing the Central Avenue district as the "melting pot" of Los Angeles, the federal government's Home Owners Loan Corporation deemed it "thoroughly blighted" and a "fit location for a slum clearance project."[12]

Although segregation, absentee slumlords, and economic hardship formed the root cause of social ills, the ideological construction of the ghetto as a "problem area" focused increasingly on pejorative characterizations of southern Black working-class migrants. White and Black leaders alike fretted that rural migrants lacked the cultural resources to adjust to life in the city. Once a Black middle-class outpost, the Furlong neighborhood became a part of the growing Central Avenue district during the interwar era. But it deteriorated notably as industries in the adjacent municipality of Vernon externalized their social costs and pollution. By the middle of the Depression, only low-income rural Black migrants were moving into Furlong. The African American social scientist J. Max Bond commented, "Already on a low cultural level, these people have been reduced by the evils of the city—poverty and vice and the numerous other menaces that lurk in a vicious environment—to an even lower level." Social workers in Central Avenue remarked that they were overwhelmed by an outburst of juvenile delinquency caused by broken homes, poor living conditions, and the rise of "associations" (gangs). In fact, reform efforts failed not because the situation was hopeless; they did so in large measure because the system was set up to fail. The offenses committed by African American youth were mostly nonviolent. Yet, as the Urban League's Floyd Covington noted, Black youth on probation were denied service by youth delinquency agencies funded by the Community Chest (forerunner to the United Way). Reflecting the Catch-22 situation, judges sometimes imposed harsher sentences on African Americans because they lacked confidence that the youth would receive proper oversight while on probation.[13]

As racial stereotypes and segregation linked their fates to the inhabitants of the "ghetto," Black and Japanese American elites advanced models of racial uplift to promote internal community policing. Reflecting white notions of Progressive reform, ethnic leaders believed that maintaining the moral integrity of their communities was critical not only to making their own individual members virtuous and productive but also to demonstrating their races' overall fitness for civilization. Both the Forum and the Japanese Association, leading community organizations launched around the turn of the twentieth century, advanced an agenda rooted in racial uplift that stressed virtue and shunned vice. Founded in 1903 as the Los Angeles Men's Forum, the former worked with churches, the Negro press, and law enforcement to suppress the "vicious element" within the community. Forum leaders further offered tutelage to new migrants to ensure they would "become useful members of society." While the Forum developed into a mass participatory organization by providing the Black community's principal meeting ground for political debate, it became less and less functional as segregation advanced and the community grew larger and more complex over the course of the interwar period. The Japanese Association functioned as a mutual aid society, an institution commonly found in Mexican and European immigrant communities too. It sought to assist Issei adjustment to American society by providing social services and organizing social events, but the organization also provided the Japanese consulate with a means to assert control over community leadership. In conjunction with the American state, the Japanese Foreign Ministry regulated and monitored the flow of Japanese immigration. Through the 1908 Gentlemen's Agreement, Japan promised to halt labor migration, and the United States allowed for the entry of "picture brides." Consular control of "picture bride" migration, expressed through directives issued to the Japanese Association, legitimated the representative function of that quasi-official body while granting the foreign ministry leverage over the Issei community. Japan established its Los Angeles consulate in 1916 and around the same time worked with Issei leaders to bring local community organizations under the regional authority of the Central Japanese Association. Neither, however, proved able to dictate the moral behavior of the immigrant population. The Yamato Club gambling hall, for instance, reigned as the social center of Little Tokyo, and leaders of organized crime became respected community figures by tending to the social welfare of the indigent.[14]

To distance themselves from the stigma of the ghetto, elite Black and Japanese Americans sought to cross over from the Eastside to the Westside. Their failure, while Jewish professionals and entrepreneurs largely succeeded, revealed the boundaries of whiteness in the Westside. Anthropologist Karen Brodkin has noted that anti-Semitism on the East Coast peaked during the interwar period before giving way and allowing Jews to "become white folks" during the postwar era. This process of assimilation, however, seems to have been accelerated in Los Angeles. Although present, anti-Semitism was less pervasive, and Jews frequently evaded the purview of racial covenants. According to historians Max Vorspan and Lloyd P. Gartner, many of the "most prosperous and acculturated Jews" relocated from Boyle Heights to suburban neighborhoods such as Hollywood and Fairfax during the 1920s and 1930s. While some gentiles most certainly harbored prejudices against Jews, they nevertheless lived interspersed with Jewish neighbors. In addition, a handful of descendants of the Californios joined in the settlement of upscale Westside neighborhoods like West Adams and the Wilshire district and were followed by exiles from the Diaz regime. This tiny subsection of the Los Angeles elite, many of whom were the living embodiment of the city's cherished "Spanish heritage," comprised the exception that proved the rule of barrioization.[15]

The Politics of Housing

At a 1926 East Adams Improvement and Protective Association meeting, C. H. Alston, a lawyer and the body's president, declared that buying and occupying homes "wherever money will permit" was "the proper thing for [African Americans] to do" even if it required "the aid of a gun and some good powder." He was among a class of elite Black homeowners who led campaigns for "better" housing during the interwar period by deploying a variety of tactics ranging from grassroots organizing to blockbusting, legal wrangling, and even armed self-defense. African Americans like Alston upheld citizenship rights that were denied Japanese immigrants. Whereas the Issei would become a symbol of entrepreneurial prowess, Black activists provided a model of residential struggle in Los Angeles. Conservative and progressive tendencies shaped these housing struggles. From the perspective of race, they unquestionably promoted democratic access to housing by challenging race restrictions. Neighborhood exclusion campaigns designed to harden racial divisions promoted solidarity among whites and Blacks alike. Regardless of political ideology, African Americans frequently rallied around community members who resisted racist attacks on homeownership. From the perspective of class, however, housing "improvement" campaigns were driven by the sort of "bourgeois agents of civilization" identified by historian Kevin Gaines in his study of racial uplift. Rather than directly confront the living conditions within the inner city, they believed that by divorcing themselves from the problem "ghetto," they could demonstrate that their race was capable of maintaining the same standards upheld by white homeowners.[16]

Three main factors situated African Americans in the vanguard of the fight for "better" housing. First, Black homeowners were simply greater in number and more tightly organized than were Japanese Americans. Even as they shed a sojourner mentality, Japanese immigrants were reluctant, because of their marginal legal status, to enter into the detailed negotiations required for home purchases, especially from whites. By contrast, the Black community had an established history in the region and a legacy of owning and selling real estate dating back to early pioneers like Biddy Mason. In 1930, one out of every three African Americans in Los Angeles owned a home—more than double the rate in Detroit, triple the rate in Chicago, and six times the rate in New York. While the Black homeownership rate nearly matched the city's overall rate of 36.7 percent, only 18.6 percent of Mexican Americans, 8.6 percent of Chinese Americans, and 4.8 percent of Japanese Americans in Los Angeles owned homes. The proliferation of Black improvement associations demonstrated the high degree to which African Americans not only took pride in homeownership but linked residence to broader conceptions of dignity and status. Flourishing first in the mid-1920s, at least eight Black improvement associations existed in 1926. Although most were rooted in the Central Avenue district, one was based in Boyle Heights, and two were in older sections of the Westside (Pico Heights and West Jefferson). In many respects, they fulfilled the same functions as their white counterparts. Typically, the associations were founded and run by business owners and professionals. Meetings were held once or twice a week. In addition to hosting social and cultural events, association members routinely concerned themselves with monitoring the condition of streets, sponsoring home beautification contests, electing block captains, and advocating that tunnels be built for children to avoid crossing busy streets on their way to school. They handled neighborhood chores themselves and lobbied the city to undertake the larger construction projects. These efforts likely factored into a 1939 survey's finding that African Americans were only half as likely as Asians and Mexicans (though still nearly twice as likely as whites) to live in substandard housing. While concerned with individual property rights and interests, African American improvement associations also joined forces to vindicate the humanity of the race. The citywide Progressive Federation of Improvement Associations passed resolutions denouncing the 1926 *Buckley* decision that upheld restrictive covenants. It also challenged the city's practice of preventing Blacks from using public swimming pools on "white" days (usually six days of the week).[17]

Second, African American leaders actively promoted housing struggles within the community. The *California Eagle* especially acted as the primary vehicle for transmitting this knowledge. John Neimore had founded the city's longest-standing Black newspaper, previously known as the *Owl*, in 1879. On his deathbed in February 1912, Neimore reportedly asked his young staffer Charlotta A. Spears—who had arrived from Providence, Rhode Island, less than two years prior—to take over the *Eagle*. Having initially planned for only a "two-year health-recuperation stay" in Los Angeles, Spears instead began four decades at the helm of the *Eagle*, during which time she would become one of the most prominent denizens of Black Los Angeles. Appending *California* to the newspaper's title, she hired Kansas migrant Joseph B. Bass as editor and married him for good measure. As publisher and managing editor, Charlotta Bass strove to uphold Neimore's vision of the *Eagle* "as a new Underground Railway, an agency to attract Negroes to California, where they would enjoy a greater portion of freedom and human rights than in their former slave environs." She ensured that every fight against restrictive covenants received ample publicity within its pages.[18]

An organized team of civil rights lawyers with a well-developed litigation strategy comprised the third factor placing African Americans in the leadership of housing struggles. A few Issei nationwide possessed an American legal education, but they were generally restricted from membership in the bar as "aliens ineligible to citizenship." Officially, they could only assist other lawyers before the court. By contrast, men like Harvard Law graduate Willis O. Tyler led Black legal struggles in Los Angeles. They were part of a strong organizational network of African American lawyers, many of whom belonged to the NAACP. Formed in the aftermath of W.E.B. Du Bois's 1913 visit, the Los Angeles NAACP chapter, initially composed of African American elites and their white allies, prioritized the legal battle against discrimination. In conjunction with the civil rights organization's national leadership, local attorneys developed carefully thought-out campaigns against restrictions. Their "admirably efficient technique" was detailed in a pamphlet written by Lloyd H. Fisher for the American Council on Race Relations. First, Black realtors purchased houses not covered by a restrictive covenant. Second, they sought out lots where "technical flaws" existed in the covenant. Faulty wording in a document would be grounds for a covenant to be deemed unenforceable by the courts. Third, they searched for lots covered by minor covenants, in other words, those in areas where only a small number of homes were restricted. These covenants were likely to be defended by associations with fewer members, a lower level of organization, and fewer resources to pursue legal action. By judiciously plotting a course of action to break down several minor covenants, Black homeowners' advocates prepared for challenges to larger covenants.[19]

Fisher, however, was writing in hindsight about a process that had unfolded over the course of the interwar period in a manner that was anything but smooth. The burden of "covenant breaking" fell on the shoulders of a few courageous souls. These activist-minded homeowners supported a far greater number of "passive dues-paying beneficiaries" who feared ruffling feathers and went along "solely because the only alternative was really wretched housing." In fact, many of the earliest test cases were lost. The victims of some of the most egregious rulings lived in and around the Entwistle tract, a majority Black section of the Central Avenue district near the Dunbar Hotel. A white woman named Lulu Letteau had placed racial restrictive covenants over three blocks covering 180 lots in 1905. The covenants were largely ignored, however, as African Americans began moving into the neighborhood by 1907. When Letteau's heirs realized they could seize forfeited Black-owned properties, they conveniently rediscovered the covenants and filed suit over deed violations in the mid-1920s. African Americans William H. and Eunice Long were the first to be taken to court. Not only did they lose their home; William had a nervous breakdown and died in the process, as did his lawyer, NAACP leader Burton Ceruti. Eunice suffered a debilitating illness. The Letteaus continued to sue the rest of the tract's Black owners, while the "Home Protection League" launched a broader campaign to impose restrictions on nearby homes, including the East Forty-fifth Street residence of African American minister Sally Trainor. Self-described as "a poor feeble widow, a half-blind old woman," Trainor had reached "seventy years of age by hard works, tears and struggles for myself and others." In 1927, she was immediately sued upon taking occupancy of her home, wherein she called on "every home loving, honest Ethiopian person [to] stand together and plead, and pray for the mercy of God, that God Almighty will help to fight this evil in our city." Although Trainor won her initial case on a technicality, she lost a second in 1930. Like others before her, she was ordered to vacate a house she owned. By this time, Los Angeles NAACP president Claude Hudson declared the chapter to be "swamped with [covenant] cases." Finally, in April 1932, the court of appeals ruled against the Letteau heirs, and the state supreme court denied their appeal two months later. Five days later, Sally Trainor won her appeal, as well. Although the judges had still refused to rule that racial restrictive covenants violated the Fourteenth Amendment, Black housing activists had nonetheless established a meaningful precedent. From now on, covenants would not be enforced when an already transpired racial transition rendered their original purpose moot. Beyond achieving key legal victories, these struggles heightened political awareness and provided valuable organizing experience that accumulated within the collective memory of African Americans.[20]

While establishing respect for the fundamental rights of citizenship required constant struggle by African Americans, the US Supreme Court's

1922 *Ozawa* decision declared Japanese immigrants ineligible for naturalized American citizenship and confirmed their status as political pariahs. As Japan was the only government willing to recognize them as its subjects, the Issei, much like other ethnic groups, relied on the consulate as an extraparliamentary vehicle through which disenfranchised immigrants could bring their concerns to American state officials. Although the consulate and the local Japanese Association had a symbiotic relationship, they were often at odds with each other. The foreign ministry lent the Japanese Association clout by recognizing it as a quasi-official body and requiring Issei seeking to bring wives and children from Japan to register with the community organization. In turn, the foreign ministry expected that Japanese Association leaders would use this clout to promote the interests of the Japanese government. To be certain, immigrants from all parts of the world often shared the homeland concerns of their nation of origin. In the end, however, foreign consulates privileged the concerns of the government they represented when handling immigrant community issues. The government of Japan was no exception: it repeatedly agreed to American calls for immigration restriction so long as this was done in a manner that allowed it to "save face." The concessions, however, inevitably proved insufficient to quell white American hostility. When a wave of attacks on Issei again crested in the 1920s, Japanese diplomats were preoccupied by their concern that abrasive race relations not disrupt negotiations with the United States. Guided by "Shidehara diplomacy," the foreign ministry stressed international cooperation as a critical element of Japan's development. Calling on the Issei to be patient once more, it advised them to refrain from challenging racial restrictions while the diplomatic process worked itself out. Japanese diplomats refused to support the *Ozawa* test case and accused Issei leaders who pushed it forward of acting rashly. Ultimately, the Immigration Act of 1924 forced most Issei leaders to the sobering realization that Japan could do relatively little to stem the tide of American racism. While introducing "national origins" quotas on immigration from southern and eastern Europe, the act legislated a total ban on immigration from Japan.[21]

The Issei response to racist attacks in Belvedere, an unincorporated district east of Boyle Heights, demonstrated both Japanese immigrants' shifting relationship to consular authority and their changing conception of their racial identity. In February 1923, Mitsuhiko Shimizu moved to Belvedere from the nearby and relatively unrestricted Evergreen neighborhood. Shimizu had immigrated to the United States sixteen years prior, working initially as a gardener for a wealthy white family in Pasadena before opening Little Tokyo's Asahi Shoe Store in 1910. A leading member of the Issei community, he would later serve as Japanese Association president in 1937. Fearing the fragility of his property rights as an "alien ineligible to citizenship," Shimizu worked closely with his friend Katsutaro Tanigoshi, a graduate of law school at Northwestern University, to pursue his housing interests. It would have been difficult for Shimizu to locate anyone else in the community who championed the Issei's acceptance in America more than Tanigoshi. Married to a white woman, the Issei attorney had convinced his in-laws to purchase Shimizu's Evergreen house in their name. He subsequently arranged the purchase of the Belvedere house from a white homeowner in the name of Shimizu's American-born children. But the Japanese family entered a district in the midst of a great racial transition that had begun several years earlier. Originally a working-class suburb planned for white single-family residences, Belvedere would be home to more than twenty thousand Mexicans by 1930. In 1923, defensive white residents believed they could halt a Japanese "invasion" in its tracks. Before the Shimizu family set foot in the house, a hostile grouping of whites tried to coerce the current owners not to sell and also sought a court injunction against the sale. When these methods failed, a swarm of white agitators mobilized to intimidate the new arrivals. The Japanese Exclusion Committee even went so far as to hire an Issei interpreter to ensure the Shimizus knew that their presence was not welcome. Within a brief period of time, twenty anti-Japanese signs sprang up near the home along with a large bulletin board reading "Japs: Don't Let the Sun Set on You Here." Approached by a "huge man," a *Rafu Shimpo* reporter examining the sign claimed he was told, "If you hang around here, I will hang you from a tree."[22]

Shimizu and Tanigoshi stood firm in their convictions. The lawyer demanded the exclusion committee pay Shimizu more than double the house's original price—in cash and within ten days. When white neighborhood representatives suggested that moving into a neighborhood with strong anti-Japanese feelings was likely to result in Shimizu being physically harmed, Tanigoshi declared, "If you were to intimidate us, we could convict you and have you put in jail at any time." But tragically, the law in 1920s Los Angeles was more likely to side with the white supremacists. Calling Tanigoshi's bluff, members of a white mob reorganized and threatened to kill Shimizu. Past midnight on February 28, while the family was away, they piled wood, poured gasoline, and set fire to the house. By the time the fire truck arrived, flames had engulfed the window and porch. To put terror in the family's heart, the assailants deliberately left behind coal tar, feathers, and ropes—items, the *Rafu* noted, that "members of the secret society in a white gown used for execution."[23]

With less than a year having passed since the *Ozawa* decision, Issei leaders were still debating how to deal with their seemingly permanent status as foreigners. What was the proper response to such a heinous and overtly white supremacist attack? "Since housing is an essential issue for our survival," the *Rafu Shimpo* assessed, "each of us needs to reflect on the arson incident carefully." Initially, the newspaper and most immigrant community leaders stood with Shimizu and called on local authorities to intervene. A local Issei identified only as an "influential person" demanded "severe punishment" of the "irrational perpetrators" to prevent attacks of this nature from recurring. Since he lived amicably among whites following an initial period of white "discomfort," this man's own experience symbolized the Issei belief that Americans would accept them once they dispelled superficial stereotypes. "Because of a language barrier, we appeared to be mysterious," he remarked. "But once Americans get to know our hearts, we are no comparison to the low-grade southern European immigrants." Nevertheless, as local authorities brushed off Japanese American concerns, Japanese immigrant leaders grew more reticent and white exclusionists more emboldened. Shimizu and Tanigoshi appealed to law enforcement for protection but received little response. An assistant district attorney told Shimizu that he had brought the attacks on himself by moving into a white neighborhood. He then provoked a heated exchange with Tanigoshi by suggesting that the arson was motivated by an insurance scam. A brief ensuing investigation by the sheriff's office resulted in a conclusion notable for its internal contradiction. The incident report "confirmed that it was arson" and identified the names of several men who "incited other citizens to act, using intimidation." The sheriff's office, however, failed to make any arrests. It claimed, "Unfortunately, until we find clear evidence we cannot do anything." Unfettered, the Japanese Exclusion Committee pressed on. Asserting the racial boundaries of its nationalism, it staked a large American flag in a vacant lot down the street from the Shimizu home and organized a huge rally of its forces—including women and children—around a bonfire.[24]

Authorities granted Japanese consul Oyama a response only slightly more respectful than they had given the Issei community representatives. While the sheriff proclaimed a personal hatred of the Japanese, he stated he would do what he could to ensure public safety. In response, the consulate directed Issei leaders to drop the case. Accepting the consular directive, Japanese Association president Sei Fujii told the community it must "act calmly and modestly." "Tough positions are not the only option to protect the rights of Japanese people," he remarked. Tanigoshi was criticized for taking a "hard line" stance. The lawyer was, truth be told, one of the community's most prominent members but also something of a maverick. As Japanese Association president in 1919, Tanigoshi once punched another board member in the face during a heated exchange. Still, even the friendliest effort to prove that Japanese Americans were clean, responsible, law-abiding neighbors was now considered a "hard line" response by Fujii, who offered an all-too-convenient story to rationalize his position. The case, Fujii claimed, principally stemmed from gentile animosity toward the Jewish seller of the Shimizu home and would have been resolved had Tanigoshi not requested the Japanese Exclusion Committee pay a $500 fee for his legal services. The story's pedagogical function for the Issei was unmistakable: A "Jew" had initiated the conflict, and the brash Tanigoshi had aborted its resolution. Shimizu was an unfortunate victim, but others could easily avoid his fate. The Japanese Association thus advocated a "moderate" stance, which rested on the assertion—shared by most whites—that Issei moving into white neighborhoods in the face of opposition drew antagonism to themselves and the entire community. The impact of this policy registered immediately. The Sato family had recently purchased a home two blocks from the Shimizu house. Even though some white neighbors had expressed tolerance toward them, they chose to vacate after receiving threats from the exclusion committee. By March 29, the "moderate" position had been formalized into a resolution adopted by Japanese residents of the Boyle Heights/Belvedere area as a "countermeasure to Japanese exclusion." No more Japanese were to move into white neighborhoods. Existing residents were directed to patronize white businesses and refrain from any conflict with whites.[25]

Within little more than a year, however, the *pax Americana* in Belvedere unraveled. Mokichi Kawamoto, manager of a Little Tokyo auto dealership and renter of a house in Belvedere, had been one of the neighborhood's few remaining Issei in the aftermath of the Shimizu incident. His white landlord had explained to the exclusion committee that Kawamoto had one year remaining on a two-year lease. When Kawamoto stayed beyond his lease, signs reading "Shall It Be America or Japan?" and "Keep Japs Out of Belvedere" were planted outside his house on June 19, 1924. That evening, a mob of sixteen to twenty white men and women showed up at his doorstep and demanded, "You better move or we'll move you." When he refused, Kawamoto was dragged outside and beaten by several white men. If the Issei resident did not leave, mob leaders vowed, they would tie him to a tree, coat him with tar and feathers, and kill him. Once again, local authorities, including an officer who was a former president of the Anti-Asiatic Association, sided with the assailants. Kawamoto moved out rather than risk further injury, and the brutal beating forced Issei leaders to acknowledge the failure of "moderate" tactics. Sei Fujii argued that the Issei community should be "outraged." Their policy of local restraint could do little to quell an exclusion movement that was national in scope, as demonstrated by the recent passage of the 1924 Immigration Act placing a total ban on immigration from Japan. With his community viewing the exclusion as evidence of their ultimate failure to garner acceptance from whites, the Japanese

Association head declared the Issei must now recognize that they were members of the degraded "colored races" alongside Chinese and Blacks, who were treated like "dogs and cats" in America. Fujii called on the Issei to file complaints with law enforcement, but he advised them to expect the police to side with white racists. To support his point, he noted that whites had lynched hundreds of African Americans with no reproach. Still, with little reason left for caution, the community had to take action against racist attacks "win or lose." While Fujii suspected the Kawamoto beating was the action of the Klan and "lower-class" whites, he insisted that the mob action was consistent with the racist attitudes of white legislators. The effort by the *Los Angeles Times* to draw a distinction between "low-class" and "high-class" attitudes only served to validate this point. Its July 3, 1924, editorial asserted that the Japanese "should be made to understand that it is not because America deems them inferior, but because it finds them unassimilable, that it makes the exclusion absolute."[26]

Moderates in the Japanese Foreign Ministry were now being pushed to defend the Issei from both sides of the Pacific. As Issei throughout the United States developed a common sense of themselves as an oppressed racial minority, an arguably stronger wave of militant anti-American voices in Japan seized on their plight. Through a far-reaching grassroots movement, the people of Japan declared "American Peril Day" and "National Humiliation Day" for the first of July, when the 1924 Immigration Act would take effect. The fervor of 1924 altered the political culture of Japan, encouraging chauvinistic nationalists whose call to overthrow white supremacy would ultimately serve as the rallying cry for militarism and imperial expansion. Newspapers in Japan fueled the indignation of the Japanese citizenry by circulating reports of the Kawamoto beating and any incident that could be interpreted as a racist attack. In Los Angeles, Fujii asserted that the Japanese consulate had a duty to uphold the Issei's right to housing under bilateral treaty. Forced to respond to the insurgent community leadership, the Japanese consulate remained scarcely willing and even less able to go out on a limb on the Issei's behalf. Los Angeles consul Wakasugi primarily wrote letters regarding the Kawamoto beating to the governor and attorney general, asking them to be mindful of "the constant protection and security of the persons and the property of the Japanese subjects in this part of your state." They were signed "Your obedient servant." Like his predecessor handling the Shimizu arson, he received the trite answer that local authorities were already pledged to uphold the law. But law enforcement officials in Los Angeles, at best, viewed peace and justice as something akin to the original Belvedere resolutions. While the authorities may or may not have approved of the exclusion committee's brazen tactics, they supported its ends by consciously allowing white mobs to escape recrimination for their acts of violence and intimidation.[27]

As the Issei recognized the common fate they shared with African Americans, they took greater notice of Black models of resistance. People all across the nation scrutinized the case of Ossian Sweet, an African American doctor in Detroit. In 1925, Sweet, his wife, and nine codefendants escaped a murder conviction after firing on a white mob seeking to force the Black family out of their home. Their action was part of a wave of militant stands African Americans took against housing restrictions and neighborhood-based white supremacist violence during the interwar period. A self-assertive Black nationalist, Mentis Carrere, provided a local model. Preaching a doctrine of economic self-reliance and racial solidarity, he believed African Americans were past due to shed their "inferiority complexes" and "fear of tackling our own problems." Having purchased a house with no restrictions in the Green Meadows neighborhood during the 1920s housing boom, Carrere was one of a handful of Blacks living in the western half of South Los Angeles. In 1926, the Southwest Chamber of Commerce organized a campaign to drive his family out of their West Eighty-fifth Street home. Led by Los Angeles County deputy sheriff F. C. Finkle, the white exclusionists issued a series of threats. They gathered a mob in front of Carrere's house, vowed to "tie [him] to a telegraph pole," and promised "a Black coat of Tar and Feathers" for any race traitor who sold a house to an African American. When Carrere steadfastly refused to move, Finkle organized mass rallies to whip the neighborhood into a racist frenzy. Joyously referencing the deadly anti-Black riot of June 1921, a white resident "from Tulsa, Oklahoma," advised his neighbors to remember "what they did there." The mob pelted the Carrere house with bricks on a nightly basis, leading Carrere to arm himself with several guns. Supporters took turns backing him up, and on one night Black community leader Frank Whitley emptied a round of pistol shots to make the crowd of agitators disperse. Harry Grund, a white friend and coworker at the Oakley Paint Company, regularly aided Carrere and vowed to fight against racist restrictions. On August 5, he fired a revolver above the crowd with one bullet piercing a neighbor's front window. Taking no action against the racist mob, local authorities arrested Grund for disturbing the peace and carrying a concealed weapon.[28]

WEST JEFFERSON

While the Issei could admire the fighting *bushido* spirit of African Americans like Mentis Carrere, they could not exactly emulate his specific form of militancy. Their status as resident aliens heightened their sense of insecurity, and they feared the repressive power of the state. In fact, since few African Americans were ready to go to the lengths Carrere went to maintain his residence, his neighborhood remained nearly all white for at least the next two decades. But where they saw an opening, Black and Japanese Americans were willing to wage a nonviolent struggle for "better" housing. They were also willing to work somewhat cooperatively. In general, the housing arena exhibited far less of the petty interethnic competitiveness engendered by entrepreneurialism. Unlike the small-business world, there were practically no ethnic-specific housing niches. Most neighborhoods were restricted to whites. When they opened, they usually did so for all people of color.

During the interwar period, West Jefferson became the principal site where Black and Japanese Americans both lived in close quarters and shared a common front in the battle against white racism and restricted covenants. Located in an older section of the near Westside, the neighborhood was a suburban outpost at the turn of the twentieth century. While predominantly white before World War I, it housed a long-standing Black population mostly centered in a section of poorly managed subdivisions that had failed to attract white homeowners. By the 1920s, West Jefferson stood relatively close to downtown and was growing more densely populated as property owners converted homes to rental units. As it decayed in the eyes of whites, it offered people of color a rare opportunity for Westside living. Given that costly struggles against racial covenants were required simply to move in and maintain occupancy, community leaders from the professional and business classes were at the core of African American migration to the neighborhood. They used the initial Black foothold as a base from which to expand the range of unrestricted housing. Simultaneously, they formed improvement associations to police the moral and physical standards of the neighborhood. J. Max Bond noted in the mid-1930s that Westside Blacks were concerned that their neighborhoods be reserved only for "respectable" types. They were "representative of those families that had attempted to escape from the masses and attain a higher level of culture." The Deteriorating Zone Committee's 1940 survey singled West Jefferson out as the "best district" of African Americans because they were "not only geographically but socially separated from the large population of their race in the original 'Central Avenue' area." But as the wealthiest Blacks moved to progressively better housing, they were replaced by relatively well-off wage earners, including civil servants, mail carriers, retired soldiers, teachers, policemen, and even better-paid domestics and service workers. As a result, West Jefferson's Black population reached 3,500 persons in 1931 and surpassed 5,000 by 1940. A large group of Japanese Americans—roughly half the size of the Black population—also moved into these same areas where Blacks resided during the 1920s and 1930s. They were accompanied by smaller numbers of Chinese and Korean Americans. The new Japanese American residents were primarily gardeners (seeking to live closer to their suburban clients), merchants, and professionals. They dubbed the community *Seinan* ("Southwest") and set up churches, Japanese-language schools, and small businesses, many of which relocated from Little Tokyo.[29]

West Jefferson epitomized the racial frontier in interwar-era Los Angeles; the initial site of Black and Japanese American settlement was surrounded on all sides by Westside neighborhoods that were practically all white. The more attractive West Jefferson became to people of color, the more of a problem neighborhood it became to a growing number of white property owners. Despite the efforts of Black and Japanese American elites to distinguish themselves by their bourgeois standing and upright moral behavior, researchers in the 1920s found that whites interviewed anonymously were quick to make sweeping racial generalizations. Stereotypes of the two groups were often interchangeable. One white resident stated that she preferred living among Japanese because they were "cleaner and neater" than Blacks. "Besides they never bother white people," she added, "and Negroes sometimes become offensive." Another white neighbor drew the opposite conclusion. "I like the Negroes better," she opined, "because they tend to their own business and leave the whites alone. They are neat looking and have nice homes and keep them nice. I never had any use for the Japanese." Denying the depth of their own racist animosity, some whites in West Jefferson exhibited discriminatory behavior while distancing themselves from white supremacist agitators. Asserting she had "never had any trouble" with Black or Japanese American neighbors, one woman argued the neighborhood would be fine "if folks would only be intelligently tolerant." She nevertheless declared she would invite neither Blacks nor Japanese Americans into her own house. Another white woman, who claimed she bore "no prejudice against the colored people," was appalled by what she perceived to be uppity behavior. When a Black family invited her children to view their Christmas tree, the riled-up woman exclaimed, "As if I would allow my children to go down there to 'Nigger' town to see their tree!" Above everything else, whites associated Black and Japanese American residency with a belief that West Jefferson had "changed for the worse" and was "becoming run down." Whites had moved to the onetime suburban neighborhood "to get away from noise and traffic and to be on the outskirts of the city." Now they feared their property values were in jeopardy. "We neighbors must really stand together," declared a white man, "for it is clear that if the man next door sold his house to a Negro or a Japanese my property would immediately become worth a thousand dollars less." On July 19, 1922, white residents living near the University of Southern California organized the Anti-African Housing Association, launching one of the first of many racist homeowners' campaigns in the Westside. The group soon after renamed itself the University District Property Owners Association. Though its title aroused less controversy, its racist agenda broadened to attack Japanese Americans.[30]

As in other existing neighborhoods, efforts to blanket West Jefferson with restrictive covenants were less than fully effective because contested neighborhoods were the perfect target for "blockbusting" by opportunistic realtors. Realtors sold houses to people of color, usually African Americans, on all-white blocks in order to provoke white anxieties and trigger panic selling. Sometimes, they merely had to hire Blacks to walk down the street. Blockbusting delivered windfall profits, in some cases to Black realtors who were party to these operations. However, far from simply being manipulated, white residents often benefited themselves from these sales, particularly when economic hardship heightened during the Depression. Because housing opportunities were distributed unequally, demand for housing by people of color far outpaced white demand in open occupancy neighborhoods. In West Jefferson, it was not uncommon for people of color to be charged 50 percent more than the offering price to whites for the same house. Whites could sell houses to people of color for as much as $10,000, then purchase newer homes in white neighborhoods considered more desirable for the same or less. Once started, neighborhood transition often proceeded swiftly—so swiftly that the pace of white out-migration sometimes surpassed that of in-migration by people of color.[31]

The most dogged battle over restrictive covenants took place in the Crestmore tract, which housed the choicest homes in West Jefferson. Chester Himes described the subdivision in his wartime novel *If He Hollers Let Him Go*. "The houses were well kept, mostly white stucco or frame, typical one-storey California bungalows, averaging from six to ten rooms; here and there was a three- or four-storey apartment building," Himes added. "The lawns were green and well trimmed, bordered with various local plants and flowers. It was a pleasant neighborhood, clean, quiet, well bred." While the area had been almost exclusively white until 1925, it developed a multiracial makeup over the course of the next decade. On Twenty-ninth Street and Twenty-ninth Place alone, there were twenty-nine Black, sixteen Mexican, and fifteen Japanese households in 1933. Elite people of color coveted the most expensive homes in the neighborhood. Actresses Louise Beavers and Hattie McDaniel lived here during the Depression, as did many less famous but well-educated residents. According to the 1940 census, people of color in this area were three times more likely to have attended college than those found in the city as a whole. The rate of homeownership surpassed 50 percent for African Americans and approached 30 percent for Asians. Both figures far outnumbered respective citywide rates.[32]

The earliest Black residents of the area paved the way for others by waging a legal and political struggle. Their primary antagonist was the Crestmore Improvement Association, an all-white group that placed twenty-five-year renewals on expiring race restrictions in 1925. Describing segregation as the "law of nature," its president, L. G. Fellows, asserted that the Negro's "selfish and unnatural effort at self advancement" was "dragging the Caucasian race down to his own level." Sued for violating racial covenants, fifteen African American families joined together in the Equal Rights Protective Association. They defended their homes and their rights with the aid of the Blackstone Club, a group the *California Eagle* noted was "composed of the leading Race lawyers of the city." The *Eagle* was particularly alarmed, characterizing the lawsuit as "the boldest attempt of its kind yet instituted in California" given "the exceedingly high character" of the Black residents under attack. As the case continued into 1926 and garnered momentum from the *Buckley* decision, other African American homeowners' associations supported the fight. The West Side Improvement Association warned the community, "If you have any race pride prepare to use it now." The "Negro race [would become] a dead issue in this city" unless Black Angelenos were ready to "make real sacrifices."[33]

A tug-of-war ensued with neither side achieving total victory, and the Crestmore tract split at Cimarron Street. Restrictions broke down in the eastern section. But a 1928 California Supreme Court order forced Black residents A. D. and Mattie Kinchlow to vacate their home in the larger western section, which remained nearly all white until the postwar era. With battles in West Jefferson ongoing between the 1920s and 1940s, Japanese Americans came under attack in proportion to their growing presence. In July 1933, two hundred property owners, including local judges, launched a campaign to drive out all "Mongolians" and "Negroes" from homes near the Thirty-sixth Street Elementary School by the end of the year. Mrs. Tsurue Kuranaga refused to move from her rented house but was forcibly dislodged by court order in November 1933. In 1940, a committee to uphold restrictive covenants successfully sued to oust a Nisei (second-generation Japanese American) homeowner and his tenants from the Crestmore tract, as well. Margaret Walker, the white group's spokesperson, boasted that for sixteen years she had "championed the cause of restrictions to keep these people [of color] out of the district known as the Westside." Over that time the identification between the Westside and white supremacy had become commonsense knowledge in white Los Angeles. "We shall have all Caucasians by themselves in residential districts and we should certainly restrict property against the Japanese," Walker declared. "I don't see why we can't save our part of town for our own people."[34]

Fig. 2.3. Thirty-sixth Street Elementary School. Japanese American children in kimonos pose for Halloween picture with African American students in West Jefferson, ca. 1941. Shades of L.A. Archives/Los Angeles Public Library.

But shared experiences with white racism also created a nascent sense of interethnic solidarity in the Westside. The same researchers who documented white hostility in West Jefferson found that Black and Japanese Americans generally held a favorable view of each other. A married woman proclaimed African Americans like herself were "treated [by whites] as if they were a race of lepers or rattlesnakes." Fearing "the inevitable progress of the darker races," whites in her eyes acted to defend the privileges afforded them by a racist society. "With white skin, one can have education and positions and better jobs and more comfortable homes," she stated. "They have more freedom to enjoy life without being humiliated always." An Issei resident concurred: "We are called 'Japs' [by whites] and things are often blamed on us that we didn't do." Many Japanese, including this resident, thus sought to live in West Jefferson because African Americans were already there. "We move in here with Negroes because they have less prejudice against us than whites," he stated. "They befriend us, and act glad that we are here." Interaction between Black and Japanese Americans was increasingly commonplace. As early as 1927, researcher Koyoshi Uono documented nine specific instances of multiunit dwellings being home to both African Americans and Japanese Americans and found one case of Black/Japanese intermarriage. While communication between adults may not have often risen above cordialities, children routinely developed close friendships across the color line. At Thirty-sixth Street Elementary, joyous Black students posed for pictures with kimono-clad Nisei girls, who were dressed in traditional Japanese clothes for Halloween.[35]

It would ultimately be this younger generation that would help build multiracial political coalitions in later years. Ironically, however, the economic success that brought the children of relatively well-off Black and Japanese Americans together in the old Westside had stemmed from divergent approaches that inhibited greater cooperation during the interwar era.

CHAPTER 3

Racial Progress and Class Formation

IN 1926, KATSUTARO TANIGOSHI, president of the Los Angeles Japanese Association, "electrified" members of the Los Angeles Negro Business Men's League by delivering what the *California Eagle* described as "one of the most illuminating and instructive of addresses which falls the lot of any man to hear." Advocating a self-assertive brand of economic nationalism, the *Eagle* remarked that the Issei response to racism of "more and better business" helped the "lowly Japanese" to command "the greatest respect and consideration from the white man." If the smaller Japanese population could build "great business institutions" in spite of racist laws, the *Eagle* propositioned, "why is it that our group claiming from 45,000 to 50,000 falls so far behind in the march of progress for business activity?" Inviting Tanigoshi to address the Business League was a "master stroke" that promised to strengthen interethnic cooperation and heighten the prospects for Black economic development. The *Eagle* concluded, "The Japanese or as sometimes called, the little brown men, cannot help but have a sympathetic feeling for his Black brother and will as a consequence, if called upon, give to him any information possible to assist him in gaining a foothold along business lines."[1]

This chapter begins with a comparison of nationalist survival strategies that Black and Japanese Americans employed during the interwar era. As white boosters hinged the city's development to racism and segregation, leaders of both groups responded with their own race-centered models of progress and prosperity. They established ethnic enclaves and business classes that revered the concepts of self-help and racial uplift. But in a reversal of relationships within the housing struggle, African Americans posited Japanese immigrants as a model of economic success. Issei entrepreneurs managed to transcend the segregated ethnic market and capture a significant share of rising white consumer spending. This was in large measure due to what historian Eiichiro Azuma has characterized as their "dual nationalist" sensibility, which embraced both the practical necessity to become Americanized and Japan's nationalist impulse to prove it was equal to the West. A common national origin provided Japanese merchants the basis for carving their own cooperatively established ethnic niches within the local economy. Viewing their activities as vital contributions to Japanese national development, the Issei were further sustained by pride in their heritage as they humbly served white clientele.[2]

The Depression-era activism discussed in the latter half of the chapter exposed the contradictions of entrepreneurial survival strategies. First, as symbolized by the *Eagle*'s awkward praise for the Issei, Black and Japanese American business leaders' focus on *intra*ethnic solidarity inhibited the creation of extensive *inter*ethnic political cooperation. Each group primarily used achievements of the other group to provide models of striving to the members of their respective races or to rationalize their own comparative lack of advancement. By contrast, Black and Japanese American radicals propagated an internationalist vision that stressed multiracial solidarity through grassroots organizing. Second, the survival of Issei enterprises was contingent on a paternalistic employer/worker relationship through which the former encouraged intraethnic solidarity to blunt the latter's class consciousness. Japanese American workers responded by asserting a greater degree of autonomy but generally shied from the radical challenges necessary to integrate themselves into the city's white-dominated labor movement. While hundreds joined unions, Japanese Americans, like their African American counterparts, at most enjoyed auxiliary and second-class membership. Finally, the growing prominence of retailing in the city correspondingly expanded the power of consumer activism. Because most served a white clientele, Issei merchants proved particularly susceptible to a racialized boycott initiated by white labor leaders. African Americans, however, deployed selective buying as a weapon to combat discrimination by white employers in the Central Avenue district. Collectively, the events of the 1930s introduced new modes of activism that expanded the political discourse within communities of color while simultaneously revealing the immediate limits of resistance.

NATIONALISM AND ECONOMIC DEVELOPMENT

Despite the rise of segregation, Los Angeles continued to represent a site of progress to Black and Japanese Americans that beckoned those with an entrepreneurial spirit. In a 1927 oration, young Ralph Bunche told the story of a "Texas colored man who had been in a virtual state of slavery to his Southern white 'boss.'" On a trip to Los Angeles, he experienced "the freedom and grandeur of the Southland and, more particularly, the pure liberty-inspiring atmosphere of our own Central Avenue." Upon returning, the man was "truant and rebellious" as he refused to return to his job. When the "boss" tried to entice him back to work by offering hog jowls, the man replied, "Uh uh boss. You ain't talkin' to me, no suh. I've been to Los Angeles and I don' want yo' old hog-jowls, cuz I'm eatin'

High up on de hog now!" A bit less sanguine, a 1928 editorial of the *California Eagle* declared, "While Los Angeles has by no means reached 'the perfect state,' we believe that Los Angeles has the best opportunity to become that city." Black Los Angeles also had its share of outright boosters. Realtor H. A. Howard proclaimed the city "one of the cosmopolitan centers of America, the mecca of millions of persons; the Promised Land for a variety of races of all complexions and cultures."[3]

Early Japanese American community fortunes, more so than those of Blacks, were tied explicitly to western agricultural bounty. For a brief period, African American adherents to the economic nationalist philosophy of Booker T. Washington sought to revive the Black Town movement, most prominently through the 1908 founding of Allensworth north of Bakersfield. As demonstrated by a 1925 advertisement for the Eureka Villa project, these rural colonies sought to build self-governing communities and to mold leaders whose "love and loyalty to the race [was] unquestioned." Black efforts to achieve self-sufficiency through agriculture, however, generally foundered because of undercapitalization. Although the alien Japanese could not hope to construct politically autonomous communities, farming established the foundation of their economic and social life. Issei conceived of themselves as contributing to the progress of two different nations by settling a dual frontier. As historian Yuji Ichioka has noted, agriculture, in the eyes of the California Japanese pioneer Kyutaro Abiko, provided a means for the Issei to establish permanent settlement in America and shed their *dekasegi*, or sojourner, orientation. By demonstrating the productive capacity and productive ethos of the Japanese people to white Americans (an Issei approach to the Jeffersonian ideal), the Issei might disprove the arguments of anti-Japanese agitators who deemed them unassimilable foreigners. As they moved from laborer to producer, most Japanese immigrant farmers in Southern California engaged in "truck farming," carving a literal and figurative niche within the region's vast agricultural landscape. While they established truck farms in the early twentieth century, many Issei were stripped of landownership and leasing rights by the state Alien Land Laws of 1913 and 1920. As a result, they often arranged to work surplus lands of absentee landlords, subdividers, homeowners with large plots, oil companies, and utility companies looking for short-term profits. Although such land proved plentiful, its speculative value drove up rental costs. Whereas some Japanese immigrant farmers like George Shima (the "Potato King") achieved success with large-scale farms in other parts of the state, Southland truck farmers typically succeeded by working small plots of land intensively. Focused on the local market, they specialized in relatively perishable crops whose production had not been rationalized by corporate growers. By 1915, Issei were planting three-fourths of all vegetables consumed in Los Angeles, such as sugar beets, lettuce, tomatoes, cabbage, and celery.[4]

Entrepreneurialism became increasingly central to Black and Japanese American visions of urban economic advancement and racial progress because of the extensive problem of labor discrimination. Employers and trade unions conspired to restrict most of the city's jobs to whites. Social scientist Charles S. Johnson's local surveys in 1926 revealed that many of the region's employers believed that African Americans lacked the capacities to do required work; that white workers objected to working with Blacks; and that white customers or clients objected to the hiring of Blacks. Those who hired African Americans generally offered them little chance for promotion. Although employers imbibed the racial stereotypes and biases of that time, they never reached a consensus on how to rank Black, Japanese, and Mexican American workers. White racism thus varied in response to particular social and economic situations. A white representative from a meatpacking plant stated African Americans made "better butchers than Mexicans." An ironworks reported that whites were willing to work with Mexican Americans but would "not stand working with Japs." Some employers said that they hired recent Mexican immigrants because they were willing to work for cheap wages. (On the basis of this response, Johnson correctly predicted rising white opposition to Mexican immigration.) Others, relying on biological stereotypes, said Mexicans were suited only to particular work. A brick company claimed they were most adapted to dust, while an ice company claimed they could best withstand the cold. Of course, even the same stereotype could be contradicted. Many factories hired African Americans to work the foundries on the basis that they were suited for "heat" work. However, the asbestos workers' union claimed that Blacks were not employed in the industry, because "they cannot stand the excessive heat." That small craft union went to great lengths to keep the asbestos jobs solely in the hands of a protected class of white workers, even to the point of excluding Italian immigrants.[5]

Although the so-called radical wing of the labor movement (the Wobblies excepted) generally toed the same racist line as exclusionary craft unions, the 1911 defeat of the labor militants held indirectly negative consequences for workers of color in Los Angeles. In response to the "open shop," white labor enacted a conservative strategy that revolved around strengthening its exclusive hold on the crafts and monopolizing nearly every union in the city. As labor and capital reached an accommodation, white workers directed their antagonism toward people of color, whom they saw as competitors for jobs or pawns in management's push to downgrade labor. Trade unions took up the call for Japanese exclusion with greater fervor. Squeezed out of artisan work in which they had been previously rooted,

Black residents found themselves scrambling for unskilled work at the margins of the local economy. The consolidation of white labor's control of the building trades, for instance, closed off what had been a significant source of skilled work for African Americans. Despite the huge rise in construction during the boom of the early 1920s, fewer Black carpenters, brick and stonemasons, and plasterers found jobs in the city.[6]

While most Issei searched for alternatives to employment by whites, the local Urban League attempted to secure jobs for African Americans by maintaining a cooperative relationship with white employers and persuading them to break down racial inequality gradually. Established in 1921 and led by social workers and other professionals, the Los Angeles chapter found even incremental advances difficult to attain. While jobs in the growing retail, entertainment, and professional services sectors attracted tens of thousands of white migrants to Los Angeles, these same fields failed to add much to Black employment options. Retail establishments came under greater control of larger, white-owned businesses that believed Jim Crow policies were necessary to retain the desired white clientele. Of all the city's major banks in 1935, only two branches in the Central Avenue district employed Black tellers. While the film industry discovered ways to market Black acting talent (critics deemed it exploitation) in the 1930s, the total number of African Americans in the motion picture industry remained "negligible." In a report to the Urban League, William T. Smith wrote, "Hollywood has not yet opened its doors to any Negro workers except actors. He may not swing a pick and shovel in the studio lots, nor may he swing a mop." The prospects for future generations did not appear much brighter. The Urban League's Floyd Covington noted that a "vicious circle" victimized Black youth. Parents encouraged their children to get ahead by studying, but schools tracked Black students onto vocational paths. However, without job skills or union membership, Black youth were denied factory work and then were denied admittance to trade schools because they lacked employer sponsorship. Administrators at the Frank Wiggins Trade School, for example, deemed African Americans "too slow and emotional to do the technical, careful, accurate and rapid work required in many of the skilled occupations."[7]

Self-employment became the primary means by which striving Black and Japanese Americans sought to obtain the rewards of hard work in the face of a discriminatory labor market. In different ways, they responded to patterns of consumption that were shaped by suburbanization and racism. Japanese immigrants shifted from rural to urban enterprises because of economic and political factors. While the Alien Land Laws did not totally preclude truck farming, they made it an increasingly difficult and tenuous venture. At the same time, suburban development devoured the Southland's agricultural land. But whereas the Supreme Court upheld restrictions barring the Issei from owning and leasing farmland, their right to wholesale and retail trade was protected by treaty between the United States and Japan. Forsaking the Little Tokyo market as it was stifled by the demise of immigration, they set up new businesses to pursue the prosperous white suburban consumer. Although whites regularly refused the Issei as neighbors, most had little trouble accepting them as merchants and servile labor, especially in quest of the suburban ideal. Catapulted by white residents' voracious appetite for manicured lawns and inexpensive labor, Japanese Americans became almost synonymous with gardening in Southern California. More Issei toiled as gardeners than in any other line of work during the interwar period. Following suit, Issei in other industries, particularly operators of hotels and restaurants, shifted their emphasis from serving Japanese to serving white patrons. A survey in 1934 found twice as many Japanese-run restaurants and cafes serving non-Japanese food as there were serving Japanese cuisine. One of the cultural oddities to emerge from this development was the faux-Chinese "chop suey" house staffed by Issei labor.[8]

Japanese produce stands and groceries became another ubiquitous symbol of suburban Los Angeles. Although the Alien Land Laws precluded horizontal integration of farms, the relative success of Issei agriculture provided a crucial source of capital for expansion through vertical integration. Ethnic producers thus made connections with ethnic distributors and retailers. By the outbreak of the Pacific War, Japanese American wholesale produce operations had developed into a $26 million industry. These wholesalers often served as creditors to Issei farmers, on the one hand, and suppliers of Issei retailers, on the other. Scarcely found in the years before World War I, Japanese produce stands proliferated by providing easy consumer access to food in an era predating the domination of supermarkets and refrigeration. Over the course of the interwar period, one thousand Issei produce retailers built a $25 million industry serving as the direct source of employment for several thousand Japanese Americans. As the writer Ayako Ishigaki vividly described in the late 1930s, Issei merchants went to great lengths to appeal to their predominantly white clientele. "Wet spinach, brightly green and with the shining red stem-ends bundled, purple lotus roots, and pure white radishes were piled up high in rows," she wrote. "Even the arrangement of vegetables, unlike that in American stores, was planned skillfully and ingeniously with a view to color." Produce stands also hired English-speaking Nisei to promote good relations with non-Japanese customers. Still, as self-service became a marker of consumer freedom, whites were increasingly content to maintain less personal relations with retailers. The relative prosperity of the produce industry, which the Issei claimed was of their unique making, generated a special pride. "Any one who has lived or visited the Southland knows [what] the Japanese fruit-and-vegetable stand is," proclaimed one Issei community history. "It has become an American institution. Like Drive-in-restaurants, these Japanese fruit-and-vegetable stands are the Southland's unique attractions. Time and again, you will hear housewives of Southern California remark like this: 'Nobody can handle vegetables and fruit the way Japanese people can!' And you know that they are not exaggerating, either."[9]

Issei entrepreneurialism was sustained by a dual nationalist ideology that marshaled intraethnic solidarity to provide services to white American society. As Japanese subjects, immigrant elites saw themselves as overseas pioneers of national development. While their pride in their Japanese heritage often smacked of ethnic chauvinism, it was a crucial element of psychic survival in a hostile country. Immigrant leaders believed that white animosity toward them was unwarranted and would dissipate once Americans were exposed to the true Japanese subject through experience and proper education. Leaders in Japan followed a similar line of thought. They believed their nation's modernization proved that Japan and the Japanese race deserved to be accepted on par with the great powers and white peoples comprising Western civilization. Herein lay the other side of dual nationalism. Viewing assimilation to American society as consistent with Japanese nationalist development, immigrant entrepreneurs willingly and eagerly discovered creative means to demonstrate their value to white consumers. In general, the typical Issei during the interwar period entered small-business fields where requirements for capital and training were low and where limited English-speaking skills would not prove detrimental. Local Japanese community leaders identified niche markets—such as nurseries, gardening, wholesale and retail flower sales, wholesale and retail produce—that were underserved by large businesses and white merchants. They then formed cooperative ethnic associations to discourage intraethnic rivalry and strengthen their standing in the market. By offering small levels of credit and entry-level trade know-how, these ethnic community networks laid a foundation for a greater dispersion of Issei within these chosen niches.[10]

Viewing self-reliance and entrepreneurialism as crucial to racial progress, African American leaders similarly embraced economic nationalism. In the eclectic political culture of Black Los Angeles, nationalism peacefully coexisted alongside other seemingly divergent philosophies deemed situationally appropriate. Marcus Garvey's nationalism, for instance, inspired a considerable following in the 1920s. Although internal clashes hastened its downfall, the Los Angeles chapter of the United Negro Improvement Association claimed one thousand members at its peak. Still, *California Eagle* publisher Charlotta Bass could be a leader in both the integrationist NAACP and the nationalist UNIA. It was less Garvey's "Back to Africa" message than it was the assertive voice with which he spoke that resonated with those seeking to affirm and enhance their place in the city.[11]

Black nationalism in Los Angeles was anchored by a pragmatic sense that self-reliance and entrepreneurialism were crucial to racial progress. The histories of two prominent Black businesses established during the 1920s (and still in operation today) illuminate this point. Founded in 1925 as "the first insurance company in California owned and controlled by Negroes," Golden State Mutual Life Insurance developed both a profitable business and multiple generations of community and civic leaders. The company's humble beginnings can be traced to a small twelve-by-fourteen-foot office at 1435 Central Avenue. Founder William Nickerson, Jr., the son of former slaves, arrived in California with his wife and eight children in 1921. Nickerson had been pushed out of Houston when his lawsuit challenging the all-white Democratic primary provoked death threats from the Klan. This activist mentality translated into a self-help philosophy fueled by economic nationalism. "When a member of the Negro race spends one dollar for Negro insurance," Nickerson professed, "he affects the whole order of Negro social life." In creating Golden State, he set out to find men who shared his combination of entrepreneurial sprit and race pride. His first two hires, Norman O. Houston and George Beavers, Jr., became lifelong employees who would inherit the firm's management. Significantly, both would also serve on the boards of many local corporations and community organizations, as well as assume numerous roles in government agencies and commissions well into the postwar era. Recognizing Golden State's founding as a milestone of community development, the city's African American leadership hailed the new company. Rev. Napoleon P. Greggs of the influential People's Independent Church argued that it would stop white-owned companies from "getting fat on the money they are collecting from our people" and provide job "opportunities which no white company on earth" offered African Americans. Two weeks later, W.E.B. Du Bois came to the First AME Church to praise the upstart Black business. Asserting that economic advancement would provide far more than "the pleasures that wealth can buy," he contended that an African American "voice in the industrial world" would "make industry more democratic." Success came quickly to the new company, which boasted multiple branches and policies totaling $2.7 million by 1935.[12]

Symbolizing the fusion of economic and political aspirations, the creation of the Angelus Funeral Home demonstrated the public sector's impact on Black entrepreneurship and civil society. As African Americans had no elected officials at the municipal or county level, not even for the

Central Avenue district, a handful of civil service workers acted as its political brokers. With the public sector workforce in Los Angeles County growing nearly eightfold during the interwar period, African Americans especially coveted civil service positions. Denied high-level managerial appointments, they held janitorial positions with particular regard. Janitors were among the best remunerated within the Black community, and L. G. Robinson stood atop them all. Arriving from Barnsville, Georgia, in January 1904, Robinson held the position of "chief janitor and custodian of the county buildings" for three decades, during which time the routine allocation of janitorial jobs was about the biggest largesse of patronage white politicians offered their Black constituency. As the late African American politician and former janitor Gil "Goober" Lindsay noted, Robinson became "the spokesman for the Negro community!" Whenever "the power structure wanted to know anything about Blacks in Los Angeles," Lindsay recounted, "they would say 'Call L. G.'" Robinson parlayed his economic and political clout into ownership of the Angelus Funeral Home, making him a prominent stakeholder in both the public and private sectors.[13]

Unlike Japanese entrepreneurialism, Black business development was heavily contingent on the segregated African American consumer market. While whites freely crossed over into Black establishments, Jim Crow practices restricted the retail and service options of African Americans primarily to businesses and services in the Central Avenue district. Although whites owned much of the district's real estate, Black doctors, dentists, pharmacists, insurance agents, realtors, cleaners, service stations, and funeral parlors provided the main source of services for Black patrons. Hosting the most prominent Black figures of the time, the Dunbar Hotel flourished because of the racist policies of downtown hotels. For instance, the financial district's lavish Biltmore Hotel refused to serve African Americans—something Gunnar Myrdal was embarrassed to discover in the spring of 1940. Believing the landmark hotel was integrated, Myrdal invited the Urban League's Floyd Covington to dinner to discuss the epic Carnegie Corporation study that would become *An American Dilemma*. When the Biltmore turned his African American guest away, the Swedish social scientist received an unexpected lesson in the nature of the "Negro problem" in Los Angeles. Begging Covington's forgiveness, Myrdal wrote, "Let me tell you again, that I did not ask you to come there for an experiment." The segregated market, however, also fostered interethnic exchanges, as certain categories of Issei professionals shunned by whites actively courted Black patronage. Japanese physicians and dentists, for instance, regularly advertised in the *California Eagle*. In January 1921, a Black doctor named J. T. Whittaker was invited to perform surgeries in the local Japanese Hospital. Impressed by the facilities and the

Issei support staff, the *California Eagle* declared, "The Japanese people know no race, no creed and they stand up for us as no other people of this nation. Our soul went out in appreciation for this demonstration of good will and genuine brotherhood of a great people."[14]

African Americans often questioned why their race failed to match the seeming economic prowess of the Japanese. Searching the entire Los Angeles area in 1935, one would find only twenty-five grocery stores operated by African Americans. More broadly, the 1940 Census revealed that only 3.0 percent of employed Black males and 1.7 percent of Black females were "proprietors, managers, and officials (except farm)" compared to 19.8 and 8.9 percent of Japanese American men and women, respectively. Ethnic employment also shielded Japanese American workers from the harshest effects of the Depression. In 1940 (already beyond the worst years of the Depression), more than one in four African Americans were unemployed or on relief work. This was nearly double the rate for whites and nine times the rate for Japanese Americans. Only domestic servants seemed capable of capitalizing on growing consumer demand from the white suburbs. Black and Issei men were often employed as servants and chauffeurs, and many Japanese American women toiled as domestic workers. Nevertheless, African American women's labor was uniquely synonymous with domestic work during the interwar period. Six thousand Black female domestics accounted for one-sixth of the community's total 1930 population. Unlike whites, the majority of Black women held jobs. But six of seven were low-wage service jobs. Community leaders viewed this as evidence of discrimination rather than opportunity. Reports in 1932 revealed that both the California Employment Bureau and the "colored" branch of the YWCA tracked nearly every Black woman applicant into domestic service. By contrast with the incorporation of white women into the clerical fields during the 1920s, fewer than 2 percent of all Black women employed in Los Angeles held clerical positions, mostly in Black-owned businesses. The Southern California Telephone Company became a target of protest in May 1933 for its refusal to hire African American operators—even to serve predominantly Black neighborhoods. Only a few African American women worked in manufacturing, while a select grouping of Black teachers and social workers were regarded as occupying high-status positions.[15]

Sometimes puzzled and other times indignant, African American community leaders offered various explanations for the interethnic business disparity. First, they asserted that hostility toward the Issei was restrained by American respect for Japan as a rising power. For instance, when the Japanese Association protested the "Yellow Peril" story line of *The Cheat*, the *Eagle* asserted the Issei would wield more leverage than the Black community could in its fight against *The Birth of a Nation*. "The nation itself, as well as the state, have been known to BACK UP when Japan gets busy," declared the newspaper. Second, African Americans often recognized the Japanese community's high degree of internal solidarity. Reginald Kearney, who has systematically documented Black images of Japan and Japanese Americans more than any previous scholar, has remarked, "Contrasting the image of the Japanese as a cohesive people with their own circumstances, some African Americans criticized their leaders for failure to unify them." Since race unity was central to their agenda, Black nationalists across America especially presented the Japanese as a model for their brethren. T. Thomas Fortune, for instance, noted that Japanese maintained "their pride of race and manhood" where Africans and other Asians failed to do so. Third, Black leaders argued that deeply ingrained cultural traits conditioned Japanese behavior. In a 1939 address, Charlotta Bass reasoned that Japanese succeeded in economic endeavors because they were "descendants of the ancient laboring classes, trained by ruthless overlords for centuries into a submissive acceptance of their duties." The "remarkable sameness of thought and action" that made possible "the economic advancement of L.A.'s Orientals" stemmed from a cultural essence lacking among descendants of slaves "abducted against their will" and cut off from African roots.[16]

Thus, in a somewhat overlapping manner, Japanese immigrants and Black observers alike viewed ethnic ties and national heritage as keys to Issei entrepreneurial prowess. Structural factors, however, revealed that it was more than culturally determined. As economic historian Masao Suzuki has shown, the class character of the Issei community had been shaped by selective immigration, return migration, and family formation patterns. Drawn from the upper ranks of the peasantry, Japanese immigrants in the early twentieth century averaged eight years of schooling and possessed a 90 percent rate of literacy (in Japanese). Moreover, the typical school year in Japan lasted seven weeks longer than that in California. Thus, the Issei who came to America and then settled permanently in California generally had relatively high levels of education. Furthermore, those who remained in America and raised children were more likely to be those who had achieved some degree of economic prosperity. In sum, many of the Japanese immigrants who seemingly attained "middle-class" status had in fact started out as "middle-class" in Japan. Structural and cultural factors must both be weighed when comparing Black and Japanese American economic accomplishment.[17]

It should be clear then that Black views of Asians (much like Japanese views of Blacks) were largely abstractions that were slotted into preexisting narratives. In the case of Charlotta Bass, Orientalism and slavery provided a rationalization to whites and other African Americans for the seemingly slow economic progress of Blacks vis-à-vis Japanese. More "positive" portrayals of Japan stemmed in large measure from efforts to rally fellow Blacks to a cause or ideology. Whereas Japan's growing military power, best symbolized by the defeat of Russia in 1905, raised white fears of a "Yellow Peril," it provided hope to some Black nationalists that white supremacy could be overturned. In order to share the Issei's nationalist sense of pride in Japan's strength, African Americans recast Japan as the "champion of the darker races." In 1921, J. D. Gordon of the Garvey movement urged an audience of nearly two thousand Blacks in Los Angeles not to lend support to anti-Japanese campaigns. "The Japanese are our best friends," declared Gordon, "because they injected into the [Paris] peace conference the equality of races without regard to color, and now this country is trying to prevent them having what they won." But nationalists were not alone, as mainstream civil rights leaders at the national level embraced similar ideas. James Weldon Johnson called Japan "perhaps the greatest hope for the colored races of the world." These leaders were optimistically interpreting (some would argue misreading) Japan's actions on the world stage. Japan's 1919 effort to place a "racial equality" clause into the League of Nations charter drew special attention from African Americans. Yet, as historian Naoko Shimazu has written, it was not a universal declaration of human rights but instead a reflection of the internal contradictions of Japanese nationalism. On the one hand, a rising bloc of Japanese political actors, some on the left but many right-wing nationalists, conceived of Japan as the leader of colored peoples against white supremacy. On the other hand, the campaign for "racial equality" was a plea for the Euro-American powers to accept the Japanese as a uniquely Westernized and civilized example of a nonwhite people. In 1915, Foreign Minister Komei Kato stated that his people were particularly disturbed by the Alien Land Law, less because of its material effect and more because of the means by which it singled out the Japanese for stigmatization. (While the law's euphemistic attack on "aliens ineligible to citizenship" affected other Asian nationalities, its proponents made clear that the Issei were its target.) "We would not mind disabilities if they were equally applicable to all nations," Kato remarked, "but . . . we thought ourselves ahead of any other Asiatic people and as good as some of the European nations." In this manner, Japanese nationalism both promoted and repelled solidarity among the racially oppressed.[18]

While most African Americans knew of Japanese people only through global abstractions, Blacks in Los Angeles developed their attitudes more in response to local matters—attitudes that were sometimes but not necessarily less abstract. To be certain, a more tangible form of Black sympathy for Japanese Americans developed from concrete interpersonal relations. An October 1927 obituary in the *California Eagle*, for instance, revealed the close bonds that African Americans had developed with Sanshiro Fujita, a resident of the Central Avenue district killed in a car accident. It noted that Fujita and his wife had "endeared themselves to the neighborhood by their touch of human kindness and little friendly acts that make for better understanding between all mankind regardless of race, creed or color." Characterizing him as a man who had "lived an exemplary life in a country whose laws unjustly denied him freedom and citizenship," Golden State Insurance executive E. L. Dorsey used the occasion of the Issei man's passing to express empathy with the entire Japanese American community. " 'Tis to be hoped," wrote Dorsey, "that America may yet see the injustice being done this enterprising colony of people by its methods of dealing with immigration and colonization, for truly they are a deserving group."[19]

But in multiethnic Los Angeles, Blacks were also more likely to come into interpersonal conflict with Japanese individuals. Living on the West Coast off and on during the Depression, Langston Hughes noted that many African Americans believed "Japan might be the savior of the darker peoples of the world." Yet, he added, some with more direct contact contended Japanese Americans did "not care to associate with Negroes." Triangulation, the distinguished writer reasoned, was likely at work. "The Japanese in America don't suffer all the inconveniences we do," said Hughes, "so I can understand why they might not want to be identified with us—and perhaps Jim Crowed as a result." African Americans could utilize triangulation in return. Whereas some Black nationalists viewed Japanese Americans as a model of economic success, others were just as likely to see them as economic and political competitors. During the campaign for the 1920 Alien Land Law, for instance, W. H. Sanders of the Industrial and Commercial Council of People of African Descent proclaimed he had contact with five thousand southern Blacks who were ready and able to take the place of Japanese truck farmers. Exercising more restraint, the *California Eagle* waited until after Congress had passed the exclusionary 1924 Immigration Act to highlight similar opportunities. "While we played no part nor did we ask for exclusion for anybody; it is here," read its editorial. "Without the asking, a tremendous opportunity is at hand."[20]

Beyond questions of interethnic relations, economic nationalist strategies of the Issei were a less than ideal model because of their gendered contradictions. The household served not just as the moral foundation of community organization but also as the material foundation of the ethnic economy. Issei women's labor was scarcely valued by the city's primary labor market. A plurality of female Japanese wage laborers were domestics, and others were generally restricted to unskilled work related to food packaging and distribution. Depression-era workers at the Ralph Nut Shelling Company, for instance, were required to take home twenty-pound bags of nuts daily and crack them by hand for compensation at the measly rate of seven cents per pound. To survive and sometimes prosper economically, most Japanese immigrant households thus relied heavily on self-exploitation, characterized by the employment of unpaid family labor within both agriculture (where unpaid laborers outnumbered wage earners) and small businesses. In fact, self-sacrifice was often rationalized as a cultural trait. An Issei hotel owner surmised that more Japanese-operated businesses survived the Depression than others because all household members were "quite willing to do odd jobs for the sake of their families." These arrangements, however, not only forced students to choose between school and the family business (or try to juggle both); they also put great strain on husband/wife relationships. Moreover, despite women's critical contributions to the economic health of the community, political authority within the community rested primarily in the hands of male leaders. As the Depression intensified economic hardship, radical activists would put the contradictions of economic nationalist strategies under increasing scrutiny.[21]

The Promise and Perils of Radicalism

In 1932, Loren Miller declared in the *Daily Worker* that only "cringing and sniveling Uncle Toms" supported Republicans and Democrats. By contrast with the two major parties, the American Communists, he stated, came "right to the front with a bold demand for equal rights and, without beating about the bush . . . emphasize[d] social equality for Negroes." Ending the capitalist-induced misery of the Depression ultimately mandated a struggle "to overthrow the system" that condemned workers "to soup lines and flop houses, while the rich heave potatoes in the ocean and pour milk down the gutters." Miller's fiery proletarian rhetoric belied the fact that he was himself a member of the city's Black elite. The son of a former slave and a white schoolteacher, he was born in the small Nebraska town of Pender. Highly educated and articulate, Miller attended Howard University and the Washburn College of Law in Topeka, Kansas. In the early years of the Depression, he followed his mother and younger siblings to Los Angeles, where he was hired by Charlotta Bass to write for the *California Eagle*. The young lawyer's passion for organizing led him to work closely with the city's most prominent African American leaders to combat discrimination. Nevertheless, Black leftists like Miller, as well as their Japanese American counterparts, drew critical distinctions between their radical agenda and bourgeois conceptions of racial progress. They asserted that nationalist survival strategies failed to address the new concerns created by a rising working-class population of color during the Depression. Furthermore, Black and Japanese American leftists prioritized grassroots protest over moral uplift, negotiation, and entrepreneurship. Above all, they propagated a multiracial vision of full equality that had never been seriously entertained by the political mainstream.[22]

Viewing themselves as participants in a global class struggle, Black and Japanese American Communists and "fellow travelers" in Depression-era Los Angeles were guided by an internationalist vision that tied the rise of the Soviet Union to the overthrow of reactionaries in Japan and the fight against white supremacy and capitalism in the United States. Their orientation reflected broader trends in Left organizing. When the Russian Revolution failed to catalyze proletarian revolution in the developed nations of Europe, the Bolshevik leader V. I. Lenin concluded that the future of the global socialist movement rested with the struggle of the colonized against imperialism. The Soviet-led international body of Left parties known as the Comintern prioritized the mobilization of "oppressed nationalities" during what it designated as the "Third Period" during the late 1920s and early 1930s. Although this period is most recalled as a notorious time of Stalinist orthodoxy and rank sectarianism, the campaign to combat "right opportunists" in the labor movement and seek unity only "from below" created greater space for people of color to operate within the American Communist Party (CPUSA). It was during this "Third Period" that the CPUSA embraced the "Negro nation" thesis characterizing the Black Belt South as an oppressed nation of African Americans with the right to secede from the United States. Such an orientation led the party to issue directives calling on its cadre throughout the nation to devote special attention to African American issues. The CPUSA also promoted vehicles of worker organizing that were independent of the AFL and its legacy of racism. Only when it feared Black or Asian workers could be deployed as lackeys of management did the AFL support organizing them, and even then it encouraged the formation of segregated unions or auxiliaries. By contrast, the Communist-led Trade Union Unity League (TUUL) explicitly embraced "social equality for the Negro people" and recruited Japanese and Mexican immigrants through its effort to establish an independent base of workers. In 1935, the "ultraleft" orientation of the "Third Period" gave way to the coalition-minded "Popular Front." But the new dynamics of this period set in motion a transformation of the Communist movement in Los Angeles. At the outset of the Depression, the party's small local organization consisted mainly of Jewish workers from Boyle Heights, reflecting in part that community's relationship to Russia. By the end of the decade, however, the Los Angeles CP would grow to nearly three thousand members and include significant numbers of Asian, Mexican, and African Americans.[23]

The Communist movement became a meeting ground for "oppressed nationalities" living as exiles in Los Angeles. Exile was literal in the case of the Issei. By the 1930s, repression and internal factionalism brought the Communist Party to the brink of extinction in Japan, where a series of governments had branded party membership illegal. With its freedom of mobility and expression curtailed, the Japanese Communist movement came to depend on exiles, who thus remained staunch foes of the Japanese nation-state. Historian Robert Scalapino has noted, "Japanese Communists were unable to capture and use nationalism, but instead were forced to fight it because it was a deadly weapon in the hands of their opponents." Rejecting the ethnic solidarity tactics of the Issei merchant class, Japanese radicals transplanted their homeland conflict to America, where they attacked Issei community leaders' promotion of Japan's interests as support for fascism. This limited the inroads they could make in a community guided by dual nationalism. Still, their numbers were noteworthy. During the Depression nearly two hundred Japanese Americans held CPUSA membership, and one thousand more were "fellow travelers" generally in alignment with the party's actions. While roughly one out of every five thousand persons in the US population had membership in the CPUSA, nearly one Communist could be found for every six hundred persons in the Japanese American community. (By comparison, the Communist Party of Japan's entire membership never reached one thousand prior to World War II.) Southern California housed the greatest concentration of Japanese CPUSA supporters. During the 1920s, Okinawan immigrants proved particularly crucial to leftist study and organization in Los Angeles. A collective eventually congealed around the Japanese Workers Association (Rafu Nihonjin Rodo Kyokai), which officially became the CPUSA's "Japanese section" in 1928. Through the *Rodo Shimbun*, a national Japanese-language newspaper published from San Francisco, the Japanese section made special efforts to foster Black/Japanese solidarity.[24]

Though citizens by birth, Black leftists fought for "self-determination" from the rule of the American nation-state. A select few directly engaged the Soviet Union. Loren Miller traveled to Russia in 1932 with a group invited to create an epic motion picture on the struggle of southern Blacks. Miller's Central Avenue district home served as the California headquarters of the delegation's most prominent member, Langston Hughes, who judged it "the swellest apartment in a street of palms and flowers." The two developed a close friendship, such that the noted poet and writer deemed Miller his "representative on the coast." Although the film never came to fruition, Miller proclaimed the Soviet Union "the best friend of the Negro and all oppressed peoples" and "the one country where all races and peoples are free and have achieved real equality including the right of self-government." Although he denied he was ever a member of the CPUSA (especially when attacked during the McCarthy era), Miller's consciousness of the struggles of "all oppressed peoples" made him a generally reliable supporter of Japanese American battles against racism through his long career as a civil rights attorney and writer for the Black press. Meanwhile, Japanese American leftists built direct ties to Hughes during his West Coast forays. For instance, the *Rodo Shimbun* sponsored a March 1934 "Japan Nite" featuring jujitsu performances, theater, dancing, and a chop suey dinner—all supporting a keynote speech by special guest Hughes on the "the Japanese and Darker Races."[25]

Most African Americans, however, judged the CPUSA by its domestic behavior. The Soviet Union's appeal was symbolic—its challenge to American power providing a psychic boost in the fight against Jim Crow somewhat analogous to the way Japan functioned as the "champion of the darker races." More concrete were instances where the CPUSA dared to take actions that mainstream race leaders approached more timidly. The defense of the "Scottsboro Boys" particularly stood out. In the early 1930s, nine Black youths were imprisoned and charged with rape in Scottsboro, Alabama. African Americans of diverse political persuasions across the nation kept a watchful eye on their case. For some, the grassroots organizing of the Communist-led International Labor Defense (ILD) provided the main vehicle for both gathering information and getting involved. Japanese American Communists in Los Angeles contributed to the multiracial effort by producing and distributing bilingual English/Japanese flyers declaring "Scottsboro Boys Must Be Freed." Contending that the rape charges were dubious and that the trials resulting in eight death sentences were stained by racism, they called on members of the local Japanese community to donate funds to the ILD and to attend its political forum featuring southern Black activist Angelo Herndon.[26]

Although the headquarters of various ethnically and racially identified leftist groups were based in the city, multiracial solidarity may have developed strongest from the shared marginality of migrant workers. The TUUL placed special emphasis on organizing California's multiracial farm labor. In 1933, its Cannery and Agricultural Workers Industrial Union led twenty-four of California's thirty-seven agricultural strikes, the majority of which centered on immigrant workers. A spring 1933 strike launched by Japanese, Mexican, and Filipino American strawberry workers near Orange County's Stanton district gave rise to the union's main Southern California formation. Twenty-eight Japanese American workers from ten different camps served as delegates to its founding conference in April 1933. Japanese radicals played a special role in agricultural struggles because some Issei had become larger growers by the 1930s and had learned the old management tactic of divide and conquer by ethnicity. At the same time, many Japanese immigrants were veterans of countless labor struggles and connected to a legacy of solidarity that included the historic 1903 Oxnard strike of the Japanese-Mexican Labor Alliance. When Issei growers appealed to workers of their nationality and offered them unique inducements, radicals responded by circulating handbills that read "DO NOT SCAB!" During the Stanton strawberry workers' strike, the *Western Worker* praised the Issei for resisting the "move to split the growing unity of Japanese, Mexican and Filipino workers" and for "realizing it was their unity with all the other pickers which won the concessions they gained." Three years later, the Venice Celery Strike drew together one thousand workers from the California Japanese Agricultural Workers Union and the Federation of Farm Workers of America, which was composed of Mexican and Filipino immigrants. They demanded raises and collective bargaining recognition from a series of Issei truck farmers. When eight hundred Japanese farmers comprising the Southern California Farm Federation backed the celery growers, labor organizers mobilized a community-wide Japanese American boycott of crops grown by the growers' association, denying management the old argument that what was good for Issei proprietors was good for all Japanese Americans. Ultimately, the growers broke the strike by giving a favorable deal to the Mexican workers and having Issei labor leaders arrested. Despite their incomplete success, however, the agricultural labor campaigns exposed the divergent class interests within the local Japanese community and highlighted the potential for innovative multiracial organizing that combined community outreach with action at the point of production.[27]

Comparatively few Black migrants toiled in California agriculture; perhaps if more like Pettis Perry had, a stronger basis for Black and Japanese American working-class solidarity would have developed. Through his many travels, Perry developed a militant posture of resistance to white supremacy and capitalism along with a strong sense of brotherhood with workers of other races and nationalities. Born into a family of sharecroppers on January 4, 1897, near Marion, Alabama, he worked as a farm laborer most of his childhood and received only fifteen months of formal education. Growing up in the rural South exposed Perry to racist terror. He witnessed a Black chain gang worker "beaten until the blood ran down from him like water running down a stream" and a preacher shot "so full of holes his intestines were hanging out." By the age of fourteen, Perry concluded that it was "a difficult thing for a Negro to keep alive in the South." Three years later, he was nearly lynched. Seeing a Black coal miner beaten to death before his eyes, he at last decided, "I was leaving the South forever. I was taking my hand from that deck never to play it again." Between 1917 and 1932, Perry roamed the country looking for work, making stops at various points in the Midwest, Southwest, and Pacific Northwest and passing through no fewer than forty-five states. He worked in such diverse places as a Muskegon auto plant, a Chicago packinghouse, and an Alaskan cannery before gravitating to California. Like many Issei "blanket boys," he spent winters in Los Angeles and the rest of the year following the agricultural harvest northward from the Imperial Valley to Sacramento. Sharing bonds of friendship and solidarity with migrant workers of all races, he developed a reputation as a tireless organizer. Perry claimed to know at least twenty-five hundred agricultural workers by name. Carrying that experience in his back pocket, he sought industrial employment in Los Angeles, where he found a job as a "jack puller" in a cottonseed mill during the spring of 1932. The onerous work required him to pull down a 2,200-pound hydraulic press to make six cotton meal cakes per minute. "Every time you pull that weight down the meal pops into your clothing, down your neck, and there's a big puff of steam right in your face," recalled Perry. "We worked twelve hours a day. It was as rough as any man's penitentiary." Inside the plant, he soon encountered Communists, discovering in their party a vehicle to confront the oppressive conditions he had faced in life. Describing Scottsboro as "the thing that really developed my national consciousness," he quit his industrial job to become as a full-time organizer for the Los Angeles branch of the International Labor Defense. Unpaid but given free room and board from his comrades, Perry quickly ascended the ranks of the CPUSA largely because of its "special approach to the Negro," which functioned as a form of affirmative action. By diligently listening and memorizing speeches and resolutions, he overcame his lack of formal education and eventually "learned to read by reading the *Communist Manifesto* and *Capital*." By 1938, the self-educated worker from the Black Belt nation had become the head of the entire CPUSA apparatus in Los Angeles County.[28]

Communist-inspired "independent" organizing attracted those seeking radical alternatives to American capitalism, but the government would not sit idly by while they plotted against it. Heavily backed by the "open shop" forces, the "Red Squad" of the Los Angeles Police Department (LAPD) was experienced in antiradicalism. After squashing the Wobblies during the years following World War I, it focused attention on the CPUSA. Emboldened by the 1929 election of ex-Klansman John Porter as mayor of Los Angeles, LAPD commissioner Mark Pierce declared, "Communists have no constitutional rights and I won't listen to anyone who defends them." As one of the appointees responsible for police oversight, Pierce added, "The more the police beat them up and wreck their headquarters, the better." Pettis Perry claimed radicals were "beaten, jailed, [and] some maimed for life."[29]

Although Black and white Communists were routinely abused, immigrants proved especially vulnerable. While the hardships of the Depression strengthened the bonds of solidarity between many Americans, nonwhite immigrants served as a scapegoat for white anxiety. Nativist groups and local governments in Los Angeles pushed for the repatriation of Mexicans, as did others throughout the Southwest and Midwest. Although some immigrants left voluntarily, many felt coerced to return to Mexico in the wake of mass arrests and intimidation campaigns cooperatively arranged by media outlets and public officials. An estimated one-third of Los Angeles's Mexican population was repatriated during the 1930s, including American citizens technically expatriated. Meanwhile, Congress curtailed immigration from the Philippines in 1934. Senator Millard Tydings, cosponsor of the legislation, declared that it was "absolutely illogical . . . to exclude Japanese and Chinese and permit Filipinos en masse to come into the country." The following year, California passed a law prohibiting aliens from obtaining forms of public relief. While nativists hoped such a measure would speed repatriation, the agricultural industry believed it would make its evaporating pool of immigrant laborers more desperate for work.[30]

Within this nativist climate, Japanese immigrants were particularly susceptible to state repression as "aliens ineligible to citizenship." In December 1929, two years after the high-profile execution of radicals Sacco and Vanzetti sent shock waves throughout America, Sadaichi Kenmotsu became one of the first Issei radicals to be arrested and eventually deported for being a CPUSA member. Prominent among leftists in Los Angeles, Kenmotsu had recently moved to San Francisco to lead the Japanese section of the CPUSA and edit the *Rodo Shimbun*. While the ILD rallied to his defense, it was unable to prevent his conviction, imprisonment, or deportation. Nevertheless, he felt blessed that it had prevented his return to "fascist" Japan by raising money for what the state deemed "voluntary" relocation. Released from the Angel Island Detention Center in 1931, Kenmotsu set sail for what he called the Soviet "Fatherland." A series of Issei activists, including Communist leader Tetsuji Horiuchi and other workers, were arrested, defended, and "voluntarily" relocated to the Soviet Union in similar fashion over the next two years. Included in this group were nine Japanese CPUSA members nabbed by the Red Squad and local authorities alongside 120 others attending a party function in Long Beach on January 16, 1932.[31]

Although ILD organizing generated new interest in the CPUSA, the endless need to defend immigrants from state repression hampered organizing efforts—that is, of course, after the "chilling effects" of the repression itself took effect. Moreover, Issei radicals found themselves isolated from the mainstream ethnic community and its anticommunist leadership. Togo Tanaka, a Nisei journalist for the *Rafu Shimpo* in the 1930s, noted that the staffs of the city's three Japanese vernacular newspapers "generally acknowledged that to become tainted with the label 'Aka' or Communist was a cardinal sin." Literally meaning "red," *aka* was a stigma applied not only to CPUSA members but also to any advocate of workers' rights or critic of Japanese militarism. Finally, as outspoken opponents of the Japanese emperor, a deportation order was particularly dire for Issei radicals, who faced certain imprisonment and possible execution in Japan. Worse yet, the symbolic dream of proletarian utopia became a living nightmare for those who successfully struggled for "voluntary" relocation to the Soviet Union. During Stalin's reign, at least five of the expatriated Issei radicals were imprisoned and executed as "infiltrators."[32]

RACE AND LABOR POLITICS

As state repression hindered independent forms of organizing, Black and Japanese American activists sought to connect with mainstream institutions. They were further prompted by international and domestic developments. On the basis of a new assessment that fascism posed the key danger to the Soviet Union and workers around the world, the Comintern in mid-1935 ordered its member parties to dissolve the "united front from below" approach and adopt a "Popular Front" orientation. Communists were now directed to create the broadest possible level of unity against fascism, working particularly with the very "reformist" forces—trade unions, liberals, and social democrats—they had previously attacked. Furthermore, under Earl Browder's leadership, the CPUSA advocated a nonviolent American path to socialism that distanced itself from the Bolshevik revolution. It especially saw union organizing as the key to reforming mainstream society. The 1935 Wagner Act created the basis for state intervention to legitimize collective bargaining rights of workers. Around the same time, the creation of the Committee of Industrial Organizations (CIO—later renamed the Congress of Industrial Organizations), advancing an innovative form of industrial unionism, lent Communists and social democrats a vehicle to integrate workers into a common organization and provide them a basis to shape the American social order.[33]

For Black and Japanese Americans in Los Angeles, the promise of Depression-era trade union organizing outweighed its practical accomplishments. On a national level, the CIO helped give rise to an inclusive model of industrial organizing that unified workers from diverse backgrounds. Through participation in the Los Angeles CIO, Mexican American workers fostered what George Sánchez has termed "a new politics of opposition" that situated "racial and ethnic justice" at the center of "the American dream." But whereas Black and Asian Americans joined the CIO in significant numbers, they did so mainly outside Los Angeles, where production remained largely craft-oriented and conservative AFL leadership guided the labor movement. Although the CIO did establish its Los Angeles Industrial Union Council in 1937, its efforts here proved far less potent than in Harry Bridges's San Francisco region. Moreover, its Southern California locals (with the partial exception of the maritime unions) were tied primarily to manufacturing sectors that excluded Black and Japanese American workers. Hence, when Black workers struggled to form unions, they generally ended up in segregated locals or auxiliaries within the AFL. Japanese American calls for AFL recognition led at best to similar results and at worst to downright rejection.[34]

Railroad workers were at the forefront of AFL unionism among African Americans. Historian Beth Tompkins Bates has credited A. Philip Randolph's Brotherhood of Sleeping Car Porters with giving rise to mass participatory "protest politics" in Black America. In part, segregation fostered a labor consciousness that drew on the militant tendencies of Black nationalism. But while the Brotherhood was one of three Black railroad unions in Los Angeles the AFL recognized during the Depression (as seventeen other AFL transportation unions barred African Americans from membership), it bore little mark of this militancy. The Pullman Company summarily fired leading organizers and intimidated much of the rank and file. It preferred to hire African Americans because it prejudged them to be less "antagonistic" than Mexicans and more suited than whites for service work. Until the Brotherhood's recognition in 1935, porters were forced to join a company union, whose privileges of membership included long shifts, low wages, a harsh disciplinary process, and payroll deductions for meals and uniforms. In spite of this, many sided with the company out of fear they would otherwise lose their job. In fact, it was primarily porters from Northern California rather than the Southland that drove the Brotherhood's struggle for recognition. As continued evidence of their reticence, only half of all Pullman porters in Los Angeles had joined the union by 1938.[35]

Nisei radicals argued that labor unions were the primary vehicle for Japanese Americans to integrate themselves into American society. Less susceptible to repression than the alien Issei, they focused on organizing Japanese produce workers. Shuji Fujii, probably the most prominent American-born Japanese radical in Los Angeles, argued that a multiracial labor movement offered the best prospects for improving the life chances of Japanese American workers. Fujii was a CPUSA member and editor of the Popular Front *Doho* newspaper (succeeding the *Rodo Shimbun*). More specifically, he was a Kibei—born in the United States but raised in Japan. Culturally and linguistically Japanese, the Kibei could better relate to the Japanese immigrant community than could the Americanized Nisei. Radical Kibei generally grew up during the Taisho era (1912–1925), experiencing a relatively liberal and open Japanese society. This group stood in stark contrast to Kibei who came of age amid the nationalism and indoctrination haunting imperial Japan of the 1930s. Reaching out to fellow produce workers, Fujii declared, "Negro, Mexican, American workers stretch out their hands to clasp yours and welcome you as a brother and as an equal in our fight to get decent working conditions—conditions that all other American workers enjoy. This invitation is a challenge to our race." But he and other activists were forced to contend with both paternalistic Issei employers and chauvinistic white union leaders. Seeking to organize the wholesale and retail industries where Japanese American workers were concentrated, Nisei activists resigned themselves to working with the AFL. Scarcely interested in fostering a multiracial culture of unity, the AFL committed only cursory efforts to organize Japanese Americans when the poor conditions of the ethnic labor market undermined the status of white workers. While Mexican American leftists successfully organized independent unions of industrial workers that later merged into the CIO, Nisei activists could not count on the Los Angeles CIO to provide them with the resources and clout necessary to challenge the AFL in service sectors where the AFL was firmly entrenched.[36]

In the end, the shared antiradicalism of the mainstream trade unions and ethnic-based associations led to a marriage of convenience, whereby Japanese American workers were organized into segregated AFL units controlled by ethnic leaders. Such was the disappointing outcome of an organizing drive in wholesale produce that began with great promise. Led by Shuji Fujii, Japanese American activists played a leading role establishing the independent, multiracial Market Workers Union (MWU) in 1936. MWU leaders pointed to their sincere embrace of "Brother Fujii," twice elected secretary, as proof that their union was "open to all the workers of the market regardless of race and [would create] better conditions for all." Indeed, more than five hundred Japanese Americans signed with the MWU following its affiliation with the AFL. There was a catch, however. The moderate Nisei leadership of the City Market Employees Association chose to maintain their ethnic-based association and join only as adherent members of the AFL local. Moreover, Nisei radicals, many of whom had been charter members, were subsequently purged from the union by the ultraconservative leaders of Teamsters Local 630, which absorbed the MWU after raising a jurisdictional dispute.[37]

The fragmented Japanese American workforce of the retail produce industry proved even more difficult to organize. The retail produce enterprise was fraught with insecurity and low profit margins. Businesses changed hands frequently, jobs turned over rapidly, and the survival of many shops rested on the work of unpaid family labor. As Issei employers came to rely on the inexpensive labor of Japanese workers with limited options, they actually developed a vested interest in keeping Japanese

Americans segregated from workers of other backgrounds and excluded from both the primary labor market and AFL unions. They further drew on their shared ethnicity to encourage a paternalistic identification with their workforce. At the same time, societal discrimination had made Japanese American wage laborers dependent on the ethnic economy and suspicious of white labor. Japanese were only one-third as likely as whites to be jobless in 1940, and low wages seemed preferable to unemployment. Furthermore, some Nisei leaders warned Japanese American workers of the risks of associating with the AFL given its legacy of racial exclusion. Larry Tajiri, a Nisei journalist who spent the Depression years in Los Angeles and San Francisco, wrote, "Many Nisei are considered permanently ineligible to union membership because they have acted as 'scabs' or strike-breakers in previous strikes." He concluded, "Should the unions triumph in their demand for preferential hiring, which is virtually 'closed shop,' the second-generation Japanese may be locked out of industry." While educated Nisei were almost equally reliant on the Issei for employment, they saw even less utility in the unions than did their less educated brethren. One study done on the eve of World War II found that one out of four Nisei produce workers had at least some college education. Their parents had labored overtime to give them opportunities the immigrant generation had been denied, even as the parents realized these opportunities might be off in the distant future. Journalist T. John Fujii lamented that "hundreds of college graduates [were] wasting their education and talents in fruit markets under unreasonable conditions." But as one Little Tokyo merchant reasoned, "A college man polishing apples usually can see far beyond polishing apples. The grammar school graduate can only think of the apple he is polishing." This sense of deferred upward mobility dulled the proletarian consciousness of educated Nisei workers, who felt their most likely future in the produce industry rested with managerial duties.[38]

A drive to organize the Japanese American retail produce industry started auspiciously but ended with a frustrated AFL calling instead for a race-based boycott of all "Japanese" merchants. Teaming with AFL Retail Clerks 770 in 1937, radical Nisei, as was the case in wholesale produce, found many Japanese workers initially willing to strike against Issei retailers. In response, the cooperative association of Issei produce merchants created the Southern California Retail Produce Workers Union (SCRPWU) as a sort of company union for the industry's Japanese American employees. For reasons previously cited, most workers opted for the employers' ethnic association over the AFL. To be fair, the SCRPWU did provide some moderate new benefits and opportunities for Japanese American workers to socialize among their own kind. Most likely, however, employers sent overt and implicit threats that workers would make their jobs more difficult or face termination if they sided with the AFL. Outraged by the tactics of the merchants' cooperative, the AFL Retail Clerks pushed the AFL's Central Labor Council to launch a boycott of "non-union Japanese operated markets" in January 1939. A would-be strength of the Issei economic development strategy—its focus on the white consumer market—was now exposed as a critical vulnerability. Local president Joseph DeSilva called on his AFL brothers to spend their money "with a merchant who hires American workers." In fact, it was well known to DeSilva and the AFL that they were boycotting markets employing mostly American-born Nisei. His appeal was thus made on the basis of race rather than nationality. Tragically, an effort to promote the integration of Nisei workers had devolved into a xenophobic anti-Japanese crusade. In March 1941, the mostly Nisei SCRPWU membership shunned both DeSilva's Local 770 and the Issei merchants' association by affiliating with the AFL as segregated Local 1510. By this time, even Shuji Fujii was forced to concede there was little hope of wresting control of produce industry unions from their conservative, racist leaders. As such, he acceded to the interim necessity of ethnic worker associations.[39]

While Japanese merchants were susceptible to mass political pressure from white labor, Black consumers and business leaders launched their own selective buying campaign in an effort to overcome discriminatory hiring patterns within the Central Avenue district. Charlotta Bass claimed that the Industrial Council, an organization that she founded in 1930, first advanced the "Don't Spend Your Money Where You Can't Work" campaign. However, *Los Angeles Sentinel* publisher Leon Washington apparently assumed control of it later in the decade. A dispute with Bass had prompted Washington to quit a marketing job at the *California Eagle*, leading him to found the *Sentinel* (originally titled the *Eastside Shopper*) with assistance from a white publisher from the South named Dickson Bell. His benefactor was quite likely a Democrat seeking to counter the *Eagle*'s Republican influence. While the Urban League had been nudging white merchants to hire Blacks, the "Don't Spend" campaign called on African Americans to boycott businesses on Central Avenue between Second and Fortieth streets that were not integrated. Two types of businesses became targets. Among the first were corporate-owned retail and financial establishments. In 1934, *Eagle* writer John R. Williams declared, "Chain store invasions by large white corporations have sounded the death knell for Negro grocery stores and Negro markets, and they are slowly but surely closing out the Negro drug stores in the so-called Black belt of Los Angeles." The second type of business target consisted of smaller white retailer operations, many Jewish-owned, that were seen as direct competitors with Black-owned businesses. These included stores selling furniture, housewares, clothing, drugs, and liquor. While Japanese

American entrepreneurs used ethnic solidarity to create their own economic niche, Black efforts to form trade associations collapsed, and many Black-owned businesses fell into crisis during the Depression. Through the selective buying campaign, African American entrepreneurs fostered cross-class solidarity with their Central Avenue district customer base, oftentimes in an effort just to stay afloat.[40]

Overall, the campaign produced mixed results. On the one hand, the rallying cry of "Don't Spend Your Money Where You Can't Work" proved capable of rousing militant protests and heightening race consciousness. Washington himself was arrested in January 1934 for violating an antipicketing ordinance when he parked with a sign brandishing the campaign slogan in front of the Zerg Furniture Company. After three to four hundred protesters rallied to his defense, Zerg withdrew its complaint against Washington. Protests against chain stores reportedly drew broader participation. In his stint as CPUSA "Section Organizer for the Negro Community," Pettis Perry maintained that five thousand people supported demonstrations in 1937 against Five and Ten and Kress, forcing the latter to employ Black women in eight of its sixteen sales clerk positions. Summing up the campaign's results at the end of the Depression, Loren Miller considered it a "fairly successful organizational drive" that generated the "employment of numerous Negroes by local business institutions." On the other hand, the Urban League's Floyd Covington replied that such success was "somewhat overstated." He noted that some cases of new Black hires "led to reprisals which have lost more for the Negro than they have gained" and cited evidence of widespread layoffs of African American "stock girls" across the city. Covington concluded, "The Negro is not yet concentrated in sufficiently large numbers to make this type of campaign effective here." In the end, the "Don't Spend" campaign was not a means to alleviate the severe poverty and unemployment of the Depression. As historian Manning Marable has noted, the movement began in the early Depression years in Chicago and spread rapidly to Pittsburgh, Atlanta, Boston, Baltimore, Richmond, and Harlem. Yet Marable questions the impact of these campaigns. While the stigma of Jim Crow exclusion from employment in white-owned businesses was very real, the remedy advanced was largely symbolic. The few jobs that might be gained were barely incremental steps forward, and such potential could be more than offset by the costs of ethnic strife and heightened anti-Semitism.[41]

The labor activism of the Depression exposed the racial dynamics of class formation. The CIO's democratizing influence had yet to achieve its full impact in Los Angeles, which still lacked a large base of industrial workers. As represented by the dominant AFL, white labor continued to commit to exclusionary organizing strategies that precluded a true sense of multiracial solidarity among the working class. Moreover, the AFL boycott of "Japanese operated markets" demonstrated how dependence on white patronage curtailed the political leverage of the Issei outside the ethnic community. With the Pacific War looming on the horizon, the seemingly more lucrative strategy of Issei entrepreneurs would ultimately prove more susceptible to undermining. Though far smaller in number, African American business owners slowly began to develop a degree of political independence that was rooted in support from a Black customer base. While the "Don't Spend" campaign may not have improved the employment prospects of the average African American worker in Los Angeles, it introduced a new brand of mass mobilization and protest that united disparate elements of the Black community in a manner that would ultimately prove crucial to the fight for political empowerment.

CHAPTER 4

In the Shadow of War

IN THE SUMMER OF 1940, white opponents assailed Nisei efforts to build the Jefferson Park subdivision. On the surface, this represented yet another instance of white suburban interests acting to exclude people of color from the Westside. This conflict, however, stood out for two reasons. First, the Nisei subdivision's foes invoked not only the specter of a nonwhite invasion of their neighborhood; they also went so far as to insist that its construction could lead to an actual foreign invasion. Heading the Los Angeles City Council's opposition to Jefferson Park, Evan Lewis declared, "This subdivision might get us into war with Japan." In council chambers, he shouted that the Japanese were "planning to stab America in the back" and called the Nisei project "an entering wedge" for the "Trojan Horse." Second, through the creation of the Equality Committee, Nisei leaders of the Japanese American Citizens League (JACL) began a mass campaign against discrimination and "Yellow Peril" jingoism unlike any in the organization's brief history. These young Americans of Japanese ancestry believed that their birthright citizenship entitled them to opportunities denied their immigrant parents.[1]

Their campaign drew the attention of civil rights activist Loren Miller, who had been the key figure promoting African American political mobilization through the founding of the Los Angeles chapter of the National Negro Congress (NNC). Miller shaped the editorial response of the Black-run *Los Angeles Sentinel*, which expressed solidarity with the Nisei while condemning the "age-old attempt to confine minority groups to undesirable sections of the city." Councilman Evan Lewis, it further noted, had "long been" a leader in the campaign for racial restrictive covenants, and his race-baiting "hogwash" had been "raised against Japanese in the same manner and with as much justice, or rather lack of justice, as the cry of 'rapists' [had been] raised against Negroes." Since it was a "safe assumption" that a politician who would deny the rights of Japanese Americans would do likewise to Blacks, Miller assured the Nisei that African American voters would strongly support their efforts to defeat Jefferson Park's political opponents at the polls. With NNC and JACL activists seemingly poised to challenge white hegemony and traditional models of ethnic leadership, the Jefferson Park episode raised the prospect of Nisei efforts to secure the rights of American citizenship fusing with Black struggles to overcome racial discrimination. The notion of such a coalition, however, would quickly become overshadowed by the looming prospect of war.[2]

Examining the prelude to World War II, this chapter provides context for the following two wartime chapters respectively analyzing Japanese American responses to the call for mass internment and African American "Negro Victory" activism. Black and Japanese Americans' distinct relationships to the nation-state pushed the two groups onto divergent political trajectories. In the early 1930s, Japanese immigrant activists had proven especially vulnerable to repression. As relations between the United States and Japan grew increasingly belligerent, the state cast an eye of suspicion over the second-generation Nisei, as well. Mass Japanese American protest against racism yielded to a traumatic search for an identity to fit the increasingly narrowed parameters of Americanism. Seemingly deprived of collective models of resistance, Japanese Americans came to view the US nation-state as a repressive body that one must either submit to or renounce. While African American activism during the Depression failed to stem the tide of segregation or close the economic inequality gap with whites, it laid the bases for unity across class and ideological lines. Moreover, as the New Deal created a dawning sense of hope in the power of remedial state action, the Black community developed a new relationship to the governing Democrats. As the war created a pressing need for national unity and defense production, African Americans would call on these politicians to deploy state power in the name of civil rights. Responding to pressure by Black activists, President Franklin D. Roosevelt established the Committee on Fair Employment Practice (FEPC). The FEPC's oversight of the defense industries promised to expand economic opportunities for all people of color, yet Japanese Americans were slated for mass internment by the time its impact was felt in Los Angeles. The dominant racial ideology during World War II would debilitate Japanese American agency while creating openings for African Americans to assert greater claims for full citizenship.

POLITICAL MOBILIZATION

On Valentine's Day in 1936, hundreds of civil rights leaders, trade unionists, intellectuals, and radicals gathered in Chicago for the first national political summit convened under the banner of the National Negro Congress (NNC). "Now is the time to close ranks for freedom and equality," read the NNC's call. "Let us unite the Negro organizations and friends of Negro freedom on a program for security and manhood for the Negroes in America." Black leftists viewed the NNC as the key to mobilizing an African American Popular Front. Although Los Angeles sent five delegates to the founding conference, Loren Miller stayed home. It was not for lack of interest, given the central role he played in promoting the NNC. As expressed in a July 1935 article for the left-wing journal *New Masses*, Miller saw the NNC as a direct challenge to the moderate politics of the NAACP. In his assessment, the ILD's grassroots Scottsboro campaign had exposed the limits of the NAACP's "purely legal approach to the question of Negro rights" and the bankruptcy of "old obstructionist leaders" who were "self-perpetuating and responsible to nobody." While the NAACP offered a "grandiose theory" of racial equality, he assured his readers the NNC would "translate this fine talk into positive action." Yet, to achieve its purpose, the NNC would require more than the involvement of a small circle of leftists. Miller thus sought to maximize the participation of others to achieve diverse representation of the Black community's political elements. In a "Confidential Report" to NNC national organizer and nonpublic CPUSA member John P. Davis, he wrote, "As you know, this is a very reactionary community and the mere fact that we were able to get organizations from Communist Party to Legion is a big step forward."[3]

An examination of two of the Los Angeles delegates provides a more detailed sense of the political unity the NNC accomplished. A loyal Republican, Norman Houston of Golden State Insurance was a prominent representative of the city's Black business leadership. He simultaneously espoused economic nationalism and opposed racial discrimination. While Houston's presence signified the community's previously reliable GOP support, state assemblyman Augustus Hawkins embodied its new party loyalty. In 1934, the Democrat Hawkins had defeated seven-term Republican Frederick Roberts, who was at the time the only African American in Los Angeles holding elected office. During his first campaign, the city's Black Republican establishment had shunned Hawkins, while Roberts and the *Eagle* red-baited Loren Miller, his campaign manager. However, they quickly sensed the shifting political balance of power as Black voters switched en masse to the Democratic Party and five out of six African American residents of the Central Avenue district voted for Franklin D. Roosevelt in 1936. Although its track record was decidedly uneven, the New Deal offered hope to Black Los Angeles. On the one hand, with public-sector employment growing exponentially, some greater rewards of patronage became evident. In 1938, Black workers in the Works Progress Administration (WPA) represented double their share of the population at-large. Moreover, the standardization of wages and government checks on discrimination made "emergency" employment in New Deal programs relatively attractive. On the other hand, there were limits to New Deal reformism. Even as it offered white workers—especially the descendants of recent European immigrants—a new sense of belonging and participation in a democratic America, its sins of omission and commission provided cover for the savage rule of Jim Crow over the South while aiding the advance of residential segregation and racial inequality in the North. In Los Angeles, the WPA routinely assigned all African Americans to manual labor jobs, and the National Youth Administration acceded to the requests of employers who refused to hire Blacks. Gus Hawkins had campaigned as an upstart candidate willing to push the envelope of the Democratic Party. In 1934, he had mounted an insurgent campaign attached to socialist Upton Sinclair's drive to "End Poverty in California," which found its main base of support in a Los Angeles that harbored three hundred thousand unemployed persons. Miller privately remarked to NNC coordinators that the young, popular, and left-leaning Hawkins was "destined to be one of the most important figures in People's Front movement."[4]

Los Angeles NNC organizers built a broad coalition that grew to encompass over one hundred organizational sponsors reflecting the social and ideological diversity of the Black community. Consistent with Popular Front strategy, the CPUSA and ILD were involved from the outset. Yet, as Miller pointed out, it was novel to see their names listed beside stalwart community groups like the Forum, NAACP, Urban League, and YMCA. Furthermore, sponsors included all of the city's major Black newspapers (including the *Eagle* and *Sentinel*), Republicans and Democrats, as well as labor unions, churches, fraternities, sororities, and veterans' groups. Even a number of societies and social clubs like the "What's Your Bid Bridge Club" were official sponsors. The local NNC chapter agreed to a long-term focus on improving employment and relief options, especially for youth. Demanding that Los Angeles compete for federal dollars provided by the 1937 Housing Act, the NNC's advocacy for public housing best reflected its challenge to local Black politics. While it was not necessarily incompatible with the ideology of housing improvement, homeowners' associations had never prioritized public housing advocacy. They were conspicuously absent from the list of NNC sponsors. Launched by a "packed house" meeting in April 1938, the NNC's campaign for decent housing emphasized the needs of low-income residents with an ultimate goal of securing a housing project for the Central Avenue district. Encouraging grassroots mobilization, it called on African Americans to be "active and vigilant" to ensure they would not be "overlooked when the time for the building of projects arrives." At best, however, social change in the interwar era occurred in a contradictory manner. While the city did set up the Los Angeles Housing Authority, it imposed segregated living arrangements on top of strict quotas limiting

Black residency within the projects that eventually opened during the 1940s.[5]

The enthusiasm generated by the expansiveness of the NNC's vision ultimately could not translate into organizational growth or movement building. It was hampered by the contradictions that occur when trying to organize simultaneously at different geographical scales. Similar problems would confront the El Congreso del Pueblo de Habla Española (The Congress of Spanish-Speaking Peoples)—a Latino Popular Front vehicle founded in Los Angeles on April 29, 1939—and the wartime March on Washington movement. On the one hand, these national movements captured the imagination of thousands of people who would not commit to joining the CPUSA or other radical groups but were dissatisfied with the timid political expressions the two major parties offered on issues of race and class. The mass turnout for the NNC and Congreso del Pueblo founding events signaled the hunger for alternatives felt by oppressed people. On the other hand, the actual function of these "intermediary" organizations (i.e., a formation that is not a political party but also not a local community organization) proved difficult to define. Leaders hoped they could at least serve as a national platform for progressive consciousness-raising and policy proposals. Yet the fact that the NNC's Los Angeles chapter reported constant financial difficulties suggests that people at the grass roots lacked the resources or commitment to sustain such an endeavor. Its shortcomings were so dramatic they were almost comical. In May 1936, the Los Angeles Council requested that the national office send one hundred copies of the NNC program "on consignment." With "exactly $1.65 in our local treasury," it regretted it could send only one dollar for postage. The national office's reply noted the local had failed to enclose the dollar. Two years later, the council's corresponding secretary–treasurer, Lillian Jones, remarked that "everyone [felt] terrible about our lack of support for the national office" but could do little to improve the situation. While Los Angeles was "not trying to dodge the responsibility of securing sponsors," there were "just so many things which could be done." Sectarian and ideological divisions also reared their heads. Loren Miller's interest in building the NNC waned as he became disillusioned with the CPUSA in the wake of the Nazi-Soviet pact of 1939. Like the "Don't Spend" selective buying campaign, the National Negro Congress was less than a complete success. Nevertheless, both laid down bases for African Americans to unite in the struggle against racial discrimination.[6]

As deteriorating relations between the United States and Japan cast a shadow over the entire Japanese community, Nisei leaders witnessed their community fracture along the lines of generation, class, and ideology.

With the bulk of Japanese immigrant families having been established between the 1908 Gentlemen's Agreement barring labor migration and the 1920 "Ladies Agreement" ending the "picture bride" migration, the first large second-generation grouping entered adulthood during the hardship years of the Depression. Backed by the Fourteenth Amendment's guarantee of birthright citizenship, a fledgling core of Nisei from educated and professional backgrounds organized the Japanese American Citizens League (JACL) to promote their own mobility and tackle the community burdens inherited from the Issei. Although this organization's strident assimilationism has most shaped popular cultural perceptions of the Nisei, the JACL in practice was far from uniform and was instead a site of intense political debate among the Nisei during critical periods of history. Like its counterparts in the Latino community, such as the League of United Latin American Citizens and the Mexican American Movement, the JACL stressed participation in American democratic institutions as the primary avenue for overcoming the handicap of race. Ironically, as Yuji Ichioka has demonstrated, Nisei initially approached this work from within the Issei paradigm of dual nationalism. Togo Tanaka's wartime reports for the Japanese Evacuation and Resettlement Study best recorded the history of this era. In its developmental stages, the JACL relied heavily on Issei leaders for material aid and turned to the Japanese consulate for political guidance. Seeking to act as a "bridge of understanding," many Nisei took upon themselves the duty of teaching American audiences about Japan. But this was no ordinary period in Japanese history; it was one defined by imperial expansion. While Nisei leftists sharply condemned the rise of Japanese militarism during the 1920s and 1930s, a significant number of early JACL leaders served as near mouthpieces for Japanese propaganda. Rising tensions between the United States and Japan would preclude the possibility of reconciling this particular configuration of "twoness."[7]

Retreating from dual nationalism, the JACL focused on the Americanist aspect of its work. As the Sino-Japanese War intensified during 1937, it adopted a position of "neutrality" stressing "sympathy" with but not allegiance to Japan. Franklin D. Roosevelt's July 1939 announcement that the United States was abrogating the American-Japanese Trade Treaty put further pressure on the JACL to distance itself from Japan. For the alien Issei, as historian Brian Hayashi has noted, the loss of treaty protection stripped them of "their last line of defense against racial discrimination." Determined to cling to their citizenship, the JACL's leaders made promoting loyalty to America their nearly exclusive priority. To be certain, "Americanism" had been a central organizational tenet from its outset, when fulfillment of citizenship rights was deemed consistent with promoting the "economic and self-protection" of the community. The JACL claimed a role in securing a 1931 amendment to the Cable Act, thereby discontinuing a provision that had stripped citizenship from Nisei and all other US citizens married to "aliens ineligible to citizenship." Its resolution in support of this reform, however, professed a naive faith in the American political system. "We Americans of Japanese ancestry believe that Congress is unaware of the conditions now existing," the JACL stated, "and believe that the wrong will be remedied once this matter is called to the attention of Congress, in whose sense of justice and fair play we have absolute confidence." The organization also took credit for passage of the 1935 Nye-Lea bill granting citizenship to "Oriental" World War I veterans. This had stemmed largely from the one-man crusade of Tokutaro Nishimura Slocum, a veteran of the Great War who preached the slogan "my Country, right or wrong!"[8]

While Nisei leaders, like most children of immigrants, possessed an anxious desire to be accepted as Americans, the Jefferson Park controversy forced them to recognize that promoting "Americanism" entailed more than making an individual effort to assimilate and keeping faith in the goodwill of elected representatives. The project began with ambitious economic goals and conservative housing improvement aims. In early 1940, leading Nisei members of the JACL and the *Rafu Shimpo* English section announced plans to build a fifty-one-acre subdivision. Jefferson Park was set to rise on a hay field near the intersection of Jefferson Boulevard and La Brea Avenue, a few miles northwest of Leimert Park. Its bright-eyed Nisei boosters had been versed in Herbert Hoover's 1922 best seller, *American Individualism*, which did not simply promote the economic benefits of homeownership but actually equated owning a home with being an American. They convinced themselves that a model subdivision would promote both better living standards and "better Americanism" among their cohort. Maintaining their own homes in a morally upright neighborhood would ostensibly improve the Japanese image in the eyes of whites and thereby curtail racial prejudice against Nisei professionals. Following the standard moral uplift tenets of nonwhite elites, the Nisei developers did not openly challenge racial segregation. They sought only to build housing for members of their race and imposed class-based deed restrictions. Nisei selling agent James Hisatomi asserted that Jefferson Park would be "an exclusive Japanese residential district, with beautiful surroundings." *Rafu Shimpo* columnist Tad Uyeno remarked that Japanese Americans now had an opportunity to depart from "the sordid existence in 'China-towns' and other squalid quarters" and move into "a clean community of homes." Doing so would "create a much healthier environment for the future generations to grow up in" and preclude them from "mingling with the class of people who are in dire circumstances." What Uyeno failed to recognize, however, was that the "ghetto" was not a fixed geographical marker but an ideological designation that followed Japanese Americans and people of color of any standing wherever they went.[9]

The venomous nature of white hostility toward Jefferson Park stunned Nisei leaders, moving them to mass political mobilization to defend both their project and their standing as American citizens. Representing the opinion of white residents in adjacent neighborhoods, Mr. and Mrs. Maurice L. Young demanded that the city council "do something to keep those Japs from moving in on us" and called for the deliberative body to "protect us from this particular Japanese invasion." Echoing these comments, the district's state assemblyman, Ernest Voigt, asserted that Jefferson Park would harm "adjoining property values." The Nisei's standing as citizens was irrelevant to Voigt, whose opposition was rooted in his belief there was a "fundamental and irreconcilable difference between the races." In response to these complaints, the Los Angeles City Council rejected approval of the tract map for Jefferson Park. In turn, the JACL created the Equality Committee to organize mass rallies in support of Americanism and Jefferson Park during July and August 1940. Its vision was shaped by JACL member and Harvard Law School graduate John F. Aiso, who asserted that the issue of civil rights was "a matter of great importance which dwarf[ed] the Nisei Week Festival and the National Conventions in consequence." Instead of spending their money solely on "comfort bags" and banquets, Aiso admonished the Nisei to devote funds to support legal battles against racism. Printing multiple daily articles and large headlines on the theme of combating discrimination, the *Rafu Shimpo* English section became a vehicle of agitation to bolster the Equality Committee's efforts. Lawsuits filed by the Nisei developers and their white financial backers ultimately forced the city council to approve the subdivision. By this time, however, the controversy had given many Nisei cold feet. As many as half of the lots had been reserved, but an unstoppable stream of withdrawals killed the project. The white residents had lost the legal battle but succeeded in convincing Nisei that Jefferson Park homeowners would have obnoxious racists for neighbors. Realty agent James Hisatomi concluded the West Coast was "all shot to hell as far as the Nisei are concerned." Hastily preparing a move to Texas, he remarked, "I'm getting out while the pulling out is good." The ensuing wartime assault on the civil liberties of Japanese Americans would prove him sadly prescient.[10]

While it may have been hyperbole for Jefferson Park's opponents to declare that the subdivision comprised a "Jap invasion," the stark reality was that the rising specter of war between the United States and Japan was becoming the determinative factor shaping local relations between whites and Japanese Americans. As the state cast a growing pall of racial suspicion over the ethnic Japanese community, JACL leaders went to greater and greater lengths to prioritize Americanism education—employing language that was almost identical to that of the American Legion, Veterans of Foreign Wars, and Daughters of the American Revolution. Tanaka characterized the 1940 national JACL convention as a "dizzy swirl of oratory replete with references to 'Old Glory.'" It reflected, to him, the "defensive character" of an organization living in perpetual fear "that Caucasians would not recognize in the Nisei an American, but would rather see a Japanese." As the political costs of its previous support for Japanese nationalism became all too apparent, the JACL broke ties with Issei leadership and the Japanese consulate. In fact, the immigrant leaders of the Japanese Association were pushing the concept of loyalty to America, as well. For the most superpatriotic JACL leaders, however, what some Issei leaders did to promote loyalty to America was ultimately irrelevant. Although most Nisei defined "loyalty" as being a "law-abiding person," a vocal minority believed that "loyalty" to America mandated rooting out the "nationalistic" pro-Japan elements among the Issei. The JACL continued to sponsor "Americanism" rallies, but the concept of a critical Americanist vision revolving around the defense of civil rights was now completely overshadowed by the goal of enforcing loyalty. At least as early as the spring of 1941, JACL leaders in Southern California established regular contact with local and federal law enforcement. They kept an especially close connection with the Naval Intelligence Bureau, routinely providing its officers information about community organizations and leaders.[11]

Young, naive, and confused, JACL leaders had been thrown on the defensive such that they answered foremost to the concerns of white authorities. Several factors explain why they bent over backward to accommodate government officials. First, they were anxious to expunge the legacy of dual nationalism. What had once served as a basis to promote transnational harmony became the source of accusations of divided loyalty. The resurgence of Japanese nationalism in the 1930s circulated among the Issei largely because they had lost all hope of becoming American citizens. At the same time, segregation kept most Nisei tied to the world the Issei had created and largely ignorant of what lay beyond it. As late as 1940, the *Rafu Shimpo* English section was still printing news releases from the Japanese government touting the puppet state Manchukuo as a "miracle of the 20th Century." For eight years, it had spread propaganda that invading Japanese soldiers had been greeted as liberators, not conquerors. Many Nisei leaders thus felt a burning need to atone for this stain on their record. Second, they received encouragement from prominent officials convincing them they were doing what was right. On August 31, 1941, California governor Culbert Olson spoke at a dinner following the Southern District JACL Convention. In front of hundreds of Nisei but also the Japanese consul of Los Angeles, Olson chastised the militaristic leaders of Japan for leading their people down a self-destructive path. Because of their race, Olson declared, the Nisei were now "marked" men in a unique position to make an "extraordinary contribution to the cause of democracy and to demonstrate [their] loyalty to [their] American citizenship." The governor then called on the Nisei to root out the "Japanese who, whether openly or secretly, swear fealty to the Japanese government." Hearing these words, Japanese Association leader Gongoro Nakamura could only sit in disbelief. Arriving in Los Angeles as a teenager in 1906, Nakamura had been educated at Los Angeles High School, Los Angeles City College, and USC Law School. Generally the most prominent Issei voice favoring "Americanization," he had arranged the dinner to smooth relations between the Japanese community and mainstream political leaders. Instead, the speech emboldened those JACL leaders who embraced the role of informant and pushed most others toward their position. Above all, it was the severe pressure of American racism that shaped the JACL leaders' mind-set. In the face of unimaginable hostility, the Nisei desperately wanted to believe that men like Olson were not only endorsing their actions but also validating their very existence. But their birthright citizenship provided a false sense of security. Less than six months later, they would be stunned by the governor's imperative that they help lead the call for mass internment.[12]

DIVERGENT WAR PATHS

The racialized nature of World War II altered the political calculus of wartime mobilization. Fearful that an antiracist demonstration would embarrass him in his front yard as America upheld the banner of democracy against Nazi fascism, Franklin D. Roosevelt conceded to Black activist demands for an antidiscrimination order in the middle of 1941. African American frustration with the president had been building since the Depression. As FDR made his fabled transition from "Dr. New Deal" to "Dr. Win-the-War," he shifted the focus of economic stimulation from the public programs of the Depression to the defense outlays of World War II. In Los Angeles and nationwide, however, Blacks found themselves on the short end of both sticks—suffering layoffs and cutbacks from public works projects and relief programs while shut out of war industry employment. FDR's statements against racism had been largely symbolic, and even the New Deal's expansive labor policies failed to confront racial discrimination on the job. At the same time, local and statewide civil rights efforts, including Gus Hawkins's proposed legislation banning discrimination within defense industries, had failed to make headway. It was ultimately A. Philip Randolph's January 1941 call for a demonstration to "shake up Washington" and "gain respect for the Negro people" that forced the president to intervene. The labor leader demanded an executive order to desegregrate the military and war-related industries. Mainstream Black organizations, notably the Urban League and the NAACP, were initially cool to the proposal for a July 1 March on Washington. But as the movement drew mass support, President Roosevelt sought to placate its organizers, who stood firm until he issued Executive Order (EO) 8802 on June 25, 1941. Making a tactical compromise to stave off the protest, FDR maintained Jim Crow policies in the military but outlawed discrimination by defense contractors.[13]

The President's Committee on Fair Employment Practice (also known as the Fair Employment Practices Committee, or FEPC) emerged as the nation's most significant vehicle to promote equal employment opportunity through state intervention. Created one month after the issuance of EO 8802, the FEPC was charged with enforcing the order. To be certain, it barely outlived the war and was a constant target of criticism from all sides during its brief life. While FDR hoped its mere existence would satisfy concerns of liberals and progressives, he sought to appease southern Democrats by limiting its scope. As Herbert Hill has noted, the FEPC had "no direct enforcement power." Instead, it operated largely by collecting data and urging employers to develop nondiscriminatory hiring plans. Nevertheless, FEPC hearings proved to have a dramatic impact for two key reasons. First, they provided a public forum for workers and civil rights advocates to testify about racism. Reflecting the significance of the city to the war production drive, the inaugural hearings were held in Los Angeles on October 20 and 21, 1941. In response, the first wave of what would become hundreds of African Americans came forward to lodge complaints against defense contractors and governmental placement agencies. A high school graduate seeking training, Jack Montgomery reported that Douglas Aircraft informed him in May 1941 that it "would not accept members of Negro race under any circumstances." Thomas Williams and Harry Madison both charged that California Shipbuilding interviewed only whites and turned away Blacks with no explanation. After reading a leaflet in which the governor reported a need to fill seventy-five thousand jobs, Jesse Battey visited the California State Employment Service's Huntington Park bureau in August 1941. Despite Battey's twenty years of experience as a cement finisher, representatives failed to inquire about his "qualifications, experience or training" as they informed him there were no "calls for colored workers in national defense work." Lloyd Owens was at least administered a test by the employment service, but he "never heard from them after." His job search led him to the city's major aircraft producers, including Douglas, Vultee, Lockheed, and North American. The response was universal. "They wanted men," declared Owens, "but not Negroes."[14]

The second major consequence of FEPC hearings was that they forced employers to disclose the stark statistics confirming the systemic exclusion of African Americans and other persons of color from employment up and down the West Coast. With forty-eight thousand workers on its payroll, half of whom had been added within the past twelve months, Lockheed was Southern California's largest defense employer. Only fifty-four members of its entire workforce were African American. Most were skilled workers recently hired through a training program developed with the Urban League. Douglas employed only ten Blacks out of thirty-three thousand total employees in three Los Angeles plants and a fourth in Tulsa, Oklahoma. All had exceptional qualifications for the jobs to which they were hired. Douglas's talented ten were joined on the workforce by "four or five Japanese, four or five Chinese, seven or eight Indians, a large number of Mexicans and several hundred Jewish people." Some companies with poor track records in minority hiring became sudden converts to equal opportunity employment at the FEPC hearings. Vultee Aircraft was the best example. The Downey-based firm had zero African Americans among a workforce of six thousand. Its 1940 statement to the NNC that it did not wish to hire African Americans had been widely distributed among the Black press and became a symbol of war industry racism. However, the same representative who had signed the letter to the NNC testified to the FEPC that Vultee now had no discriminatory policy. He even added that he "didn't think that the fact that the company has never hired Negroes was prima facie evidence of discrimination against Negroes." Bethlehem Steel scrambled to hire two skilled Black workers to fill unskilled laborer positions on the day of the hearing. Management representative Rodney Edward VanDevander reported without shame that his company gave workers of color the "same consideration based upon qualification and experience as any other person." After testifying "No Japanese have applied for work," he was surprised to hear that a Nisei had filed a discrimination complaint.[15]

While the FEPC findings established grounds for Black and Japanese American unity in the fight against employment discrimination, the bombing of Pearl Harbor drove a wedge between the two communities. Their relationships to the white majority and to the nation-state now diverged acutely. While similar on the surface, two statements released in the immediate aftermath of the Japanese offensive exemplified this widening divergence. Published by African American community leader Charlotta Bass, the *California Eagle* signaled its patriotic support for the war in its first weekly edition following December 7, 1941. "We must defend this democracy, for it is the child of our blood and suffering," its editorial read. "Despite their disheartening shortcomings, their instances of savagery and hypocrisy, America's people are the freest in the world." Yet the *Eagle* also specified that it would not capitulate to racism. "Actually, Negroes will continue to petition for their rights throughout the conflict," it declared, "so long as it does not interfere with the vigorous prosecution of an all-out war." By this time, editor Shuji Fujii had already rushed out a special issue of the Japanese American *Doho*. The December 7 edition spotlighted Fujii's telegram to President Roosevelt from Los Angeles: "As editor-publisher of 'DOHO,' I urge immediate declaration of war on Japan and pledge fullest support to the US government and towards extermination of un-American elements amongst us. Stop. May I request reiteration of promise of fair and democratic treatment of loyal resident and citizen Japanese?"[16]

Both the *Eagle* and *Doho* gave editorial support to the Popular Front orientation that promoted all-out resistance to fascism, support for FDR, and participation in the war on all fronts. Moreover, Bass and Fujii both recognized the importance of civil rights for their respective communities. However, whereas the *Eagle* emphasized that African Americans themselves would be engaged in the struggle against discrimination on the home front, Fujii offered only an appeal for fairness to the federal government. If politics is the art of the possible, this distinction is especially telling, for it surely reflects the different sense of possibilities that Black and Japanese Americans envisioned during World War II. While American nationalism and state action during World War II enabled Black civil rights activism, those same factors curtailed the freedom and ultimately nullified the citizenship rights of Japanese Americans.

State suspicion of pro-Axis sympathies affected Black and Japanese Americans in opposite ways. Not only did the Pearl Harbor attack occur on "home soil"; its "surprise" nature followed by an ominous sign of sweeping Japanese victories in the Pacific sent a chill through the American public. Pacific Coast voices now demanded the attention of the nation, as California political leaders screamed that their state and their cities were the imminent target of a "second Pearl Harbor." Clamoring for political and military action to corral the "Japs" within their midst, they pushed FDR to issue Executive Order 9066 authorizing the mass removal of Japanese Americans from the West Coast.

While most African American leaders delivered loud proclamations of patriotic support for the war and distanced themselves from pro-Axis sentiment, official concerns about "Negro morale" actually provided leverage to be wielded against the federal government. In April 1942, military intelligence concluded, "Japanese-sponsored agents and organizations are active among the Negroes of the United States, successfully promoting sedition and espionage." As historian Robert A. Hill has documented, this led FBI director J. Edgar Hoover to launch an extensive investigation of the African American community. While some Black pro-Axis agitators—primarily in the Midwest and East Coast—were detained and prosecuted, agents reported that there was little trace of fifth-column activity in Los Angeles. Federal officials nonetheless feared that both subtle and acute forms of home front disruption could occur throughout the nation. As scholar Reginald Kearney has argued, many African Americans greeted the American declaration of war against Japan with skepticism and cynicism that was not limited to fringe elements. Throughout the 1930s, W.E.B. Du Bois had been particularly unabashed in his praise of imperial Japan as the scourge of white supremacy. Characterizing the Chinese as the Uncle Toms of the Far East, he declared Japan was "showing the way to freedom" through its invasion of Manchuria. This sentiment had spread through portions of Black America. As the American military fretted that Black soldiers' resentment of Jim Crow outweighed their animosity toward Japanese militarism, the Negro press fueled this concern by widely recounting the reputed quote of a young Black inductee: "Just carve on my tombstone, 'Here lies a black man killed fighting the yellow man for the protection of the white man.'" Even moderate Black leaders routinely concluded white America's racism was the principal cause of the war. Langston Hughes wrote of a "distinguished Negro member of the Black Cabinet" who privately cheered Japan when its army was "beating back the British in Asia." Hughes also relayed a joke reflecting grassroots sentiment. A white representative from the Red Cross told a Black church audience in the South, "Why, you know, these Japs are really trying to wipe us white folks off the face of the earth." To which, a "dark and wrinkled old grandma in the amen corner" responded, "It's about time!"[17]

If African American leaders gained clout with government officials because the state needed their active involvement to sell the war to the Black masses, then challenging an "evacuation" order the government deemed a "military necessity" might undermine that clout. In fact, some Blacks in Los Angeles saw opportunity in the potential removal of thousands of Japanese residents. Rumors of plans by African Americans to take over the farms of uprooted Japanese Americans, for instance, had circulated for months, and this possibility especially piqued the interest of economic nationalists. In mid-December 1941, members of the National Negro Business League meeting at Golden State Mutual Life Insurance asserted, "Negroes have the greatest opportunity ever offered by the State of California." One member remarked, "You don't have to distrust a Negro face in a boat plying in California waters; nor would you need to fear a traitor in our lettuce fields." The group concluded, "Somebody must take the place of these alien farmers and fishermen, for we must not be dependent on their produce when we are at war with them." At the opposite end of the spectrum stood African Americans who denounced the call for internment as racist. The *Los Angeles Tribune* claimed to be the city's only Black newspaper that took a firm stand against the Japanese American internment. (Unfortunately, the bulk of its wartime publications are unavailable in existing archives.) Attorney Hugh MacBeth organized a "Negro-white committee" whose mission was "to champion the cause of the disenfranchised Americans of Japanese ancestry." The NAACP's stance was ambiguous. One longtime member of the Los Angeles chapter urged the national civil rights organization to take a stand against the internment in both the broad interest of justice and in the self-interest of African Americans who could be the next target. In a delayed and tepid response, the NAACP passed a July 1942 resolution accepting the government's claim that military concerns necessitated an "evacuation" but criticizing the "arbitrary classification" of evacuees on the basis of "race and color." It concluded that under these circumstances "American citizens of Japanese extraction" were "being unfairly treated." As Japanese Americans had already been confined at this point, NAACP leadership's primary concern—expressed only in private to federal officials—was that the internees be afforded humane treatment. Still, after surveying the records of seven national Jewish and African American organizations, historian Cheryl Greenberg maintained the NAACP's "muted and at times oblique . . . critique of the internment was the most forceful of any at the time." By comparison, the Urban League took no position, while the Los Angeles chapter of the Anti-Defamation League "apparently supported internment (but not publicly)." In general, these organizations did not take a firm antigovernment stand, because their own political status was insecure—especially given the expanded repressive powers of the state during wartime. They would not risk jeopardizing the state support they felt was necessary to achieve their own civil rights priorities.[18]

While some grassroots African American opposition to the internment must have coincided with resentment toward mainstream America and/or hidden sympathy with Japan, some exceptional individuals empathized deeply with the persecuted and went to considerable lengths to support them in the face of public scorn. Their stories (likely quite numerous) need to be more properly recovered. For example, Thomas Robinson, a Black teenager, traveled by public transportation to the Santa Anita racetrack-cum-detention center to visit the Shimakochi family and other friends on opposite sides of the barbed wire in spring 1942. Robinson had been a full-fledged member of the youth groups associated with the Japanese Christian Church near his residence in the multiethnic Central Avenue district. He selflessly retrieved supplies from the outside and passed them through fences to internees.[19]

Most Black leaders in Los Angeles chose neither to join the racist agitation led by whites nor to independently speak out against the internment order. African Americans generally expressed apprehension in the immediate aftermath of Pearl Harbor but not to the point of hysteria. Some, for instance, lodged complaints that air-raid sirens were placed in white neighborhoods rather than the Central Avenue district. With relation to Japanese Americans, African Americans joined the small chorus of voices expressing greatest sympathy in the month following December 7. The Junior Council of the NAACP sent a December 22 letter to the Los Angeles JACL conveying its "whole-hearted sympathy to the members of your organization in the struggles they must be undergoing in these troubled times." It further offered to provide any assistance possible to stop Japanese Americans from being victimized by "un-American" attacks. Responding to a JACL statement of loyalty, the *Eagle* declared on New Year's Day 1942, "We urge all people of our great country to adopt an attitude of friendliness, sympathy and courtesy toward all Japanese." It added, "Our people, therefore, should continue their normal relations in schools, in business and in our social groups with the Japanese residents of our communities." These statements came, however, at a time when the federal government had indicated that a mass internment was not likely. Indeed, the *Eagle*'s call for "normal relations" with Japanese Americans rested on government assurances that it could handle any problems with disloyalty on a case-by-case basis. As the internment unfolded, Black leaders in Los Angeles would not be particularly concerned about the fate of Japanese Americans until their potential midwar return to the city ignited a new round of debate and controversy.[20]

As World War II commenced, most Black and Japanese Americans had little sense of how dramatically their lives were about to be changed. War is a time when the issue of *national security* casts its shadow over every corner of society. Definitions of security, however, are far from universal or self-evident. They are instead highly contested, especially when the question turns to defining domestic threats to national security. Here, the issue of *national identity* becomes crucial, particularly as it relates to the ultimate power of the state to determine who rightfully belongs to the nation. Liberal elements inside and outside the Roosevelt administration came to the conclusion that proactive measures to improve race relations were necessary both to maintain good wartime morale among white Americans and to project a democratic image of America to its allies abroad. But while they advanced the theory of universal human equality to advocate the removal of discriminatory barriers preventing Black incorporation into mainstream society, Japanese Americans would remain subject to crude biological conceptions of race that linked the most assimilationist Nisei to the most fanatic and savage purveyors of fascism in Japan. As EO 8802 and EO 9066 demonstrate, the nation-state made a clear determination: *national unity* on the home front would be defined by efforts to integrate African Americans and exclude Japanese Americans.

These national imperatives occupied a commanding presence in the local construction of multiracial relations as the war marked a watershed moment in the city's history. Los Angeles housed the largest concentration of public figures advancing the popular call for Japanese American internment. As the JACL's prewar experience demonstrated, Japanese Americans had been coerced into a submissive form of patriotism portending their eventual cooperation with the government's internment order. At the same time the war brought about the mass removal of Japanese Americans, it provided the city's African American community with an opportunity to express a critical form of patriotism driven by mass activism. The city became a strategic site for war-related production just as the threat of Black protest compelled FDR to desegregate the defense industries. The rise of an industrial workforce transformed the size and character of the Black community, creating new bases for political action and multiracial labor organizing. Although the NNC had failed to remedy African American suffering during the Depression, its coalition of nationalists and internationalists prefigured the formation of the "Negro Victory" movement that would bring forth a new level of civil rights struggle in Black Los Angeles.

CHAPTER 5

Japanese American Internment

BOTH POPULAR AND SCHOLARLY treatments of Japanese American internment have tended to focus on either the federal government's role in order-
ing and implementing the mass incarceration or the experience of Japanese
Americans behind barbed wire. These research projects and writings
played a key role in debunking the once widely accepted claim that the
internment was justified by "military necessity" while revealing the deep
level of suffering and trauma that Japanese American internees endured.
In this regard, they served to support the long and ultimately successful
campaign for redress and reparations from the federal government. Nevertheless, we still lack a thorough understanding of how local actors built
the anti-Japanese movement, how Japanese Americans deliberated in the
period between Pearl Harbor and the start of internment, and how the
internment shaped the postwar Japanese community. For Los Angeles
mayor Fletcher Bowron, relocating Japanese Americans into concentration camps became a matter of "common sense." His masterful and ne-
farious accomplishment was to shift the primary focus of suspicion from
the immigrant and alien Issei to the American-born and citizen Nisei,
transforming a highly problematic witch hunt for "disloyal enemy aliens"
into an indiscriminate concentration of 120,000 Japanese Americans.

This chapter explores how the drive for internment reordered the internal politics of the city's Japanese community, as it was forced to confront
both state repression and popular racist animosity posing as patriotism.
Thrown into a state of fear and chaos, Japanese Americans struggled to
formulate an effective response or even obtain accurate information. On
December 7, 1941, the FBI began detaining immigrant leaders, initiating
a process that prematurely elevated Nisei of the Japanese American Citizens League (JACL) to fill the leadership vacuum. While JACL representatives had been promoting "Americanism" for over a decade, they had
little experience working with the multiple generations that comprised
the Japanese community and thus lacked a true sensitivity to its concerns.
As the drive for internment intensified, they became consumed with the
task of proving the Nisei's loyalty to the government. Thrust into harrowing straits and fearing resistance would be futile and self-destructive,
JACL leaders found themselves in the difficult position of having to explain why Japanese Americans should cooperate with the state-sponsored

internment. Although their position can be justified in hindsight, it proved intensely unpopular at the time and was often distorted to make it appear that some Nisei had actually helped to engineer the internment. The sadder truth was that JACL leaders, lacking popular community support and reduced to a powerless position in relation to the state, had become increasingly reliant on the sponsorship of manipulative government officials. This disciplining of one community's leadership would ultimately affect the city's broader multiracial order.

LIVING WITH INFAMY

"It couldn't be true! The mythical Japanese-American war which we Nisei and Japanese had never dreamed could really happen." This was Nisei writer Mary Oyama's reaction to Japan's attack on Pearl Harbor. "There was a hard paralyzing stone inside of me," she added. In the immediate aftermath of December 7, chaos reigned over the Japanese American community. Hundreds of Japanese American workers were suspended from their jobs, while many ethnic businesses struggled to attract customers. Half of Local 1510's twelve hundred Japanese American produce workers were laid off, and the Treasury Department shut down all Issei commission merchants in the wholesale markets. Perhaps most disorienting was the FBI's wholesale roundup of Issei community leaders. On the day of the attack alone, 736 Japanese immigrants were taken into custody nationwide on the basis of a hastily issued and loosely worded blanket presidential warrant targeting "dangerous" enemy aliens.[1]

What is often overlooked, however, is that anti-Japanese sentiment for the duration of December 1941 was relatively mild compared to what would transpire the following year. Although the "surprise attack" on Pearl Harbor generated an overwhelming sense of anxiety in America, this did not immediately translate into an organized campaign of agitation against Japanese living in America. Many of the Nisei layoffs proved to be temporary, and the *Rafu Shimpo* noted there was "no anti-Japanese hysteria in Southern California" for the "first few weeks" following December 7. The public "was more or less sympathetic to the Nisei for the unfortunate plight the war had suddenly brought about them." Reflecting gender divisions among Japanese Americans, women writers commissioned by the *Rafu* for "feminine" topics like society and fashion wrote of how domestic life would go on as before. Characterizing herself as "your little ray of sunshine" whose job was to "chase away the nasty glooms," Ayako Ellen Noguchi remarked, "Regardless of the bomb bursting over in the Philippines, or the blackout in the neighboring cities, the dishes must still be washed and put away." Her point was that such duties provided "gals" the "greatest opportunity to serve" the national cause. "Women have always been expected to furnish the spiritual stamina that backs up the physical courage of their men," Noguchi concluded. "In times of stress, it is a woman's privilege and her duty to keep the home fires burning and banners of faith, hope, courage and love flying." For some, interethnic conflicts were the primary concern. Japanese Americans fretted that other Asians wore badges to distinguish themselves from them. The *Rafu* argued that they were committing "a grave injustice" that was "making life harder" for "fellow Americans." "What they should do now," it declared, "is to forget that they are Chinese or Filipinos or Koreans and think [of] themselves as true Americans." Some Asian Americans did sport these badges, although the extent of their prevalence is unclear. When the *Rafu*'s Edith Kodama surveyed Filipino American community leaders in Los Angeles, she reported no animosity. Filipino vigilantes did attack Japanese Americans in rural areas where the two groups had clashed as farmworkers and growers respectively. But Filipino leaders, such as Melecio Dellota of the Pacific Coast Filipino Inter-Community Organization, condemned the attacks. Viewing them as isolated incidents, Dellota assured Japanese Americans that the Filipino community of Los Angeles had "an attitude of friendship" toward them. Rev. Casiano Coloma of the Filipino Christian Church added that Japanese Americans were by no means responsible for Japan's invasion of the Philippines and that his congregation included "many" Japanese Americans married to Filipinos.[2]

The first official policy statements after Pearl Harbor had a more soothing than alarming effect on many Japanese Americans. At the federal level, the government assured the citizenry that with the confinement of Issei leaders, it had achieved complete control of homeland security. Primarily concerned about potential disruptions to production or public order, FDR issued a general statement opposing discrimination against aliens. Furthermore, Attorney General Francis Biddle and numerous federal, state, and local officials issued specific statements promoting tolerance of Japanese Americans and ensuring domestic peace. The Los Angeles County Board of Supervisors passed a December 9 resolution that recognized Japanese Americans had "proven their loyalty to the United States by service in the [First] World War and in other ways." It called on the public schools to promote "an attitude of sanity and fairness toward all children" and urged that "every effort be made to show a real American spirit toward American born children of Japanese blood and their parents."[3]

Given reassurances of fair treatment, Nisei leaders confidently set out on their quest to promote Americanism, and their carefully chosen spokespersons were given opportunities to address the public. Togo Tanaka represented the Nisei on radio station KMTR at 11:00 PM on December 7. Born in Portland, Oregon, in 1916, Tanaka moved with his parents to Los Angeles three years later. They were among the earliest Japanese settlers in Hollywood, where Togo wound up living down the street from Cecil B. DeMille and attending schools nearly devoid of other students of color. As a result, nearly all of his childhood friends were white, and he developed a particular ability to cultivate interracial friendships and relations. Physically small but academically precocious, Tanaka graduated from Hollywood High School at the age of sixteen and entered the University of California at Los Angeles (UCLA). After working on the *Kashu Mainichi* newspaper during college, he was lured by publisher H. T. Komai to the more established *Rafu Shimpo* upon his 1936 graduation. Under Tanaka's stewardship, the *Rafu* English section expanded dramatically and became the primary medium for Nisei thought and debate. Repeating words that had become the mantra of the JACL, Tanaka assured radio listeners on December 7, right after the Pearl Harbor attack, that Japanese Americans were "all Americans pledged to the defense of the United States" and that all were willingly functioning as "counterespionage" to aid the authorities. Major newspapers conducted interviews with Nisei leaders the following day. Several posed for a picture with Los Angeles mayor Bowron that was featured above a *Los Angeles Times* story headlined "Japanese-Americans Ready to Aid Nation." "Treat us like Americans," the *New York Times* quoted the JACL's Fred Tayama: "give us a chance to prove our loyalty." Meanwhile, the *Rafu* characterized the war as a "crucial test" of the loyalty of Japanese Americans as it denounced Japan's "treacherous slaughtering of Americans" and called for an "all-out victory" over "her ruthless, barbaric leaders." The publicity was largely the product of the JACL's Anti-Axis Committee (AAC), a reworking of the Equality Committee that Nisei leaders had put into motion almost immediately after learning the war had begun. Its first meeting was held at the Japanese Union Church and opened with a flag salute at 8:15 PM on December 8. With representation from eleven JACL chapters across Southern California, ranging from Santa Maria to San Diego, the AAC named Fred Tayama its chairman, Mas Satow coordinator, and Kay Sugahara executive secretary. Attracting seven hundred attendees, the AAC's second meeting on December 13 demonstrated the body's potential mass appeal.[4]

Although able to bring community members together in quick fashion, the Nisei of the JACL faced a stiff challenge given their lack of experience as mass leaders. The organization's budget and membership paled in comparison to that of leading Issei groups, and what popularity it enjoyed among the younger generation stemmed largely from hosting dances and other social events. With their social and economic life defined primarily by the ethnic community, many Nisei had not found the politics of the wider world intensely relevant. Others felt their involvement would not make a difference. As Togo Tanaka privately confessed, the JACL "had always been an organized minority within the Japanese community seeking to make claims in the Caucasian community that it spoke on behalf of all Americans of Japanese ancestry." It was "the mouse trying to cast the shadow of the elephant." The initial broad-based showing of support for the AAC served mainly to reinforce the existing leadership style of JACL leaders rather than provoke them to alter it. On paper, the AAC's objectives were threefold: (1) to promote Japanese American cooperation with the government; (2) to coordinate the Japanese American community; and (3) "to secure National unity by fair treatment of loyal Americans." In practice, however, all tasks were subordinate to promoting loyalty. AAC leaders reasoned that demonstrations of loyalty were necessary to bolster a case for fair treatment. At the same time, they feared acts of disloyalty would undermine any effort to promote the interests of the community. The committee temporarily censored the local Japanese press and removed books connected to the nationalistic Black Dragon Society from some local retailers. It even considered producing buttons to distinguish "Japanese" persons from "Americans of Japanese ancestry" but took no action in this regard. Above all, members of its Intelligence Committee brought the AAC its greatest notoriety. Their charge was "to investigate all cases where loyalty to America is questioned and to report to the office of Mr. R. H. Hood of the Federal Bureau of Investigation." This was a panicky response to an unprecedented crisis. To the degree these Nisei leaders were working with any strategy, they were guided by a belief in taking the actions they deemed most likely to be looked on favorably by white authorities. The AAC developed an advisory board that included county supervisor John Anson Ford, Rabbi Edgar Magnin, Los Angeles school district supervisor Vierling Kersey, federal Department of Justice attorney William Fleet Palmer, and the ubiquitous Carey McWilliams. Maintaining a good relationship with such prominent figures seemed for Nisei leaders to be the best defense against attacks on the community.[5]

But the AAC's goal of impressing white authorities with demonstrations of patriotism ultimately conflicted with its goal of uniting the community. Japan had engaged in espionage during the prewar era. The arrest of Japanese naval officer Itaru Tachibana, who had posed as a USC student, on charges of espionage caused commotion in the community. Japanese Americans must admit, Tanaka remarked, that Tachibana "was headquartered right in 'Little Tokio.' Right under our noses!" Totally uncorroborated, however, were reports that Japanese Americans had committed or planned to commit sabotage and suggestions that espionage was a common activity of both Issei and Nisei. There was little subtlety in state actions or public sentiment. The FBI detained hundreds of Issei who had done nothing remotely illegal, and even Togo Tanaka and former JACL president Eiji Tanabe were among those arrested within the first twenty-four hours following Pearl Harbor. Because a pall of suspicion was cast over the entire community, JACL leaders believed they had to go to great lengths to root out disloyal elements. They may have sympathized with the plight of the immigrant generation, but they viewed the "enemy alien" Issei as a political liability and excluded them from participation in the AAC. Even those Nisei who had previously worked with Issei leaders were viewed suspiciously by some of their peers. Tanaka suspected he spent eleven days in jail, unjustly, because he had been "bird-dogged" by a "couple of fellow Nisei, prominent in the national JACL and overzealous in their American patriotism." Army and navy intelligence officers became a regular presence at AAC meetings. JACL leaders asked, "How can we know what is suspicious?" The general answer came back, "When a man has been living and spending beyond his means, something may be fishy." While AAC leaders drew quick conclusions about community members, some community members returned the favor. The Tachibana episode and the arrest of community leaders heightened sentiment that JACL leaders were acting as informants, a role many Japanese Americans judged despicable regardless of whether the information being passed was accurate. In his diary entry for January 9, 1942, Tanaka observed, "There is already considerable suspicion that the Anti-Axis Committee is an 'inu' (dog) organization; there is, it seems to me, tremendous growing resentment against unfair 'finger-pointing' resulting in the arrest and detention of men whose families insist are completely innocent and will be exonerated."[6]

While stories of opportunistic whites swindling Japanese American farmers, merchants, and households on the eve of internment have often been repeated, it is less well known that growing anger within the Japanese American community was aimed at Nisei who were accused of taking advantage of Issei families caught in a bind by legal and economic restrictions. It is difficult to assess in hindsight whether these were justified allegations or a result of redirecting frustration from state repression and white racism toward more accessible targets within the community. The effect, in any case, was a further discrediting of the JACL leadership. Fred Tayama of the AAC and JACL was a prime target of Japanese nationalists at the Manzanar internment camp, but his image had already been sullied before the internment. Tayama was alleged to have gouged Issei farmers seeking travel permits and families looking to record assets placed into storage.[7]

More commonly, community members resented JACL leaders because they felt those claiming the mantle of spokespersons for the entire community were acting presumptuously. Tokutaro Nishimura Slocum, the AAC's new choice for chairman in mid-January 1942, created even greater friction. "Tokie" Slocum is without a doubt one of the most curious characters in Japanese American history. His greatest assets in the eyes of the AAC simultaneously proved his greatest liabilities within the broader Japanese community. Although born in Japan in 1895, he lived most of his life in the United States among whites, rarely interacting with ethnic Japanese. When US exclusionary practices pushed Slocum's father to resettle in Canada, young Tokie was adopted by Ansel Perry Slocum of Minot, North Dakota. After graduating from the University of Minnesota, he enrolled in law school at Columbia University. But he cut his studies short during World War I, when he signed up to fight in the 328th Infantry. Slocum's campaign for naturalization rights through the Nye-Lea bill, considered one of the biggest Japanese American civil rights successes of the prewar era, endeared him to a number of prominent JACL leaders in the mid-1930s. However, a brief effort to involve him in the leadership of the Los Angeles Japanese American community ended with him denouncing Issei organizations as "tools of the Imperial Japanese government" and castigating Nisei institutions as "Jap-indoctrinated." With the outbreak of the war, JACL leaders again courted Slocum because of his relationship with white American authorities and veterans' groups like the American Legion. While JACL leaders all along the West Coast embraced the mandate to police the community's loyalty, Slocum and his biggest supporters especially intensified the effort in Los Angeles. He proclaimed that he was "proud" to have reported names of presumably disloyal Japanese to his "buddies" from the FBI and naval intelligence. "I was personally responsible for the arrest of the Central Japanese Association members," Slocum further boasted, including "everyone from that lecherous Gongoro Nakamura down." Nakamura had been the immigrant community's most prominent leader and its greatest proponent of Americanism. Under Slocum's leadership, "education" (which others might have termed indoctrination) became a central function of the AAC. At the January 23, 1942, meeting of the AAC, two white representatives of the American Legion spoke venomously of traitorous Japanese in America and praised those who turned them in. A few weeks later, a still unsatisfied Slocum complained, "Nobody's turning in any names; we're not getting any cooperation in this vital work."[8]

Togo Tanaka is the rare insider who has left an almost unmatched analysis of the JACL's internal contradictions. Tanaka did not so much question the sincerity of Slocum and other leaders like him—who, he wrote, believed they were carrying out "a brave service and contribution to the war effort"—but he was sharply critical of their hostility toward members of the Japanese American community and the divisive impact of their leadership. Reserving particular scorn for Slocum, who was ushered to the head of JACL leadership while Tanaka sat in prison, Tanaka identified him as the Japanese community's "bitterest pre-war non-Caucasian antagonist." On January 11, 1942, Tanaka confided to his diary: "Disowned, discredited, and shunned by the J.A.C.L. generally for so long, he has now returned as the prodigal son, his inordinate vanity bloated in his own self-esteem. The fact that the J.A.C.L.-ers who before war were calling Slocum such choice names as 'drunken bastard' 'wife beater' 'bird dog' 'sonufabitch' now accept him as a leader and elect him chairman of committees is a pretty good indication of the confused and muddled state of J.A.C.L. leadership."[9]

For generations to come, white American leaders would proclaim that Japan failed to crush the nation's spirit on December 7, 1941. But the impact of Pearl Harbor was dramatic and everlasting on the Nisei community. The morphing of the JACL Equality Committee into the Anti-Axis Committee provided unquestionable proof that the nascent spirit of progressive activism that JACL leaders had demonstrated in founding that committee less than two years prior had died a tragic death.

Making a Case for Internment

As many other officials did, Los Angeles mayor Fletcher Bowron made an appearance at the first meeting of the Anti-Axis Committee on December 8. Released earlier that day, Bowron's first public statement after Pearl Harbor followed the general contours of the federal government's line urging calm and reassuring the citizenry that domestic security was under control. The mayor stated that he was not expecting an attack on the city and that there was "no reason why this public concern should develop into an apprehension bordering on hysteria." Correspondingly, the minutes of the AAC meeting reported that Bowron "expressed that he didn't doubt the Nisei's sincerity and patriotism." He assured the Nisei that local government would provide them with "all the knowledge and protection accorded any other citizen." Generally maintaining this position through the end of 1941, he expressed no interest in joining radio commentator John B. Hughes's early campaign to remove Japanese Americans from the West Coast. Such a stance was not out of character for Bowron, who was in the midst of fifteen years and four terms as a liberal Republican mayor who enjoyed bipartisan support. Campaigning on a platform of "clean government," he had swept into office through a 1938 recall election against Frank Shaw. He supported New Deal programs and prided himself on being a civil libertarian. Bowron dismantled the LAPD's notorious "Red Squads" and warned an audience of officers that police abuse turned upright citizens into supporters of communism. In June 1940, he remarked, "We are going through a period of stress and hysteria, within a whirlpool of propaganda, where too frequently the appeal is to the emotions and prejudices rather than reason." Emphatically stating that "civil liberties" would "not be abridged in the City of Los Angeles," Bowron proclaimed: "I believe in the letter and spirit and purpose of the Constitution of the United States." In yet another August 1940 speech against anticommunist witch hunts, Bowron commented, "The true patriot is not a flag waver." Further: "The real American, the real patriot, the one who is actuated by love of country, is not one who shouts the loudest in trying or unsettled times. He works quietly to protect American institutions, to see that the guarantees of the United States Constitution are carried into effect rather than be forgotten and disregarded by mob hysteria."[10]

Given his strong record on civil liberties, how was it possible that Bowron—like Earl Warren and so many "moderate" public figures—could turn so virulently against the entire Japanese American community and lead the call to place the whole lot of them in concentration camps? Speaking on the first anniversary of Pearl Harbor, Bowron explained that a 1940 trip through the Asia-Pacific region—in which he had met General Douglas MacArthur, Philippine president Manuel Quezon, and Chinese officials—had alerted him to the special danger that Japanese militarism posed to humanity. Seeing the strength of America's Pacific Fleet had provided him with a "sense of security" that was obliterated by the Japanese attack. Bowron thus claimed that his immediate reaction to Pearl Harbor was fear that Los Angeles could face an imminent assault resulting in "a slaughter of the innocents." In this regard, the mayor justified his stance within the frame of "military necessity," the main argument the Supreme Court would later validate in the 1944 *Korematsu* case. This retrospective argument, however, contradicted Bowron's earlier public assurances that the city was secure. Indeed, through the end of December 1941, the army had no plan for mass internment of Japanese Americans. More importantly, while Bowron's comments might rationalize his strident agitation against Japanese militarism, they fail to account for why he would deem the American-born Nisei the greatest threat to national security. As dissenting justice Frank Murphy argued in the Supreme Court's *Korematsu* decision, the assertion that the mass internment of Japanese Americans constituted a "military necessity" rested ultimately on the "erroneous assumption of racial guilt." Murphy, in fact, was the only justice among three in the minority to declare that the majority's decision amounted to the "legalization of racism."[11]

Drawing on Justice Murphy's insight, what must be explained is how the nation's military and civilian leaders came to embrace the assumption of Japanese American "racial guilt" between the end of 1941 and February 19, 1942—the day President Roosevelt issued Executive Order 9066. Given that the government's primary concern—as evidenced both inside and outside the military—during the first month after December 7 had been identifying and detaining those particular "enemy aliens" who posed a threat, why did debate by February 1942 revolve around what to do about a problem "race"? Why did Secretary of War Henry L. Stimson validate the mass internment proposal of General John L. DeWitt? Historian Roger Daniels has characterized DeWitt, head of the Western Defense Command, as an aging and prejudiced man who gathered dubious evidence of Japanese American "disloyalty" in an attempt to escalate his personal role in the war. Why did FDR side with Stimson over the serious reservations Attorney General Francis Biddle voiced about the necessity and legality of mass internment? Part of the reason for the shift in public and political opinion can be attributed to latent prejudice brought to the fore and magnified by the tremendous sense of insecurity caused not by Japan's initiation of the war but by its early victories. Legal scholar Peter Irons—who has also argued that Stimson's seniority over Biddle influenced FDR's decision—has noted that "graphic reports of brutality by Japanese troops as they overran the Philippines shocked the American public" during the weeks *following* Pearl Harbor. As the conflict intensified and it became clear it would be protracted, millions of Americans viewed the war against Japan as a crusade to exterminate the Japanese race.[12]

Although the most critical political decisions of World War II were made at the federal level, an analysis of local activity is crucial to understanding how racial ideology and multiracial relations were constructed. In large measure, local agitation tapped currents that had been flowing over the extended history of the Japanese exclusion movement. Political expediency accounted for much of the demagoguery exhibited by elected officials, especially as the 1942 campaign season approached. Moreover, economic interest led those forces labeled "pressure groups" by scholar Morton Grodzins to call for removing Japanese Americans from the West Coast. The influential Los Angeles Chamber of Commerce, most notably through its Agricultural Committee, lobbied behind the scenes for repressive measures, while the Western Growers Protective Association boasted that its members' profits soared as "prices sky-rocketed to almost unheard of values" owing to the demise of Japanese farming. It should be stressed, however, that the cultural and political impact of the drive for internment transcended such blatant opportunism and cut to the heart of the American psyche. As scholar Emily S. Rosenberg has argued, Americans justified the Pacific War "in terms of national character rather than national interest." At the local level, this meant that whites—not just the longtime agitators but almost universally—developed a new level of repulsion toward Japanese Americans. People who had for a generation shopped at Japanese American markets and taken in stride the mark that Issei gardeners had left on the Southern California landscape now feared that every yellow face was a potential enemy saboteur.[13]

It was not just that white fear and prejudice increased. Political leaders created a lethal combination by encouraging anti-Japanese racism as an expression of wartime patriotism. No figure typified such behavior better than Los Angeles mayor Fletcher Bowron, whose racial paranoia nullified any concern he may have previously held for the sanctity of civil liberties. His central contribution to the argument for internment was his insistence that the American-born Nisei posed the greatest threat to national security. In this sense, he helped to escalate the magnitude of the "Japanese problem" in public eyes. The mayor seems to have reacted quite strongly to internal reports he solicited from police commissioner Al Cohn. In memos dated January 10 and January 21, 1942, Cohn stated that there was "no doubt that in this horde of alien born Japanese, espionage activities have been in progress for several decades." Yet he argued that the Nisei posed the "greatest menace." While the Nisei "outwardly" appeared to be "thoroughgoing Americans," Cohn discerned that "it would be foolish to look for any great degree of loyalty among them." He believed only one-fourth of Japanese Americans were loyal to the United States while one-fourth were loyal to Japan and half were "on the fence." After learning of Cohn's findings, Bowron quickly retracted his reassuring comments to the December 8 Anti-Axis Committee's meeting. Indeed, he became convinced that the pro-American event had been staged "for the purpose of misleading those in local official life."[14]

Unsatisfied with the FBI's response to the "Japanese problem" but reluctant to reproach a federal agency, Bowron turned toward city government. He commissioned another report, which aroused suspicion about a 1934 request by the Japanese consulate for information about the city's water system. He then discovered there were thirty-seven Japanese Americans working for the city, including its Department of Water and Power. These were the same Nisei whom the *Rafu*'s Nisei Business Bureau had hailed as pioneers because they used their college degrees to work in civil service rather than produce markets. Bowron, however, saw the situation quite differently. "I discovered to my amazement," he reported publicly, "that Japanese by schooling themselves and taking civil service examinations had filtered into the most important positions where they not only had all of the information relative to our water works system but also our electric power development and distribution system as well." On the basis of this one isolated inquiry made eight years prior into details unspecified and for reasons unknown, the mayor of Los Angeles developed a deep fear that Nisei were plotting to sabotage the city's water and power supplies. Japanese American civil servants soon became the scapegoats of a public propaganda campaign. On January 27, 1942, Bowron politely informed all of the city's Nisei employees they were no longer wanted. Officially, he requested they take a "voluntary" leave of absence, deploying the same measure Los Angeles County used to remove its forty-nine Japanese American employees. Publicly, the mayor was still handling the "Japanese problem" with kid gloves. He declared the dismissals of the Nisei were "not to be construed as any indication that any of them [were] dangerous or that their loyalty [had] been questioned." Privately, Bowron feared the worst from the Nisei, especially city personnel technician Kiyoshi Patrick Okura. Japanese Americans, by contrast, regarded Okura as a shining example of Nisei achievement. A star baseball player, he had graduated from UCLA as the first Nisei to earn a varsity letter and an MA degree from the university. Okura had also served as the first executive director of the Los Angeles JACL. His "crime" was having a father arrested during the FBI roundup. Bowron asserted that Okura was "known" to be the son of a former Japanese admiral, who lived near the city's harbor and aided the entry of illegal aliens. He argued that the Nisei civil servant had intentionally secured a job that strategically positioned him to hire other Japanese to aid potential sabotage of the city's water and power systems.[15]

Following the removal of Nisei city employees, the mayor sharply escalated his rhetoric and demands. Three central themes could be identified in Bowron's case for casting a broad net of suspicion over the Japanese American community. First, he asserted, disputing federal law enforcement and intelligence agencies, that the domestic threat posed by Japanese in America was far from contained. In mid-January 1942, Bowron argued that a "second Pearl Harbor" was likely to occur in Southern California and that Japanese Americans would be part of any enemy plan. "We here are most vitally concerned," he declared, "because we are the ones who are going to get the bombs if our seeming patriotic little Japanese brothers swing into action at a pre-arranged signal at an appointed time." Al Cohn asserted to Togo Tanaka in a January 12 meeting at City Hall that they both "knew" that "more planes [were] wrecked at Pearl Harbor" by Nisei driving trucks than by Japanese bombers. Bowron and Cohn found justification for their comments with the January 25 release of the Roberts Report, which FDR commissioned to find the cause of the military's lack of preparedness at Pearl Harbor. Valorizing faulty rumors passed by military officers, the report attributed the surprise nature of the attack to the work of "Japanese spies and saboteurs," including those with "no open relations with the Japanese foreign service"—in other words, common Japanese immigrants and Nisei. Bowron's second contention was that it was impossible to discern Japanese American loyalty.

"No one may look into the mind of an Oriental," he remarked in a January 29 broadcast on radio station KCEA. Two weeks later, he added, "All of them must go, good and bad alike, for the safety of the nation, because there is no way to determine those loyal to this country and those loyal to Japan." The Nisei did not escape suspicion, because they were "non-assimilable" and they were certainly not white, "regardless of how many generations may have been born in America." Bowron, in fact, accused the Nisei of harboring "a secret loyalty to the Japanese Emperor, while enjoying the privileges and immunities of American citizenship as a constitutional right." Indeed, Bowron would have used any convenient argument to make his point. In private correspondence to the Justice Department's Tom C. Clark, Bowron emphasized that Nisei who were "otherwise . . . entirely docile" and "who had previously indicated a pro-American and anti-Axis viewpoint" were now in a "hostile frame of mind." The "agitation to remove them" had only now convinced them that they were "a race apart" and could "never be considered American citizens in the full sense of being accepted by other Americans." Not only did Bowron report in this letter that he could discern the loyalty of the American-born Japanese; after three weeks of constantly barraging the public with anti-Japanese rhetoric, he warned that racist exclusion was breeding dangerous Nisei who felt they had no place in America.[16]

Finally and perhaps most shamelessly, Bowron advanced the Catch-22 argument that an *absence* of evidence of sabotage by Japanese Americans signaled that a sneak attack was imminent. The Japanese in America, he insisted, were "too smart" to blow their cover by committing "isolated acts of violence" that could do "little damage." Rather, he noted, they "could serve the cause of Japan most effectively" if they were "to lay low [and] appear docile, entirely harmless." In the mayor's mind, the basic phenomenon of Japanese immigration represented "the infiltration of Japanese into this country during times of peace." Nevertheless, he concluded, Japanese immigrants were "far less dangerous than many of the American born Japanese." Employing twisted logic that could be sustained only by unabashed racism, Bowron declared, "The most natural thing would be for the most dangerous of them to condemn the Japanese war clique, the Axis powers, to loudly declare a prejudice against Japan and proclaim a belief in American Democracy with an emotional pledge of allegiance to the Stars and Stripes." These comments, delivered on the radio in February 1942, must have particularly incensed the Nisei, for there was no way to defend against them. As one Nisei stated shortly afterward, "I thought the Mayor was a liberal and a man who had a scrupulous record for human justice and honesty. He's more of a pompous jackass and hypocrite from what I can gather." Bowron himself was nonplussed by these Nisei reactions and took direct aim at their white allies. World War II was "not a time for sentimentality or for our people to be so actuated by a mistaken sense of brotherly love." He offered these famous last words: "Those little men who prate of civil liberties . . . will be forgotten in the pages of history."[17]

Bowron played a pivotal role in formulating and propagating the assumption of racial guilt, yet students of Japanese American history will recognize that his arguments were not unique. While focusing on the effects of his agitation and exposing the remarkable hypocrisy of his positions provides a detailed view of anti-Japanese politics at the local level, it should not follow that he was singularly or uniquely responsible for what was a broad and popular assault on Japanese American civil liberties. Earl Warren similarly judged the Nisei the gravest danger to security and ruled that a lack of Japanese American sabotage was a "disturbing and confirming indication that such action [would] be taken." As attorney general of California, the future governor and chief justice developed his greatest act of grandstanding by commissioning law enforcement agencies throughout the state to compile data demonstrating the proximity of Japanese Americans to potential military targets. Truck farmers, of course, had little choice over where they toiled and thus often ended up in sites near industry, power lines, major highways, airports, and other locations shunned by residential developers. But racial suspicion trumped any such logic in the mind of Warren, who shocked the public with his "discovery" that the Japanese had surreptitiously insinuated themselves onto land near dozens of sensitive sites, such as the Standard Oil refinery in El Segundo, the Vultee aircraft factory in Downey, and the Hughes aviation plant in Culver City. It was another no-win situation for Japanese Americans. Even farmers in the desolate Antelope Valley were accused of staking out the perfect spot for an invading Japanese air force to build a landing strip. Like Bowron, John L. DeWitt also used the impossibility of discerning loyal from disloyal Japanese as the basis for the army's claim that mass internment was a "military necessity." As the mayor publicly took "pride in feeling that [he had played] some small part" in "getting every Jap out of this area," he contended his "most effective argument was made to Lieutenant General John L. DeWitt."[18]

According to Bowron, military leaders like DeWitt worked with local, state, and federal officials "to formulate and to put into effect a rather definite propaganda campaign" to handle the "Japanese problem." Their efforts made Japanese American internment a matter of what the mayor termed "common sense." In a February 3 letter to the Office of Facts and Figures, he disclosed that the goal was to have public officials "all saying much the same thing." One week later, Bowron met late into the night with Earl Warren, Tom Clark of the federal Department of Justice (whom Truman would later appoint attorney general and Supreme Court justice), and an attorney from the San Francisco Department of Justice to work out a legal plan for the exclusion and internment order, which they immediately conveyed to DeWitt. The anti-Nisei propaganda was stunningly effective. In all of December 1941, the federal attorney general's office received only four letters calling for the removal or internment of Japanese Americans. Scarcely thirty such letters arrived from across the nation between January 1 and January 18, 1942. The situation, however, turned rapidly. By February 20, 1942, the office had received 671 anti–Japanese American letters, the majority from Los Angeles County. Yielding his original stance, Attorney General Biddle agreed to a series of increasingly repressive measures against Japanese immigrants before ultimately relenting to the mass internment order in mid-February 1942. Congress altered course, as well. Prior to the first week of January 1942, no representative had publicly advocated any sort of mass internment. In mid-January, Southern California's Leland Ford was the first to call for Japanese Americans to be "placed in inland concentration camps." By the end of January, when Bowron, Warren, and California's governor Culbert Olson stood in unison to advocate some form of mass "evacuation" of Japanese Americans, most of the Pacific Coast congressional delegation agreed with them. (Senator Sheridan Downey of California was the most notable exception.) All the major corporate newspapers in Los Angeles signed on, as well. When FDR issued EO 9066, Congressman John M. Costello, a Democrat from Los Angeles, told Mayor Bowron that it was "the outgrowth of our consultations back here and the extensive discussions between yourself and General DeWitt and others out there." As some form of internment was now guaranteed, civilian and military officials wrestled with a new central question: what kind of "evacuation" should be carried out, and how extensive should it be?[19]

CORNERED INTO COOPERATION

It is hard to overestimate the impact that the propaganda campaign of Bowron and his ilk had on the Nisei themselves. Anxious to provide information, JACL leaders developed personal relationships with members of the intelligence community. Some lent the Nisei sincere but ultimately false assurances that their informant activity would demonstrate to military and civilian officials that the Japanese American community posed no general threat to national security. "I still have faith in the Nisei of the United States," Kenneth D. Ringle, chief of naval intelligence for Los Angeles and San Pedro, proclaimed at a January 11, 1942, JACL meeting. "I don't think you'll let us down. To a certain extent I've gambled my professional reputation on that score." Ringle's informants had helped him crack the Tachibana espionage case. A State Department report further emphasized the Nisei harbored a "pathetic eagerness to be Americans." Embracing the role of informant, however, created dangers beyond the risk of alienating fellow Japanese Americans. The arrest of more than five thousand Japanese Americans prior to the mass internment actually helped legitimize Bowron's and DeWitt's unsubstantiated allegations that espionage and subversion were widespread throughout the Japanese American community. The detained had no trials, no opportunity to prove their innocence or cross-examine their accusers. Moreover, stories of the arrests continuously appeared in the media through April 1942, fueling speculation that the threat had yet to be contained. Worse still, playing the role of informant did not satisfy the loyalty criteria of Bowron or other agitators.[20]

Authorities like Bowron quickly recognized how easily the desire of Nisei leaders for acceptance could be manipulated. Their message to the Nisei was that they should do whatever the government asked of them to prove their loyalty. Al Cohn's report proposed that "fear propaganda" be used to "keep [the Nisei] in line" and "obtain information" from them. On February 5, Bowron publicly informed Japanese Americans that if they wanted to remain in America they not only had to behave themselves but also had to ensure that no other ethnic Japanese deviated in any way, shape, or form. He declared that "one single act"—in other words, "anything that might assist the Japanese government in time of war"—would "brand the entire Japanese population, not only during the existence of a state of war, but at least for a generation." Restating what was by then becoming a popular argument, Bowron remarked that voluntarily moving to relocation camps would signify the truest sign of loyalty. There was, he assured, "nothing that could be considered inhumane in connection with this plan." Desperately wanting to believe that the government would implement only the minimal relocation plan that was absolutely necessary to winning the war, most Nisei leaders looked for ways to cooperate with the "evacuation." Called to Sacramento, the state capital, for a February 6 meeting, Japanese American leaders from across the state anticipated words of assuagement from Governor Olson, a liberal Democrat who served as the honorary chairman of the "Northern California Committee on Fair Play for Citizens and Aliens of Japanese Ancestry." Their hopes, however, were quickly dashed as Olson made clear the occasion was designed to secure their approval of his relocation plan. While the Nisei attempted to offer diplomatic protests, they resigned themselves to working with the governor and left the meeting in a mood of "gloom and bitter disappointment." Politicians from across the ideological spectrum had closed ranks behind the "evacuation" and varied only in their sense of how it should proceed. Ironically, the national JACL had just released a statement cautioning Nisei not to "become panicky" and assuring them that the government had no plans for a mass evacuation of the American-born.[21]

Not only did Nisei leftists refrain from contesting the internment; they were quite possibly the only force within the Japanese American community that promoted cooperation with the government more stridently than the JACL did. Their behavior was, in part, driven by their belief that defeating fascism and defending Soviet Russia should be the principal goals of those who believed in human freedom. Beyond ideology, however, they were put in an even more precarious political position when the CPUSA suspended its Nisei "comrades" and supported the internment as a manifestation of the party line "Everything for National Unity!" Longtime CPUSA member and labor historian Karl Yoneda stated in retrospect why he and other leftists acquiesced to these policies. "We had no choice but to accept the racist US dictum at that time over Hitler's ovens and Japan's military rapists of Nanking," Yoneda remarked. "We would thrash out the question of rights after victory." Shortly after Pearl Harbor, the *Doho* deemed the JACL "the logical and best qualified to assume such leadership in this crisis." In fact, Shuji Fujii's main critique was that the JACL was not doing enough to purge its ranks of all "who had ever been even slightly suspected of any connection, willfully or otherwise with the old Japanese leadership." Fujii applauded when the hyperpatriotic Tokie Slocum took the chairmanship of the Anti-Axis Committee and saw his own membership in the committee restored.[22]

But as their following within the Japanese American community diminished in the face of the crushing Depression-era defeats, Nisei leftists' biggest mark may have been made on their white liberal and left-wing allies. In early February 1942, the Popular Front–oriented Nisei Writers' and Artists' Mobilization for Democracy distributed a statement from twelve Nisei and Rev. Fred Fertig, a white pastor at the Japanese Christian Church and member of the Fellowship of Reconciliation. It outlined the essential stance of the antifascist left. The authors expressed concern that restrictions placed on "enemy aliens" had combined with discrimination and uncertainty to devastate the economic health of the Japanese American community and dampen its morale. In their eyes, the best solution was an evacuation of Issei and their nonadult children from areas where such action was essential for public safety or the safety of the Issei themselves. They specified, however, that any evacuation should be limited and that the government should provide evacuees with subsidized housing and fair employment. If done properly, the evacuation could be carried out in a manner that ultimately improved human relations. Isamu Noguchi—the son of an Issei poet but raised primarily by his white American mother—served as the group's spokesman. Already renowned for his sculptures,

Noguchi was an unquestionably brilliant artist. He had worked as an assistant to the famed sculptor Brancusi in Paris and returned to produce busts of American celebrities like Martha Graham and George Gershwin. In Mexico, Noguchi assisted muralist Diego Rivera—that is, until the master discovered he was having an affair with Frida Kahlo. While Noguchi's fusion of Eastern and Western traditions drew raves from critics and artistic peers, this same cosmopolitan sensibility left him ill prepared for community leadership. Though he willingly transgressed borders in his art and personal life, political conditions in wartime America bore little resemblance to those he had experienced among the cultural avant-garde. Thus, his faith in modern progress led him to coauthor a document that was politically naive. "Some say they would rather be interned," reported the Nisei Writers' and Artists' Mobilization. The fact that this comment was underlined in county supervisor John Anson Ford's copy suggests the most immediate as well as perhaps lasting impact of the document.[23]

It was probably impossible to support any kind of state-sponsored "evacuation" or "relocation" plan without opening the door to the mass, forced internment that took place. Once they conceded there was an uncontained threat to national security, neither Nisei supporters of a limited, voluntary evacuation nor their white advocates possessed enough political clout to ensure it was carried out in a manner that pleased them. Practically nothing resembling the Nisei writers' and artists' recommendations was implemented—at least before programs to reincorporate interned Nisei back into mainstream society began. The Nisei left's general support for "evacuation," however, provided cover to white liberal politicians looking for reasons to avoid taking a stand against the internment policy the federal government actually carried out. "The general acceptance of this procedure by those who [were] proud to call themselves liberals," decried Socialist Party leader Norman Thomas, was "as ominous as the evacuation of the Japanese." Though he would later change his position, Supervisor Ford, a liberal, supported the internment as a "quarantine" of Japanese Americans undertaken for their own protection and commended the federal government for its superb handling of the "Japanese crisis." Meanwhile, politicians like Olson were concerned mainly with assuring the public they were taking care of the "Japanese problem." They were not going to stick their necks out over the question of a limited versus mass "evacuation."[24]

Although individuals denounced the rising tide of racism, oppositional voices never congealed into a sustained and coordinated movement to stop the internment. Clifford E. Clinton, the white proprietor of popular downtown Los Angeles cafeterias, wrote in an open letter to major politicians dated February 1, "We must avoid the costly mistakes that may follow

Fig. 5.1. Nisei leaders. *Left to right*: Tokutaro Nishimura Slocum, Togo Tanaka, Fred Tayama, and Joseph Shinoda testify before the Tolan Congressional Committee on March 7, 1942. Herald Examiner Collection/Los Angeles Public Library.

hysterical action and snap judgment." Recall also that while conscientious African Americans stood with Japanese Americans, the community lacked a collective response. Such individual voices were drowned out by the stampede clamoring for internment, which came thundering to a new peak after events of the last week of February 1942. Bold headlines declared that Japanese submarines had shelled oil wells in Santa Barbara. Down the coast, the "Battle of Los Angeles" erupted. Although the "battle" consisted of blaring air-raid sirens, antiaircraft fire, and reports of phantom Japanese planes that never materialized, this nonevent had serious consequences. Twenty Japanese Americans in the Los Angeles area were arrested; most were accused of "suspicious" activity that included turning apartment lights or car headlights off and on in a manner befitting signals to bomber pilots. In this context, Carey McWilliams's plan to create a congressional forum for sober deliberation by sound minds fizzled. The Tolan Committee hearings of March 1942, which he hoped would allow patriotic Nisei to state their case to a national audience, ultimately provided a greater platform for pro-internment voices. As it happened, little positive outcome could have resulted, since FDR had already committed to De-Witt's plan by the time the hearings were held. In the end, what aroused the greatest concern, especially among liberal and religious organizations, was that the "evacuation" be carried out humanely. Activity designed to support Japanese Americans thus intensified after the internment began and efforts to resettle Nisei in the Midwest and East Coast were undertaken. McWilliams remained critical of the racist treatment of Japanese Americans, but even he initially supported what he regarded as the government's surprisingly well-executed and just implementation and administration of the internment.[25]

As the ink was drying on EO 9066, Togo Tanaka was making one last-ditch effort to mobilize the Japanese American community under coordinated Nisei leadership. Twelve "major" Nisei groups came together to issue a call for a mass meeting under the banner of the United Citizens Federation (UCF) on February 19. Sponsoring members included the American Legion's Commodore Perry Post (based in Little Tokyo), the retail produce workers' union, Buddhists, Christians, and the Los Angeles and Southern District branches of the JACL. A follow-up announcement asked any organizations that had been left out to "be sure to contact The Rafu Shimpo." Over fifteen hundred Nisei jammed the auditorium of the Maryknoll Japanese Catholic Church. For the sake of unity, Tanaka "made up" with Slocum by appearing with him onstage. However, Tanaka had spurred the creation of the UCF in order to challenge the narrow and misguided leadership he attributed to Slocum's wing of the AAC and JACL. Whereas some JACL leaders feared that unleashing the community's collective potential for activism might lead their brethren to wittingly or unwittingly jeopardize the organization's efforts to maintain loyalty, Tanaka believed that mass mobilization and diplomatic protest stood a remote chance of staving off the internment. At minimum, he recognized that the community needed an opportunity to debate competing positions in an open forum. The UCF meeting thus became an occasion for alternative Nisei voices to be heard. Joe Shinoda remarked, "I think that in time to come the complete and utter disregard for our right to make a living, to share in the defense effort in this area where we make our homes, where we pay our taxes, will some day appear as a very black page in American history." A Nisei who wrote a letter to the *Rafu* praised the UCF as "the first good thing our Nisei leaders have done since Pearl Harbor." In fact, the writer called for it to "be enlarged so as to invite all other minority groups to join in the movement."[26]

To be sure, steps to implement EO 9066 were already being taken when the UCF began meeting, and little or nothing it did could change that. However, a great deal was still at stake, for what had yet to be determined was what kind of leader would represent Japanese Americans, or even the JACL, during the war. Would it be a community insider like Togo Tanaka? Or would it be a Nisei from outside the community—namely Mike Masaoka, the young lawyer raised in Utah? To be certain, both were liberals, not radicals. They were highly educated men from middle-class backgrounds, and both had continuously advocated cooperation with rather than overt resistance to the government. Yet there were sharp distinctions between them. Tanaka had intimate knowledge of the Issei's social and political culture, and he had the ability to unite Nisei from a range of class and ideological backgrounds. He believed that every law-abiding Nisei had the right to have his opinion heard and that leaders should do their best to respect diverse views and reach a consensus. Finally, while he considered it the duty of the Nisei to provide information to the authorities, he charged finger-pointers like Slocum with going overboard and harming dozens of respectable members of the community. After a January 11, 1942, meeting of the JACL, he confided to his diary, "Seldom have I felt more out of place. I must have lost a great deal more faith in the J.A.C.L. during those days in jail than I suspected." By contrast, Masaoka represented the type of JACL leader admired for his charisma, oratorical skills, and forcefulness. He had remained in Utah for law school after his family moved to Los Angeles. Above all, Masaoka, like Slocum, was valued for his ability to win the trust of white Americans. In actuality, he may not have been any more skilled than Tanaka at this; however, Tanaka's connection to the Issei and to dissident Nisei branded him as problematic. The JACL, Masaoka asserted, must distance itself from those elements to keep pure its message and patriotic reputation. He was more willing to do what he himself believed was correct, even if it made him as an individual or the JACL as an organization unpopular with Japanese Americans. Because of this, he acted with unflinching conviction but without a sense of diplomacy. Standing somewhere in between was Shuji Fujii, who supported the participatory structure of the UCF but believed the community's best interests lay in cooperating with the government. As such, he harbored little sympathy for Nisei who asserted their "citizenship rights" by opposing evacuation.[27]

Believing their organization to be the dominant voice of "loyal" Japanese Americans, most JACL leaders closed ranks around Mike Masaoka. Once the government's decision to "evacuate" the West Coast Japanese had been made, they sought to end debate about protest, silence dissidents, and unite the community in a show of loyalty. In their eyes, Tanaka's relatively inclusive approach exemplified by the broad-based UCF would needlessly allow "disloyal" elements to challenge the JACL's standing and tarnish the community's reputation. For instance, Kay Sugahara, quoted in the *New York Times*, told a UCF gathering that the community should abide by military orders but fight the scheming of political demagogues "to the last ditch." Such comments were a particular source of embarrassment for JACL leaders when they met with government officials.[28]

Passively involved at the UCF's outset, the JACL withdrew on March 2. This act cemented the coalition's demise—but not before one more historic gathering took place. On February 27, 1942, the UCF held an even larger meeting at the Maryknoll Church, which had become the central site for Japanese Americans seeking any information about or assistance preparing for their possible internment. Although an "evacuation" had been *authorized*, the actual orders to "evacuate" had not yet been issued. The community was thus still in the dark as to who would be forced to leave, where they would be going, and when it would take place. Federal officials provided a small group of JACL leaders with advance knowledge of the order for a wholesale, forced internment and instructed them to use the mass meeting to prepare the audience to receive it. Also informed that internment was imminent, Maryknoll's Hugh Lavery, a white priest considered a trustworthy ally and relative community insider, urged Japanese Americans to cooperate with the government for their own safety. Mike Masaoka represented the JACL's conciliatory position. "If we must move, let us do so without bitterness," he stated. "Let us do it in the spirit of adventure. If we have the stuff, we can take this without whining and prove our loyalty beyond all sense of doubt." But far from uniting the community, the meeting hardened divisions. Rumors spread, not just that the JACL had advance knowledge of and would be *cooperating* with the internment, but that the organization had *collaborated* with the government to intern its own people.[29]

The difference was critical. The JACL's position was that internment might be an unfair and unjust policy, but that the organization was in no position to contest it. Therefore, it could best promote Japanese American interests by working with the government to make the internment as safe and tolerable as possible and then vigorously pursuing redress and civil rights upon the war's conclusion. It was a position that could have been defended if delivered by a trusted messenger. Viewed as an outsider to Little Tokyo, Masaoka was, tragically, not that person. The reputation of the JACL as *inu*—stool pigeons—had already stuck with much of the community, which was now ready to attribute the worst possible motivations and actions to the organization. Successive events only compounded the problem. The JACL distanced itself from Nisei who challenged different aspects of the exclusion orders and internment in court, as well as those who resisted the draft. Elevating the call to demonstrate loyalty, Masaoka advocated the formation of all-Nisei "suicide battalions" to serve in the most dangerous frontline combat while the government held their families and friends as hostages to guarantee their loyalty. Meanwhile, JACL leaders continued to point fingers at other Japanese Americans, especially the Kibei. This prompted Tanaka to confess privately, "The practise of sitting in judgment of more vulnerable members of the Japanese community appears to have become in a sense a conditioned reflex of Nisei behavior." Lacking a popular base and placed in an even more vulnerable position in the internment camps, the JACL would become even more dependent on its state sponsors.[30]

As the community braced itself for the inevitable, some hoped for the best. It is difficult to assess in retrospect how many levels of irony lay beneath the cheerful tone of their language during this harrowing period. The *Rafu*'s Sadae Nomura wrote, "We think it's rather fun, going to Manzanar center, for instance, with all our families and friends. It will be an experience that we can turn to our advantage. We hope to gain a new sense of values." Maryknoll's Father Lavery, the JACL, and the *Doho* aggressively recruited participants for the first group of "voluntary" evacuees to Manzanar. One thousand persons left from Little Tokyo on March 24, 1942. Published by the "voluntary" residents, the inaugural issue of the *Manzanar Free Press* expressed "sincere appreciation" to government officials for the "excellent comforts" they had provided. " 'Can't be better,' is the general feeling of the Manzanar citizen," concluded the *Free Press*. Calling Manzanar the "Li'l Tokyo of the Desert," the *Doho* described the weather as "terrifically windy" and "very dusty" but reported the food there was "first quality." After watching volunteers help build the barracks at a rapid pace, the *Doho* reporter was moved to marvel at "the efficiency of machine-age America." Shuji Fujii and Isamu Noguchi worked with a USC film professor to document the "evacuation." On April 6, "an enthusiastic audience" of twenty-five hundred people came to a film screening to preview "their future home and environment." The final preinternment issue of the *Doho* cautioned that Manzanar's "open" latrines and showers breached privacy but expressed optimism that this would be remedied soon. Above all, the Popular Front newspaper asserted that the Manzanar center provided Japanese Americans with an opportunity to see "how democracy works in evacuation." The community's earliest and most strident opponents of the militaristic Japanese government, many Nisei leftists enlisted in every facet of the American war mobilization. They especially aided the Office of War Information in a campaign to "teach democracy" to the people of Japan and to translate enemy communications for the Military Intelligence Service. Their bilingual skills thus proved invaluable to the war effort. Others, such as Noguchi, who tried to establish art classes at the Poston camp, became disillusioned with the "evacuation" and moved east. Resettlement, however, was a luxury most were initially denied.[31]

Of course, the majority prepared for the worst, selling businesses and property at severely deflated prices. "Have you ever heard so many sarcastic references to our 'democracy'?" the *Rafu* asked. Some internees from Los Angeles were first sent to the fairgrounds of Pomona, a temporary "assembly center." Mary Oyama joined eighteen thousand others taken to the "swank Santa Anita track with its 'super' turquoise grandstand, from which cheering thousands once witnessed the lightning grace of 'Seabiscuit.'" Both Pomona and Santa Anita provided animal stalls among their accommodations. At least in a relative sense, living conditions eventually improved as the more permanent War Relocation Authority (WRA) "relocation centers" were completed. Socially and politically, however, the full tragedy of the internment would be played out at WRA camps like Manzanar. Government officials attempted to place the early "volunteer" relocatees in charge of internal Japanese American community relations. But this effort to pacify the internee population instead provoked extreme polarization, as the repressed voices came back to haunt the JACL in the form of right-wing nationalists demanding loyalty to the Japanese emperor. Lacking effective means to overturn the actions of the US government, these internees directed much of their animosity inward, toward ethnic leaders, and sought violent revenge on the *inu*. In particular, Joe Kurihara, a Hawaiian-born World War I veteran, felt so betrayed by America that he began rallying Japanese nationalists and other dissident internees. Kurihara had come to Los Angeles in February 1942 vowing to "sacrifice my personal liberty" and looking to work with other Nisei leaders to fight an unjust incarceration. Rebuffed by the JACL, he thus made no distinction between leaders like Tokie Slocum or Togo Tanaka, both of whom were attacked by Kurihara's grouping at Manzanar. JACL leaders who spearheaded the WRA governing councils were branded as collaborators, as were the leftist *aka* and those hired as participant-observer researchers by white social scientists. A notable target of the dissidents, the JACL's Fred Tayama was severely beaten, touching off an escalated round of arrests and protests. In the culminating "Manzanar riot" on December 6, 1942, federal soldiers fired on the protestors, killing two and wounding many others. Barely escaping the violent crowd, Tanaka hid in the car of a Brethren missionary, who smuggled him out of the camp. Other "pro-American" leaders pleaded with WRA officials to take them into their immediate custody for eventual resettlement elsewhere. Never had the traumatic effects that state-sponsored racism had on the Japanese American community been more apparent.[32]

CHAPTER 6

The "Negro Victory" Movement

ON NOVEMBER 18, 1943, from the confines of a jail cell, Thomas Madison Doram recounted his tumultuous experiences as an African American shipyard worker in a sworn statement to the Fair Employment Practices Committee (FEPC). Three weeks after the attack on Pearl Harbor, Doram had been hired as a janitor by California Shipbuilding, one of the three major shipbuilders in California that had agreed to a closed shop arrangement with the AFL Boilermakers Local 92. Founded in 1880, the International Brotherhood of Boilermakers, Iron Shipbuilders, Welders and Helpers of America was a craft union whose central purpose was to govern access to employment. Typical of many AFL unions, Black workers were restricted to joining segregated auxiliaries, which provided them few of the benefits of union membership and no role in decision making. Thus, at the outset of the war, African Americans rarely found work in the shipyards—fewer than 2 percent of all workers placed into shipyards by the US Employment Service in 1941 were African American. Those that did find work were often relegated to the lowest-paying, least desirable positions. With the war boosting demand for production, battleships arose from the yards of Terminal Island, an island on the southern tip of Los Angeles where a Japanese American fishing community had recently been uprooted. Doram was determined to gain opportunities for himself and end the racial discrimination resulting from the collaboration of employers and trade unions. Other than whites, the Boilermakers allowed only token Asian and Latino shipyard workers to become members of Local 92. Black worker Fred Washington signed up for full membership as a "Hindu," and Doram was initially admitted because of his apparently being misidentified as "Mexican." However, upon discovering that Doram was Black, union officials refused his request to enter training programs for higher-paid positions.[1]

Whereas charges of "disloyalty" branded Japanese Americans as pariahs, African Americans in Los Angeles situated themselves at the forefront of the drive for national unity. "My unrelenting desire to serve my country better and my overwhelming patriotism," declared Doram, "impelled me to learn to be a 'Burner' whatever the sacrifice, to continually improve my effectiveness in helping the war effort." With some support of white fellow workers, the union promoted him to work as a "burner" provided he stayed on the night shift and kept his racial identity concealed. But instead of remaining quiet, Doram helped to organize a mass campaign for the full rights of union membership. Three hundred Black shipyard workers on the West Coast were fired during the war because they refused to join Jim Crow auxiliaries. White workers resented these challenges to the established order. "I was mutely threatened time after time with injury or even my life if I did not leave my job," Doram declared. He was ostracized, repeatedly called "Nigger," and ultimately assaulted by two white workers in June 1943. In a perversity of justice, Doram was the only one arrested. Yet he and his associates continued their struggle and won three California Supreme Court rulings during 1945 and 1946 outlawing the segregated auxiliaries. Their words and deeds typified the militant brand of patriotism that characterized the Negro Victory movement in Los Angeles and the transformation of African American consciousness and politics during World War II. By favorably altering the terrain of struggle, wartime social and political conditions set the stage for the breakdown of Jim Crow employment patterns in the North and West. The massive wartime investment in production created a windfall demand for labor, while the creation of the FEPC gave African American workers a new weapon to wield in the fight against job discrimination. Seizing upon the federal government's pressing need to contain domestic racial unrest and maintain the moral high ground in the war against fascism, Black community leaders like Clayton Russell and Charlotta Bass joined forces with workers like Doram to reconstruct the "loyalty" discourse.[2]

Although local Black community protest dated back at least to *Birth of a Nation*, a qualitatively different form of activism developed in response to the historic opportunity of World War II. Claiming the mantle of patriotism under the banner of "Negro Victory," visionary African American leaders argued that their community's participation in wartime efforts mandated the abolition of segregation, discrimination, and social inequality. By making the Black defense worker the primary subject of "victory" discourse, left-leaning activists pushed working-class concerns to the fore of a Black leadership agenda that had previously revolved around middle-class notions of moral uplift and housing improvement. They built demonstrations far outweighing the scale of the Depression-era "Don't Spend Your Money Where You Can't Work" campaign and developed strategies to utilize direct confrontation tactics more effectively. While African Americans offered no organized opposition to the onset of the Japanese American internment, Black activists over the course of the war years developed a broad political scope that transcended narrow self-interest and minority rights. They joined with progressive CIO activists to advance an expansive view of movement building that pushed forward new questions about the value and meaning of interracial organizing. Finally, Black leaders demanded that the state intervene on the side of those fighting to eliminate discrimination. A "hate strike" by white workers protesting the upgrading of African Americans by the Los Angeles Railway revealed both the benefits and limits of state intervention. In the end, the wartime mobilization represented only one step in the Black community's long quest for racial equality, but it clearly signaled that a new day in Los Angeles had arrived.

Constructing the Movement

In spite of President Roosevelt's June 1941 order banning racially discriminatory employment within the nation's defense industries, the war-related production plants of Southern California had scarcely been integrated when Japan attacked Pearl Harbor. Like Japanese Americans, Blacks must have spent the following weeks pondering what fates the war years would hold. Just as the Nisei had been given little evidence to suggest that mass internment was a serious possibility, African Americans had been given little reason to believe that mass employment in manufacturing was likely. In early 1942, people of color held no more than 3 percent of all jobs in war-related industries nationwide. Discrimination against Blacks within defense employment was as bad in Southern California as in any other place in the country, or worse. Even African Americans inspired to enlist after Pearl Harbor were rejected by local military officials waiting for instructions from Washington on how to handle segregated induction. The army recruitment office in downtown Los Angeles turned away so many African American volunteers that it was forced to issue a statement to the Black press: "IT IS ABSOLUTELY UNTRUE THAT WE ARE RECRUITING NEGROES INTO THE REGULAR ARMY." When the FEPC released its January 1942 report on the basis of the Los Angeles hearings held three months prior, this record of rampant racial discrimination became available for all to read. Using carefully worded language, the committee reported that Blacks had been excluded from entire plants, banned from entire job categorizations, and routinely barred from trade unions. Where employed, they were severely underrepresented and denied jobs commensurate with their skill levels. The FEPC called on companies to advertise to prospective applicants that they were nondiscriminatory employers. Praising the report, the *California Eagle* declared that the FEPC hearings combined with the issuance of EO 8802 had "done more to advance the dignity and opportunity of Negro skilled workers than anything similar which [had] occurred in the last quarter-century." Even at this watershed moment, however, the crux of the struggle lay ahead. "The

Negro's foot may be in the door," noted the *Eagle*, "but the bulk of him remains tragically out in the cold."[3]

Economic and political conditions in Los Angeles transformed over the course of 1942. Despite rapid manufacturing growth, the city's industrial employment levels had lagged behind those in the rest of the nation. Prewar production had been weighted toward the crafts and required the importation of semifinished goods. Wartime demand, however, created a new base of Fordist production. Los Angeles County garnered roughly 5 percent of all federal contracting funds awarded during the war. By January 1945, local employers had received $10.6 billion in war production and facilities contracts. While much of America's workforce was fighting overseas, the federal government announced that it would need ten million additional defense workers nationwide between July 1942 and July 1943. Led by the durable goods sector, manufacturing employment in metropolitan Los Angeles soared from 94,000 wage earners in 1935 to a wartime peak of 540,000 in June 1944. The unemployment rate shrank to 1.4 percent, pushing the region's wages above the national average and leading federal officials to designate Los Angeles the nation's "No. 1 critical labor shortage area" on two occasions during the war. While industrial growth reflected the diverse demands of wartime production, Southern California proved to be an especially critical site for aircraft manufacturing. With Detroit's converted auto plants providing engines, airframe construction centered on Los Angeles, which had jump-started the aviation industry during the Progressive Era and was strategically located with relation to the Pacific theater of operations. But while the region claimed 60 percent of the nation's airframe production by the eve of World War II, local industries had employed only 20,000 workers. By July 1944, 190,000 persons were on the payroll of local airframe construction plants. Parts suppliers, as well as the shipyards, each employed another 85,000.[4]

African American activists mobilized to ensure that the racist hiring practices disclosed by the FEPC would not stop their community from getting its fair share of this windfall of job openings. Launching what would become the most dynamic element of Black wartime organizing, a coalition of African American community leaders convened the Los Angeles Negro Victory Committee (NVC) in April 1941. The NVC realized its potential under the leadership of Rev. Clayton D. Russell. A Los Angeles native and Jefferson High School graduate, Russell was born in 1910, making him one of the youngest Black community leaders during the war. Educated at USC and Chapman College, he continued his studies during the early 1930s in Denmark, where he developed a keen awareness of the danger Nazi fascism posed to humanity. Viewed as a "maverick" preacher because of his activist tendency to focus on earth as much as heaven, Russell became pastor of the People's Independent Church of Christ (PIC) in 1935. Emerging from a break with First AME in 1915, the activist-minded PIC had been founded by parishioners seeking to free themselves "from the greed and avariciousness of church despots." Located in an older section of the Central Avenue district at Eighteenth and Paloma, it had several thousand African American members, who provided a significant base for the NVC. Attracting entrepreneurs, workers, and recent migrants, PIC's congregation combined the assertiveness of economic nationalists with the hunger of those seeking jobs. Church sustainers were drawn from the leading ranks of the Black bourgeoisie, including managers of Golden State Insurance. Black patronage provided them with a degree of independence necessary to challenge the white establishment without fear of reproach. At the same time, PIC established a social welfare network to address the needs of low-income African Americans that went largely unaddressed by white social service agencies and traditional Black organizations. By the middle of the Depression, it rivaled older, established congregations at churches like First AME and Second Baptist in both size and influence. CIO organizer and NVC leader Walter Williams characterized PIC as "an ideal place for mobilization." He noted that the NVC "automatically had a large mass of people who were willing to, at the drop of a hat, move behind Russell's leadership."[5]

Progressive activists like Clayton Russell and Charlotta Bass challenged their community to embrace militant, oppositional politics. As relayed to author R. J. Smith, Russell's contemporaries characterized him as a sharp dresser who always drove a luxury Packard car. He entered a room like a prizefighter stepping into a sold-out arena, deacons trailing behind him like an entourage. The spirited preacher possessed the charisma and charm to draw a large following, be it for religious worship or political action. With the war providing unique opportunities for African American social, economic, and political advancement, Russell called for "the fullest unity of action, nationally and locally," from the Black community. "Negro ministers, regardless of denomination or size of church, must get together now!" he declared. "Negro newspapers must get together now! Negro business, Negro leadership must get together now!" Bass's *California Eagle* served as the principal print medium to deliver such messages. While the newspaper and its matriarch had been at the center of Black Los Angeles since the early twentieth century, both undertook an ideological reorientation during the war. Bass had always been an unrelenting foe of the Klan and an outspoken critic of restrictive covenants, but she had supported a rather conservative economic agenda. During the Depression, she referred to the New Deal as "the new-fangled Red-baiting socialistic idea that is eating in on American ideals like a cancer." The *Eagle*'s wartime pages reflected her turn to the left, which some

Fig. 6.1. Leaders of the "Negro Victory" movement. *Left to right*: J. Raymond Henderson, Charlotta A. Bass, and Clayton D. Russell. Photo from the California Eagle Photograph Collection. Courtesy of the Southern California Library for Social Studies and Research.

charged was the result of the CPUSA bailing Bass out of bankruptcy. Other observers believed the paper's left turn stemmed from the influence of staff member John Kinloch. A brash writer from Harlem, Kinloch was the beloved nephew of Bass (more like her son) and a CPUSA fellow traveler. Not only did Bass become similarly friendly with the CPUSA, she articulated the Popular Front line more eloquently and effectively than just about any of its members. Instead of alienating herself from the mainstream of the community, she used her words and deeds to transform local Black political culture. "Mass movements are the very spearhead of the Negro's struggle," she proclaimed.[6]

The city's African American community leaders and thousands of workers answered her call. In early April 1942, the grouping that launched the NVC gathered for an "emergency" meeting in response to racist violence in other parts of the country. But their underlying concern was job discrimination. In their first public appeal, the sponsoring coalition of community leaders announced, "We are the representatives of most of your organizations, your civic bodies, your business institutions. We are Democrats and Republicans and Left-wingers. We have not always agreed with each other on all points, and we do not agree on all points now. But on the most important issue facing our people today WE STAND UNITED!" NVC organizers claimed their inaugural mass meeting at Second Baptist Church drew thirty-five hundred people. The body resolved to petition the army to accept volunteers without racial discrimination; to demand Black representation on local and state policy boards; to support India's fight for freedom; and to protest housing restrictions in the city of Maywood, a white working-class suburb southeast of Los Angeles. After tasks were outlined and taken up by committees, a follow-up meeting on June 21 reportedly drew fifteen hundred people and made significant progress toward these goals.[7]

Through both the NVC and broader coalitions of Black individuals and organizations, Negro Victory activists united the community around a basic proposition: African Americans supported the war 100 percent and called for the removal of all racial barriers to participation in the war effort. While this would echo the "Double V" campaign popularized by the *Pittsburgh Courier*, Black politics in Los Angeles took shape in a particular multiracial context. On the one hand, Negro Victory proponents had no qualms about declaring African Americans the most patriotic Americans in the land. This was more than a defensive wartime gesture. In fact, it was a strategic offensive maneuver. As Black leaders recognized the federal government needed their voices to help sell the war, high patriotism became a basis for critiquing domestic racism. Interviewed a generation later by scholar E. Frederick Anderson, Russell recalled, "In order to gain employment which was the number one need for Blacks at the time, we exploited the war. We charged those who were discriminating with hurting the war industry." On the other hand, what this meant was that Negro Victory proponents took initial advantage of racial triangulation. In practice, much of the space for the Negro Victory argument to be articulated came from the dominant culture's intense focus on rallying American nationalism to combat enemy "Japs"—a task frequently carried out in a virulently racist manner. Seeking to win the support of reluctant Black masses, Popular Front–oriented Negro Victory leaders felt compelled to debunk the notion that Japan's expansionism comprised a blow to white supremacy. For example, Black leftist Revels Cayton reportedly drew "frequent outbursts of applause" at the first NVC mass meeting, where he declared, "Japs in America would ally themselves with the KKK, not with us." These comments, however, conveyed little concern for the slippery slope that led to Japanese Americans becoming the target of a generalized race war. Identifying the Nisei as "U.S. Japs," the *Eagle*, strangely enough, reported next to nothing about the internment. The American Communist Party actually supported the internment and suspended its Japanese American members. By contrast, those who criticized the war, including anti-Stalinists and some Black nationalists, were less inhibited from condemning the government's incarceration of Japanese Americans than those whose strategy relied on displays of patriotism and alliance with FDR.[8]

Negro Victory work encompassed a creative mix of self-help and mass protest activities that was testimony to the breadth of participation in wartime coalitions. Clayton Russell and the People's Independent Church mobilized five hundred people in early 1942 to launch the Negro Victory Market, a cooperative grocery begun with $1,700 of pooled funds. Observing that the vacuum created by restrictions on Japanese Americans had left the "whole marketing situation in Los Angeles . . . at a great crossroads," the *Eagle* considered this a brilliant and well-timed move that had "fired the enthusiasm and the imagination of rank-and-file Black people here as nothing has done in the last ten years." Stressing the importance of economic self-initiative, it characterized the market as "a genuine effort of all the PEOPLE of the Eastside to OWN THEIR COMMUNITY." By war's end, five Negro Victory Markets had been established, all funded by NVC stockholders. While the cooperative markets struggled to compete with the city's established groceries, they served as a vehicle to awaken the consciousness of Black consumers and challenge the unequal distribution of rationed food between white and Black neighborhoods in the city. As one female member remarked, "I know that the Victory Markets do not have the same big stock of the white chains, but how can they when the Negro people haven't got foresight and loyalty enough to spend their money with them."[9]

While the cooperatives fused economic nationalism and participatory democracy, the NVC further enlarged Black political discourse by addressing the concerns of an expanding working class. As the demand for labor intensified, the opening of industrial employment accelerated the Great Migration to the urban North and West. Metropolitan Los Angeles drew the greatest share of the 1.4 million total persons who arrived in California during the war. The Golden State registered a net wartime increase of over a quarter million African Americans, the largest of any state nationwide. Although Blacks comprised only 2 percent of all migrants to Los Angeles during 1941, the Black population of the Los Angeles area expanded by 59,000 persons between April 1940 and April 1944—an increase of 78.2 percent that more than tripled the overall rate of population growth for the region. By January 1946, the number of African Americans within the city limits alone reached 133,082, raising the Black share of the city's population to 7.4 percent—a jump from 4.2 percent in 1940.[10]

Notwithstanding a tightening labor market and FEPC oversight, the new migrants continued to encounter serious difficulties on and off the job, as exemplified by the plight of railroad workers recruited to California from various parts of the South. Public awareness of their problems arose in July 1942 after Carey McWilliams, chief of California's Division of Immigration and Housing, held hearings in Los Angeles. McWilliams found that Southern Pacific, which had arranged with government agencies to hire five thousand employees, was flagrantly violating its agreement to maintain decent working conditions, wages, and health standards. Most recruits, who included minors, had no experience working on the railroads and little knowledge of the type of work they were hired to do. Some were placed in grueling desert work with no advanced notice. With medical examinations lax or nonexistent, many workers had advanced cases of gonorrhea and syphilis, and some had physical handicaps. McWilliams concluded that Southern Pacific's failure to plan and coordinate properly "made for utter confusion on the part of the worker and equal confusion on the part of the recruiting government agencies." During a three-week period in the summer of 1942, thirty-one hundred out-of-state migrants, 98 percent of whom were African American, were brought to California. Arriving in Los Angeles with no directions, workers were often arrested for vagrancy. Even the Southern Pacific's representative admitted the recruitment program was a "practical failure." He acknowledged that only 50 percent of the migrants actually went to work, while 15 percent deserted en route, another 15 percent refused to work upon arrival, and 20 percent quit after a short time. Exasperated, forty to fifty workers testified that they had been defrauded and wished to return home. The railroads, however, refused to provide many their entire return passage. Charlotta Bass chastised the "labor racketeers" for luring "innocent young Negro men" to the city with "false promises." This in her eyes was nothing more than an "old and rotten stunt" designed to create "an over-supply of workers to force down all wage levels." Leaders of social agencies contended that the railroads were deliberately sabotaging the program in order to renew their original request for Mexican labor.[11]

Black leaders in the era of racial uplift had often condemned migrant workers for causing a deterioration of community standards. Characterized by Clayton Russell as a "fighting organization," the NVC instead placed working-class concerns at the center of Black community politics. By mobilizing a large base of African Americans around a proletarian agenda, the NVC forced established leaders, such as Russell's ministerial peers, to get involved if only not to lose touch with their flock. One of its first major campaigns demonstrated the crucial role African American women played in the development of working-class organizing. In mid-July 1942, the NVC reported that a United States Employment Service (USES) official had described Black women as deficient in defense work because they either lacked support for the war effort or were born to be domestic workers. Although the USES denied the comment had been made, Russell asserted at the next NVC meeting that community leaders had heard it with their own ears. Furthermore, the minister reached an extended audience through his popular Sunday night radio show called *The Visitor*, which was sponsored by the Black-owned Angelus Funeral Home. He broadcast a call for every African American woman in Los Angeles who wanted a job in the defense industry to go to the downtown USES branch the next day. Monday morning, USES officials discovered between two thousand and twenty-five hundred Black women at their front door demanding to be employed. Most had arrived before the offices opened. The NVC used the occasion to host a speak-out. "This is our war! We must win it!" declared Mrs. Lou Rosser, leader of the NVC's Ladies Auxiliary. "We cannot win it in the kitchen! We must win it on the assembly line!" A long line of African American women then recounted how they had been shut out of defense work. In the mix was the widow of a Pearl Harbor casualty, Irene Jackson, who condemned the Huntington Park branch of the USES for denying to place her in suitable employment. So many women applied for jobs that morning that the bureau was forced to shut its doors just after noon. While the crowds rallied, NVC leaders met with USES representatives. A defensive official responded, "I think we have gone beyond our instructions in breaking down discrimination." However, USES area supervisor Arthur Woods agreed to recommend to his higher-ups that training classes be relocated from Long Beach to Los Angeles to accommodate Central Avenue residents.[12]

Having won a commitment for training classes, the NVC turned its attention to the Los Angeles school district to ensure the training would be implemented. Civil rights advocates had long harbored complaints that officials were insensitive to Black educational concerns. In a harsh letter to school district supervisor Vierling Kersey dated July 29, 1942, a coalition of African American leaders charged, "You ignored every committee, every petition and every complaint that we made to improve the conditions in and around the schools and in the community." Russell contended that training centers had been consciously placed in white areas like Inglewood ("home of the Ku Klux Klan") and Glendale (where police "would question a Negro if he or she were caught on the streets after 6 o'clock in the evening"). On August 2, 1942, one thousand people discussed the issue at the regular Sunday NVC meeting. The next day they descended in large numbers on the Los Angeles Board of Education's meeting to insist that training classes be implemented at Jefferson High for Central Avenue residents. (They also protested the school board's decision to remove areas of Black settlement in the Westside from the attendance boundaries of newly built Dorsey High and place them with Polytechnic instead.) Supervisor Kersey offered a plethora of excuses for the lack of training classes at Jefferson, citing a lack of coordination and resources, as well as the old rationale that schools were forbidden to train students unless their employment was guaranteed. Assemblyman Gus Hawkins and Clayton Russell responded by assuming their respective roles as negotiator and agitator. As the latter recalled, "The strategy was for Gus to talk smooth and for me to talk tough." The quick-witted Russell pointed out that the problems Kersey cited had not prevented the school district from starting up fifty training classes in other areas. "Hitler is not waiting for the opening of the fall semester," he quipped. While the board promised nothing, it showed respect for the NVC's organizing power by agreeing to devote special time to address the issue at its next meeting.[13]

By mid-August, the school district had started defense industry training classes at Jefferson. Women, however, were still denied admission. In response, Charlotta Bass devoted her next On the Sidewalk column to the issue. Opening with a call for women to stand up and fight, Bass reminded readers that Black women were "the mothers of a hundred rebellions." With this history of struggle came a responsibility. "Black women have a tradition which they must not forget and which they must not fail," she argued. Her vision of sisterhood was consciously internationalist. "I devoutly believe that we stand in this moment on the threshold of a great new day and the final liberation of Women," she asserted. "All over the world, women, Black, white, yellow, red—women in China—women in India—women in Africa—are joining and LEADING the fight for freedom, the fight against that brutal Fascism which would forever degrade all the women of the world." Buoyed by these words, the NVC removed the barriers to training classes for Black women, too. The victories signaled a new

Fig. 6.2. Aviation plant worker. African American women entered defense industries during World War II. Security Pacific Collection/Los Angeles Public Library.

dawn in Black Los Angeles history. Clayton Russell noted that "the steps taken by the women of our community" were responsible for the new opportunities. He declared, "The future of democracy in the world and for the American Negro depends to a great extent on the role of Negro women during these war years and the responsibilities which they will accept."

Next to Russell's words, the *Eagle*'s pictorial spread "From 'Street Car Blues' to Real Victory Job" portrayed proletarianization as a marker of modern progress. On the left was the "familiar malady of overworked Negro domestics . . . during high point of Eastside disembarkation for Hollywood 'service' drudgery." On the right lay the "NEW INDUSTRIAL WORKER." The caption read, "She is expert at a highly technical job . . . draws good pay . . . leaves her children at a fine nursery and is protected on the job by union membership."[14]

The retreat of Jim Crow employment patterns during the war appeared striking. Nationally, 1.25 million African Americans (including 300,000 women) held manufacturing jobs by 1944. Starting from next to nothing at the time of Pearl Harbor, Black defense industry employment in the Los Angeles area reached 30,000 in 1943. As a result, the African American share of the city's war-related production work grew from scarcely 1 percent in May 1942 to more than 5 percent in 1944. As craft work was replaced by wartime assembly lines, aircraft production drew a far higher percentage of unskilled and semiskilled workers. In early 1942, Douglas, North American, and Lockheed were nearly bereft of Black workers. By May, they collectively employed over 1,000. The following year, there were 2,000 African Americans at Douglas plus 1,693 at North American and 1,189 at Lockheed. These opportunities continued to draw southern Blacks to Los Angeles. In late 1942, Floyd Covington noted, "We have now for the first time in [Urban] League history more jobs than people to apply and qualify for same." He conservatively estimated that ten thousand Black migrants had arrived in the city over the course of the previous year. To be certain, the invocation of FDR's executive order in a tight labor market had provided the requisite condition for breaking down racial barriers. But the significance of mass activism should not be discounted. The level of community organizing and agitation determined the speed at which Blacks were integrated into industry, the volume in which they were hired, and the conditions under which they labored. Yet, for progressive Black activists, securing jobs was not the ultimate end. Building the fight against employment discrimination was a step toward creating a social democratic movement.[15]

BLACK ACTIVISM AND ORGANIZED LABOR

In November 1942, Black community leaders worked with CIO organizers to coordinate what was arguably the labor movement's most innovative and visionary wartime campaign in Los Angeles. The "Eastside" organizing drive comprised a "joint community-union campaign" aimed at African Americans in the Central Avenue district. It sought to build on the growing Black affinity for the CIO, whose leaders had addressed thousands at Negro Victory rallies. "In CIO, Jim Crow is a dead bird," proclaimed Black CIO officer Revels Cayton as he kicked off the drive in January 1943. The campaign encompassed fifteen unions, including the United Auto Workers (UAW); Mine and Mill; State, County and Municipal Workers; United Electrical Workers; and Packinghouse Workers. But the unions did not act alone. The CIO reached out to Black churches, social clubs, and small businesses to join the campaign. By involving multiple unions, organizing multiple sectors, and engaging African American institutions, the goal was to create a "buzz" in the Central Avenue district. At the core of campaign planning lay an understanding that while wages and labor conditions deeply concerned all workers, the specific problem of racism hung over the head of Black workers. But more than this, organizers recognized that the oppression of African Americans transcended the workplace. The Eastside organizing drive at its height promised to redefine the role of unions by addressing the off-the-job needs of workers, families, and communities. For instance, dozens of volunteers from the CIO Social Service Workers union went canvassing door-to-door in Black neighborhoods to offer five days of free child care to working mothers. Their stated goal was demonstrating the great and unmet need for state-subsidized child care. The program, however, not only served the practical purpose of building a database of workers' names and addresses; it also helped solidify the CIO's reputation as an organization that understood the special concerns of African Americans.[16]

The Eastside organizing drive was born out of the close relationship that the regional CIO's left-wing leadership established with Black progressives in Los Angeles during World War II. San Francisco longshoreman Harry Bridges had been named West Coast director of the CIO by national leaders coveting the base of membership he had built in the AFL. Though his actual membership status in the party was purposefully vague, Bridges's practice generally adhered to the shifting line of the CPUSA. In Los Angeles, the CPUSA exerted considerable influence, especially through the regional CIO's Los Angeles Industrial Union Council (LA CIO Council), which had formed in June 1937 following the CIO's ouster from the AFL Central Labor Council. Early in its history, a high-ranking official had warned that the CIO was "fast becoming" a Communist outpost in Los Angeles. In truth, LA CIO Council secretary-treasurer Philip Connelly was a leading member of the CPUSA. His nickname, "Slim," was an ironic reference to his hefty frame. A white radical from the newspaper guild, he also held the presidency of the California State CIO Council for part of the war's duration. Paralleling the local CP, the CIO in Los Angeles opted not to march completely in step with its parent body during the war. For example, it supported a Communist-led wildcat strike of four thousand UAW workers at the North American–Inglewood plant. The CIO had practical as well as ideological reasons to expand its mass base and support worker initiative. In August 1939, its sixty unions in Los Angeles totaled fifty thousand members—less than half the membership of the rival AFL. Reflecting leftist influence, CIO efforts to organize Black workers in Los Angeles went above and beyond what was typical in other parts of the country. Correspondingly, the Black presence within the local CP expanded exponentially. The FBI claimed that Communists were responsible for "the majority of agitation among the Negroes by outside sources." Between February and May of 1943, the CPUSA set a goal of recruiting 60 new African American members in Los Angeles and wound up drawing in 115. Beyond Slim Connelly, the key personal link between the CIO and Negro Victory work was Black Communist Revels Cayton, who had joined the party in Seattle during the Depression. The younger brother of the noted intellectual Horace Cayton, he moved to Los Angeles just as local organizing was taking off in the spring of 1942. Rising to become the most prominent African American in the West Coast CIO during this period, Revels served as state federation vice president and headed just about every union initiative involving "minorities." With an expanded dues base providing new resources for the CIO's aggressive organizing drives, leftists urged moderates to recognize that winning over the burgeoning ranks of African American workers was crucial to challenging the long-standing AFL hegemony over the local labor movement. At the Goodyear Plant in South Los Angeles, for instance, the CIO called on management to end its racist hiring practices and filed a complaint with the War Manpower Commission. Its actions helped give rise by the end of January 1943 to the hiring of two hundred Black women covered by the CIO Rubber Workers union.[17]

In June 1943, African American leaders vigorously endorsed the CIO's United Auto Workers in the National Labor Relations Board (NLRB) election scheduled for Douglas plants in Vernon and El Segundo. A diverse body of Black leaders, including many who stated they did not normally "take sides" in union conflicts, drafted a full-page ad in the *Eagle* to urge all workers to vote for the UAW. The grouping included representatives of the NAACP, NVC, *Eagle*, *Sentinel*, Golden State Insurance, Urban League, First AME Church, and Second Baptist Church. It was a coup for the UAW to have every prominent African American leader in the city lining up behind it. First AME and Second Baptist, both founded in the early 1870s, were the two oldest, most well-established Black churches in Los Angeles. A recent transplant from the East Coast, J. Raymond Henderson, head minister at Second Baptist, especially helped coordinate a citywide effort to promote the CIO among Black churches. The Negro press actively aided the CIO, as did many of the city's most prominent African American businessmen. Finally, the NAACP represented a well-respected voice on the issue of civil rights dating back three decades, and its president, Thomas Griffith, Jr., was a well-known attorney and the son of Second Baptist's former pastor. During the war, the NAACP's membership swelled above ten thousand persons as progressives like Bass and Russell worked closely with Griffith to orient it toward working-class interests. The *Eagle* commented that the NAACP had "grown from a small select 'association' [into] a major mass movement of Negro people in Los Angeles."[18]

The coming together of this coalition demonstrated the degree to which the African American community had closed ranks in support of a Negro Victory agenda centered on the struggle of workers. Not for another generation would a Black movement of this magnitude unify actors from this spectrum of ideological perspectives. In late 1942, Floyd Covington noted that the NVC by itself had brought together "labor, communistic, and conservative and radical elements of community." This common front had been constructed by creative leaders responding to a historic economic and political conjuncture and demonstrating a willingness to seize unique opportunities for Black advancement. Wartime national unity gave rise to a consensus economy that did not eliminate conflict between labor and management but most certainly narrowed the practical parameters of ideological difference. In exchange for a "no-strike pledge," unions were granted a "maintenance of membership" agreement by the National War Labor Board starting in June 1942. Effectively, the ordinance replicated a closed shop by requiring all workers covered by a union contract to remain union members and pay dues for the duration of the contract. In this context, it was more likely than not that defense workers would be unionized. Thus, the choice they and their advocates confronted was not "union, yes or no?" but "AFL or CIO?" Nationally, the wartime arrangement fueled the CIO's expansive growth, as it grew from 1.8 million members in 1939 to 3.9 million in 1944. The UAW alone claimed 1 million members. Although the weak Los Angeles CIO had rarely offered Black workers a viable alternative to the AFL during the Depression, the war created new openings.[19]

The AFL's history of racism served to galvanize Black support for the CIO. While the Boilermakers' overt insistence on Jim Crow unionism among shipyard workers was public knowledge, the AFL's International Association of Machinists (IAM) maintained a policy of racial exclusion through custom and ritual. Like most internationals within the AFL, the IAM began as a nineteenth-century craft union, and fewer than 1 percent of its 310,000 members were African American in 1941. Its largest Southern California affiliate, Local 727, covered 30,000 aviation workers at Lockheed Burbank, where the wartime introduction of mass production gave the craft union jurisdiction over an industrial workforce. In fact, the relatively progressive leadership of Local 727 supported integration and raised the issue at the national IAM convention three times before winning removal of racial barriers in 1948. During the war, however, Black workers were repeatedly denied jobs and upgrading at Lockheed. Given their knowledge of that situation, the coalition of African American leaders stressed the gravity of the election contest at Douglas between the UAW and IAM. They chastised the latter's discriminatory practice as "a dagger at the heart of the future of every Negro industrial worker in Southern California" that threatened "to leave Negro workers naked and unprotected to be hired or fired at will." Employing Negro Victory discourse, the coalition emphasized above all that the racism of the IAM was "a bitter wedge driven into the national unity without which full production against the nation's enemies [was] impossible." By contrast, as African Americans penetrating the lily-white field of airframe production encountered resistance, the CIO emerged as a potential ally. For instance, it stood behind them at North American, which had a greater concentration of Black workers (7.2 percent in summer 1944) than any other major aircraft company but maintained segregated departments and discriminatory policies. In one egregious case, Horace Dickey was fired in March 1942 for violating an order that African American male workers refrain from talking to white women at North American. With the support of the UAW, he won a reinstatement with back pay through arbitration.[20]

The NLRB elections of June 8, 1943, revealed the impact of African American support for the CIO. At the Vernon plant (southeast of Los Angeles), where there was a large concentration of Blacks, the UAW won the election with 60 percent of the vote. But at the El Segundo plant (in the Westside), where there was only a small percentage of Black workers, neither union won a majority, and the "no union" position prevailed. Even in this instance, however, bloc voting by Black workers likely prevented white supporters from claiming an IAM victory. The UAW victory at Vernon and the defeat of the IAM at El Segundo symbolized the monumental changes that had occurred over two years. Black apathy toward unions, which had been caused by decades of AFL racism, was replaced by a community-wide campaign to win an NLRB election. For the time being, at least, African American workers had demonstrated their importance to union success, and the CIO had demonstrated the importance of building ties to the Black community. At its wartime peak, the CIO nationwide had three hundred thousand Black members, who accounted for 7.7 percent of its total membership. More than half belonged to the UAW or Steel Workers. There were limits, however, to this "Negro-labor" alliance. Just as some Black workers and leaders supported the CIO largely because the AFL was intolerable, many of the CIO's national leaders likewise recognized the ease with which they might gain a competitive advantage with African Americans. The CIO need not be a vigorous champion of civil rights, only a tolerable alternative to the AFL. While the CIO supported the FEPC and the insertion of antidiscrimination clauses into union contracts, its leaders did not advocate that special measures be adopted to address the plight of African Americans. Instead, they generally clung to the position that the status of Black workers would improve through a general raising of working standards. For instance, the CIO established the Committee Against Racial Discrimination (CARD) at its November 1942 convention, but it never prioritized this body's work. Furthermore, CARD was unwilling to remedy racial inequity between white and nonwhite CIO union members if it meant that the seniority system, which primarily served established white workers, would have to be challenged. Symbolic of the committee's status, its African American director, George Weaver, lacked an office in CIO national headquarters and was forced to carry out his work in its hallways.[21]

Charlotta Bass typified the view of Black progressives that the CIO must do more. "The simple statement that Labor believes in 'equality' isn't worth a tinker's dam," the *Eagle* publisher declared in December 1942. It was "imperative" that organized labor "recognize its SPECIAL duties to Negro workers" by standing at the "forefront of the struggle" and waging "a militant campaign to hoist colored workers up to the levels of equal treatment before the law." Simultaneously, she challenged African Americans to shed inherent biases against unions for the sake of both groups' self-interest, as well as the future of humankind. "That there has ever been division between labor in a Black skin and labor in a white skin has been a prime stumbling block in the way of all American progress," Bass concluded. "It is only through such unity that victory may be won and a durable peace DEMANDED at the war's end." To a large degree, Bass saw her vision come to fruition through the Eastside organizing drive and the UAW election. In their efforts to organize plant workers and community members, Black progressives and leftist labor leaders had coalesced around the notion that interracial cooperation could produce a movement to address the shared concerns of the city's marginalized elements. Their resolve was quickly put to the test by a race riot and a hate strike.[22]

INTERRACIAL CONFLICT, INTERRACIAL ORGANIZING

Despite citizen and state-sponsored efforts to promote home front unity, a wave of wartime racial conflicts swept through the nation. White neighborhoods continued to resist the entrance of people of color, white workers launched "hate strikes" to protest the hiring or upgrading of African Americans, and some notable instances of urban unrest occurred. Race riots in Detroit left 34 dead and 675 seriously injured in June 1943. The majority of the casualties resulted from white civilian and police assaults on African Americans. In Los Angeles, social conflicts took on a more explicitly multiracial dimension. "It was a foregone conclusion," remarked Carey McWilliams, "that Mexicans would be substituted as the major scapegoat group once the Japanese were removed." Hostility toward Mexican Americans surfaced in summer 1942, building toward the Sleepy Lagoon trial and boiling over in the following year's zoot suit riots. These events forced both community activists and leaders of the political establishment to develop ideas and plans for interracial organizing. The two groups respectively espoused bottom-up and top-down visions of racial integration that held together in fragile alliance during the war.[23]

On January 12, 1943, following a trial fraught with irregularities, seventeen Mexican American youths alleged to be gang members were convicted of crimes related to the death of a man found by an Eastside mud reservoir known as "Sleepy Lagoon." Spurred by sensational media reports of an urban crime wave caused by *pachucos*—Mexican gang members—prosecutors charged that Mexicans were prone to violence and criminality owing to the Aztec warrior blood pulsing through their veins. The sheriff's office further asserted that Indians possessed "Oriental characteristics, especially so in [their] utter disregard for the value of life." Quite incredibly, therefore, Mexican Americans bore the burden of racist stereotyping of at least three different cultures. Responding to the convictions, the *California Eagle* asserted, "In Los Angeles, it is the Mexican minority which faces the most vicious discrimination, its contribution to the war effort brutally circumscribed, its youth hounded by police, its citizenship and loyalty attacked." The newspaper urged African Americans to take the struggle of the Sleepy Lagoon defendants to heart. "Why are we Negroes interested in what happens to our Mexican neighbors?" it posed. "Well, we've had a lot of experience along the same lines. We've felt the whip-lash of oppression and we know how and where it stings. Besides, it would be us if the Mexicans weren't more convenient. It's us in Harlem and Detroit. It's us in Meridian, Miss. It's us on that damn bridge from which six Black bodies hung." Charlotta Bass called on African Americans to donate money to the Sleepy Lagoon Defense Committee, write protest letters to elected officials, and learn more about the case by reading the committee's pamphlet. A multiethnic community campaign led by the Sleepy Lagoon Defense Committee, initiated by CPUSA member LaRue McCormick and chaired by Carey McWilliams, helped win a reversal of the convictions in October 1944.[24]

As the defendants languished in jail during the spring of 1943, Black leaders fretted that rising tensions would lead to an outbreak of interracial violence. Their concerns especially heightened when an LAPD officer

shot and killed thirty-six-year-old African American defense worker
Lenza Smith in the Central Avenue district on May 23. Having seen
Smith shot in the back, a large crowd gathered around the scene to protest
the police actions. Meeting the next day, the NAACP condemned the
"police killing of an unarmed man who had committed no crime." But
the officer faced no charges, and the only eyewitness willing to come forward and dispute the police account was never called to testify. Instead,
three African American men among the onlookers were arrested and convicted of "inciting a riot." William E. Harrison, a deacon and World War
I veteran, was severely beaten in the police station until his face was reportedly "swollen on one side into a huge brown knot." He accused one cop of
threatening to kill him for being "one of those smart Eastern n——s . . .
down on Central Avenue listening to a bunch of Russian Communists who
are trying to convince you that the American white people aren't treating
you all right." Working with the NAACP and the CIO Anti-Discrimination
Committee, the Negro Victory Committee mobilized fifteen hundred
people (including non-Blacks) for a mass meeting to protest police misconduct. "We're here to tell the officer who beat and cursed Deacon
William Harrison that we don't need any 'Reds' to tell us that white folks
sometimes don't treat us right," declared NVC leader Clayton Russell.
Contending that authorities were engaged in "a deliberate effort to goad
the Negro people into rioting and bloodshed," Russell warned that the
state would use a riot as a pretext for repressive measures to erode the
gains the community had won through wartime activism. Charlotta Bass
linked police brutality against Blacks to the multiracial "smear of 'zoot
suits.' " Through "an organized effort to stimulate prejudice against minority groups," the corporate media had generated "a steady stream of
colored news to hold up the Mexican and Negro communities as dens of
corruption, vice, murder and sabotage." Demonstrating a tragically un-
canny ability to keep her finger on the pulse of the community, Bass headlined her June 3 editorial "NO RIOT HERE!" It was published the very day
the zoot suit riots broke out.[25]

The disturbance reportedly began with an altercation between off-duty
sailors and a group of Mexican Americans in East Los Angeles. Returning
that evening, the sailors broke into a movie theater and randomly assaulted youths, especially targeting those wearing flashy "zoot suits." By
cracking down only on Mexican Americans, the police signaled that it
was open season on pachucos. The following night two hundred sailors
cruised through the Eastside in taxis, jumping out regularly to beat local
youths. The riot lasted a total of five days, during which time thousands
of sailors, soldiers, and civilians joined the hunt for "zoot suiters" before
military police and shore patrol intervened to quell the violence. Although
a majority of the victims were Mexican Americans, Blacks and Asians

were attacked as the disturbance spread. In one instance, shipyard worker Lewis W. Jackson, a recent African American migrant from Louisiana, found himself surrounded by two hundred soldiers and sailors as he walked down East First Street to his Little Tokyo home. One assailant held him down while another gouged his eye out with a knife. Jackson was left lying on the street to die until a passerby called an ambulance.[26]

In the aftermath of the riots, progressive Black leaders saw a necessity and opportunity to expand the bases and prospects for social change. How the grass roots actually responded is difficult to assess. A rather pessimistic Loren Miller suggested, "Negroes very probably increased their contempt of Mexicans because they thought the Mexicans did not fight back enough." But regardless of whether this represented a majority view, the fact that prominent African Americans were publicly advocating multiracial organizing was a historic development. Charlotta Bass fired off a letter to Mayor Fletcher Bowron demanding he take action against divisive elements that were terrorizing communities of color and damaging the war effort. The Junior Council of the NAACP teamed with the Mexican Youth Defense Committee to launch the Working Youth Committee to End Discrimination Against Minorities. Its first meeting attracted "Mexican, Jewish, Negro, Chinese, church, school, and civic leaders." Not to be outdone, the People's Victory Market issued an inspiring statement declaring "SALUDOS AMIGOS!" Chastising the "bald-faced lie" that Mexicans were biologically predisposed to criminality, it called for "an intelligent rehabilitation program, fitting delinquent youth into America's war for survival, enabling them to understand that 'the whole world' is not against them." Later in June, two thousand persons at a mass meeting of Negro Victory movement forces agreed to demand justice for riot victims, disciplining of officers, and a removal of all racist elements from the military. Clayton Russell, who had grown up in multiethnic Boyle Heights, asserted that the rioting had taught "a great lesson" to African Americans. "It has welded us ever closer to the Mexican community of this city," he remarked. "That is good, for one of the clear requisites for victory is the unity of all minority groups, Jews, Chinese, Negroes, Mexicans and the oppressed people of the world."[27]

The war had transformed the consciousness of Negro Victory movement leaders, such that they now viewed the empowerment of other oppressed peoples as not only consistent with Black advancement but indeed a requirement for it. As Penny Von Eschen has highlighted, this expansive view of Black struggle arose in part from the fostering of an anticolonial consciousness by figures like Paul Robeson working through the Council on African Affairs. In front of a standing room only Los Angeles crowd in September 1942, Robeson had proclaimed, "We, the great mass of Negro people, are a part of that common humanity which is today fighting for a new world. If this war means anything, it means we should no longer ask for favors from above, but that we should fight to enter a new world whose millions shall determine their own destiny." Robeson's audience resolved to support not only Indian independence and the opening of a second front but also the arming of the people of Africa for participation in the war against fascism and for their "full democratic rights." The following year, the *Eagle* reported that "hundreds of colored citizens" enthusiastically listened to Madame Chiang Kai-shek discuss "Democracy and interracial understanding," as the NVC organized Black support for the repeal of the Chinese Exclusion Act. But although informed by world events, African American activists in Los Angeles were responding at least as much to the demands of struggle on the multiracial domestic terrain. An ongoing feud between Charlotta Bass and A. Philip Randolph was fueled in large measure by the former's embrace of the Popular Front orientation and the latter's scorn for the CPUSA. Yet it ultimately manifested itself as a debate on the propriety of Randolph's assertion that the March on Washington movement must be "all-Negro." Negative experiences with the CPUSA inside the National Negro Congress had led him to the conclusion that excluding whites was necessary to preserve Black political independence. Bass, of course, courted relations with white leftist allies, but she also asserted that Randolph's vision was constrained by a bipolar framework of race relations. Making a case for multiracial solidarity, Bass argued that the African American community could achieve its goals "only by welcoming with open arms other minorities willing to work with us." In February 1943, her *California Eagle* declared, "The 70,000 Negroes, 250,000 Mexicans and 125,000 Jewish citizens of this county of Los Angeles represent a force capable of determining great things in the Southland." Notable for their absence from this statement were Japanese Americans. The city's most notorious outcasts, they must still have seemed a liability to some Black proponents of multiracial organizing. But this was also about to change. In fact, Japanese Americans would enter into the *Eagle*'s political calculus the following year.[28]

Placed into context with the Detroit riots and other race-based conflicts, the zoot suit riots that spurred Black progressives like Bass to demand multiracial organizing provoked a simultaneous sense of urgency among the political establishment. Until quite recently, public officials had most often ignored or encouraged racism. But given the disruptive effect of home front tensions during the war, they began putting their names on record against racial hatred. Moreover, white supremacist outbursts against Mexican, Asian, and African Americans embarrassed the United States in its relations with international allies and provided fodder for pro-Axis forces. Hence, all levels of government took up the cause of improving race relations. With more than a hundred local, state, and national commissions springing up by the end of 1943, interracialism, in the words of historian Harvard Sitkoff "became an overnight fad." In January 1944, Mayor Bowron expanded his Negro advisory committee into the multiracial Committee for Home Front Unity, and Los Angeles County established its own interracial committee shortly thereafter. In a sign of their political clout, Negro Victory leaders comprised half of the mayor's twelve original committee appointees. Five others were white, including the city's Catholic bishop and a Jewish lawyer. None were Asian. Despite the fact that he had been particularly prompted by the zoot suit riots, Bowron appointed only one Mexican American. The committee's composition provided rough evidence that the city's white elites saw "home front unity" primarily as a biracial concern and judged African Americans best suited among the minorities for political leadership. Believing governmental action was required to spur the changes they envisioned, civil rights activists cheered the formation of the interracial committees they had long requested. Yet, as Carey McWilliams argued, they were created largely in a fit of "crisis patriotism." Their ultimate mission was not to empower communities of color but merely to assuage social tensions.[29]

The struggle over discrimination within the Los Angeles Railway (LARY) highlighted both the significance of state intervention and the limits of "crisis patriotism." Through an arrangement between LARY management and the AFL's Amalgamated Association of Street and Electric Railway and Motor Coach Employees of America Local 1277, African Americans were limited to menial positions at the city's primary mass transportation company. Since none worked as operators, the Negro Victory coalition took aim at LARY during its December 1942 mass meeting. Wary that "semi-official Negro groups" were scheming to cut a deal with management for "token employment," Charlotta Bass proposed a mass march on LARY headquarters. Arguing it was "no accident that employment of Negroes in aircraft industries has boomed," she declared, "The railway fight has become a struggle of the people. Let them fight it!" Eschewing a traditional march, the coalition held a New Year's Eve win-the-war rally. Ethel Waters sang the national anthem, while Clarence Muse and other African American entertainment stars joined her onstage. Legendary boxing champion Jack Johnson showed up and cheered, "I was proud of my boys before. I am proud of them today." As activists sold $62,000 worth of war bonds, Clayton Russell declared LARY's discrimination against "loyal, patriotic, Negroes" was depriving defense workers of transportation and endangering national security. After holding two more "giant mass meetings," the NVC garnered a pledge of support from the Minorities Division of the War Manpower Commission and an agreement by the AFL Railway Employees to help end discrimination at LARY. In exchange, the NVC promised to back the railway union's fight for higher wages.[30]

In response, LARY began a gradual process by upgrading a few Black workers in February 1943. Resentful of the agreement made by their union leaders, however, white rank-and-file workers walked off the job at LARY. They joined a wave of "hate strikes" against the hiring or upgrading of African American workers that swept the nation during the war. Thousands of white workers struck at plants like Detroit's Packard Main, Cincinnati's Curtis-Wright, and Toledo's General Motors. To appease the hate strikers, LARY ceased upgrading African Americans. Both the union and management claimed that if the upgrading program resumed, 90 percent of white workers would strike again. When the FEPC asked LARY to upgrade some Black workers voluntarily, the company played the patriotism card just as the NVC had. It contended that complying with the FEPC request would *"seriously jeopardize the continued operation of our transportation*, which [was] so vital to the defense industries." The company's lawyer stated, "Our employees with very few exceptions have indicated a firm intention to quit work if we engage Negroes for platform service." Discrimination against African American workers thus continued well into 1944. Even though the streetcars were operating at half their capacity and the War Manpower Commission designated the situation a top priority concern, LARY continued to reject hundreds of Blacks referred by the USES. Nona Slayden, a twenty-six-year-old African American woman, had worked as a conductor in San Francisco. Disregarding her experience, a LARY representative told her, "The Negro is happier in domestic service." Another Black applicant asserted, "They gave me a driving test and I drove longer and better than the white fellow, but when the instructor told me the results he said I had not passed."[31]

As the conflict intensified, local and federal government officials were pushed to take bolder action. African American community leaders pressed the FEPC to hold hearings on the LARY matter. Worried such hearings would inflame tensions and draw negative publicity to the city, Mayor Bowron balked. In yet another display of its preference for voluntary action, the FEPC allowed him time to negotiate a settlement. Accepting management's claim that it was willing to upgrade African Americans if the hostility of white workers could be stemmed, Bowron worked with the nongovernmental Council for Civic Unity on a plan to educate the LARY workforce. Hollywood screenwriters were commissioned to draft scripts promoting the acceptance of upgraded Black workers as a patriotic duty. Olivia DeHavilland, Rex Ingram, and Orson Welles, as well as officers from the army and navy, agreed to address the white LARY workers. But rejecting the scripts as "too inflammatory" and "too Red," the union torpedoed the mayor's plan. Catholic bishop Joseph T. McGucken, chair of the mayor's Committee for Home Front Unity, warned that "racial tensions that have caused no small degree of alarm among civic-minded people here in Los Angeles [were] being dangerously aggravated by discrimination in employment." Rumors spread that an African American "Bumpers" gang, incensed at LARY's intransigence, was attacking white conductors and patrons on streetcars passing through the Central Avenue district. FBI director J. Edgar Hoover noted that the LAPD placed blame for the incidents on "the 'hoodlum' type of Negro recently migrating from southern States." Declaring they had been especially targeted by the "Bumpers," white women conductors led nearly two hundred female LARY employees who now vowed to strike if Blacks were upgraded. While it is true that some racial tensions did surface on LARY streetcars, the notion of a systematic intimidation campaign by African Americans may have stemmed from white hate strike advocates attempting to portray themselves as the real victims. Nevertheless, the rumors stoked federal officials' fears of the growing potential for another race riot just as FEPC staff members became convinced LARY management was acting out of racial prejudice.[32]

These concerns finally led the FEPC to order hearings on the LARY matter, which began on August 8, 1944. Several days prior, the federal government had halted the hate strike of white Philadelphia transit workers by declaring their walkout illegal and threatening to replace the strikers with soldiers, cancel their draft deferments, and prevent them from being reemployed in war-related jobs. With the Philadelphia settlement lending extra gravity to its actions, the FEPC soon convinced LARY and the Railway Employees union to agree not to discriminate against African Americans. By June 1945, though the majority of Black workers remained car cleaners and janitors, African Americans comprised 113 of 2,016 operators. Stirring the emotions of thousands of African Americans in Los Angeles, the LARY struggle had achieved a major victory in the fight to break down Jim Crow employment practices. The *Sentinel*'s Leon H. Washington hoped the LARY settlement would lead to the creation of "a model plan for the integration of Negroes."[33]

As wartime mobilizations gave rise to a variety of new coalitions and bolstered the political stature of African Americans, racial integration—a concept scarcely articulated before the war—had pushed its way into the center of public policy concerns. Facing near total exclusion at the outset of war, Black workers had opened doors throughout the defense industries. Moreover, politicians, union leaders, and the mainstream media were now paying attention to the voices and concerns of African Americans like never before. The war, however, had produced two contrasting models of integration. Progressive Negro Victory activists championed grassroots mobilization, multiracial solidarity, and social democratic reform. Commenting in September 1945 on the close working relationship that these "high quality" Black leaders had developed with "the liberal-labor-progressive forces," writer Carey McWilliams proclaimed, "It is my firm conviction that the Negro community in Los Angeles is destined to write a new chapter in the history of the Negro in urban communities in America." Establishment figures, however, took a different perspective. Mayor Bowron argued that integration should proceed voluntarily through educational efforts to increase white tolerance of minorities. Yet the federal government's breakdown of the hate strikes in Philadelphia and Los Angeles strongly suggested that antidiscriminatory measures required firm state intervention. Where there were no teeth behind its orders, the FEPC had made little headway. When the AFL's Boilermakers refused to appear at the agency's November 1943 Los Angeles hearings, for example, the FEPC remarked that it had no power to compel them to do so. Called to answer charges of racial discrimination, the union snubbed the FEPC seemingly without fear of reprisal. In addition, whereas the FEPC secured an April 1944 agreement with Northrop Aircraft to end discrimination, one year later it had yet to achieve the hiring of the first African American at the company's Hawthorne plant.[34]

In the end, the Black community by itself lacked the ability to define the future direction of integration, which would instead be shaped by struggles at the level of both state action and grassroots action. While Japanese Americans had been excluded from residence in Los Angeles during the formative years of the Negro Victory movement, their impending return promised to complicate even further the multiracial context in which these struggles would take place.

CHAPTER 7

Bronzeville and Little Tokyo

"No state in the union, not even the most unreconstructed southern one, faces the enormous and complicated racial problem California will have for some time," the *Los Angeles Tribune* argued in June 1946. "The South mainly just has Negroes and antebellum whites. California has Negroes, whites, Japanese, Mexicans and Chinese, all of whom must learn to live together, or the whole shebang might as well be chucked on a KKK bonfire." Like many other representatives of Black Los Angeles in the 1940s, the *Tribune* came to the conclusion that the problems of African Americans were situated within a multiracial matrix. The issue of Black-Japanese relations drew particular attention as the communities' previously divergent wartime trajectories collided in the overlapping geographies of Little Tokyo and Bronzeville. During the internment, Black business owners and thousands of recent African American arrivals to the city had taken root in spaces previously occupied by Japanese Americans.[1]

As the intersection of the "Negro problem" and the "Japanese problem" could not be evaded, the real question was whether it would produce more interethnic cooperation or conflict. In practice, conscious efforts to promote cooperation stemmed mainly from efforts to avoid overt instances of conflict. Opportunistic white politicians and sensationalistic corporate media outlets raised public alarm that the return of Japanese Americans to a Little Tokyo occupied by Blacks would incite a riot. Through projects such as Common Ground, African American and Nisei leaders worked with their respective communities to promote interracial education and forums for cross-cultural interaction. Although some quarrels broke out between Black and Japanese American individuals, the vast majority of Little Tokyo/Bronzeville denizens coexisted with nothing more than differences of opinion. Frequently reflecting the frustration of oppressed subjects lacking the power to rework the dominant social order, these differences of opinion, however, were significant. While some Japanese Americans felt that Blacks had taken no stand against the internment, Blacks in turn accused Japanese Americans of neglecting to support civil rights struggles. These frictions resulted in part from each group's relative ignorance of the other. What both needed most to appreciate was how the racialization of World War II had respectively positioned them in relation to the nation-state.

As the nation's white majority contemplated the incorporation of its minorities, integration connoted conflicting notions to Black and Japanese Americans in the war's immediate aftermath. For the former, integration was a progressive vision thrust forward by the Negro Victory movement. It had emerged from a participatory struggle of the African American working class to end racism and fight for jobs and dignity. State intervention was deemed the crucial force to ensure fair treatment. Though they often needed to be pushed to act, white liberals were assumed to be natural allies in the quest for social democratic reform. Integration, however, was an alien concept to the vast majority of Japanese Americans, who were behind barbed wire when the Negro Victory movement and interracial efforts to fight racism had been launched. Moreover, Japanese Americans had been taught to fear official power, making them at best suspicious of an interventionist state. They became equally suspicious of the motives of white liberals, whose "integration" plans struck many Japanese in Los Angeles as compulsory assimilation. Ultimately, the quest to improve multiethnic relations in Little Tokyo/Bronzeville demonstrated both the expansive vision of solidarity and civic unity that had arisen from the war, as well as the limits of an integrationism that seemed forced and imposed.

THE NEIGHBORHOOD OF LAST RESORT

"This is Bronzeville. Watch us grow." These signs, produced by the Bronzeville Chamber of Commerce, filled storefront windows and marked the African American presence in the neighborhood in 1943. When the removal of Japanese Americans began, there had been some talk of turning Little Tokyo into the city's "Latin Quarter," which would be both a center of Mexican American life and a conduit for inter-American trade. But these plans never came to fruition. Instead, Black business owners seized the opportunity. Considered the pioneer of Bronzeville, Leonard Christmas purchased the one-hundred-room Digby Hotel. Several others followed course, including Clara Brown. A New Orleans transplant, Brown advertised that her "group of serious, progressive women" investors had taken "just thirty-two breathtaking days" to transform a Japanese retailer's East First Street premises into the "first Negro department store in the Far West." Other Black southern migrants operated restaurants, barbershops, laundries, and hotels. Perhaps the aspect of Bronzeville most often recalled today is its nightlife. The district featured dance spots, such as the Samba Club and Finale. Above all, club goers were drawn to Shepp's Playhouse, an elaborately decorated place that hosted early bebop performances by Charlie Parker and Miles Davis among others. As noncommercial institutions also changed from Japanese to Black American hands, the Los Angeles Hompa Hongwanji Buddhist Temple leased its property to Providence Baptist Church. A similar process of transition occurred in West Jefferson, as well. In an act it characterized as "Turning Crisis Into Opportunity," the African American congregation of Trinity Baptist took control of Centenary Methodist Church. Trinity's pastor recognized a "moral obligation [to] safeguard Japanese interests" in the property, but he simultaneously noted that the church was "proceeding on the assumption that the Japanese [would] never be back in this area in large enough numbers to justify a property of this magnitude." Former beautician Gail Thompson took over the Taiki Cafe and maintained the Chinese food menu of its previous Issei operators. Gail's Chop Suey boasted that its frequent Chinese patrons complimented the owner-chef for "the authenticity and taste of her dishes," which were served by a "pretty young oriental 'type' brownskin waitress . . . in a Mandarin coat and cherry blossoms." Thompson declared her team comprised "the only colored [sic] folks in the U.S. actually cooking and serving" Chinese food.[2]

Negating the optimism of Black entrepreneurs, depictions of Little Tokyo as the city's most notorious problem neighborhood quickly overshadowed Bronzeville boosterism. Southern Black working-class migrants comprised the overwhelming majority of its inhabitants. A 1943 Haynes Foundation survey of African Americans in Little Tokyo reported that 85 percent of residents had arrived within the past year, and most were between the ages of twenty and forty-four. Half had family or friends in Los Angeles, and a majority of migrants had come from either Louisiana (35 percent) or Texas (25 percent). Typically, one or two migrants settled in before sending for family members. In the middle of 1943, an estimated five thousand Black migrants per month were arriving in the city. "The people in Louisiana [are] all coming up here," declared a recent African American arrival to Bronzeville. "The white folks done got too rough." An official from the War Manpower Commission remarked that the city of Shreveport, Louisiana, had "been practically depopulated of its Negro workers as they have all been coming to Los Angeles." If pushed by southern racism, Black migrants were pulled by the prospect of a robust and relatively nondiscriminatory job market. One migrant, however, reported that he had been recruited to work as a mechanic for up to ninety cents per hour but was hired as a driver for less than half that wage. Still, the job market represented a fountain of opportunity compared to the tight and discriminatory housing market. On one occasion, after receiving but a half day's worth of applications, federal officials reported that the African American allocation of public housing units was oversubscribed. Given such chronic shortages, the Little Tokyo district, now devoid of its

Japanese founders, served as housing of last resort for many migrants and some long-term residents, as well. "Don't tell me any of that stuff about helping the negroes in this town," a Bronzeville denizen told a government official. "I been here [in Los Angeles] 25 years and I am still sleeping in doorways and theaters."[3]

The transient nature of residence in the district makes it possible only to approximate its demographics. A city agency estimated in July 1943 that 3,000 persons, mainly African Americans, were living in the former business section of Little Tokyo. In May 1944, the *Los Angeles Times*, apparently citing new data from city officials, reported that Blacks comprised the bulk of 79,800 people jammed into the neighborhood. This, however, seems a vast overstatement, since closer to 10,000 residents were living in the area before the war. Drawing from multiple sources, we can estimate that the one-square-mile Little Tokyo was home to perhaps 25,000 persons during the war. What is clear is that the district's makeshift dwellings were primarily occupied by recent Black migrants, who caused the greatest sense of panic among authorities. City health officer George Uhl hastily ordered 140 units in Little Tokyo condemned because of unsanitary conditions. Claiming the residents had caused outbreaks of venereal disease and tuberculosis, Uhl remarked, "Many of these people who come from Louisiana and Texas have no knowledge of sanitation and health standards."[4]

In the eyes of African American leaders, the city's racist housing restrictions rather than its new Black settlers were the root cause of problems in Little Tokyo-cum-Bronzeville. "With 95 percent of our town locked, bolted and barred against us," asserted the *California Eagle*, "the Negro is bound into a ghetto as fast as any which binds the Jewish people in Germany today." State action had forcibly removed Japanese Americans from Los Angeles, and racism now confined desperate Black families to the degraded spaces they had vacated. "In the rancid, rat-infested area once known as 'Little Tokyo,'" the *Eagle* further remarked, "the great migration of Negroes from all over the nation is finding a home, one reeking with filth and dilapidation." Although a certain level of crowding could not be avoided during the war, the federal government was in fact rushing to meet the housing needs of defense workers. But it did nothing to prevent the maintenance of separate and unequal residential patterns. While thousands of African American workers were squeezing into shacks, sheds, and storefronts, thousands of whites given a helping hand by the government were moving into new suburban homes with modern amenities.[5]

Although most other urban centers received federal funds mainly for public housing construction, discriminatory private developers received vast portions of the wartime housing largesse directed to Los Angeles.

Boosted by Federal Housing Administration subsidies legislated by the 1941 Housing Act, Fritz B. Burns built and sold thousands of Westside homes. As historian Greg Hise has documented, these new homes were strategically sited near new mass-production airframe assembly facilities that were built in outlying areas to maximize accessibility to landing strips. Through the construction of vast suburban housing tracts, the developer sought to uplift "industrious" workers to a middle-class standard of living. A leading figure in the Los Angeles Realty Board, Burns—much like Walter Leimert and other contemporaries—assumed that racial segregation was necessary for healthy communities. In conjunction with postwar business partner Henry Kaiser, he would go on to develop massive neighborhoods like Panorama City, located near General Motors's San Fernando Valley plant, which opened in 1948. This pattern of uneven and racially discriminatory development, however, was set in motion during the war. Adjacent to the airport and aircraft plants on the city's far Westside, Westchester exemplified the sort of pervasive exclusion, championed by Burns, that flew directly in the face of the wartime civic unity discourse. To be certain, its entry-level offerings were not lavish. They provided the rising population of industrial workers access to cozy ranch houses built on small lots with backyards scarcely large enough for fathers to pitch batting practice to little leaguers. Still, nonwhites were completely shut out. As Westchester's total population skyrocketed from 353 to 33,459 persons between 1940 and 1950, the percentage of people of color living there declined from 5.3 percent to a negligible 0.1 percent. In the mid-1950s, a white owner refused to sell his Westchester house to James H. Kirk despite the fact that the prospective African American buyer was a professor and chair of sociology at a nearby college. "One of the paradoxes of my position," Kirk retorted, "is that I can teach at Loyola which is in Westchester, but I'm not allowed to live in Westchester."[6]

Meanwhile, the long fight against housing restrictions continued in established neighborhoods without decisive victory. As wartime rationing set strict limits on new home construction, the influx of migrants caused a severe housing shortage that strengthened the resolve of white neighborhood exclusionists. In places like Watts and Venice, white residents demanded that proposed public housing projects exclude people of color. In South Los Angeles, a white homeowners' association drove African Americans Henry and Anna Laws out of the house they built in 1942. For three years, civil rights advocates battled proponents of restrictive covenants until the municipal court ordered the Laws to vacate in November 1945. Defying the order, the Laws were sent to jail for living in their own home. Proving that no Black homeowner was untouchable, perhaps the only case drawing greater publicity was that of the star-studded inhabitants of "Sugar Hill," a collection of mansions on Harvard and

Hobart streets in Adams Heights (north of West Jefferson). Long after the city's wealthiest late-nineteenth-century residents had founded the neighborhood, some of their descendants sold aging homes during the 1930s to actresses Hattie McDaniel, Louise Beavers, and Ethel Waters; actor Ben Carter; musician Noble Sissle; insurance executive Norman Houston; and about a dozen other African American households. Outraged white neighbors moved to extend old and expiring racial restrictive covenants for another century. Real estate attorney Le Compte Davis ("a stout gentleman from Kentucky") rallied a gathering of over one hundred whites to the cause of restrictions. "Your wife and children will be safe," he declared. "You won't see a big Black man there, you won't have to feel any fear for your children." When the campaign failed to produce unanimous white support, white property owners sued Black residents to chase them out of the neighborhood. The cases drew increased public attention to restrictive covenants, which Negro Victory activists denounced during the war as "sabotage." In response, civic leaders provided an educational platform to civil rights lawyers like Loren Miller but took no concerted action. Left largely in the hands of the court, the racial covenant cases would not be fully resolved until the federal Supreme Court outlawed their enforcement in 1948.[7]

While ending Westside patterns of exclusion eluded their grasp, Negro Victory activists sought governmental action to enhance the quantity and quality of Eastside housing. Pushing the Los Angeles Housing Authority to meet the needs of Black defense workers, a coalition of community leaders declared in September 1943 that "the 'Little Tokyo' Negro neighborhood [was] a threat not only to the health of its Negro occupants, but to all the people of Los Angeles." In the aftermath of the zoot suit riots, city officials responded primarily within the context of crisis aversion. First, with Mayor Bowron declaring that Little Tokyo was struck by "very extreme and complex problems . . . almost beyond description," the city initiated antislum measures in early 1944. In addition to condemning buildings and removing their occupants, health officials aggressively screened Bronzeville residents for syphilis and gonorrhea. Black leaders cooperated with both efforts. The *Eagle* was encouraged to find that condemned buildings were being "rehabilitated and re-occupied." Charlotta Bass, moreover, stated that she would be checking in with local doctors on a regular basis to see how many persons had been treated. She even called on her readers to report neighbors who were ill. Second, the city housing authority chairman promised to "liberalize" race restrictions on public housing that had been determined on the basis of prewar population patterns. Following a mass meeting of fifteen hundred community residents in December 1942, the Negro Victory movement pressured the agency to raise its African American quota. A Black female defense worker, the wife of a disabled man and mother of six children, testified that she lived in a condemned building in the Central Avenue district that was infested by cat-size rats. Despite vacancies at the Pico Gardens housing project, she was denied housing because the "Negro quota" was full. Though slow to act, officials were driven by consistent agitation from Black activists and their own fears of unrest to open up additional units. By February 1946, African Americans occupied 27 percent of the city's 11,170 units of public housing. By this time, however, Japanese Americans released from internment camps had boosted the demand for housing.[8]

JAPANESE AMERICANS RETURN

After a tidal wave of racist clamoring had prompted the internment in 1942, mass detention did little to calm public officials who were continuing to pound away at the "Japanese problem." The following year, a new wave of anti-Japanese agitation crested as the army began inducting Nisei deemed "loyal" and the War Relocation Authority (WRA) moved to resettle other "loyal" adult Nisei for schooling in the Midwest and East Coast. Aided by the mainstream media, prominent officials railed against the specter of Japanese Americans returning to California. John L. DeWitt, commanding general of the Western Defense Command, testified to Congress in April 1943 that he would oppose "by every means" the return of any Japanese Americans to the West Coast. "A Jap's a Jap," he added. "It makes no difference whether he is an American citizen or not." Italians and Germans in America posed no serious threat in DeWitt's eyes, but the "Japs" would produce scorn until they were "wiped off the face of the map." Calling the release of internees "stupid and dangerous," the *Los Angeles Times* surmised that "as a race, the Japanese have made for themselves a record for conscienceless treachery unsurpassed in history." Civic organizations old and new took up "Jap-hating" as a virtually full-time occupation. "Oust the Japs from California Forever" went the rallying cry of the California Citizens Council. In his radio address of June 2, 1943, Los Angeles mayor Fletcher Bowron elevated his already vituperative rhetoric to new heights. "We in Los Angeles ought to know our Japs," Bowron declared. "We are not going to be fooled, if others are. And those Japanese released through warm human sympathy of the administrators of the War Relocation Authority had better not come back to Los Angeles." Unabashed, he went so far as to argue that Japanese Americans posed a threat to national security from behind barbed wire at Manzanar. With the city siphoning fresh water from the Owens Valley, the mayor fretted that potential saboteurs were being held "near the source of the domestic water supply of more than a million and a half people in Los Angeles." For the former judge, the final solution lay in intricate legal schemes he crafted to strip the Nisei of their birthright citizenship and to permanently bar all Japanese Americans from the West Coast. Although these schemes never came to fruition, the Los Angeles County Grand Jury passed a resolution in support of the first idea, and the secretary of the Los Angeles Chamber of Commerce backed the second.[9]

In the attacks on returning Japanese Americans, Black activists saw a new opportunity to express interethnic solidarity. The *California Eagle* signaled a shift in its stance on the "Japanese question" with an editorial on November 11, 1943. Apologizing for its "past omissions," it called the "persecution of the Japanese-American minority . . . one of the disgraceful aspects of the nation's conduct of the People's War." Furthermore, the *Eagle* discontinued using the pejorative term "Jap" at a time when the city's major corporate newspapers regularly labeled persons in both Japan and the United States with the epithet. Throughout the following year, *Eagle* columnist Rev. Hamilton T. Boswell devoted considerable effort to educating his readers about the problems confronting Japanese Americans and encouraging Blacks to develop greater cooperative bonds with other communities of color. He condemned "the undemocratic evacuation of Japanese-Americans" as the "greatest disgrace of Democracy since slavery." If African Americans allowed the sort of "race mongering" typified by the internment and "the zoot suit riots against Mexican people" to go "unquestioned," Boswell further asserted, they could "expect similar action against us." As they came to view multiracial solidarity as both an ideal principle lending moral force to their activism and a practical necessity of politics in Los Angeles, Blacks approached the "Japanese question" with special interest. "Nowhere else in the nation is there such an intriguing mixture of economic and social problems," declared the *California Eagle*. Under the headline "The Eyes of the World Are Focused on California," its first editorial of 1945 opined that public response to the return of Japanese Americans would determine whether the state would "live up to its tradition of democracy" or "become a breeding place for Fascism." In large measure, it echoed the line of the WRA, focusing not on whether the internment was ever justified but on the potential for Japanese American rehabilitation. In its zealousness to portray them as loyal, it argued that internees had "gladly" and "willingly" given up their homes before proving their patriotism "in the fire and smoke of battle." However, the *Eagle's* rigorous defense of the rights of Japanese Americans marked a departure from its earlier stance of complicity in the face of anti-Japanese agitation. It condemned "the usual arrogance born of ignorance and bigotry" exhibited by those insisting "that these Americans born of a different race than their own [should] not return to their former homes." By highlighting the racist nature of the opposition to internee resettlement, the *Eagle* prodded its African American readers to recognize that they stood in a common struggle with Japanese Americans.[10]

The *Eagle*'s call for Japanese Americans to reclaim "their former homes" was particularly noteworthy because the full-scale release of internees made them direct competitors with Blacks for housing amid a citywide crisis. In March 1945, Mayor Bowron announced that Los Angeles needed 114,075 more units of housing. The deficit was "unequalled in any other major city in the United States" and was "growing more acute daily." Two years later, the Los Angeles Citizens Housing Council estimated that 162,000 families in the city were living in "tents, garages, cabins, trailers, hotel rooms, or doubled-up in single-family dwellings." Black and Japanese Americans especially felt the sting of the housing crunch. "Negro families are crowded together in wholly inadequate living quarters," said the mayor. "They have filled the houses, rooming houses, hotels and even storerooms formerly occupied by Japanese." In fact, an April 1945 survey by the county revealed that the majority (6,000) of the more than 11,000 African American families lacking permanent housing were living in residences of uprooted Japanese Americans. Occupying one of the choicest of these spaces, author Chester Himes noted that he and his wife Jean were, "by the purest of luck, living in the cutest little house in L.A."[11]

Compounding the problem for internees were reports filtering back to the camps of vitriolic hatred on the West Coast. When the internment order was lifted on January 2, 1945, there were 80,000 Japanese Americans living in concentration camps under the WRA. By the end of June, only 1,100 Japanese Americans, comprising a scant 3.2 percent of the prewar population, had returned to Los Angeles County. During this period, the WRA documented thirty-four acts of terrorism against Japanese American residences on the West Coast, as assailants firebombed the homes of some returnees and shot at others. In the face of such hostility and uncertainty, so many internees chose to remain in the camps that the WRA finally forced them to leave in fall 1945. Subsequently, the Japanese American population of Los Angeles area grew to 23,000—about two-thirds its prewar size—by the start of the next year. Although violent attacks declined in frequency, restrictive covenants continued to limit housing options. In May 1946, white West Jefferson residents Bertha Kenyon and Clara McCormick successfully petitioned Judge Henry M. Willis for an injunction barring Takeshi Saito and his family from moving into their recently purchased home. One month later, the California Supreme Court upheld the ruling.[12]

Although the federal government had created a mass population of homeless Japanese Americans, neither the WRA nor local officials desired

taking responsibility for their public welfare. Isolated and politically disenfranchised, Japanese Americans struggled to find living quarters on the
margins of society. Only because he was anxious to empty the internment
camps of those least willing to leave did WRA director Dillon Myer very
reluctantly agree to set up provisional housing in Southern California.
Those most in need of publicly assisted housing included families with
young children, returning veterans, the elderly, and the infirm. During
1945, roughly three thousand Japanese Americans moved into WRA
trailer parks in Burbank, Santa Monica, Lomita, Hawthorne, El Segundo,
and Santa Ana. In March 1946, insisting these were temporary residences, the agency announced their imminent closure despite the fact that
most occupants had yet to secure permanent homes. With its director asserting there were "no real problems of importance left," the WRA began
shutting down the trailer parks, keeping only Burbank's Winona camp
open until December 1947. To force trailer residents out, the WRA intentionally kept living quarters small, cramped, and nonprivate while depriving the residents of water, electricity, and adequate latrine facilities.
A Japanese American committee representing the Lomita tenants wrote,
"Such cruel, inhuman, and uncivilized way of life should not be enforced
upon anyone!" A coalition of white religious and civic organizations
chastised the "comfortless, almost primitive conditions into which this
final evacuation has forced these people" and accused the WRA of inhu-
manely casting off a population that the state had stripped of the means of
subsistence. Dismissing these charges, Myer argued that the former internees needed to be cured of their dependence on "welfare funds." In the
end, he responded only to the angry outbursts of local politicians, who
charged the WRA with dumping the federal government's problem onto
their doorstep. While this helped forestall the final closure of the trailer
parks, it also meant that indigent returnees were persona non grata with
no possibility of integrating into the multiracial public housing that was
central to the Negro Victory agenda. Mayor Bowron insisted that he had
no resources to aid Japanese Americans and that even attempting to provide aid would be political suicide. The Burbank City Council opposed
closing Winona only because it did not want to see its residents released.
"Japs were in Burbank before the war," it declared, "and we can't handle
any more." While Los Angeles County reluctantly provided minimal relief, its Board of Supervisors demanded to be reimbursed by the federal
government.[13]

With only half the returnees securing permanent housing, Japanese
Americans resorted to makeshift housing, "doubling up," or transient
boardinghouses and residential hotels. While this harked back to the
community's Issei bachelor origins, whole families now lived in such

accommodations. When young George Takei (later to find television fame as *Star Trek*'s Mr. Sulu) returned to Los Angeles from Tule Lake in March 1946, his family called home two connected rooms in "the derelict Alta Hotel." "The walls had brown stains so old that they were starting to fade to a fuzzy beige," he recalled. "The linoleum on the floor was cracked and torn. Everything about the rooms was tired and worn out. 'It's not the Biltmore,' Daddy joked, 'but, remember, it's only temporary. I promise.'" At the start of 1946, fifteen hundred Japanese Americans lived in over thirty different hostels, another form of emergency housing. Several thousand returnees passed through the Evergreen Hostel, the city's largest such facility, operated by the American Friends Service Committee and Presbyterian Church inside a former Boyle Heights boarding school. Its stated purpose was "to provide temporarily a quiet and inexpensive place where those who return may live during the period of adjustment." For many Japanese Americans, however, the hostels were a notch below residential hotels in status. Conditions reminded families of concentration camp barracks, as even the most well-kept hostels were simply large buildings with living areas divided by standing curtains. Moreover, living in a relief shelter was considered a source of shame for some residents. The population of the hostels dropped sharply after their public funding was cut off owing to the June 1946 termination of the WRA.[14]

Squalid living conditions gave rise to widespread fears of rising delinquency, reinforcing the idea that the internment had torn apart the social fabric of the Japanese American community. The notebooks of social scientist Tom Sasaki, commissioned to study Los Angeles by the Japanese Evacuation and Resettlement Study, provide a particularly rare insight into the internal dynamics of the Japanese community during this critical period. According to Sasaki's notes, the *Rafu Shimpo*'s Henry Mori described Little Tokyo as "a breeding place for delinquents." Prostitutes and hustlers loitered in the district, and younger Nisei formed gangs. Believing the key task was getting "these boys off the streets," Nisei veteran John Yasukochi proposed forming sports leagues to keep the youths active. "If there was a gym in Japanese town," he argued, "it would be just the thing." (Nothing came of his proposal. Six decades later, activists are still fighting to secure a gym in Little Tokyo.) Concerns about delinquency were gendered, and several respondents reserved their harshest criticism for Nisei women. An Issei merchant complained, "It is not so bad for the boys, but the girls, they go out with anybody that can show them a good time, and throw money away on them. It doesn't make any difference whether they are Negroes, Mexicans, hakujins [whites]." Sasaki himself asserted that domestic workers would "do anything to get married to a fellow." He added, "They hand out left and right, because that is one way they think they can hold a fellow, and eventually marry them."[15]

SEARCHING FOR COMMON GROUND

For African Americans, the workplace had become a critical site of activism not only for economic justice but also for the forging of multiracial labor organizing. The internment, however, had precluded the possibility of Japanese American workers securing jobs in defense plants, depriving them access to the pivotal site of wartime "integration." They recalled mainly the racist behavior of organized labor rather than its more recent efforts to advance interracial unity. Thus, if unity between Black and Japanese Americans was to be built, the community rather than the factory would be the principle arena for struggle. As the end of the war approached, it was clear that two communities, Bronzeville and Little Tokyo, were standing on the same geographic location. Leaders of both groups were taken aback by rumors spread on the street and in the press that the release of Japanese Americans from the internment camps would cause tension in the district. In December 1944, Mayor Bowron led a chorus of voices warning that race riots could result from Japanese attempts to reclaim space occupied by African Americans. Bronzeville leaders, however, actively disavowed media reports linking them to anti-Japanese sentiments and promised to welcome Little Tokyo returnees. "I have nothing against the return of the Japanese [or] against any minority group," stated Rev. Leonard B. Brown of First Street Baptist Church. "I'd be crazy if I did, considering that I am a member of a minority group myself." Later that year, Bronzeville club owner Sam Evans hired "an attractive Nisei waitress" as a gesture of interethnic solidarity. Still, in August 1945, community leaders noted an incident during which "white workers had incited negroes against Japanese." The following month, social worker Samuel Ishikawa reported, "The Negroes seem to want to keep the 'Japs' from returning, and the Japanese want to 'Kick the niggers out.'" He told of African Americans who threatened to boycott Japanese businesses that did not hire Blacks and Japanese Americans who organized their own private security force to crack down on Black criminals.[16]

While tensions were prevalent below the surface, the reports of an impending riot and organized racial clashes were sensationalized. Amidst general complaints by Issei leaders of rising crime, the greatest friction seems to have been generated by the robbery of an elderly Japanese American couple, allegedly by an African American assailant. As word of the incident spread distress throughout the community, a group of Little Tokyo merchants hired two Nisei vets to patrol the district. This, in turn, spawned resentment among African Americans. Community representatives, however, settled their differences in a meeting sponsored by the Council for Civic Unity, and no similar incidents were repeated. Beyond that, some friction also resulted as control of property changed hands. In January 1945, the Hongwanji Buddhist Temple evicted the Providence Baptist Church despite the latter's contention that it had leased the property for the duration of the war. Four months later, Providence won the right to occupancy and $5,000 in damages from the court. But though it hoped to purchase the building outright, its stay, like that of most Bronzeville residents, would prove temporary. A JACL staff member confidentially admitted that some "pretty ruthless" Japanese Americans were buying leases to Little Tokyo properties and evicting Black merchants and tenants. One African American observer, however, remarked it was the "Negroes own damned fault for selling." In addition, a number of Japanese Americans were accused of setting up residential hotels as privately owned "hostels" to evade rent control laws, and some reportedly evicted Black and Mexican American tenants to complete the makeover. Community leaders became incensed at the gouging that occurred in these facilities. The JACL's Scotty Tsuchiya accused one operator of charging $40 per month for each room within a hotel he rented in total for $50 per month. Tenants refrained from protest out of fear of being evicted, but Tsuchiya himself also noted that the JACL's reliance on the support of Issei merchants precluded him from speaking out against the abuses. He instead hoped "to see some red make a big stink and turn some of these people in." The Union Church's Rev. Sohei Kowta observed that some landlords "would line up four to six in a single room and charge the individuals per bed." One Issei owner admitted privately that "easy" and "tremendous" profits could be made in the hotel business by purchasing a condemned hotel on the cheap and making "a little repair, here and there." While he asserted it was most profitable to restrict tenancy to whites and Japanese Americans, a rival insisted he preferred residents of color to "white trash."[17]

On the whole, interethnic relations in Little Tokyo/Bronzeville were cordial. A special census taken in January 1946, one year after internees began returning, found 6,800 African Americans and 1,500 Japanese Americans residing in two census tracts encompassing the district and surrounding areas. Although they outnumbered Japanese Americans, there is no evidence that Blacks acted to hamper their return. Despite the fact that many harbored racial stereotypes, Japanese American merchants relying heavily on non-Japanese patronage got along with Black customers if for none other than practical reasons. "The Japanese . . . have brains, and they don't spend their money around," an Issei drugstore

Fig. 7.1. Bronzeville/Little Tokyo. Merchant Kiichi Uyeda (posed on the far right, May 14, 1945) was reportedly the first Japanese American internee to return to the district. National Archives.

owner privately remarked in July 1946. "Mexicans and Negroes make the money, but spend it fast. That is what makes my business good now." Some African American observers in fact concurred with the sentiment that recent Black migrants, feeling flush with cash from new jobs, were especially loose spenders. Such generalizing, however, failed to take into account the reality that consumer patterns in Little Tokyo had less to do with race and more to do with the district's status as a borderline red-light district. On the basis of an interview with a longtime Black resident of the city, author R. J. Smith characterized Bronzeville as the roughest and loosest part of town, where the hustlers were "quicker, more broke," and the "pimps spoke in harsher tones." On the more upscale Westside, a Japanese American launderer said his initial image of African Americans as "dirty people" had been displaced by a perception that most were "very nice" and "very clean." In fact, he preferred doing business with Blacks rather than whites.[18]

The most concerted effort to promote unity between African Americans and Japanese Americans in Little Tokyo/Bronzeville was launched in mid-1945 by the "Common Ground Committee of Caucasians, Japanese and Negroes." It was a project of the Pilgrim House youth service agency, which a coalition of "race relations" advocates from local government, the private sector, and religious charities had formed two years prior. Responding to the perceived crisis in the "Negro district" of Little Tokyo, social workers and public health officials helped document neighborhood service needs. The Congregational Conference and Presbyterian Church, which legally controlled the home of the Japanese Union Church, offered the vacated building to house the agency. With political backing from liberals like county supervisor John Anson Ford, Los Angeles city and county governments combined resources to provide Pilgrim House's first three staff. Moving beyond service providing to engage community organizing, Common Ground was in large measure part of the wave of interracial committees created to promote home front unity in the aftermath of the zoot suit riots. Unlike those found in most parts of the nation that stressed Black and white cooperation, Common Ground promoted multiracial solidarity through sponsorship of mass meetings and conflict resolution between leaders of the different ethnic groups. This in part reflected the heightened civic role of African American community activists and their commitment to multiracial coalition building. Pilgrim House's founding director, Rev. Harold Kingsley, an extremely fair-skinned Creole, was brought over from Chicago because of his experience doing similar "interracial" work for the church back there. The agency also hired Nisei Samuel Ishikawa specifically to develop Common Ground. Part of the generation thrust into community leadership by the war, Ishikawa drew from the JACL network to identify one hundred Japanese Americans "interested in interracial activities" to assist the project. He further brought Japanese American children from the Koyasan Hostel into Pilgrim House's nursery school and reported that children of different races played together with "no prejudice toward one another." Characterizing itself as "Los Angeles' Plymouth Rock in a Drifting Community," the agency noted in its pamphlet (ca. 1946), "Although most of the children who come to Pilgrim House for their 'daily fun' are Negroes, there are some of Mexican and Caucasian origin, and the returning Japanese Americans are happy to find its doors wide open to them."[19]

These activities became the focal point of a new public relations campaign by the proponents of racial integration, who now invoked the Little Tokyo/Bronzeville story as "a miracle in race relations." In July 1946, the upstart *Ebony* magazine characterized the nonriot as "THE RACE WAR THAT FLOPPED," while noting there had "not been a single case of violence, [or] a single disturbance between the two minorities." Instead, it asserted that from "the mixture of chitterlings and sukiyaki, of jive and Japanese," a "heartfelt kinship [had] grown between the two minorities, both victims of race hate." Beyond Pilgrim House, *Ebony* told of how Blacks, Japanese, and whites ate side by side at Leonard Christmas's Digby Hotel and of how the neighborhood health clinic housed "Mexican, Chinese, Negro, Filipino, Irish, East Indian, Jewish, Gentile [and] Japanese patients, doctors, technicians and nurses." The article's depiction of multiethnic interaction was firmly rooted in reality. But like the warnings of an imminent riot, its portrayal of multiethnic harmony was exaggerated. Many liberals seem to have been especially taken in by the novelty of it all. Nevertheless, even as propaganda, these narratives likely played a role in curbing tensions if only by not exacerbating or exploiting any underlying racialized sense of mistrust that already existed. Moreover, the simple fact that Black/Japanese relations commanded so much attention represented a changing dynamic in the popular discourse of race.[20]

THE POLITICS OF INTEGRATION

Readers of *Ebony* could be forgiven for thinking that a strong political bond might have grown from the "Negro-Nisei" exchange in Little Tokyo. The reality was that little formal political cooperation of the sort developed during the early postwar years. African American observers frequently attributed this to the failure of Japanese Americans to appreciate the civil rights concerns raised by the Black struggle. For instance, a 1944 housing report from the National Urban League stated that African Americans had "fought the hardest" against housing discrimination and thus were the "most often frustrated." By contrast, it asserted, "The strong ethnic ties among Orientals have generally precluded any major attempts on their part to escape the ghetto." Some local African Americans issued harsher criticism, suggesting that Japanese Americans were betraying Black allies. Harold Kingsley remarked, "The Negroes at the outbreak of the evacuation and all through the war have been the most vocal group fighting against any discrimination focused on the Japanese." He believed that Japanese were less inclined to political protest because of their "stoic" nature, fostered by a "long history of subjugation under authority." A Black laborer in Bronzeville further contended that African Americans were "the best friends [of] the Japanese" and had repeatedly "stood up" and "spoken out" on their behalf. Yet, despite loyal Black patronage in their establishments, it seemed to him that Japanese Americans were "trying to drive the Negroes out" of the district. All three statements carried a bit of truth. Some bitter competition for space had occurred in the transition of Bronzeville back to Little Tokyo, and most of the city's Japanese residents were reluctant to join multiracial political organizations. Moreover, through the combination of such statements, a seemingly logical conclusion circulated among sectors of the Black community—instead of joining the struggle against racial segregation in the city at-large, Japanese Americans focused on reclaiming Little Tokyo from African Americans.[21]

While not rooted in racial hatred per se, such "common sense" reflected racial stereotyping. The Issei emphasis on ethnic solidarity had been part of an economic strategy fostered under historically specific conditions of racial segregation and oppression. Indeed, Black self-help proponents had often aspired to achieve the same level of unity. Furthermore, the Urban League's characterization of Japanese American housing patterns was patently false. During the interwar period, many of the city's Japanese elites had expressed the exact same desire as their Black counterparts to escape the "ghetto" and had also been drawn into struggles beside them. Without necessarily embracing the internment as policy, some African Americans had come to accept the notion of Japanese clannishness that helped justify the government's actions. Rather than ingrained cultural traits, four other factors inhibited Black and Japanese American political alliances: first, the continued weakness of both groups, despite Black wartime advances, vis-à-vis the political establishment; second, the way in which the racialization of the war drove a literal and figurative wedge between the two groups, causing them to misread each other's actions; third, the actions of white assimilationists, which led Japanese Americans to develop a negative view of "integration"; and fourth, the two groups' clashing notions about the proper role of the state in remedying social ills.

Although politicians increasingly put issues of race on their agenda, communities of color in Los Angeles with few exceptions still had little direct representation in government at any level. Given this weak overall political standing, a prospective alliance, therefore, carried the prospect of arduous struggle but few immediate rewards. The internment had created a deep sense of cynicism toward government on the part of Japanese Americans. While the African American community had more political clout and a deeper interest in politics, gerrymandered districting diminished its electoral influence. State assemblyman Gus Hawkins remained the only politician in Black Los Angeles to hold elected office at any level of government. Building on the achievements of the Negro Victory movement, the spirited but failed 1945 campaign of Charlotta Bass to become the first African American elected to the Los Angeles City Council symbolized the limits of Black political power.

Vowing to "work for the full integration of all minority groups into the life of the city," Bass advanced a social democratic vision that promised to extend the high level of state intervention and public investment that characterized the wartime political economy. She had moved considerably to the left in a short span of time. As late as 1943, Bass had "proudly worn the title Willkie Republican." Soon thereafter, however, she was alerting African Americans that the GOP was "smiling in our faces with a knife in our backs." By late 1945, she was "accused of being a Communist" simply, in her opinion, because she fought for "the rights of the people." Running for the Seventh District council seat, she dubbed herself the "Peoples Unity Candidate" in what would prove a crucial test. While the struggles of the war had given rise to a progressive conception of multiracial unity, the question remained as to whether such an agenda could actually be taken successfully to city hall. Bass highlighted her penchant "to serve all of the people of the community without regard to race, creed or color." Not only had she "led the successful [1918] campaign for employment of Negro nurses at General Hospital"; she had also led "the fight against segregated and restricted housing accommodations in the interest of people of all minority groups." In addition to her 1943 appointment as the "first Negro to serve on a local grand jury," she was "one of the earliest defenders of the 'framed' Sleepy Lagoon Boys." Borrowing the title of the popular song "Don't Fence Me In," the platform of candidate Bass grew out of her long struggle against racism yet pointedly revealed how her political views had changed. At the top of her social democratic agenda lay a goal of maintaining Los Angeles as "an industrial city with full employment" and increasing unionization. Bass further advocated public spending for construction of "large scale housing" as well as for the establishment of health clinics and child care centers; expansion of public transportation, recreational facilities, and libraries; and improvements to sanitation, streets, lighting, sewers, and the harbor. Finally, she pledged to impose price controls on utility rates and raise the wages of "the lowest paid municipal workers to a level more commensurate with the present cost of living."[22]

While Bass appealed to voters across racial lines, Black voters most of all united behind her candidacy. Through a quasi-official nomination process, a cross section of eighty-five community leaders, organized by the NAACP's Emergency Committee, settled on Bass in January 1945. Though she was a novice at electoral politics, the others who had sought the nomination from the community coalition generally endorsed Bass and expressed confidence in her abilities. As a partisan backer of its publisher, the *California Eagle* remarked, "This is the first time in the history of this community that the many interests have united and selected a candidate." The progress of the campaign brought about a level of "peoples unity" the *Eagle* deemed "beyond the fondest hopes of even the most tireless leaders." In the campaign's widest-reaching event, Paul Robeson headlined a star-studded rally drawing a reported seven thousand attendees. After promising to sing "two or three numbers," he was roused by the audience to perform an extended set capped off by crowd favorite "Ole Man River." Robeson declared the Bass campaign to be "symbolic of the struggle against racism, against Fascism that is going on all over the world."[23]

A bitter political conflict ensued. In the primary, Bass trailed incumbent Carl Rasmussen by fewer than a few thousand votes but qualified for the May runoff by finishing second. Accusing the incumbent of employing "race-baiting" tactics reminiscent of the "Nazi doctrine of persecution," the *Eagle* reported that Rasmussen was telling white residents and realtors that a Bass victory would mean death to the restrictive covenants they held dear. Notwithstanding its use of such emotional language, the *Eagle* asserted Bass would not conduct a "racial campaign." She remained convinced that an agenda targeting the general social welfare and economic needs of the community would unite the Black community and appeal to voters of other races, as well. The final tally, however, revealed Bass had lost considerable ground, and the incumbent prevailed by a two-to-one margin (16,582 to 8,386). Bass attributed her defeat to the work of the "Divide and Rule" forces who had created "a political machine of destruction" in order to prevent the incipient emergence of "*Unity in the ranks of the Negro, labor, and the liberal element.*" Declaring that Bass had built a coalition that symbolized the "determination of the people to build true unity and equality of opportunity," the *Eagle* predicted that the structures "built to support Charlotta Bass [would] endure to support the hopes and aims of the community for many years to come." This would prove to be largely the spin of a defeated campaign.[24]

Within this context of electoral failure, Black leaders further emphasized the importance of multiracial community organizing but also expressed frustration. Frequently at ideological loggerheads, the leaders of the *Eagle* and the *Los Angeles Tribune* could at least agree on the principle of Black/Japanese solidarity, though their views of why it had foundered differed. In August 1945, the *Eagle* called for Asians, Jews, Mexicans, and whites to join the NAACP. Such a proposal at the time, however, was little more than idealism. No mass membership organization brought Black and Japanese Americans together citywide. In her memoir released in 1960, Charlotta Bass lamented "the continuing failure on the part of the major Negro organizations to establish fully cooperative working relations with the main organizations of the Japanese community in our midst." Almena Davis of the *Tribune*, whose editorial content comprised an eclectic mix of anticommunism and Black nationalism, took a harsher stand. "Japanese-Negro relations do stink," she declared in September 1946. Far from seeking to feed the hysteria about interethnic conflict, Davis hoped that "unified action by Japanese and Negroes" could achieve sweeping political reforms that would serve both groups' shared interests. But she attributed blame for the failure of "attempts to integrate Japanese into Negro organizations of protest" to "indifference" on the part of Japanese Americans, whom Davis maintained held "if not contempt—certainly not effusive feeling for the Negro."[25]

Shaped by the profound social and psychological effects of exclusion and internment, Japanese American political behavior was ultimately more complex than Davis acknowledged. While African Americans would not excuse their failure to join political coalitions, Japanese Americans had not been convinced that Blacks were trusted allies. Black expressions of solidarity with Japanese Americans were potentially transformative, but they had largely been voiced *after* Japanese Americans were behind barbed wire and out of earshot. The city's Japanese community thus harbored no collective memory of Black activists fighting for its interests. It would have been interesting to see if the election of Bass, a strong potential ally, might have sparked greater Japanese American interest in local politics, but her defeat eliminated that possibility. During the early postwar years, most Japanese Americans probably believed they must confront their demons in isolation. While they bitterly resented their unjust and racist oppression, they had witnessed their protests repeatedly shut down by authorities ranging from the Los Angeles mayor to the US Supreme Court. Inside the camps, overt resistance to the internment was often channeled out of frustration and alienation into misguided Japanese nationalistic gestures. And those protesters who embraced democratic principles were shunned and neglected by the JACL and other would-be allies seeking to uphold a pristine image of Japanese American loyalty through cooperation and military service. Thus, it was Japanese Americans' marginal status more than any cultural predilection that rendered them subordinate and, in the eyes of outside observers, silent. Hisaye Yamamoto took on the burden of explaining the Nisei perspective to readers of the *Tribune*. Through an intriguing development, she had been hired as a staff writer at the end of the war in a concrete sign of Davis's commitment to promoting a cross-racial dialogue. What's more, she beat out Togo Tanaka for the job. A protofeminist with a keen critical eye and uniquely creative voice, Yamamoto was far from a typical Nisei. Nevertheless, her writings from the postwar era reflected the ambivalence with which Japanese Americans approached the issue of "race relations." The internment had severely traumatized the community and left Yamamoto "weary unto death of Race." When racist comments by white acquaintances left her speechless, she remarked, "I thought of all the cool and lovely points I might have made to persuade the man and woman of what I thought was their error. And I rued, with excruciating pains in my conscience, the hauntingly glorious specimen of Nisei womanhood I might have shown myself to be."[26]

   The strained political dialogue between Black and Japanese Americans was particularly shaped by the fact that integration meant something quite different to each respective group. The term "integration" had been put into political discourse largely by the racialization of World War II and had rarely been used previously. Its meaning was contested, such that it was less than fully embraced by Black activists. Nevertheless, most African Americans recognized that the nation was debating integration—especially following the publication of Myrdal's *American Dilemma*—because white elites had finally begun to admit that the castelike oppression of Blacks comprised the glaring contradiction undermining American democracy and national unity. At least in this regard, the focus on integration was a welcome development in the fight against white supremacy, and African American social democrats struggled for integration on their own terms. By contrast, Japanese Americans resisted "integration" because they felt it was being imposed on them by whites. While these would-be white allies hoped to increase public tolerance of the internees and aid their return to open society, they generally believed their advocacy could succeed only if Japanese Americans assimilated to Eurocentric norms. During the war, white liberals had come to a consensus that the "loyal" Japanese should be separated from the "disloyal" and released from the camps. However, they universally agreed that promoting "Americanism" necessitated tearing apart ethnic communities and breaking down what they viewed as a backward, traditional culture. Carey McWilliams, who became perhaps the most publicly outspoken white critic of the internment, embraced the notion that coercive government actions were beneficial to the degree they disrupted the "reactionary, retarding influence" of Issei family structures. These white liberals thus saw in the internment an opportunity for a grand experiment in social engineering that they regularly described as "integration." Undoubtedly, many African Americans would have had difficulty identifying with this assimilationist variant of integration.[27]

   In postinternment Los Angeles, the Japanese American encounter with integration as an everyday life experience was most directly tied to Protestant efforts to advance "interracialism." In the summer of 1945, liberal-minded whites like William Carr, Clifford Clinton, and Raymond and Gracia Booth worked with a scattering of Nisei and African Americans to form the Los Angeles Coordinating Committee for Resettlement. With a designated mission to achieve the "integration" of Japanese Americans, they particularly admired the fact that "Nisei had not segregated but had scattered into many churches" after resettling to Chicago. Such figures thus sought to enact the "Chicago plan" in their own city. But unlike individuals or couples transplanted into the Midwest, the Los Angeles returnees were largely families seeking to reclaim homes, neighborhoods, and communities they had established before the war. The white integrationists maintained that the readjustment of returnees to Los Angeles required breaking up all-Japanese congregations and opening their facilities to people of all races. Part of Japanese Americans' resistance to this form of interracialism stemmed from anti-Black prejudices some harbored, especially as they developed racial stereotypes through their interaction with transient Bronzeville residents. But the primary concern of local Japanese leaders was that their community institutions—namely the Japanese Christian Church, the Boyle Heights YWCA, and the Japanese Union Church—not be broken up by white religious leaders acting under the guise of "integration."[28]

Following the removal of Japanese Americans from the city, white authorities of the Disciples of Christ converted the Japanese Christian Church (JCC) into the "All People's Church." Founded by Issei in 1914, the JCC had moved to its Central Avenue district home at Twentieth Street and San Pedro Street in 1931. Although Japanese members had paid for the JCC's construction, ownership rested in the hands of the head church's Indiana-based United Christian Missionary Society (UCMS). The UCMS board's creation of All People's was a progressive step to promote racial integration and serve the multiethnic neighborhood surrounding the church. But its missionary nature was reflected in its top-down efforts to speed the Nisei's assimilation by eliminating the JCC and three other Japanese churches outside Los Angeles. In 1942, the UCMS appointed a young white minister from the Midwest named Dan Genung to lead All People's and also allowed him to take over the family residence of JCC head minister Kojiro Unoura. When Unoura returned after the war, the board prevented him from presiding over the church. He was relegated to serving only the older, primarily Japanese-speaking immigrant population, and Bob Kodama was hired to develop programs to integrate the Nisei into the multiethnic congregation. Genung would later write that the Issei minister was "humiliated" by this demotion. Ultimately, the tensions generated by these maneuvers were resolved with a compromise. On the one hand, a number of Nisei preferred the integrated church and embraced its idealistic mission to promote racial harmony. Some Japanese Americans such as Aki and Martha (Yaguchi) Suzuki stayed with All People's into the twenty-first century and were joined by the likes of Kei Kokubun, who replaced Genung as senior pastor in 1956. All People's became a sort of cause célèbre. Politicians like Mayor Bowron and movie stars like Ronald Reagan paid well-publicized visits to the church in the late 1940s. On the other hand, Japanese American attendance at All People's fell well short of attendance levels at the prewar JCC. The church was foundering, argued Kodama, because "the top-bracket laid a policy of non-segregation but did nothing on the action level to make it work."

Fig. 7.2. All People's Church Nursery School. A Nisei teacher with a multiethnic student group, February 4, 1950. Photograph by Toyo Miyatake Studio, Gift of the Alan Miyatake Family, Japanese American National Museum (96.267.10.3).

Japanese American members felt excluded from the decision-making process and, therefore, less enthusiastic about attending and supporting the church. Unoura was further upset that white authorities mainly pushed the Japanese to mix with "other racial minorities" while allowing whites to remain in all-white churches. A now concessionary UCMS agreed to fund the construction of the West Adams Christian Church for Japanese Americans in the Westside under Unoura's leadership. With Japanese Americans flocking to the neighborhood, the new church opened in 1948 and saw its membership peak during the late 1950s and early 1960s. But as suburbanization extended farther away from the central city, it too would eventually come to be seen as an "inner-city" church.[29]

The postwar controversy over the Boyle Heights YWCA generated perhaps even greater resentment. Unoura stated that Japanese Americans had paid "completely" for their YWCA facility and had left for the internment camps "with an understanding, in writing of course," they would repossess it when they returned. When the regional YWCA leadership sought to transform the branch into a multiracial center, Unoura argued that they had failed to "keep their word" and had acted in a manner that was "fundamentally wrong." An incensed Issei named Mrs. Sugino condemned the YWCA for implementing "their program of integration" while affording Japanese "no say in the matter." Likely releasing pent-up frustration from her wartime detainment, Sugino declared she had "lost faith in the white race." Commissioned to arbitrate the dispute, Raymond Booth, the prominent minister and leader of the Council for Civic Unity, ruled in favor of the YWCA hierarchy because he believed the prevalence of "Japanese-only" institutions was causing the Japanese community to sit passive while others engaged the fight against racism. Chastising him as "a jelly-boned man," Sugino commented in a manner that reflected not simple anger but exasperation that even white "allies" like Booth had abandoned her community. By November 1946, the YWCA had placed control of the branch back into the hands of the Japanese American leaders. Unoura, Kodama, and Sugino, however, were united in their assessment that the "integration" projects at the Japanese Christian Church and the YWCA had cost them a significant number of followers. By tending to the social needs of a community whose wounds were still fresh, the predominantly Japanese Buddhist temples drew record memberships. Their sports leagues and cultural organizations often provided the only source of recreation for Japanese Americans, whose desperate search for jobs and housing during the postwar crunch left them scarce time or space to congregate.[30]

Given the key role Pilgrim House had played in promoting harmony between Black and Japanese Americans, the conflict over the Japanese Union Church was especially significant. The Congregational Conference and Presbyterian Church, which owned the Japanese Union Church building, had offered the vacant structure to Pilgrim House during the war. Many Japanese American leaders felt the Congregational board overseeing the church had violated a "verbal agreement" to return it to its Japanese American members and was now "morally obligated" to do so. In addition, a number of the church's members were upset that goods stored there by internees had been stolen or damaged. Some (almost certainly misguidedly) held Rev. Harold Kingsley, an African American brought in from Chicago as Pilgrim House's director, responsible for the break-ins and consequently did not trust his leadership. At war's end, Pilgrim House launched another interracial church, bringing ministers Kingsley and Booth together with Nisei Royden Susu-Mago to create a novel multiracial trio to preside over services. While the church established itself for a long run in West Adams, turnout from Japanese Americans was small, causing a somewhat frustrated Susu-Mago to resettle in Hawaii. Meanwhile, the Congregational leadership alienated the Union Church's Issei members by moving Japanese-language services to the

Evergreen Hostel in Boyle Heights. Japanese members of the Union Church, however, did not reject the integrationist plans outright. In a practical sense, they had paid for only one-third of the costs of building the Union Church. Some also recognized that Pilgrim House had been doing important work. Furthermore, a specially organized interracial service in September 1946 led by Rev. Hideo Aoki generated widespread enthusiasm. At least one Issei member hailed it as one of the best services he had ever attended. Perhaps summing up the mixed general sentiments of Japanese American adult members, an Issei lay leader of the church characterized integration as a "good thing" that would take many years to become "totally successful." Japanese Americans were not "ready" for this sort of engineered race mixing while they were "still suffering from the effects of being segregated in camps." He concluded, "Many of us still want things Japanese, whether it is people, food, picture shows, etc."[31]

Local efforts to break apart the Japanese American community fell in line with the federal government's attitude toward resettlement at the national level. Forbidden from returning to California, the earliest resettled Japanese were consciously dispersed throughout the Midwest and East Coast in accordance with WRA policy. In part, this stemmed from political concerns, since no elected official welcomed the idea of disgruntled constituents clamoring about how he had let "Japs" overrun his district. President Franklin D. Roosevelt believed that sending "one or two families to each county" would "constitute a great method of avoiding public outcry." However, those who believed they were acting primarily out of benevolence were the most ardent advocates of dispersed settlement. Embracing the WRA's position, the predominantly white Committee on Resettlement of Japanese Americans gave the following instructions to its supporters: "Special attention should be given to the development of a sound program to prevent the formation of a 'Little Tokyo' or segregated district in your community. Do not plan large functions for the benefit exclusively of the Japanese Americans." Through these resettlement programs begun by whites, Nisei internees pursuing education and work were released to Midwest and East Coast destinations. These Nisei, leaving the hostile West Coast climate, comprised the members of the community who most appreciated the humanitarian gestures some whites proved capable of making. As such, they were also the strongest supporters of "integration." By design, however, their ranks were comparatively thin in Los Angeles. In the immediate aftermath of the internment, most local Japanese Americans reacted with fear and suspicion to any application of state power, and they resented the Roosevelt appointees who had administered the concentration camps.[32]

Even Nisei reaction to the planned dispersal was decidedly mixed. On the one hand, some applauded the WRA's efforts. They especially understood that public recognition that the Nisei were even *potentially capable* of assimilation represented a paradigm shift in racial discourse. During the era of exclusion, they had been considered unassimilable. The WRA's resettlement plans may have been imperfect, but they were preferable to remaining in internment camps or returning to life under prewar conditions that gave rise to anti-Japanese hostility. While interned at Jerome, Eddie Shimano wrote, "Such dispersal resettlement, I am convinced, will go far to effect with surgical thoroughness and surgical disregard for sentiment, the integration of the Japanese into American life." Larry Tajiri added, "The Little Tokyos have been shattered and—I hope—will not be put together again." On the other hand, many Nisei leaders—uniting with the majority of the community—worried that forced assimilation measures would tear apart the economic and social support mechanisms Japanese Americans had developed under decades of oppression, while leaving them with no obvious means of survival in still harsh environments. Even the JACL's Joe Grant Masaoka remarked, "Minority members resent having 'integration' constantly dinned and preached at them. The ultimate ideal is a gradual evolution of individual adaptability and social consciousness among minority members."[33]

Conflicting Black and Japanese American views of integration were ultimately rooted in their varying appreciation of state intervention. Through the Negro Victory movement, the African American community of Los Angeles had pushed the state to act as an agent of progressive change—one that could redistribute wealth and safeguard civil rights. Interned Japanese Americans, however, had experienced the state as a repressive body. As a result, those who returned to Los Angeles in the immediate aftermath of the internment were unlikely to view such "official" integration campaigns as a natural extension of their own desires for opportunity or equality. Moreover, WRA director Myer, representing a position widely held within the Roosevelt administration, sought the integration of Japanese Americans into society so they would not become an intractable burden on the state, as he believed American Indians had become. (As head of the Bureau of Indian Affairs, Myer would later promote "termination" of reservation life.) The WRA director concluded that it was not his or the government's place to assist those who, "after four years of living in barracks in relocation centers, had become institutionalized to that type of living." Given his admission that the government itself was responsible for Japanese Americans being reduced to wards of the state, Myer's was a heavy-handed posture. Nevertheless, the state's refusal to entertain postinternment calls for remedial action undermined the likelihood that Black and Japanese Americans would seek common policy solutions for problems they shared, such as the pressing need for affordable housing.[34]

Fears of state intimidation hung over the Japanese community in early postwar Los Angeles. While several political organizations briefly emerged, the internment had a chilling effect on activism. A small group of Issei initiated the Civil Rights Defense Union to wage campaigns for naturalization rights and to fight state confiscation of land from Issei accused of circumventing the Alien Land Laws. Cleared of charges after fourteen months in federal prison, former Heart Mountain draft resister Kiyoshi Okamoto launched Fair Play United in 1946 to continue the struggle for citizenship rights. Both groups emerged from challenges to authority, but neither was able to get far off the ground. One community leader remarked in September 1946 that many Issei feared restarting or joining organizations of any kind because the FBI was "constantly watching" them. A dentist in Little Tokyo added his concern that rising anticommunist repression made life even harder for activists. Whether these suspicions were true, the fear they generated was all too real.[35]

By the time a coalition of Black and Japanese American social democratic activists found common cause, local government planners had largely sealed the fate of Little Tokyo/Bronzeville. Pilgrim House's demise served as a microcosm of the devastating toll postwar redevelopment would take on communities of color. The Japanese Union Church allowed the multiethnic organization to share its building until early 1949. Throughout this period of uncertainty, it desperately lobbied for public support of its efforts to secure a permanent site. "Pilgrim House is a port of entry, of interpretation, of adjustment, a proven instrument for preventing racial friction," the youth agency argued. "We are also the only playground as well as community center for about 5,000 people; 150 children a day use our facilities." But as the city condemned a large swath of the area for development of a new civic center, Pilgrim House was twice uprooted from nearby locations. Director Kingsley again reached out to city and state officials to help the agency survive this trauma. The slated demolition "would take away the only center for the underprivileged" in the densely populated district. Its pleas unheeded, Pilgrim House held a closing ceremony on October 15, 1950. It shut its doors the next day, never to recover. In its place, the LAPD erected a parking garage.[36]

The most significant effects of government efforts to clean up Little Tokyo both during and after the war proved to be demolition and eviction. When the city condemned property near First and San Pedro in the spring of 1949 to develop new LAPD headquarters, it ordered the eviction of twenty-five hundred of the area's residents. Over half were African American; the rest were mainly Japanese American. A new formation, the Nisei Progressives, organized resistance to the evictions. Led by Sakae Ishihara, Art Takei, and Sue Kunitomi, this grouping provided the best glimpse of the postwar Nisei left that emerged for a fleeting moment during and immediately after Henry Wallace's third-party presidential campaign of 1948. Pledged to "further the economic, political and social rights" of Japanese Americans, the new organization resolved to fight for immigration and naturalization rights and for the redress of internee losses. Also committed to a broad agenda of "peace, prosperity and freedom for all," the Nisei Progressives prioritized instituting a new FEPC, creating affordable housing, and ending restrictive covenants. Generally born a half generation after those in the prewar Doho, members of the Nisei Progressives seem to have been politicized more by the internment experience and less by the Bolshevik revolution. They worked with other Progressive Party organizers to raise awareness of the problems brought about by the civic center redevelopment and to bring a multiracial coalition together in the San Pedro Tenants' Committee. In response to their demands, Mayor Bowron committed the city to finding the tenants "suitable lodging" at a cost comparable to their current rent. Yet he refused to halt the evictions.[37]

Symbolizing the shifting relationship between two communities, Bronzeville was fast becoming a distant memory, and Little Tokyo's character was changing dramatically. Having been forced to submit to the internment, returning Japanese Americans were primarily concerned with being free of the most overt forms of hostility and repression. The idea of America as a tolerant and integrated multiracial nation seemed too far-fetched to them. Through the Negro Victory movement, bigger hopes and dreams had arisen among African Americans during the war. But the partial nature of wartime gains was crystal clear. Although Blacks gained new spots in Eastside public housing, the federal government poured far greater resources into subsidies for white workers buying racially restricted Westside homes adjacent to mass employment. And while politicians had begun to acknowledge African American concerns, representation at every level of government remained dominated by whites. Finally, the progressive vision of a multiracial social movement had gripped only a small segment of political actors. The events of the war had set in motion a divergence of experience between Black and Japanese American that would soon prove too wide to reconcile.

CHAPTER 8

Toward a Model Minority

IN A 1966 FEATURE FOR the *New York Times Magazine*, University of California sociologist William Petersen declared that Japanese Americans had achieved a "remarkable record" of unparalleled achievement "by their own almost totally unaided effort." "Even in a country whose patron saint is the Horatio Alger hero," Petersen concluded, "there is no parallel to this success story." As Asian American studies developed in the late 1960s, activists and scholars placed their condemnation of the "model minority" myth at the center of the field's critique of multiracial relations. This image of Japanese American "success," they argued, had been purposefully distorted and exaggerated to denigrate other communities of color for their failure to pick themselves up by their bootstraps. Although the "model minority" controversy first arose amid the social upheaval of the 1960s, the roots of this ideological construction lay in the generation prior.[1]

On December 8, 1945, General Joseph W. Stilwell, commander of the Tenth Army of the United States, delivered the Distinguished Service Cross Award to the family of Kazuo Masuda in Santa Ana, California. In response to a series of hate crimes against Japanese Americans returning to Orange County, a grouping of Christian women's organizations had arranged the popular general's highly publicized visit. Local and national media documented the heroic acts of Masuda, who died while fighting with the all-Nisei 442nd Regiment in Italy. The staff sergeant had single-handedly marched through two hundred yards of enemy fire to set up a mortar and attack German infantry positions in Italy. He later sacrificed his life while attempting to prevent members of his unit from entering a heavily mined area. In front of a large crowd, "Vinegar Joe" Stilwell asserted that such bravery was emblematic of Japanese American soldiers. "I've seen a good deal of the Nisei in service," he remarked, "and never yet have I found one of them who didn't do his duty right up to the handle." Presenting Masuda's posthumous award to his sister Mary, who had previously been forced out of her home by threats from a racist mob, the high-ranking general called on the local citizens to do their "very best to welcome the Japanese back into your community." In conclusion, he made sure that they understood the broader significance of racial tolerance in America. "Now, the war is over, but the responsibility of our nation is not finished," Stilwell declared. "We must build a true democracy here in our land [and] the peaceful world."[2]

In the wartime drive for internment, the military had discounted exhibitions of loyalty by Japanese Americans as it made them the most widespread domestic casualties of "national security" interests. Stilwell's ceremonial visit and others like it thus marked a turning point in history. Never before had the American government gone to such lengths to promote tolerance of Japanese Americans; now it issued an effective declaration that the favorite scapegoat of so many local and national officials was off-limits.

Through foreign and domestic considerations, a confluence of actors became invested in portraying Nisei as model American citizens during World War II. Countering Japan's race war propaganda, the United States recruited Nisei into the armed forces and highlighted their achievements. At the same time, white liberals pressing the War Relocation Authority (WRA) to release select internees back into public life insisted that Nisei loyalty was beyond reproach. With their every move closely followed by the American public and the state, Nisei soldiers and resettled internees alike recognized that they needed to make a positive impression on white America or risk permanently besmirching their entire community's reputation. Although many white Americans still despised Japanese Americans after the war, their reasons for fearing them had largely evaporated. Indeed, with occupied Japan serving as the linchpin of East Asian foreign policy, American leaders called on their citizenry to accept Japan as a special ally and to embrace things Japanese. In this context, celebrations of Nisei battlefield heroism and the "successful" Nisei assimilation reinforced official narratives of America as a land of opportunity and a nation that had defeated racial prejudice. In fact, the federal government argued that the internment itself had been a benevolent endeavor consistent with modernist notions of progress and racial integration.

SPOILAGE AND SALVAGE

For the social scientist Dorothy Swaine Thomas, the Japanese American concentration camps were "social laboratories" providing a fortuitous chance to conduct research on an ethnic population. With white academics and interned Nisei assisting her research, Thomas developed the Japanese Evacuation and Resettlement Study (JERS). She classified the internees' behavior, attitudes, and adjustments by three designations. The "salvage" group comprised those who were most assimilated and who experienced the easiest transition back into civilian life. At the opposite end of the spectrum lay the "spoilage"—the most alienated and resentful

Japanese Americans who either returned to Japan or encountered severe difficulties reentering mainstream society. In between lay the "residue." While Thomas's labels were not used in common parlance, race relations experts who studied or attempted to assist Japanese Americans almost universally accepted their substance. Under the influence of the Chicago School's theory of the race relations cycle, these experts considered assimilation to be the ultimate marker of progress for minority groups. But as the Nisei had already learned, embracing Americanism did not guarantee assimilation; the white majority would also have to accept them. To promote white acceptance of the Nisei as they were released from internment camps, the white leaders of both the WRA and volunteer resettlement committees developed a public advocacy campaign hinged on tying the image and fate of Japanese Americans to the "salvage" type while distancing them from the "spoilage." Through these efforts to combat the most thoroughly racist stereotypes of Japanese Americans, the idea that some Nisei—especially high-achieving college students and heroic war veterans—were model American citizens first began to take root in the public imagination.[3]

Student resettlement comprised the first of two primary routes by which the "salvage" were prematurely released from wartime incarceration. Although many within the military and the government shared the public's fears of sabotage and believed that mass internment of Japanese Americans should continue unabated, other federal officials had reason to welcome discharging some internees as early as 1943. WRA officials worried that the protests, disturbances, and frustration within the camps had made them difficult to manage and had severely dampened internee morale. White liberals especially raised concern that the Nisei's belief in American ideals would be permanently shattered if they remained trapped beside the "spoilage." With the WRA's blessing, the nongovernmental National Japanese American Student Relocation Council placed over four thousand internees in colleges and universities primarily in the East Coast and Midwest. As historian Allan W. Austin has noted, white coordinators of Nisei resettlement impressed on those leaving the camps that they must represent themselves as "ambassadors of goodwill." While many of these liberal-minded whites idealized assimilation, practical wartime considerations guided their thinking, as well. During the frenzy of anti-Japanese sentiment at the war's height, some voices within the federal government, higher education, and local communities expressed reservation at the thought of Nisei students reentering public life, while others flat-out opposed it. Moreover, WRA officials, themselves under attack for being "soft" on the internees, carefully screened those seeking release. Using a color-coded scheme, the government classified the internees as "white," "brown," or "black." Only "white" Japanese Americans capable of demonstrating that they were both loyal and docile Americans could harbor hope of freedom from incarceration. "Black" internees were denied clearance, and "brown" internees required further investigation. Whether consciously or unconsciously devised, the racial symbolism of these bureaucratic codes was unmistakable. In fact, no Nisei students were sent to historically Black colleges due partly to a fear—shared by JACL leader Mike Masaoka—that fostering interaction between members of two disgruntled minorities might cause "a troubled situation."[4]

Within Southern California, a grouping of Good Samaritans based in Pasadena delivered arguably the most concerted effort to promote the image of Japanese Americans as model citizens. In November 1943, Rev. Albert Edward Day of the First Methodist Church condemned the internment as "one of the most grievous violations of civil liberty and shocking assaults upon the meaning of sanctity of American citizenship in our history." By his historical account, Japanese Americans had already proven they were "a credit to our country":

> There has never been a crime problem among them. They have been conspicuously honest in business. They were never dependent upon the WPA or the PWA or any other alphabetical means of redemption from poverty. Their cleanliness is proverbial. No group has made more far-going concessions to overcome prejudice. They are industrious. They have made many a wilderness blossom as a rose.

The Friends of the American Way hoped that by securing volunteers who agreed to provide housing and jobs for Japanese Americans, it might convince the WRA to allow an initial release of some internees. Its appeals for assistance stressed the high moral character and good manners of Japanese Americans. A white friend of Yamato and Fusako Hara described the gardener and his wife as "active, efficient [and] trustworthy." "They keep themselves and their children up to a high level of morale in this Center," she added. "Their barrack room is scrupulously neat and clean and they are always neatly dressed."[5]

When the US armed forces began taking Nisei volunteers in 1943, military service comprised the second route out of camp for the "salvage." Above and beyond concern for Japanese Americans, self-interested American leaders acted out of fear that the specter of American concentration camps was fueling Japan's race war propaganda. With encouragement from JACL leaders, they called on the Nisei soldiers to demonstrate to the nation and the world that they were full-fledged American citizens. For the Nisei, combat represented an opportunity to fight for what African Americans had called a double victory over fascism abroad and discrimination at home. For the American state, the Nisei soldier served as a model of self-sacrifice on behalf of national interests. Frank T. Hachiya—a

Nisei from Hood River, Oregon—drew nationwide plaudits, including a February 17, 1945, editorial by the *New York Times*. A graduate of the Military Intelligence Service Language School (MIS), Hachiya served in the Pacific theater, where he volunteered to scout troops behind enemy lines but was struck by gunfire on his return. With his last living breaths, he delivered maps of the Japanese defenses to an American officer. Retelling these heroic feats, the *Times* chastised the Hood River American Legion post for removing the names of Hachiya and fifteen other Nisei from a monument dedicated to veterans from the area. "To be sure, his eyes slanted, his skin was yellow, his name different," declared the editorial. "But Hachiya was an American." A second notable incident focused on the 442nd Regiment, which the War Department had deliberately assembled as a segregated all-Nisei unit to magnify the "propaganda value" of Japanese-faced soldiers in American uniforms. Nearly three thousand Nisei were sent on a harrowing mission to rescue the "Lost Battalion," a white unit from Texas caught behind enemy lines in the Vosges Mountains of France. In all, 2,000 Nisei were wounded, 882 seriously, and over 200 lost their lives largely in an effort to save 211 surviving members of the "Lost Battalion." The extended campaign figured centrally in the Nisei unit becoming the most decorated of all American forces during World War II.[6]

Highly publicized accounts of Nisei heroism served multiple purposes. No doubt the battlefield accomplishments offered white Americans a positive image of Japanese Americans, who were once seen only as a threat to national security. Racist stereotypes of Japanese Americans had been so pervasive and so focused on the unassimilable nature of the Nisei that they had created what ultimately amounted to straw man targets. The Nisei veterans demonstrated in the most fundamental manner that it was in fact possible to distinguish between enemy "Japs" and "loyal" Nisei. More than that, they convinced many Americans that Japanese Americans were willing to pay the ultimate price in defense of the nation. General Stilwell remarked that the Nisei "bought an awful hunk of America with their blood." A sense of brotherhood-in-arms especially registered with some white soldiers. Representing four chapters and five hundred members, the Los Angeles Area Council of the American Veterans Committee passed a resolution in October 1945 calling for a halt to anti-Japanese hate crimes and advocating legislation to "stop such un-American persecution." While many Americans regretted that "racial guilt" had initially denied Japanese Americans the opportunity to serve their country, the most observant recognized the value of the Nisei's bicultural heritage. Frank Hachiya was one of several thousand Nisei MIS graduates providing indispensable translation skills and linguistic capabilities to the American armed forces during the Pacific War and the occupation of Japan.

Furthermore, as Stilwell's visit to the Masuda family exemplified, embrace of Nisei soldiers carried over in a gendered manner to their families, who could proudly claim to have produced the boys sent overseas. The national Committee on Resettlement had seized on these sentiments in 1944 by promoting its "adopt a war wife" campaign, which called on kindhearted American women to make contact with internees and help them find jobs and housing for their families. Spokesperson Gracia Booth wrote that as she painfully watched Japanese Americans being hauled away, "Saddest of all to see were the mothers with tight-set faces and steady hands as they quietly went about their task, breaking up their homes—'folding up housekeeping,' as they put it."[7]

By linking the political fate of Japanese Americans to decorated Nisei veterans, the JACL sought to advance its civil rights agenda and curry favor from mainstream politicians. In November 1946, it sponsored a high-profile banquet in Los Angeles that drew extensive media coverage and the attendance of many elected officials. Its guest speaker of honor was none other than Mayor Fletcher Bowron, who used the occasion to deliver a mea culpa. Especially proud of the high proportion of Nisei veterans with local origins, he praised the 442nd Regiment and admitted their deeds had proven his previous suspicions misguided. "I am glad, indeed," Bowron concluded, "to make the public declaration that I have been convinced beyond any peradventure of doubt, the Nisei have been true." Two days after this momentous occasion, the JACL won a victory at the polls. Proposition 15 was championed by state senator Jack Tenney and other forces who had agitated not only for the internment but also for the deportation and permanent exclusion of all Japanese Americans from California. The initiative, which promised to strengthen the Alien Land Laws, fell to defeat by a nearly 60–40 percent margin and failed by 350,000 votes. After decades of marginalization, the JACL also achieved a semblance of access to the nation's highest policy-making circles. Mike Masaoka was invited to join Harry S. Truman's civil rights committee, whose recommendation helped spur the passage of the first law providing limited redress for the material losses of internees. Moreover, the Justice Department and civil rights lawyers from diverse backgrounds aided successful lawsuits overturning the Alien Land Laws and other legacies of exclusion.[8]

Found within and outside the government, proponents of America as the leader of the "free world" seized on Nisei narratives to advance a celebratory notion of liberal nationalism. The young actor Ronald Reagan best expressed this sentiment during General Stilwell's ceremony honoring the fallen Kazuo Masuda. "America stands unique in the world," he proclaimed, "the only country not founded on race, but on . . . an ideal." If the segregated 442nd Regiment could serve as a model of American

Fig. 8.1. The mayor embraces Nisei leaders. *Left to right*: Los Angeles mayor
Fletcher Bowron, Mike Masaoka, Eiji Tanabe, and Scotty Tsuchiya. Photograph
#36830-51, Los Angeles Daily News Photographic Archive (Collection 1386),
Department of Special Collections, Charles E. Young Research Library,
University of California, Los Angeles.

democracy in action, it was perhaps not so far a stretch to propose that
the internment could do likewise. WRA director Dillon Myer did just
that. In his eyes, the herding of Japanese Americans into WRA "relocation centers" had launched "an exciting adventure in the democratic
method." As the smooth (by his account) postwar resettlement confirmed
his faith in American justice, he stated, "When the people of the United
States have the opportunity to understand the problems of the underdog
and those discriminated against, they really do believe in the Bill of Rights
and are ready to do something about it." Myer and other assimilationists
argued that the status of Japanese Americans improved not *in spite of*
their having been interned but *because of* their internment. While he considered the internment to be "unnecessary," he declared it had "yielded
some excellent results." Ultimately, he concluded, Japanese Americans
were "better off as a result of the evacuation." Myer even belittled or

downplayed Japanese American suffering, when he asserted that "probably at least half [of the Issei] had never had it so good" as when they were interned. Few Japanese Americans shared that assessment, but the WRA director used his power and resources during the war to cultivate an alliance with the JACL and other Nisei leaders. He solicited their input on camp governance, aided their efforts to resettle, and hired them to assist the agency. After the war, his Nisei patrons returned the favor. Kiyoharu Anzai, staff member at the Los Angeles WRA office, praised the "marvelous work" of the WRA and lauded Myer and his associates as "real friends and people we could trust." In May 1946, the JACL feted Myer and presented him with a testimonial scroll for being a "champion of human rights and common decency."[9]

The self-serving nature of Myer's comments is apparent enough. But were the Nisei offering sincere admiration to their former captor or staging an incredibly well-orchestrated act? Perhaps a little of both. The Nisei possessed a strong desire to be accepted as equals by America but also an array of masks to don when it was clear to them they were not accepted. In fact, the WRA's sharpest critics were anti-Japanese agitators, who argued that the WRA was giving in to liberal advocates and coddling its prisoners. "We have one weak spot at home which must be overcome immediately!" declared the Americanism Educational League. "Powerful—very powerful—organizations of religious and educational leaders have *Sob-sistered* the Japanese evacuation order almost out of existence." In this context, some Nisei, especially those "salvage" who most appreciated being prematurely released from camp, saw the WRA as a bulwark against racism. Moreover, given the Japanese American community's weak political status, the JACL maintained that the most it could accomplish during the war was to minimize suffering caused by the internment and secure the soonest possible release of internees. Its leaders found the WRA generally supportive in these regards.[10]

The JACL, however, was scarcely representative of the local Japanese community. During the early postwar era, the Los Angeles chapter consisted largely of a small staff and a handful of Nisei members. Its leaders acknowledged that community perceptions of the JACL as a body of informants and collaborators had done damage to its reputation that could not be easily repaired. When John Yasukochi tried to recruit members, only four out of the three hundred people he contacted signed up. "Every one of them voiced antagonism, or disinterest in the organization," he noted. Refusing to attend the JACL-sponsored veterans' banquet, Hisaye Yamamoto ghostwrote this cynical account for the *Los Angeles Tribune*: "Japanese in this country could be imagined giddy with joy this week, flashing their buck teeth and hissing, 'Banzai!' as no less an eminence than Los Angeles mayor Fletcher Bowron announced to his constituents that they could stop hating the Japanese now." Yamamoto was especially disturbed by the "exclusive" nature of "an important Japanese-white dinner [taking place] in a community where Negroes, Mexicans, Filipinos, Chinese, and who knows what other -oes, -ans, -os, and -ese dwell." Working at the Black newspaper had made her especially sensitive to the suffering of other communities of color. For instance, O'Day Short had reported to her about receiving racist threats just days before his family was burned alive in their Fontana home. In November 1946, researcher Tom Sasaki surmised that scarcely any Nisei in Los Angeles backed the JACL but that half of the Issei did. Indeed, Japanese immigrant leaders and merchants were the principal sponsors of the JACL's banquet and its political actions, most notably the campaign against Proposition 15. Even though the organization's citizenship requirement barred them from membership, the Issei believed that the citizenship rights, education, and English fluency of their children's generation rendered them the community's best representative to outsiders.[11]

Although they functioned well within mainstream society, Nisei veterans offered some of the community's staunchest cultural resistance to assimilation. Given that their formative experience had been their fighting in a segregated unit, this was not an ironic stance. By the early 1950s, returning veterans had organized six different all-Nisei posts of the Veterans of Foreign Wars in California. The Nisei were not necessarily excluded from other VFW posts but elected to maintain their independence. Having been thrust into service by the same government that held their families and friends behind barbed wire, Japanese American veterans developed an intimate awareness of the imperfections of American democracy that may have underlay their decision to remain somewhat aloof. A Nisei chaplain, for instance, privately criticized commands given on the Lost Battalion rescue. He noted that when the 442nd Regiment was ordered to march straight into the teeth of Nazi "machine gun nests and their well-prepared defense," the remaining white soldiers of the Lost Battalion's own 141st Infantry were "not forced to take the same responsibility." Frequently sent into exceptionally dangerous combat, Japanese Americans endured a one-in-three casualty rate that was six times that of the US military at-large during World War II. White commanders claimed that being assigned the toughest missions was an honor bestowed on the best soldiers. But there were clear signs of racial prejudice within the ranks of the armed forces. Interestingly, Nisei added a twist to Frank Hachiya's heroic story. In their accounts, he was killed by "friendly" fire when Americans invading Leyte mistook him for a "Jap." Hachiya had outfoxed Japanese militarism but fell casualty to American racial prejudice. Soldiers also faced public scorn upon returning to Los Angeles. Dressed in full uniform, Hideo Watanabe was denied service by a barber who refused to serve a "Jap." Some gestures of goodwill also turned sour. In January 1945, the Hollywood American Legion Post 591 made headlines when it condemned the Hood River, Oregon, chapter's snub of Hachiya and inducted Nisei veteran Harley Oka. But Oka resigned in disgust within three months because of a "malicious attack" and the general scorn of World War I veterans.[12]

Rank-and-file Japanese Americans harbored feelings that were far more complex than the unproblematic portrayals of them advanced by both white and Nisei leaders. What they essentially wanted was freedom from the stigma of racism, something that could apparently be accomplished by a moderate conception of integration. As members of a small minority whose citizenship rights could be granted or taken away at will by the state, they felt it was necessary to maintain the face of a loyal subject in public. Any resentment they felt would have to be kept hidden.

THE "PROBLEM" COMMUNITY

For those who welcomed the strides toward Nisei assimilation in Midwest and East Coast communities, Los Angeles posed a severe problem. It was nearly devoid of the "salvage" during the early postwar era. Correctly sensing that anti-Japanese sentiment was strongest on the West Coast, most resettled Nisei felt little incentive to return until conditions improved in the 1950s. Particularly discouraging to the Nisei was the fact that Japanese Americans were generally precluded from white-collar and professional employment. Los Angeles County General Hospital, for instance, barred Japanese Americans from employment until the end of 1945. Despite labor shortages, the hospital denied Dorothy Takechi a typist-clerk position even though she had passed the civil service exam. Hiro Nakamura reported being "refused for no other reason but my ancestry." The incident moved him to ask, "How can some of us rightly ask for world peace when here at home we don't practice the very principles for which we are fighting?"[13]

At the same time, racist hostility hampered efforts to reestablish the prewar Japanese community's ethnic employment and entrepreneurial niches. Owing to the obstructionism of the Teamsters—whose official magazine declared it was "senseless to argue" that "Japs are American citizens"—only a fraction of Japanese American wholesale produce workers reclaimed their jobs. The union, which had lobbied against the release of internees and for the revocation of their citizenship, banned Japanese workers—even its own prewar members—from the downtown markets. Within the nursery and cut-flower industries, Japanese Americans faced boycotts by white retailers and suppliers. Although most who experienced hostility eventually managed to stabilize their business, they were initially quite embittered. One Nisei, who deliberately overcharged white customers, professed his desire "to get back at these selfish Caucasians." Although the Japanese American flower industry association owned its wholesale market, its members encountered trouble regaining spaces they had leased to white merchants. They were greeted with signs outside the market reading "No Japs Allowed between Seventh and Eighth Streets on Wall." On February 17, 1945, Howard Otamura became the first Japanese American employee to return to the flower market. Not only did he endure harassment from whites at work; three gunshots were fired at his residence. Almost "ready to give up" and move "back east," he was inspired by the Nisei soldiers who "were dying on the battlefields, fighting for a right to come back." His plight drew the attention of Friends of the American Way activist William Carr, who helped secure a constant police presence inside the market. Given the hostile climate, fewer than one-third of all prewar Japanese American merchants had returned to the flower market by October 1946. Many had trouble obtaining land for growing and often faced discrimination in their dealings. Sears for a time refused to stock its Los Angeles stores with plants and flowers sold by Japanese Americans.[14]

Since the West Coast was the nation's final sector to have the exclusion order lifted, it was attracting primarily the "spoilage" and "residue," as they were the last to be emptied from the internment camps. While some emotionally damaged individuals continued to insist that Japan had won the war, the ranks of these and other "spoilage" were quite small. Indeed, the truest "spoilage" had returned to Japan. Hence, the majority of the Los Angeles returnees consisted of the "residue." They commonly spoke the phrase *shikata ga nai*—meaning "can't be helped"—which simultaneously connoted a sense of resignation and resilience. Whether they were relatively optimistic or pessimistic, Japanese Americans acknowledged the reality of racism, then carried on with their lives as well as possible. In numerous cases, they started from scratch. During the war, internees on the whole lost an estimated $367 million worth of assets calculated in 1949 dollars. Caught in a state of uncertainty and disenfranchisement, most Japanese Americans had sold their prewar personal and business possessions for ten cents on the dollar. Many who stored items with the federal government never recovered them, because the agencies assigned to protect the assets made little effort to secure them. Other possessions were simply abandoned, since the government placed restrictions on the quantity of materials that could be taken to the internment camps. Various factors such as government confiscation, swindle, and damage accounted for the remainder of losses.[15]

Although some Japanese Americans returned to agriculture and small businesses, the local community's prewar economic strategies had been undermined by the internment and the restructuring of the regional economy. Small businesses and enterprises in Los Angeles were especially disrupted by the internment. The entire fishing colony at Terminal Island was uprooted, and its land confiscated by the navy. In addition, nearly all truck farmers were cash tenants and thus easily replaced. From the start of war to the end of 1946, the acreage covered by Japanese farming plummeted 75 percent. Still more family farms went under after the war because of applications of the Alien Land Laws, urban expansion, and the consolidation and mechanization of agriculture. Their demise had a rippling effect, causing Japanese American declines in wholesale and retail produce. Indeed, the once ubiquitous roadside produce stands all but vanished from the Southern California landscape. As the internment hastened the ethnic economy's collapse, Japanese American workers were forced to turn to whites for jobs. Whereas fewer than 20 percent of Japanese Americans in the Los Angeles area had worked for whites before the war, 70 percent were doing so by 1948. The largest group of laborers, including many who had previously been in white-collar trades, turned to gardening and domestic work. Hundreds more toiled as busboys and dishwashers while hoping for better opportunities to come along. The newest area of wide-scale employment was in light industry, with men laboring in various fields and women particularly in garment work. But despite the large presence of these laborers, there was no political organization, other than the short-lived Nisei Progressives, advancing an explicitly working-class agenda in the Japanese community. Prewar leftists, many of whom volunteered for armed service, had scattered throughout the country. Shuji Fujii, who moved to New York, continued to organize in new locales but never returned to the CPUSA after being suspended. Karl Yoneda, one of the few remaining Nisei Communists, retreated to a Sonoma County chicken farm to escape the pressures of life as a radical during the McCarthy era.[16]

White and Japanese American advocates of the Nisei as model citizens deliberately cast the Japanese community's most distressed members into obscurity. Beneath the surface, however, lay the deeply contrasting experiences of the "spoilage" and "salvage." Sometimes dramatic examples could be found within immediate families. Togo Tanaka escaped Manzanar in 1942 to lead the "progressive" branch of educated Nisei to Chicago, where he began a successful publishing business and edited a prominent Nisei journal. Breaking a vow to never return to the city that had expelled him in a racist frenzy, he moved back to Los Angeles in 1955. Working in finance and real estate, he discovered new opportunities for his immense talents. Tanaka developed a multimillion-dollar business by leasing retail locations to the burgeoning fast-food industry and other restaurants, entering into deals with emerging giants like Carl Karcher of the Carl's Jr. burger chain. The government that once declared him a threat to national security later entrusted him as regional board member of the Federal Reserve under Paul Volcker. Tanaka's brother Jack, however, fared far less well. When he protested the internment and wrote disgruntled letters to the government, he was questioned by the FBI and later committed to a series of stays in mental institutions as a "schizophrenic with paranoid tendencies." He was repeatedly administered shock therapy, suffered severe emotional problems, and became estranged from his wife, children, and siblings. Four decades later, his daughter, a documentary filmmaker, discovered him living alone on the streets of Skid Row in Los Angeles. Did mental illness cause Jack Tanaka to lash out at the government, or was he diagnosed as a paranoid schizophrenic because he protested the internment? Was cutting himself off from the "loyal" members of his family a product of his wartime outrage, or did they distance themselves from him because he resembled the "spoilage"? As these questions are left unanswered in his daughter's film, it is likely she herself cannot answer them. Her point is that the official discourse of the postwar era allowed no room for them to be raised.[17]

Gateway to a New World

At the weekly "Town Hall" forum of Los Angeles civic leaders on November 1, 1943, Nobel Prize–winning author and social critic Pearl Buck emphasized the significance of race relations in a world standing at a crossroads. Throughout American history, she argued, the white majority had ruled the nation at the cost of terrible suffering for the colored minorities of the land. On a global scale, however, whites were severely outnumbered. Hitler's genocidal war of conquest, which was still raging at its fiercest pitch, now forced every American to choose between two potential courses. Domination of the planet by its white minority could only be sustained by "military preparation of the most barbarous and savage kind"; the use of "super-weapons," including "chemical warfare on a mass scale"; and an ultimate willingness "to destroy all civilization, even our own, in order to keep down the colored peoples." But establishing a world order shaped by the free and equal participation of all humankind could augur a new era of peace and prosperity. Through speeches like this, Buck contributed to the reformulation of racial discourse in response to the paradigmatic geopolitical developments of the evolving "American century." Leading a chorus of intellectuals during World War II, she pushed Americans to comprehend that "the battle against race prejudice" had shifted from being "a family quarrel in our own house" to becoming "part of the tremendous struggle for human freedom upon this globe."[18]

Portraying this national watershed as particularly salient to Los Angeles, Buck implored her audience to assume the responsibility that came with their region's new status as "the leader of the nation." "Imperceptibly the center of gravity in our country is moving westward," she declared. "The people in our Eastern states are already looking toward you as these great questions arise of how to deal with the people of Asia and South America." As she spoke these words, Buck knew that next week's "Town Hall" would debate "whether or not any Japanese Americans should be allowed to return to California when the war is over." Los Angeles had made itself known as the center of public agitation for the internment, and this troubled her because racial chauvinism played into the hands of Japan's propagandists. Rallying the people of Asia to its "Greater East Asia Co-Prosperity Sphere," Japan submitted that it was a liberating force marshaling resentment of Western imperialism and white supremacy. Hence, to win the hearts and minds of people in Asia, America would have to disavow its past indiscretions. "I beg of you men and women of the most important part of our country, as I now believe California is, to keep your wits and common sense," Buck pleaded. "Once in an æon a single people is given the opportunity to shape the world's direction—that opportunity is now ours. And because you in California face the Pacific and Asia, you among us have the crux in your hands. You can, by what you decide, be a barrier—or you can be a gateway to a new and better world, for us and for all peoples."[19]

Throughout the first half of the twentieth century, the Pacific Coast location of Los Angeles had inspired both boosterist visions of growth and xenophobic fears of "Yellow Peril." When Pearl Buck asked the Town Hall audience to embrace a world of interdependence, her speech's most practical implication was that the city could not have growth unless it overcame its fears and hatred. The subsequent events of the war served to quell the fears. White agitators had always portrayed the small population of Japanese in America as a symbol of a grave threat—the yellow hordes who would pollute the nation through unchecked immigration; the Japanese farmers who would take agricultural sustenance from the hands of the white race; and, above all, the scheming "Yellow Peril" saboteurs ready to strike the minute Japan gave the signal. By the end of 1945, Asian immigration remained tightly restricted, the Issei presence in farming had been curtailed by the internment, and Japan had been subdued by the atomic blasts at Hiroshima and Nagasaki. As it turned out, the anti-Japanese agitators, who for decades had warned that yellow hordes would invade California, got it reversed: the invasions occurred largely from west to east—that is, from America to Asia. The United States occupied Japan with two million personnel for nearly seven years. With a vested interest in demonstrating that the people of Japan were close friends capable of adopting the American way of life, the occupying forces carried forth an idealistic vision of Western-style democracy. Liberal behavioral scientists serving as consultants actively rejected the biological racism that had informed the dehumanizing depictions of the enemy during the war. Instead, they along with New Dealers in policy-making functions advanced the concept of "universalism," asserting that all people were inherently capable of practicing democracy. Interestingly, the American occupation authority drew directly on government-sponsored social science research conducted on Japanese American internees in an effort to make sense of the Japanese "national character." Based on data collected by Nisei ethnographers inside the camps, scholar Alexander Leighton's "community analysis" proved critical to American plans for governing the occupation. In this sense, the "salvaging" of internees provided a basis for "salvaging" Japan.[20]

In return, the occupation had a profound impact on the way people of Japanese descent were viewed and treated in postwar America. Most immediately, hostility toward Japanese Americans diminished as American foreign policy made new designations of "good" and "bad" Asians. In large measure, Japanese Americans had been victimized by racist acts because whites had linked them by "racial guilt" to Japan's belligerence. But Japan was now central to the creation of the United States' sphere of influence, otherwise known as the anticommunist "free world." As it hosted permanent American military outposts, Japan went from being a reviled enemy to a critical ally in the fight against communism in China and Korea. In this regard, as literary critic Christina Klein has argued, American Cold War policy was marked not only by the fight to contain communism but also by the attempt to create an affiliation between the United States and Asia. To secure domestic consent for transpacific intervention, American intellectuals and policy makers constructed what Klein has called a "global imaginary of integration." Just as wartime propaganda had taught Americans how and why to hate the "Japs," postwar news accounts and fictional narratives provided models of a dominant America taking Japan as a subordinate ally. Through the production of a "sentimental discourse," postwar cultural and ideological projects provided middle America with an appreciation for Cold War integrationist objectives.[21]

As the transpacific alliance relieved the Nisei from being caught in the cross fire of two hostile nations, it created economic opportunities that boded well for the acceptance of Japanese in postwar America. One of America's primary aims for incorporating Asia into the "free world" was expanded access to overseas markets. By cultivating ties to America's new special ally, Los Angeles civic leaders positioned their city to reap the benefits of transpacific commerce. In October 1951, Mayor Bowron visited Japan with a delegation of Southern California business leaders at the invitation of Japanese officials seeking to increase trade. By the 1950s, the Port of Los Angeles was receiving more tonnage from Japan than from anywhere else in the world. As Asian trade became increasingly central to the city's economy, Los Angeles boosters developed a more cosmopolitan sense of themselves, thus paving the way for the emergence of the "world city." Demonstrating their new mobility, Nisei became active in import-export trade as employees of American or Japanese firms and in some cases as entrepreneurs. While serving as a lobbyist for the JACL, Mike Masaoka simultaneously worked as a consultant for Japanese corporations looking to capture market share in America. Though he insisted that increasing Japanese imports would benefit the American economy, it is impossible to imagine Masaoka taking this stance during the divisive years leading up to the war.[22]

To the degree the social climate for Japanese Americans was enhanced by the friendly relations between Japan and the United States, it was likewise shaped by the unequal power relations dictating the terms of that alliance. As historian John Dower has demonstrated, the American nation-building campaign in postwar Japan comprised a "revolution from above" that informed the Cold War dialectic of freedom and repression. Viewing their task as a civilizing mission resembling the "white man's burden," military leaders "ruled their new domain as neocolonial overlords." Moreover, whereas Americans viewed German Nazism as a "cancer in a fundamentally mature 'Western' society, Japanese militarism and ultranationalism were construed as reflecting the essence of a feudalistic, Oriental culture that was cancerous in and of itself." Thus, while the Japanese people were deemed capable of practicing democracy, American efforts at democratization were characterized by "an ethnocentric missionary zeal" to wipe out Japan's "Oriental" essence. Japanese modernization, too, could not exceed parameters defined by the American occupiers. When a mass movement arose advocating communism as an alternative modernity, the occupiers engaged in brutal repression to stop it.[23]

Released in 1957 and garnering ten Oscar nominations, *Sayonara* served as the quintessential film depicting this new model of Japanese-American affiliation and revealing its contradictions. A writer for the *Los Angeles Times* remarked that it would "unquestionably win a large audience for its exceptional Nipponese realities and its exceedingly colorful dramatic appeal." Based on the James Michener novel of the same name, the film is set during the occupation. An emasculated Japanese nation serves as the feminine partner of white America through two interracial relationships. The first couple, played by Red Buttons and Miyoshi Umeki, gets married in violation of the military taboo on interracial romance. Their tragic double suicide serves to underscore both the unfairness of antimiscegenation laws and the evil of intolerance. The successful marriage of the second couple, played by Marlon Brando and Miiko Taka, symbolizes the malleability of race and culture. Speaking with an affected southern drawl, Brando is initially opposed to interracial dating (and thus represents the racism of the American South). His change of political and romantic heart occurs through his courtship of Taka, who must unbind herself from the traditions and prejudices that preclude her from marrying an American. In the end, *Sayonara* challenges the racist dehumanization of Japan that swept through America during the war while creating new stereotypes rooted in the postwar context. Since American racism is presented as a southern problem, what emerges most triumphant is the northern white liberal metanarrative of American progress. In promoting a strategic transpacific alliance, *Sayonara* asserts that Japan needs liberation from its indigenous culture through the modernizing efforts of the victorious United States. Its depiction of white men marrying Japanese women parallels the paternalistic relationship between America and Japan. While actresses Umeki and Taka became minor pop cultural icons, signifying a decline in hatred toward Japanese Americans, the film's portrayal of Japanese women as exotic and erotic prizes of white men reinforced gendered stereotypes rooted in affection. If hypermasculinity was a defining trait of the "Yellow Peril," feminization was just as critical to white America's embrace of the "model minority."[24]

Reflecting the contradictions of Cold War integrationism, the JACL's moderate civil rights agenda fed on the transpacific anxieties of anticommunist politicians. Nowhere was this more evident than during the debate surrounding the 1952 McCarran-Walter Act. Considered the crowning achievement of postwar Nisei activism, the law granted naturalization rights to Japanese immigrants, removing the basis of exclusionary laws that targeted Japanese and other Asians as "aliens ineligible to citizenship." It also replaced the 1924 ban on immigration from Japan with a new quota. Owing to the impact of this law and others that loosened restrictions on entry, the 1950s became the greatest decade of Japanese immigration in forty years. But the law's passage was motivated by anticommunism on two fronts. Although various Issei groups had mobilized for naturalization rights just after the war's end, the JACL assumed leadership of the campaign around 1947. It quickly discovered that the best case for ending Japanese exclusion could be made by stressing the vital role of Japan to American Cold War objectives. John Foster Dulles declared the goal of American foreign policy was "to align [Japan] with the West and alienate it from Asia." Walter Judd, a Republican from Minnesota, became the leading congressional proponent of a bill to provide Japan with a token immigration quota as a gesture of friendship and symbol of democratic relations with an ally. Lamenting the fact that America had "lost a good part of Asia to Communist control," Judd asserted that Japan could serve as "a bulwark of freedom" in the region. The commanding general of the Eighth Army in Japan agreed; so did the American ambassador to Japan, who proclaimed the proposed law would "electrify the people of Asia." Despite these endorsements, Judd's proposal languished until it was incorporated into an omnibus bill that satisfied the domestic concerns of Nevada senator and cold warrior Pat McCarran. In 1950, McCarran had pushed through a repressive internal security measure that authorized detaining subversives in the same type of concentration camps that had been used to hold Japanese Americans. Two years later, he was concerned that immigration posed a threat to national security. America was "the oasis of the world," he declared, and it was in danger of being "overrun, perverted, contaminated or destroyed" by immigrants. Joining a chorus of liberal and left-wing critics, the Los Angeles Committee for the Protection of the Foreign Born condemned McCarran's 1952 omnibus bill as a repressive device comparable to "Hitler's Nuremberg Laws." The threat of deportation or loss of naturalized citizenship, it asserted, was being held over the heads of all immigrants to force them "to conform to standards of thought set by the powerful reactionaries."[25]

While recognizing the 1952 bill was not "perfect," the JACL vigorously pushed for its passage. Its main contention was that the aging Issei could not afford to wait any longer for the long-sought rights of citizenship. Yet there were broader considerations that framed its decision. Most significantly, JACL leaders embraced the anticommunist ideology that now united the governments of the United States and Japan. (Four years later, in September 1956, an aide to President Eisenhower would tell the attendees of the organization's national convention that they were "in a unique position to help our country win the confidence of Japan" and stop the "Communists [from] making inroads.") At the same time, Nisei leaders downplayed the concern over civil liberties that provoked liberal opposition to the McCarran-Walter Act and, eventually, a veto by President Truman that Congress would override. On the surface it appeared that Nisei, because they were no longer deemed a threat to security, were more than ready to sell others down the river. The JACL's Saburo Kido, however, contended that the internal security issue was nothing more than a "smoke screen" put up by "liberal groups [that] were selfishly maneuvering to attain their own objectives." In the view of the organization, the new law would grant few repressive powers to the state that were not already on the books. The JACL's position may have been a problematic compromise, but it was entirely consistent with its behavior during the war. In both instances, it argued that Japanese Americans, as a small minority with little political clout, could not issue immediate challenges to national security directives. Rather, they could only hope to secure the best outcome within parameters dictated by the state. This time, however, the JACL acted in accordance with the Japanese American majority, which heralded the 1952 law. As the overall social status of the community improved, the JACL's reputation within it was gradually repaired.[26]

The "revolution from above" proved to be a transpacific phenomenon. Like the people of Japan, the postwar Japanese American community found greater acceptance from white America. Once ground zero for the "Japanese problem," Los Angeles was becoming a "gateway to a new and better world." But the incorporation of Japanese from both sides of the Pacific into the American way of life occurred largely through the terms dictated by the American state. In the context of both World War II and the Cold War, Nisei leaders surmised that racism would abate only if they proved they were model American citizens. Remaining consistent with official invocations of American nationalism, however, mandated that they embrace assimilation as a one-way process that would excise a corruptive racial essence. In the end, the emerging "model minority" ideology served not only to discipline the Nisei but also to raise the bar for others to qualify for full citizenship. Stories of both Black and Japanese American advancement were incorporated into propaganda circulated internationally by Americans to demonstrate their commitment to democracy. In practice, however, the political meaning of Black and Japanese American identities would reflect a new divergence. While the "successful" Nisei were becoming the poster child for a voluntarist conception of integration, the social democratic agenda that had arisen through African American wartime activism was collapsing in the face of McCarthyism. As Cold War directives made perfectly clear, sacrificing for national interests and submitting to the authority of the state were prerequisites for any group that wished to have its pursuit of civil rights taken seriously by those in power.

CHAPTER 9

Black Containment

IN MAY 1947, ROY WILKINS, then assistant secretary to Walter White of the national NAACP, called a fringe publication's assertion that the Los Angeles branch was "harboring Communists" the "funniest accusation" imaginable. He conveyed his full confidence to the local leadership, which had established a close and productive alliance with the left wing of the city's labor movement during World War II. "In this present hysterical cry about Communism," Wilkins noted, "it is natural that anyone who is connected with a protest organization and who also works with other liberal groups should be branded as a Communist." Less than three years later, Wilkins had stopped laughing and dramatic changes had occurred inside the NAACP, as it strained to maintain a semblance of access to the Truman administration. The organization's national leadership, through moves that paralleled those made by the CIO, toed the anticommunist line on American foreign policy during the Cold War and suppressed those who dissented. At its 1950 national convention, the NAACP resolved "to take the necessary action to eradicate [Communist] infiltration" even if that meant expelling entire branches. Renewing the anti-Communist pledge became an annual ritual of the organization during the Cold War era. These measures proved especially divisive. Whereas a common struggle against *segregation* had unified Black leadership in the Negro Victory movement, African American leaders would clash sharply over competing visions of racial *integration* in postwar Los Angeles. Wartime activism had been aided by special conditions, including a shortage of white labor, a pressing need to avert crisis, oversight by the federal FEPC, left-wing CIO leadership, and persecution focused on non-Black minorities. The evaporation of these conditions narrowed the parameters of African American political agency.[1]

Although civil rights activists achieved formal equality during the Cold War, domestic forms of containment set strict limits on social reform. Black and Japanese Americans occupied distinct positions within postwar multiracial discourse. Whereas Japanese Americans served as a "model minority" for a moderate integrationist agenda, African Americans were racialized as a problem minority that had to be contained. While anticommunist measures led to the overthrow of some foreign governments and manipulation of others, racial containment at home had three discernible effects. First, as both the state and corporate America unmade the social democratic elements of the wartime political economy, patterns of racial inequality persisted and intensified. With moderation and voluntarism defining integrationist policy, the state did little to ensure that African Americans enjoyed the fruits of postwar economic growth. Second, under the duress of anticommunist repression, Black political activism in Los Angeles foundered. McCarthyism disrupted the alliance between civil rights activists and left-wing union leadership underlying the social democratic movement in Los Angeles and elsewhere. Third, it was not just opponents of integration who fixated on the "Negro" as problematic; proponents of postwar liberal reforms, such as urban renewal, explicitly magnified the idea that working-class African Americans were culturally dysfunctional. Worse still, anticommunist reaction undermined the promise of modern public housing, which had been one of the central premises supporting the destruction of nonwhite neighborhoods through "slum removal."

Postwar Retrenchment

Although the postwar period was a time of prosperity in America, the benefits of economic expansion were not shared equally throughout the population. As the nation emerged from World War II with its domestic sources of production unscathed compared to European and Asian combatants, the combination of military, political, and economic power provided the basis for the United States to assume global leadership in the creation of policies for trade and development. Buoyed in part by a hefty annual trade surplus of $25 billion, the domestic economy grew at a fast clip through the early 1970s. While the average American worker's real income doubled within just one generation, the median income of all workers (not adjusted for inflation) in the Los Angeles area amazingly doubled during the 1950s alone. But as ten million veterans returned to civilian life, the postwar era began with a crisis of reconversion. By the end of 1945, one in four war workers had lost their job, and wages were tumbling downward. Because war-related industries had propelled the dramatic growth of Southern California's economy, the local rollback during the immediate postwar period was particularly severe. In 1945, economists projected that Los Angeles County would lose 250,000 manufacturing jobs owing especially to declines in aircraft and ship construction. "Reconversion" was a misnomer because unlike Steel Belt cities, such as Detroit with its auto plants, Los Angeles had no significant prewar manufacturing base to which it could return. Asserting that two decades of growth had been crammed into two years, the Merchants and

Manufacturers Association remarked that many factories were "war babies" destined to "fold up and go out of business after the war." Representatives from the United Auto Workers feared over 90 percent of all jobs created during the war would be lost. Even as the economy picked up in the late 1940s, it could not keep pace with the growth of the labor force. In 1949, the unemployment rate for Los Angeles County stood at 10.2 percent—double the national average. Hampered during the war by the tight labor market and government intervention, employers reasserted their authority. With a surplus of labor strengthening the hand of management, the California CIO Council declared that speedups and stretchouts were now "the order of the day."[2]

African Americans took special note of the changing economic and political climate. As Americans celebrated victory in the Pacific War, Second Baptist Church's J. Raymond Henderson cautioned, "Anyone who thinks . . . that all will be rosy for the Negro is indulging in delusions." He warned that "the forces of reaction" sought not only to deprive "minority groups" of "the fruits of victory, but to even take from them the liberties grudgingly extended during a world emergency." His words quickly proved prescient. Within two weeks of Japan's surrender, heavy cutbacks were occurring in defense industries employing twenty-five thousand African Americans. No industry in the Los Angeles area epitomized Black wartime gains and postwar retrenchment better than aircraft production. With demand tied to defense outlays, employment took an extended roller coaster ride throughout the Cold War era. Between 1945 and 1959, successive shifts in federal policy—brought about by the end of World War II, the onset and end of the Korean War, and the launch of the first Sputnik—caused spikes and plummets of 100,000 or more aviation industry jobs within a year's time. The lack of job security resulting from these fluctuations particularly damaged the prospects of workers of color. Those hired during the wartime "overemployment" conditions were frequently laid off when postwar cutbacks ensued. In most cases, the only thing preventing their removal was seniority under a union contract. But as the mass scale of layoffs cut deep into the workforce, workers of color who were building seniority were also eliminated. When new orders quickly generated mass hiring, they were forced to the back of the hiring line again. Between World War II and 1949, the number of African Americans employed by the aviation industry in metropolitan Los Angeles plunged from 5,000 to 1,183. Blacks now comprised but one in sixty of the industry's workers, and their ranks had fallen by 72 percent at North American and 99 percent at Douglas.[3]

As their numbers grew, African American workers were forced back to the margins of the labor market. The wartime surge in Black migration continued, pushing the city's Black population above 200,000 in the early

1950s. Most came to Los Angeles from urban areas in the western half of the South, especially Texas and Louisiana, and to a lesser extent from Dust Bowl regions. During the postwar era, as the combination of white supremacy and the mechanization of agriculture undermined the livelihoods of southern rural Blacks, Jim Crow employment patterns severely curtailed the prospects of those seeking work in southern cities. Los Angeles thus remained a site of potential opportunity despite the fact that median wages of Blacks (and Asians) trailed those of whites by 30 percent. Census data for 1949 detailed the limited job options underlying this low wage rate. A cluster of Black women worked in education and health care, but the greatest number (more than two in five) were employed as domestics. With the exception of 3,000 garment workers, African American women were seldom found in factories. Meanwhile, Black men often found nothing better than dead-end unskilled labor and service work. While the growing Los Angeles auto industry provided 15,000 jobs, Blacks held scarcely 2 percent. Suburban plants rarely hired African Americans, who comprised only 22 of General Motors' 3,100 workers in South Gate and Van Nuys and 75 of Ford's 1,121 employees in Long Beach. Although over 1,000 African Americans worked in the iron and steel industry, companies like Bethlehem Steel frequently restricted them and other nonwhites to unskilled jobs. An Urban League survey of the early 1950s found African Americans could also obtain no better than custodial jobs at seven major petroleum companies, four major brewing companies, sixteen major insurance companies, and the Automobile Club. Some department stores made token Black hires, but they continued to reserve "public contact" jobs for whites. Similarly, the Southern California Gas Company refused to let people of color make service calls to the houses of whites. While Black-owned businesses employed Black managerial staff, they generally failed to produce mass employment opportunities. Given these market conditions, public employment remained highly coveted. Civil rights struggles had helped to open up positions, especially in the postal service, for public sector work generally providing a level of wages and job stability superior to that of the private sector.[4]

What was most striking about this situation was that Blacks were facing difficulties securing decent employment during what was not a period of deindustrialization but rather a time of record industrial expansion for the Los Angeles region. Over 300,000 jobs in "durable goods" were added between 1950 and 1960, more than doubling total employment in a sector that offered above-average wages. Growth, however, was of a new sort tied especially to the high-tech work of the "military-industrial complex." While significant numbers of Black and Japanese American professionals broke into the bustling aviation and aerospace industry, only a piece of the decade's prosperity trickled down to working-class people of color. At the end of the 1950s, whites were still close to 50 percent more likely to be employed in durable goods manufacturing than African Americans and "other nonwhites." Moreover, white median earnings in the sector surpassed those of "nonwhites" by about 35 percent. In the defense industry, employment discrimination and housing segregation reinforced each other. Government contracts improved the status of whites, who were the "first hired" into defense industries, while workers of color fought to be the "last hired" into the least desirable jobs. The greater access of whites to employment provided, in turn, greater access to new federally subsidized housing in the suburbs. Finally, the construction of formal and informal organizations in all-white communities provided the networks necessary to push for continued white control of housing and jobs. At the 1960 hearings of the Civil Rights Commission, the Los Angeles Community Relations Conference reported that the placement of new and relocated plant facilities in the suburbs "posed a serious problem for the colored minority workers in the labor force." Several large employers in the San Fernando Valley's predominantly white Canoga Park neighborhood, for example, only hired local residents.[5]

THE DEMISE OF THE "NEGRO-LABOR" ALLIANCE

Partaking in a postwar shift toward political conservatism, the labor movement retreated from the fight for civil rights. While the AFL had always harbored a reputation for racism, the loss of progressive CIO leadership dampened the prospects for mass employment gains by workers of color. The mid-to-late 1940s were a time when competing forces battled to define the meaning of American liberalism. Mainstream labor leaders, including those of the increasingly bureaucratic CIO, followed the path of the Democratic Party under Harry Truman. With union membership at a record fourteen million, their goal was to consolidate wartime gains in the face of an increasingly conservative political climate. Seeking higher wages and benefits but looking to avoid a confrontation with corporate power, mainstream labor leaders retreated from a commitment to "industrial democracy"—a concept that encompassed not just the redistribution of wealth but also the direct involvement of workers and unions in planning and production. As the New Deal devolved into consumption-oriented liberalism, the labor movement became reduced, in the words of historian Nelson Lichtenstein, to a "militant interest group" with a "Keynesian emphasis on sustained growth and productivity gain-sharing." While Truman appreciated labor-management peace, what he most expected from both was support for his foreign policy. In March 1947, the president laid down his historic doctrine pledging American intervention wherever necessary to assist "free peoples" in the fight against "terror and oppression." His call for American intervention to suppress communist forces in Greece was a global declaration escalating the Cold War. Viewing American hegemony as consistent with a prosperous economy, prominent CIO leaders such as Philip Murray and Walter Reuther backed Truman. Leftists, however, broke ranks. Emboldened by a rise in membership and a wave of wildcat strikes throughout 1945 and 1946, the Communist Party, USA (CPUSA), under William Z. Foster's stewardship abandoned its Popular Front orientation as American-Soviet relations deteriorated. In the wake of the 1947 passage of the Taft-Hartley Act, however, national CIO leaders became exhausted with left-wing dissent. The new law gave management more freedom to bust unions, and it required trade unionists appearing before the NLRB to sign an anticommunist pledge. When leftists symbolized their opposition to Truman's Cold War agenda by campaigning for Progressive Party candidate Henry Wallace in the 1948 presidential election, they were quickly disciplined by the CIO's majority leaders. Purges and resignations reduced CIO membership by 20 percent and generally stripped leftists of the most prominent leadership positions they had garnered.[6]

The CIO split had a devastating impact on the Left in Los Angeles. CPUSA member Slim Connelly, the Negro Victory movement's most prominent labor ally, had led the Los Angeles CIO for most of the 1940s. To undermine his authority, national leadership backed a breakaway group from the Los Angeles CIO Council. Connelly's council responded by denouncing its rivals for their "groveling subservience to the Democratic machine" and their participation in spreading "war hysteria." Dividing the CIO in Los Angeles would serve only to "wreck its effectiveness economically and politically." But by revoking the charter of the Left-led council and placing the district into receivership, the national CIO neutralized Connelly and his allies, who resigned in March 1949. Under Albert Lunceford, the new Greater Los Angeles CIO Council promptly condemned communism and affirmed its support for Truman's foreign policy. *California Eagle* columnist and labor activist John M. Lee chastised the "phonies, the double-standard boys, the opportunists and the boss-inspired reactionaries" that had conspired to force Connelly out. "Mark it down," he wrote, "that the loss of Slim Connelly was the first of what will be a series of devastating losses to be endured by the CIO here." Los Angeles–based CPUSA leader Dorothy Healey, who had married Connelly "for all the wrong reasons" in 1947, retrospectively offered a more sobering analysis that held the Communist leader more responsible for his own downfall. Obesity and problem drinking had wracked his health. Worse yet, Healey surmised, the CPUSA's maneuvers to make Connelly "a 'leader' in the CIO just brought out his most egocentric and self-destructive side." Her greater concern was that the CPUSA's removal from the Los Angeles and California CIO councils had permanently corroded the party. Over the next decade, it became politically isolated and increasingly irrelevant to those not on the far left or far right of the political spectrum. FBI arrests and surveillance combined with internal party purges of "white chauvinists" and "homosexuals" to drive membership down further. In spite of its efforts to build the Civil Rights Congress and mobilize opposition to McCarthyism, the Los Angeles CP lost over 90 percent of its membership during the 1950s.[7]

Most devastatingly, the demise of the Left-led CIO deprived the city of its most significant organizational vehicle for building a multiracial and class-conscious social movement. To be certain, the CIO's broad approach to organizing around both workplace and community issues in the mid-1940s had its blind spots. Laid off from relatively well-paying jobs as the war ended, African American longshoremen felt abandoned by the International Longshoremen's and Warehousemen's Union in Los Angeles. Ignoring Black protests, leftist union leader Harry Bridges allowed the local to hire whites almost exclusively because he feared defections to the AFL. Nonetheless, the CIO's efforts to connect labor with civil rights issues were substantial. The Los Angeles council organized numerous committees and conferences to address the "new and special problems" postwar conversion was creating for workers of color and to push for a permanent FEPC. It sought to train its members on "how to fight discrimination in the shop and in the community," and it intervened in cases of voter disenfranchisement, police brutality, racial harassment within schools, and attacks on homeowners of color. Furthermore, it built an alliance with the NAACP, cosponsoring its membership drives and circulating antilynching petitions. The Los Angeles CIO Council also pledged to fight for "protection of all those Mexican workers now in this country and especially in Southern California" from exploitation, discrimination, and "the threat of deportation." Although the council resolved to support Japanese Americans returning from internment camps, it could potentially have had an even greater impact on the Japanese American community. Elsewhere, the postwar CIO became known as a dependable advocate of Japanese American civil rights in Northern California and the principal organization for the empowerment of Japanese American workers in Honolulu. In the wake of the purges, however, the CIO left much to be desired. Gone were the internationals that had made the greatest advances toward breaking down racial and gender divisions, organizing new areas of employment, and orienting workers' strategy toward movement building rather than "business unionism." Although the CIO generally remained on the record as opposed to discriminatory hiring, it was far less willing to engage in struggles outside the workplace.[8]

Labor's retreat from civil rights activism became even sharper following the AFL-CIO merger in 1955. Scott Greer found rampant evidence of racism in his broad survey of Los Angeles–area AFL-CIO trade unions in the 1950s. White workers continued to use union leverage to preserve their own privileges. Defying a relatively progressive leader, one belligerently declared his rank-and-file companions would "shut the plant down" rather than allow "those niggers to come down and get jobs with us." Trade unions who recruited workers of color as a defensive measure made no effort to elevate them above the bottom levels of employment. Above all, they failed to appreciate the strategic relationship between race and class. One white labor leader explained his union could not "afford to fight for [racial] equality" instead of "simple commercial things—wages, hours and working conditions."[9]

ANTICOMMUNISM AND BLACK LEADERSHIP

Whereas the ubiquitous nature of segregation and the immediate prospect of mass job openings had acted as centripetal forces for African American political mobilization during World War II, the selective nature of postwar integration and repression generated centrifugal forces. As the unique set of wartime conditions unraveled, the clash of opinions and interests that had always been a feature of Black community politics returned to the fore. The same brand of militancy that had propelled Negro Victory leaders to prominence during the war cast them as Cold War subversives regardless of their professed ideology. At the height of his popularity in 1945, Clayton Russell presided over seven thousand members at the People's Independent Church, served as NAACP vice president, led the Negro Victory Committee, and kept watch over five cooperative markets and one bank. Within a year, the cooperative economic endeavors collapsed and grassroots support waned. Russell's failed 1946 bid for a seat on the county Board of Supervisors was an ominous sign of how the wartime momentum of Black social democrats stood on the verge of depletion. Operating under the auspices of the former NVC (renamed the People's Victory Committee), he ran a grassroots campaign that emphasized public employment, spending on social needs, and regulation of industry and investment. Despite endorsements from the Los Angeles CIO Council and prominent Black ministers and business owners, Russell garnered only three thousand votes while losing to incumbent Leonard Roach. Convinced that the Victory Committee and allied groups had become a victim of their own success, he surmised that the accomplishment of activists' immediate wartime objectives, particularly the opening up of jobs, had dampened the masses' urgency to fight. Quite possibly, many shared some of white America's consumer ethos and believed that continued economic growth was the best remedy for their troubles. Although Russell remained loyal to Truman and the Democrats in the late 1940s, the fiery minister was soon relieved of the numerous positions of authority and ceremonial prestige he once held. He was stripped of his KOWL radio program, which had been a cornerstone of his popularity. Amidst accusations he was too "friendly with communism," he even resigned his post at People's Independent Church. Scaling down his activities, he charged the FBI and the IRS were harassing him. He later launched a new broadcast and the smaller Church of Divine Guidance on the Westside in October 1953, but Russell vowed his sermons would not address "extra-religious matters." The *Tribune* celebrated his downfall, labeling him as a "demagogic pastor" and one of a long line of charlatan Black leaders who proclaimed themselves "a Messiah come to save the Negro." It argued that Russell's agitation was senselessly polarizing, swelling the list of the Black community's enemies and generating internal discord. Only after the radicalism of the 1960s reopened space for Black activism would he reemerge as a protest leader.[10]

While some African Americans argued that Negro Victory leaders had fallen out of touch with the community, others retorted that a repressive climate stymied those who followed their conscience. The saga of Charlotta Bass provides fodder for both points of view. She became a sharp critic of American Cold War policies, while asserting that the masses were waking up to recognize that communists did "wonderful things for the common people." The *Eagle*'s steadfast support for left-wing activists and their causes brought notoriety for Bass, who was nominated for vice president by the Progressive Party in 1952. Although she stridently repudiated allegations she was a member of the Communist Party, Bass was an outspoken anti-imperialist and openly celebrated the Chinese Revolution for inspiring "hope for freedom in the world." But the base of support for leftist politics in Black Los Angeles dissipated quickly after the war. Revels Cayton's fizzled attempt to revitalize the National Negro Congress as a radical alternative to both the Democratic Party and the "nationalistic jive" of Randolph's March on Washington movement was a telling sign. Despite a promotional tour headed by Paul Robeson, support from prominent African American trade unionists, and the backing of the *Eagle*, the National Negro Congress dissolved in November 1947. Having moved to New York, Cayton "drifted out of the Party" over the next five years. Many others, claiming it had shortchanged the Black struggle, broke sharply with the CPUSA, leaving outspoken leftists like Bass even more isolated. The *Los Angeles Tribune* castigated her for being a "Stalin-whatchamacallit" who wore "a Joseph's coat that literally shrouds the color of her skin." In a move that was heretofore unimaginable, Bass was purged from the NAACP, as both the local and national bodies passed anticommunist measures during the McCarthy era. Citing evidence of subversive activity, as documented by a 1951 state of California "Report on Un-American Activities," the Black sorority Iota Phi Lambda rescinded her honorary membership in August 1956. That the honor had been bestowed on her only eight years prior, a time when her identity as a fellow traveler of the CPUSA was more than obvious, demonstrated just how quickly and abruptly the fortunes of African American leftists had turned.[11]

Perhaps the most historic Cold War shift in Black community leadership occurred when the *Eagle* changed ownership in April 1951. After owning and editing the newspaper for nearly forty years, Bass was anything but pleased to give up control to a group headed by civil rights lawyer Loren Miller. *Eagle* supporters claimed that free copies of other Black newspapers were being distributed throughout the community in a drive "to kill its circulation." Signing off on her last On the Sidewalk column, Bass remarked that "would-be American fascists" who deemed "it essential to do everything within their power to prevent the continued existence of a free press" had run her out of business. She was particularly disheartened that some of her "own people" she had helped "to become successes in business, in the professions, and in political office [had] joined forces with the enemy." In part, this must have been a thinly veiled reference to Miller, who had worked at the *Eagle* in his youth. Despite her recent chagrin, Bass was proud that she had stood with "the working people" and they had struggled alongside her. Her final line with the *Eagle* read, "I am very confident that within my lifetime yet I will see first-class citizenship achieved for all my people, true democracy for all Americans, and peace in all the world!" She remained politically active through her elder years and penned her memoirs before dying of a cerebral hemorrhage on April 12, 1969.[12]

Loren Miller used the *Eagle* to stake a claim to the political center of postwar Black Los Angeles. The talented attorney was now thoroughly disillusioned with the CPUSA, which he charged had "sold Negroes out completely" because of its subservience to Soviet interests. Chastising its former publisher for letting it become an "extreme left-wing newspaper," Miller contended that the *Eagle* had sunk to "a very low ebb." With Miller as publisher and S. Wendell Green as editor, the new *Eagle* vowed to continue pushing "for complete integration of Negroes into every phase of American life through the democratic process," as well as decent housing, social security, collective bargaining rights, and "Negro business." But respecting the narrowed parameters of Cold War political discourse, its anticommunism was explicit and its partisanship an open secret. In Miller's eyes, responsible leadership entailed supporting the Democratic Party and working with establishment figures to advance a realistic agenda of reform. When appealing for funds, the *Eagle*'s new leadership emphasized its ability to use ostensibly "non-partisan" promotions to mobilize Blacks to vote for Democratic candidates.[13]

An abrupt change in organizational tenor marked the early postwar history of the Los Angeles NAACP, whose civil rights advocacy became defined and contained by Cold War imperatives. Through cooperative recruitment with the CIO, the branch membership reached fourteen thousand by 1946. The purge of Reds from the CIO, however, altered the NAACP's tactical relationship to organized labor. As moderate labor leaders now dictated the terms of the "Negro-labor" alliance, NAACP leaders had little incentive to work with leftists. Indeed, given the repressive Cold War political climate, local and national NAACP leaders actively sought to disassociate themselves from communists, be they white or African American. For instance, the NAACP blamed the collapse of a 1948 protest against discrimination at Sears in Santa Monica on the involvement of a few white CPUSA members. Although protest organizer Frank Barnes, a Black member of the NAACP, was not a CPUSA member, Sears managed to get him fired from his job at the postal service for consorting with subversives in violation of the Smith Act. Local NAACP bodies conformed to the anticommunist policies of national leaders. The Southern California Area Council's 1953 resolution against "Communist infiltration" exemplified the NAACP's stance equating "World Communism" with "the destruction of civil liberties." Ostracized by the organization because of this stance, Charlotta Bass lamented, "It appears to me that the local N.A.A.C.P. leaders have accepted the fatal direction of the Ku Klux Klan, or the Joe McCarthy committee."[14]

By the mid-1950s, while its parent organization was scoring a major civil rights victory in *Brown v. Board of Education*, the Los Angeles NAACP had become mired in turmoil and disarray. Chapter members had cast aside their president, Thomas Griffith, as membership plummeted during the late 1940s. Griffith had already broken ties with the leftists who had been his close wartime allies, but he was charged with putting his personal interests ahead of the organization as he developed a special bond with Mayor Bowron. Although the branch harbored a reputation for being "right wing," new president E. I. Robinson was also hounded by charges that he was tied to communism. By 1954, membership fell below five thousand, and even this figure masked the branch's general level of inactivity. During the whole year, only six general meetings were held, usually with no more than forty people in attendance.

Less than a hundred dollars had been raised at all the meetings combined. Still, a divisive battle for the branch presidency heated up in December 1954. There were two main candidates, and supporters of each attacked the other as a communist sympathizer. Although Loren Miller's *Eagle* also adhered to an anticommunist line, it characterized such a use of McCarthyist tactics as "extremely unfortunate." The newspaper declared, "The charges and counter charges of Communism are playing into the hands of our enemies." Local dentist and longtime NAACP member H. Claude Hudson announced that he had been pushed "by many community leaders and organizations" to run for branch president in order to prevent "Communist infiltration." He was defeated by Thomas G. Neusom, whose "first official act" was to push through a resolution banning from branch membership "members of the Communist Party" and those of "any organization on the attorney general's list as subversive." With membership rising back to nearly fifteen thousand and the group's finances in better order by the end of 1956, Neusom argued that the communist ban had been key to the branch's recovery. In fact, the gains seem to have been mainly inspired by the Los Angeles Black community's desire to support the burgeoning civil rights movement in the South. Regional field secretary Tarea Hall Pittman reported that the controversial local election had caused "strife, misunderstanding and division."[15]

For the NAACP and other civil rights advocates, the Cold War produced contradictory tendencies. At their most effective, organizers seized on mainstream political leaders' concern for America's global image as the defender of the "free world." As Mary Dudziak contends, "While the Cold War narrowed acceptable civil rights discourse and led to sanctions against individuals who stepped outside those narrow bounds, within them it gave the movement important and effective leverage." Reflecting the new ethical-juridical discourse supporting integration, victories against formal segregation at the state and federal levels provided the greatest evidence of progress. In 1948, six years before the *Brown* decision, the NAACP stood at the center of the successful campaign to outlaw state enforcement of racial restrictive covenants. That same year, a coalition headed by the Catholic Interracial Council of Los Angeles struck down California's antimiscegenation law. Strategy to challenge the law had been formulated through multiracial forums sponsored by the California Council for Civic Unity, which had originally formed to support Japanese internees. In 1954, the Los Angeles NAACP also achieved a symbolic local victory over segregation. For more than a year, NAACP attorneys had been pressuring the city to stop confining Blacks in the fire department to two stations (No. 14 and No. 30) in the Central Avenue district. When Mayor Norris Poulson threatened to remove the defiant chief John H. Alderson if he did not comply with an integration order, two Black firemen were transferred to a Studio City station in late 1954. On a national level, civil rights were afforded a new primacy within electoral politics. By supporting American foreign policy, the NAACP maintained an amicable relationship with President Truman. With African Americans casting decisive votes in the tight 1948 election, Truman developed the most advanced civil rights platform of any major presidential candidate in history. In California, the cushion Black voters supplied was greater than his overall margin of victory. In one of his first actions following the election, Truman ordered the armed forces desegregated. His Justice Department also repeatedly filed amicus curiae briefs supporting the legal battles for civil rights. In these regards, the quests for national security and racial integration moved hand in hand.[16]

At the same time, the Cold War rendered the militant activism of World War II an increasingly distant memory. The war on leftist subversives deprived insurgent groups of membership and damned the reputations of previously effective leaders. Despite the issuance of the universal declaration of human rights and the emergence of liberation movements around the globe, most Black leaders framed their struggle within parameters constrained by national imperatives. As historian Carol Anderson points out, whenever Truman balked at meeting the NAACP's demands, the organization had "no place else to go." Its organizational development, like that of other civil rights groups, was thus stunted by an overriding concern with anticommunism. Fear of being branded subversive or opening the door to involvement of would-be subversives caused moderate leaders to curtail the participatory activities that had emboldened working-class people to see themselves as agents of change. Perhaps even more disconcertingly, using "Communists" as a scapegoat for their organizations' setbacks often precluded these leaders from self-critically examining their strategies and tactics. Outside these circles, some members of the Black community began to question the effect of Cold War accommodations to state power. In 1957, a writer for the *Los Angeles Sentinel* was moved to ask, "Are those who are qualified to be Negro leaders being 'bought off'? Are those who could be Negro leaders merely 'tools' of political parties or pressure groups?"[17]

FROM FAIR EMPLOYMENT TO INTERRACIAL TOLERANCE

Although the Cold War agenda of civil rights activists scored historic victories against legalized segregation, it made little headway toward securing fair and decent employment for tens of thousands of Black workers in Los Angeles. As anticommunist measures reined in the agitation for social democratic reform, integration became tied less to the working-class concerns of the war and more to the prospects of an emerging class of minority professionals. With the June 1946 retirement of the Fair Employment Practices Commission (FEPC), the federal government withdrew its primary mechanism to eradicate racially discriminatory hiring practices. Despite its imperfections, the FEPC had offered activists the ability to wield the power of state intervention against private employers. In this regard, the FEPC had lent political leverage to civil rights organizing similar to how the National Labor Relations Board boosted trade unionism. Searching for a way to recover the function of the federal FEPC, fair employment proponents focused on California government in the November 1946 election. Beginning what would become a protracted effort, they called on voters to create a state-level FEPC by passing Proposition 11. However, the same electorate that defeated the Proposition 15 initiative to expand the Alien Land Law soundly rejected the FEPC proposal, which garnered barely 30 percent approval. While California voters were not wont to pass an exclusionary measure, neither were they eager to authorize using state resources to combat discrimination. Whites, in particular, demonstrated their willingness to accept a new level of interracial tolerance simultaneous with their opposition to extending economic justice across racial and ethnic lines.[18]

The absence of any governmental body committed to combating discrimination facilitated the reemergence of racist hiring patterns that had retreated during the war. White workers regrouped to defend the rule of white privilege in hiring. Free of the duress imposed by wartime production imperatives, federal agencies lacked an urgent commitment to fair employment. Workers of color seeking placements from the local offices of the United States Employment Service (USES) found themselves increasingly passed over for manufacturing jobs and relegated to public sector, domestic, and low-wage service work. In 1946, a coalition of the CIO and diverse ethnic organizations charged that 95 percent of USES job orders were processed as "white only" postings. Their protests, however, were blunted by the counterprotest of industry representatives and the intransigent attitude of government officials. Arguing that state intervention was impeding market efficiency, representatives of the California Manufacturers Association called on the USES to boost the supply of labor and dampen wages by forcing workers to accept whatever job was offered. Lobbyists for industry characterized the unemployed as "conscienceless parasites," who were encouraged by lax USES operations to " 'vacation' at the wage-earner's expense." Not only did the USES director for California, Raymond Krah, unite with manufacturers in condemnation of "the lazy ones who [refused] to undertake and continue anything as obnoxious as work"; he also dismissed as "absurd" charges that his agency enabled discrimination. Civil rights groups accused him of acting "shamelessly evasive." Despite the limitations of federal agencies set up during the war, their demise certainly did not advance the cause of civil rights. Because of what it called the "reluctance of city and state government agencies to take a strong position on non-discrimination," the Los Angeles Urban League experienced extreme difficulties placing Black workers into jobs. While the California State Employment Service assumed much of the federal agency's former responsibilities, it continued to post discriminatory orders. A January 1951 study revealed that over two-thirds of all work orders at four of its Southland branches stated racial, ethnic, or religious preferences. While civil rights advocates successfully pressured the agency to stop accepting discriminatory orders, private employment agencies developed schemes to continue taking exclusive requests well into the 1960s. The B'nai Brith asserted that applications were marked with secret codes, such as "no 99's" to signal "don't hire Blacks."[19]

As civil rights activists renewed their campaign for fair employment measures in the 1950s, the anticommunist paradigm shaped the arguments of those both for and against the FEPC. With hopes for a "permanent" federal FEPC largely dashed, advocates focused on the state and local levels. Opponents of a state or local FEPC denounced it as a measure created by communists to deprive Americans of freedom. Gordon G. Hair, publisher of five local newspapers, condemned a proposed county ordinance as an "iniquitous proposal" brought forth by "people who believe in the Russian communistic way of life." Howard V. Fulton, the manager of an Anchor Hocking Glass Corporation subsidiary, agreed that any type of FEPC was unwise and unnecessary. "There just are no depressed groups in America," he noted, "except in the frenzied minds of an energetic group of communists and their fellow-travelers." Rejecting the ostensibly coercive methods they associated with communism, corporate leaders and their lobbyists maintained that a voluntary approach to integration was most effective. Insisting that they were already practicing nondiscriminatory hiring, they contended that legislating fair employment would actually inhibit progress. The wartime paradigm shift in racial discourse prompted many of them to become converts to a more liberal perspective on human nature, which they conveniently deployed to justify the status quo. Before the war, many employers had opposed the passage of antidiscrimination measures by asserting that racial inequalities and divisions were natural and immutable. In the postwar era, they argued that regulation and legislation were unnecessary because, in the words of Lockheed president Courtlandt S. Gross, "any instances of unfair employment practices which may exist can be and will be corrected in the normal course of mankind's social development." Supporting "the principle of voluntary action," Randolph Van Nostrand of the Merchants and

Manufacturers Association advocated hiring on the basis of "individual qualifications and merit . . . without regard to race, religion or national origin." Citing a 1953 survey, he stated that "members of so-called minority groups" so often failed to secure jobs because 8 percent of Asian, 28 percent of Mexican, and 44 percent of African American applicants were unqualified. The implication of his argument was that white employers felt more justified turning away African Americans seeking work than those of any other race.[20]

FEPC proponents offered their own multilayered anticommunist argument. In the 1950s, the Los Angeles Committee for Equal Employment Opportunity comprised a cross section of Black, Japanese, Jewish, and Mexican American organizations, as well as trade unions. Loren Miller served as its cochair while the JACL's Saburo Kido was an honorary chairman. The committee first argued that discrimination prevented people of color from giving their full contribution to the fight against "Communist totalitarianism." In this regard, postwar communism replaced wartime fascism as the anti-American evil used to represent the antithesis of fair employment. Second, the committee asserted that the prevalence of racism aided Communist Party agitation and recruitment efforts by providing "grist for their world-wide propaganda." Finally, it even blamed the Communists themselves for the FEPC proposal's lack of support. How was this possible? The coalition claimed that the staggering electoral defeat of the 1946 initiative for a statewide FEPC was due to the "great clamor" Communists had made *in support of* the measure. By doing so, they "created tremendous confusion among the loyal and responsible individuals and groups" that supported an FEPC. Such persons "found themselves in the dilemma of having to choose between voting *against* legislation which they sincerely favored in principle, or voting *for* a measure which had become rather thoroughly stigmatized in the public mind by the CP activity in its behalf." Some moderate FEPC supporters even accused Communists of campaigning publicly for civil rights laws as a conscious effort to poison them by association. They accused Communists of intentionally derailing reform in order to incite people of color to open rebellion. These arguments reflected the desperation of a campaign that had repeatedly fallen short before the California legislature, the Los Angeles County Board of Supervisors, and the Los Angeles City Council. The coalition came closest to local victory on January 9, 1958, when a vote on an FEPC ordinance found the fourteen members of the Los Angeles City Council deadlocked, with seven votes each way, for and against.[21]

Civil rights advocates were finally given a boost when their favored candidate, Pat Brown, was elected governor in 1958 and liberal Democrats bolstered their standing in the state legislature. The new governor, for instance, appointed Loren Miller to serve as a municipal court judge for Los Angeles County in 1960. In the realm of policy, two civil rights laws defined the most significant achievements early in Brown's first term. The 1959 Unruh Civil Rights Act prohibited discrimination in public accommodations and allowed aggrieved parties to sue for restitution plus $250 in damages. Signed into law that same year, the Fair Employment Act outlawed discrimination by employers and unions, while creating a statewide FEPC to administer the law and investigate complaints. The California FEPC was granted the authority to request court injunctions to stop discriminatory practices, and those violating its orders faced misdemeanor criminal charges. Yet its main purpose was to resolve problems through negotiation. Consequently, this long-sought body would prove far less imposing than its supporters had hoped and its detractors had feared it would be. Maintaining the primacy of voluntary steps toward integration, employers fought to curtail the FEPC's scope. North American Aviation's corporate director of personnel, Dwight R. Zook, was one of five original commissioners the governor appointed to the statewide FEPC. An active member of the Los Angeles Urban League, Zook was white, as were three other appointees. C. L. Dellums, a longtime leader of the NAACP and Pullman Porters in Northern California, was the only African American commissioner. Brown seemingly chose Zook, a Republican, to represent both Republicans and industry executives. Testifying before the Los Angeles hearings of the US Commission on Civil Rights in January 1960, Zook complained that too many "hypersensitive members of minority groups" and others with "ulterior motives" were lodging "ill-considered and baseless complaints." Defending his company's "merit employment policy," Zook concluded North American Aviation's "slow progress" toward integration was a result of "retrogression caused by over-emotionalism."[22]

Before the 1959 creation of the California FEPC, the burden of advancing civil rights issues within government had fallen on the interracial committees that had first sprung up in response to the home front crises of World War II. Until the 1960s, the City of Los Angeles even lacked one of these. Although Mayor Bowron had established a committee to advise him on home front unity issues during the war, the Los Angeles City Council in a close vote rejected a 1945 proposal for a Community Relations Board, which would have served as the city's official interracial committee. Opposition to the proposal fused red-baiting with arguments for voluntarism. Councilman Charles Allen, "convinced" the proposal was a "Communistic setup," argued that "thinking members of minority groups" had no desire for an interracial body. Lloyd Davis was one of four others who contended that the proposed committee would "create more riots and race discrimination than it would do good." These opponents were especially troubled that an official interracial committee would challenge the racial restrictive covenants that many of their white constituents held dear. Maintaining that racism could not be "removed by force," the *Los Angeles Times* offered the clearest articulation of the voluntarist principle of interracial tolerance. It stated, "Prejudice is a matter of the mind and the conscience and they cannot be controlled by legislation, though they can be influenced by education and by persuasion." As there was no "short cut" to completing this "long-time job," the *Times* concluded that "an official interracial committee to protect and advance the interests of so-called minority groups" would serve only "to rouse more prejudice and ill-feeling than it allayed, to emphasize the differences between peoples rather than to minimize them."[23]

Civil rights activists saluted the Los Angeles County Board of Supervisors' creation of the Committee for Interracial Progress (CIP) in March 1944. However, much like the California FEPC, it proved in practice to be far less potent than they had wished. While the committee did a decent job gathering data on communities of color and documenting social problems in areas such as housing, education, and employment, it was an advisory body with no authority to issue "cease and desist" orders to those who perpetuated discrimination. It had scarce resources to act much at all. During 1951, the renamed Human Relations Committee had only two staff members and an annual budget of $8,430, roughly one-tenth that of its Chicago counterpart.[24]

Although the committee was interracial in name, whites held firm control during its formative years. Its agenda was thus decided by the balance of power between white conservatives and white liberals, with both sides exerting influence that neutralized militant activists of color. While serving as the inaugural chair of the CIP, B. O. Miller, a white man who headed the Los Angeles Chamber of Commerce, advanced the voluntarism embraced by the conservative *Times* editorial board. In January 1945, Miller stated his belief that restrictive covenants were "fundamentally unjust" but were legal and "established custom." He warned that "until we have advanced much farther on the road toward" racial tolerance, serious problems would only result from the races being "suddenly thrown" together. Instead, Miller advocated actions to promote the voluntary and gradual abandonment of racial covenants. Given its resource limitations and narrow ideological parameters, the CIP's work emphasized education to reduce prejudice and promote racial harmony through moral suasion. In December 1948, its members were counseled to promote racial integration as if they were running a business and advertising "a product which meets a need." The key was delivering "a skillful sales presentation" that did not "create enemies" or seek "to defeat or embarrass opponents." Ultimately, the CIP resolved, "If we portray the democratic ideal vividly enough, the majority will subscribe to it." Unexamined, however, was the white majority's deep investment in the culture and political economy of racism. White liberals seemed particularly invested in the new and fashionable ideas about the nature of humankind in the wake of the Nazi reign of terror. An early CIP strategy session stressed that its members should know "the difference between race and culture and the basic fundamentals of anthropology." This sort of educational work, however, generally failed to address working-class priorities raised by social democrats.[25]

While they supported remedial state action to varying degrees, white moderates and liberals involved with civil rights politics sought to exclude noted African American activists, whose presence they felt would discredit the CIP and other interracial committees. A pivotal white player in the moderate civil rights nexus, George Gleason was appointed executive secretary of the CIP. He secretly expressed concern that both Charlotta Bass and Clayton Russell were "radicals" and that J. Raymond Henderson was "very pro-Negro, anti-white." These prominent Negro Victory leaders were minimally involved in the CIP. At the same time, Gleason recognized that "Uncle Tom" figures like Floyd Covington would not make effective leaders either. Gleason described the Urban League official as a "southern type of Negro who 'kowtows' to the whites. Liked by them; not liked by his own race." As interracial bodies of all kinds arose throughout the nation, some Black leaders expressed serious reservations about the rising prominence afforded the self-proclaimed white experts on race relations. National Urban League director Lester Granger, for instance, chastised the wartime emergence of what he mockingly dubbed FDR's "white cabinet on Negro affairs [that] represented no one except the individuals included." Its "half-baked and often unwise" proposals served only "to infuriate the Negro population" and "to misinform well-intentioned officials, or provide the ill-intentioned with shifty ways of evading issues."[26]

If white leaders of interracial relations work deemed "radicals" and "Uncle Toms" unbefitting allies, who among the Los Angeles Black community best fit the bill? Two types stood out. Regardless of whatever urgency to end racism these acceptable Blacks felt personally, their strategy of working with establishment figures often necessitated constraining their activism to the parameters of mainstream political discourse. Importantly, both types of African American leaders embraced the Cold War anticommunist imperative. The first was a moderate-to-liberal civil rights advocate, typically from a well-educated background, who believed in working within the system to combat racial discrimination. As Loren Miller demonstrated when he took charge of the *Eagle* and castigated Charlotta Bass's left-wing politics, such leaders also needed to prove they were willing to criticize "irresponsible" elements within communities of color. (On those occasions when race relations committees designated an "Oriental" slot, JACL officials were frequently chosen, as they had been groomed to play exactly this moderate leadership role.) The second type of minority leader commonly found on race relations committees was the socially liberal but fiscally conservative representative of the Black bourgeoisie. These "race men" embodied the struggle for African American advancement while upholding the central tenets of the American capitalist order. They had stood at the core of the Negro Victory movement and rose further in stature within the conservative Cold War climate. Demonstrating the bipartisan nature of civil rights advocacy, at least on some levels, these businessmen were often Republicans. Repeatedly appointed to serve on governmental commissions, Norman O. Houston and George A. Beavers of Golden State Mutual Life Insurance (GSM) exemplified this brand of leader. Propelled to social and political prominence by GSM's continued financial success within the Black community and beyond, Houston and Beavers participated in countless meetings and committees designed to improve race relations. They were self-assertive economic nationalists who simultaneously opposed racial separatism. While more committed than most white corporate leaders to state intervention against discrimination, their connection to members of the white establishment stemmed from a conservative economic ideology. True to the spirit of the "open shop," GSM fired 126 striking employees in early 1957 amid ongoing picketing. In a 1961 speech, Houston stated that his belief in "the doctrine of self-help" caused him to oppose "the Welfare State for any level of society."[27]

Overall, the rise of the official and nongovernmental interracial committees signified that Los Angeles residents, like many others in the nation as a whole, were striving for a new level of interracial tolerance. But as domestic containment measures squelched the momentum of the social democratic movement, postwar integratonism exhibited a predominant class bias. In a pamphlet released by the American Council on Race Relations, Lloyd Fisher commented, "Interracial organizations are almost always of white inspiration and commonly of white middle and upper class origin." He further noted that all of Southern California's interracial committees tended to appoint the same select group of minority elites as members. "What is to be built," Fisher concluded, "must be an organization of the people rather than of colored and white spokesmen for the people."[28]

REDEVELOPMENT AND THE "SLUMS" DEBATE

The postwar controversy surrounding public housing and urban renewal best revealed the political biases against working-class members of Black Los Angeles and other communities of color. A review of this history reveals how wartime efforts to foreground the self-activity of African American workers devolved into debates over how best to deal with the problem of Black and Mexican "slum" dwellers. At least initially, liberals and civil rights advocates supported a tripartite agenda of "slum" removal, public housing construction, and urban renewal deemed consistent with modernist notions of progress. Through this process, outdated and crowded structures would be replaced by clean and modern facilities. Low-income families would have an opportunity to live in decent housing, and the whole of society would ostensibly benefit from social harmony and improved public health standards. Black activists entered the postwar era fighting for access to public housing, and they proceeded to remove almost every barrier or quota in effect. By 1960, African Americans comprised 65 percent of the city's public housing residents—five times their share of the general population. Yet this was viewed not as an accomplishment but as a sign of oppression, rendering meaningless the elimination of formal segregation within the projects. Through institutional mechanisms, federal policies had promoted a two-tiered system of housing—separate and unequal. While government subsidies spurred construction of a nearly endless supply of single-family houses for suburban and white homeowners, the malnourished public housing system shouldered the stigma of poverty and ghettoization.[29]

The dramatic and well-told story of public housing's downfall in Los Angeles needs only a brief recounting here. When a Democratic US Congress passed the 1949 Housing Act as a measure of Keynesian stimulation, the city was allocated 10,000 of the 810,000 total units of public residences authorized for construction within six years. Only a fraction of the authorized units would end up being built, locally and nationally. Since the federal government placed housing management in the hands of localities, the battles that ensued were fought at the municipal level. Los Angeles foes of public housing waged an intense four-year campaign that drew on voter initiatives, lawsuits, and public propaganda to bore away the substance of the original agenda approved by the city council. The final showdown came in 1953, when their candidate, Norris Poulson, made public housing the central issue of the mayoral campaign. Accused of supporting socialism, four-term Republican mayor Fletcher Bowron was abandoned by many of his former allies and swept out of office. Poulson's victory augured the elimination of thousands of units of public housing and low-income housing from redevelopment plans. At the same time, government agencies granted private interests urban renewal subsidies, which were now divorced from obligations to the less fortunate. In line with the concerns of the new mayor's downtown sponsors, the most dramatic alterations of course took place in Chavez Ravine/Elysian Park and Bunker Hill. Nearly one thousand homes had been condemned in

Chavez Ravine to make way for over three thousand planned public housing units, two schools, four churches, and several playgrounds. During Poulson's term, the site was practically given away to the Dodgers in a sweetheart deal to lure the baseball team from Brooklyn. Authorities dragged out the last residents refusing to budge from the predominantly Mexican American community. Because the Elysian Park project had been designed to accommodate casualties of nearby urban renewal, its cancellation also affected those uprooted as the downtown elite erected cultural landmarks in place of the decaying Bunker Hill mansions that had been converted into low-rent apartments and boardinghouses.[30]

The turmoil over public housing altered the discourse of racial and class politics in two profound ways. First, it strengthened the resolve of private interests, who tied their fortunes to a conservative economic agenda. Elements of the real estate industry alongside the Chamber of Commerce, the *Los Angeles Times*, and the Hearst papers steadfastly opposed not only public housing but also rent control and regulation of the housing market. Builders, realtors, lenders, and landlords argued that mass public construction of residences would cut into their profits by increasing the housing supply. Developers were further concerned they would be hampered by new government standards for housing. Feeding on McCarthyism, these forces waged a ruthless and relentless war on "socialized housing" through front groups like the Committee for Home Protection and the Committee Against Socialist Housing (CASH) headed by megadeveloper Fritz B. Burns. They were often the same voices that denounced open housing measures, and they employed similar arguments decrying the state's intrusion into private affairs. A 1952 CASH pamphlet asserted that the government's construction of homes provided "a privileged few their rent below cost—with the rest of us paying the difference." Declaring public housing a threat to national security, CASH went so far as to claim it was "the *last rung* in the ladder toward complete *socialism*, one step this side of *Communism* and *Our* downfall." Such inflammatory rhetoric heated passions on both sides of the conflict. Condemning the city's abrogation of its commitment to public housing, a coalition of housing advocates headed by Monsignor Thomas J. O'Dwyer declared the reversal was "the result of the most disgraceful special interest propaganda and political pressure spectacles ever witnessed by the citizens of Los Angeles." But as Bowron's defeat would attest, political figures standing up for public housing could be taken down by well-financed smear campaigns. Helen Gahagan Douglas, the Broadway star turned Democratic congresswoman representing the Central Avenue district, lashed out at the leaders of the real estate industry for their failure to seek "any solution to the housing problem except on their own greed-dictated terms." She argued that developers had exerted so much control over public

Fig. 9.1. "Slum" housing in the Central Avenue district, 1952. Liberals aroused middle-class fears of "slums" to build their case for public housing and redevelopment. Security Pacific Collection/Los Angeles Public Library.

housing programs that the public was now being subjected to "the spectacle of a Veterans' Emergency Housing Program that builds only Bel-Air mansions and bowling alleys!" Her political theatrics, however, wore thin after three terms in the House. In one of the defining moments of his career, Richard Nixon crushed Douglas in the 1950 Senate race. With his supporters dubbing Douglas the "Pink Lady," Nixon rode the emerging anticommunist tidal wave to victory.[31]

Defenders of public housing may in fact have done more than its assailants to stigmatize communities of color. Historian Daryl Michael Scott has argued that postwar liberals, in their critique of biological racism, advanced a "damage thesis" highlighting the reported cultural deficiencies of African Americans. Asserting these ills were a product of detrimental environments, they sought to build a case for liberal social engineering and state intervention as remedial measures. While Scott emphasizes the manner by which such arguments appealed to white guilt, the lasting effect of these appeals may have been their rekindling of white and middle-class fears of working-class communities of color. Thrown

onto the defensive by anticommunist attacks, proponents of public housing ultimately built their case around the need to eliminate "slums." A
pamphlet by the mayoral-appointed Committee for Home Front Unity
exemplified this line of argumentation with its headline stating "This is
your fault, diseases breed in Los Angeles Slums." It co-opted the collective voice of poor people of color to issue this frightening message framed
by contrasting pictures of suburban homes and wooden shacks:

> We Live Here
> You Live There
> BUT CONTAGIOUS AND INFECTIOUS DISEASE TRAVELS WITH US

The pamphlet then showed a collage of faces and bodies representing the
city's multiracial diversity and offered these words to the well-off classes:

> Thousands of us enter your homes daily as servants, repairmen, tradesmen, etc.
> We are constantly with you and your children in schools, clubs, churches.
> Packed, overcrowded buses, streetcars and other means of public transportation.

Increasingly under fire from the right, Mayor Bowron stated he was "not
and never [had] been a champion of public housing" but that he was
merely trying to aid those "compelled to live in unsanitary housing" and
"reared amid depressing surroundings." Echoing this approach, the
NAACP's 1959 "Housing Manual" mandated that the organization's fair
housing advocates "exploit the negative aspects of segregated housing" by
warning voters and public officials they would shoulder "the tax burden
of increased municipal and social services to slum areas."[32]

The end result of the "slums" debate was a double defeat for working-
class communities of color. Rallying behind "slum" removal, the real estate lobby secured public funds through measures such as Title I of the
1949 Housing Act and the 1954 Urban Renewal Act to eliminate neighborhoods deemed a threat to public health and safety. To seize desired
land for both public use and private profit, officials readily condemned a
broad swath of urban settlement. Since a mere one-fifth of an area needed
to be classified as "blighted" to qualify for subsidies, many relatively sta-
ble communities were ravaged by urban renewal. One-time supporters,
Black leaders began to label the program "Negro removal." Between
1949 and 1968, urban renewal wiped out 425,000 units of low-income
housing nationwide while adding only 125,000 new units, the majority of
which were luxury apartments. In the Los Angeles area, urban renewal
and freeway construction were the primary reasons roughly 2,500 homes
per year were destroyed during the 1950s. The displaced were often
forced to scramble for apartments, whose rents were artificially inflated as
demolition reduced supply. Vastly overrepresented within the ranks of
the displaced, people of color suffered far more than could be measured

materially. In the end, the negative impact of racial stereotyping counteracted whatever positive effect voluntary steps to promote interracial tolerance may have had. As residents of "slum" neighborhoods were dehumanized and disenfranchised, the "damage thesis" contributed directly to the pervasion of the stereotype that African Americans were engulfed in a culture of poverty. Japanese Americans largely escaped this particular form of degradation, since the idea that the Nisei were "damaged" would have undermined the state's contention that the internment was a benevolent and successful measure. However, as biological racism lost political currency, cultural stereotypes of African Americans provided a central rationale for postwar segregation and inequality. An investigative reporter for the *Los Angeles Times* was moved to acknowledge the persistence of white racist ideologies in July 1962. "A good many whites think of the Negro community in terms of crime, slums, poverty and stupidity," he declared. "The stereotype of the shuffling, shiftless darky lingers in their minds and they are satisfied with it."[33]

Coda: Multiracial Eastside Politics

The most prominent voice in local politics to decry both the red-baiting smear of public housing and the dispossession of homeowners in urban renewal zones was that of the Mexican American political pioneer Edward Roybal. A veteran of World War II, he became the first person of color to win election to city council in modern Los Angeles history. Roybal cut his political teeth and built a Mexican American following as president of the Community Service Organization in East Los Angeles. Saul Alinsky, who had developed a national reputation for effectively applying the CIO's trade union organizing strategies to the community setting, had been influential in the Community Service Organization's creation and hired full-time organizer Fred Ross to shape its development. (Branching out across California, the Community Service Organization would also figure prominently in the early career of César Chávez.) Like Alinksy, Roybal negotiated his way through the repressive Cold War climate by supporting anticommunist foreign policy while aggressively pushing for civil rights and economic justice at home. Boosted by the Community Service Organization's registration of eleven thousand Mexican American voters, he possessed a grassroots base of power that granted him independence from the Democratic Party machinery. Roybal's victorious 1949 campaign for the Eastside's Ninth Council District united a cross section of the Mexican American community while garnering the support of leftists in the CIO. It also built a multiracial coalition from a district that included Boyle Heights, Little Tokyo, and portions of the Central Avenue district. Black and Japanese American activists were directly involved, such that a rival candidate's representative was moved to curse Roybal for running "on that unification of minorities claptrap." While Black social democrats had recognized the power and salience of multiracial working-class organizing during the war, their postwar plans never came to fruition. Propelled by the work of and the new energy generated by dozens of grassroots activists, the Roybal movement best carried forward their spirit.[34]

Roybal's historic victory and his multiracial coalition provided Eastside communities of color with a beacon of hope in an otherwise bleak Cold War political landscape. But there were also strict limits to what he and his supporters could accomplish. The alignment of forces pushing through the cutbacks to public housing and dispossession of homes through "slum removal" ensured for the time being that Roybal's voice within municipal politics would mainly be one of principled resistance. Furthermore, anticommunism eventually disrupted multiethnic coalition building in the Eastside. Carey McWilliams, for instance, noted in 1949 that activists from the "largest and most progressive Jewish community" on the West Coast had made unique contributions to multiracial civil rights advances in Los Angeles. Boyle Heights had been the incubator of Jewish radicalism in the city, and Roybal had garnered decisive political and financial backing from Jewish allies. In the 1950s, however, Jewish activist circles were torn apart by McCarthyism. In the end, the Community Service Organization's Mexican American community organizing would continue, but Eastside organizing would fail to marshal the progressive multiracial base required to stave off the polarizing effects of postwar economic restructuring and spatial reorganization. For instance, as people of all races distanced themselves from "slum" dwellers, few of the city's residents backed the Mexican American holdouts against the Dodger Stadium landgrab. Blacks, Asians, and organized labor were no exception. Dismissing the effort of those claiming to "save Chavez Ravine for the people," the *Los Angeles Sentinel* remarked that beyond the Police Academy there was "little else" of substance in the neighborhood.[35]

With bulldozers leveling the Chavez Ravine community and paving the way for Dodger Stadium, the absence of a strong and progressive multiracial movement to challenge the postwar agenda of the city's elites was readily apparent. During the postwar era, the push for racial integration would shift its focus and location. Black wartime activism had given birth to the promise of social democratic reform that was ultimately contained by new patterns of employment discrimination and repressive anticommunist measures. At the same time, liberal reformers portrayed the Eastside's communities of color not as engines of social change but as problems that needed to be eradicated. As the prospects dimmed for Eastside strategies focused on the advancement of workers of color within the industrial order, middle-class fair housing advocates renewed the campaign to integrate the predominantly white neighborhoods in the Westside. "Thus, the Westside would once again become the critical meeting ground of Black and Japanese American aspiration and community formation."

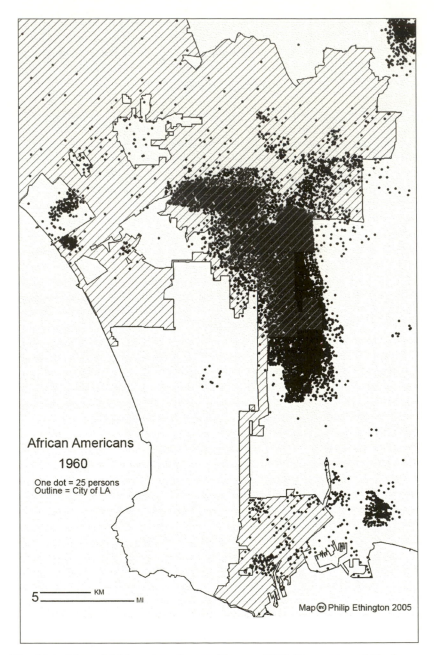

Fig. 10.1. Map of African American residences, 1960. Segregation of Blacks created the South Central Los Angeles ghetto. Ethington et al., *Los Angeles Census Tract Data*.

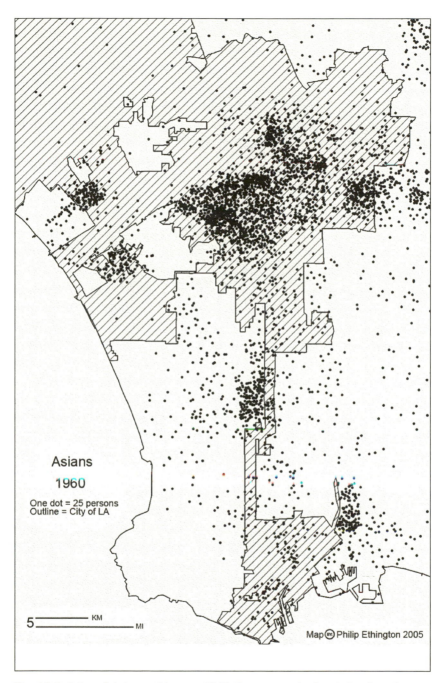

Fig. 10.2. Map of Asian residences, 1960. Japanese and other Asian Americans dispersed into outlying areas. Data drawn from "other" category of census. Ethington et al., *Los Angeles Census Tract Data*.

CHAPTER 10

The Fight for Housing Integration

STRIDING OUT OF SUPERIOR COURT on December 6, 1945, actress Hattie McDaniel declared, "That's one fine judge. [I'm] mighty happy I've still got my home." Judge Thurmond Clarke had just dismissed eight lawsuits brought by white property owners seeking to dislodge Black entrepreneurs and celebrities from the Westside's Sugar Hill neighborhood. Whereas African Americans had previously won racial covenant cases on the basis of technicalities, Clarke opined that his judicial peers had "been avoiding the real issue too long." Setting a regional precedent, he concluded that racial covenants violated the Fourteenth Amendment. As Los Angeles led the nation in legal challenges to housing restrictions, the momentum from more than twenty local cases built toward a 1948 national climax before the US Supreme Court in *Shelley v. Kraemer*. With an argument Thurgood Marshall presented with assistance from Loren Miller, the NAACP and its allies at long last struck down state enforcement of racial restrictive covenants. Although it was soon overshadowed by *Brown v. Board of Education*, *Shelley* was the pivotal case outlawing court-enforced segregation for Los Angeles residents. It was a product of the most extensive litigation effort in the NAACP's history to that point. Black and Japanese Americans alike celebrated the decision as a means to escape the crowded and deteriorating areas to which they had previously been confined.[1]

Many of these celebrations, however, were short-lived. As occurred throughout the nation, the polarizing effects of postwar development in Los Angeles counteracted civil rights gains made in the courts and legislatures. Since the federal government provided no positive mechanism to enforce *Shelley*, white homeowners and real estate interests developed new, informal methods to circumvent antidiscrimination measures. White homeowners were thus the principal beneficiaries of the substantial private investments and public subsidies favoring new suburban construction. In conjunction with racially prejudiced white behavior, callous planning that disregarded the concerns of communities of color intensified both racial divisions and the gap between the city and the suburbs. The Sugar Hill homeowners, in particular, saw their fortunes turn from better to worse in May 1954, when the California Highway Commission unanimously approved the route for what would become the Santa Monica

Freeway. Extending from downtown through the Westside, the freeway sliced Sugar Hill in half, forcing out many of its residents. Witness to the destruction of a Black community through ostensibly race-neutral governmental actions, the *California Eagle* warned that civil rights victories had provoked the creation of "a form of Jim Crow that [was] more insidious than many other forms of discrimination."[2]

In a sea of segregation, the Westside's multiethnic Crenshaw district became the pivotal site of Black/Japanese intersection and an island of integrationist hope. On a regional scale, Black and Japanese American settlement patterns diverged noticeably. Although white supremacy fed on hostility toward both groups before World War II, the postwar version of suburban racism drew conscious distinctions between "model" and "problem" minorities. Chastised for exhibiting the worst forms of biological racism, many white residents chose to accommodate integrationism by passively accepting members of the comparatively small ranks of local Japanese. While fears of the "Yellow Peril" diminished, the presence of even a single Black family continued to signify an "invasion" of white space. In postwar Crenshaw, however, it appeared as if activists had accomplished the rare feat of breaking down racial covenants while maintaining a diverse community to prevent resegregation. In subdivisions developer Walter Leimert had once promised would be permanently restricted, Black and Japanese Americans lived side by side, occupying Crenshaw's heart and soul. Their shared space represented a culmination of overlapping struggles to secure "better" housing opportunities and build a multiethnic community.

A More Insidious Form of Jim Crow

Commenting on the impact of *Shelley* nearly one decade after the 1948 ruling was released, the JACL's Harry Honda observed, "Racial restrictive covenants have been ruled invalid by the highest court in the land, but the problem only seems to be beginning as more subtle and sinister forms to circumvent the Supreme Court decision come to life." If contemporary Black and Japanese Americans needed vague descriptions like "insidious" and "subtle" to characterize discrimination, it was largely because it was impossible to pinpoint the single mechanism by which postwar racial segregation transpired. In winning *Shelley*, civil rights advocates hoped they had eliminated the decisive weapon of those who practiced housing discrimination. The Los Angeles NAACP, for example, proclaimed the 1948 courtroom triumph "the close of a long and vigorous national effort on the part of the association to knock out the vicious evil of segregated housing in the United States." The government, however, took few positive steps to eradicate housing discrimination post-*Shelley*, and Congress would not pass the Fair Housing Act for two more decades. As a result, the legal victory over restrictive covenants was neutralized by a confluence of forces ensuring the proliferation of separate and unequal housing through less overt methods. White property owners had needed to rely on lawsuits to enforce restrictive covenants only when one of their own broke ranks by selling to a person of color. Although some idealistic white activists made conscious efforts to integrate their neighborhoods post-*Shelley*, in many cases white homeowners kept their neighborhoods racially homogeneous through "gentlemen's agreements." The dissolution of white solidarity most frequently occurred in older, transition areas where white demand was evaporating. As they had during the interwar era, white developers and homeowners' associations proved far more successful at constructing and maintaining exclusively white subdivisions in the newer suburbs. In the absence of strong state intervention, racist housing patterns that had been ingrained through the customs of white real estate interests and homeowners continued—just as racist employment patterns did—throughout the postwar era. While nonwhites gained access to homes within the central city, public policies subsidizing postwar suburbanization helped create new bastions of white homogeneity on a larger metropolitan scale.[3]

The full implications of *Shelley* were indeterminate, pending follow-up battles taking place within the courts, public agencies, and private industry. Most critical to federal policy, the Federal Housing Administration (FHA)—alongside the corresponding housing section of the Veterans Administration (VA)—offered a tepid response to the *Shelley* decision that did little to disrupt the discriminatory residential patterns the agency had originally set in motion. Beginning in the 1930s, the FHA had explicitly directed lenders to employ "redlining" practices prohibiting loans for homes in integrated (or even potentially integrated) neighborhoods, while urging builders to employ deed restrictions to preserve class and racial exclusivity. Drastically reducing a homebuyer's required down payment, federally insured loans provided the financial basis for the construction and purchase of millions of suburban homes restricted to whites. Although provoked by *Shelley* to develop new policies forbidding the use of racial restrictive covenants, the FHA was scarcely vigilant against racism. It declared that it would not cover properties with covenants *after* February 15, 1950. As a result, the agency grandfathered all restrictions recorded before *Shelley* and provided property owners a three-and-a-half-month window to record as many others as they wished. Probably more significant was the fact that neither the FHA nor the VA put into place any real mechanisms to enforce their antidiscrimination measures, leaving private lenders and builders largely free to continue patterns of exclusion.

African American veterans, consequently, never reaped the full benefits provided by law. Adopted in 1944, the G.I. Bill of Rights lifted millions of white Americans into the middle class by helping veterans obtain home mortgages, as well as unemployment and pension benefits, job training, funding for education, and small business loans. However, it was standard practice, asserted Loren Miller in May 1956, for the VA to "guarantee loans for builders well knowing that they [would] bar Negro veterans." The civil rights lawyer advised, "Whenever you see a no-money down tract for veterans, you should insert the word 'white' before the word 'veterans' to get the full flavor of the advertisement."[4]

Given the federal government's reluctance to intervene, leading white realtors in Southern California developed a two-pronged postwar strategy marked by overt political resistance to *Shelley* and superficial compliance in their practical operations. Not only did they fear the 1948 decision would destroy their livelihood; they also warned that society would unravel without racial covenants. "The magnitude of the economic and social loss which confronts us is appalling," declared Los Angeles Realty Board (LARB) president Phillip M. Rea. "The insistence of some Negroes upon moving into areas previously restricted exclusively to the occupancy of Caucasians will necessarily create racial tensions and antagonisms and do much harm to our national social structure." No more than a few months had passed since the *Shelley* decision when the LARB announced it had drafted a constitutional amendment guaranteeing the right of property owners to employ racial restrictive covenants. The San Gabriel Valley and Culver City realty boards were among the numerous local branches that endorsed its proposal. They would continue their campaign into the 1960s before relenting.[5]

Meanwhile, a case corollary to *Shelley* led the industry to recognize it must adapt to the paradigm shift in race relations discourse. Civil rights advocates and real estate interests had clashed over the question of whether property owners could file civil lawsuits over racial covenant violations. In 1953, the US Supreme Court ruled in *Barrows vs. Jackson*—a test case from Southwest Los Angeles—that the state could no longer award civil damages for violations of unconstitutional covenants. Some of the covenant proponents had espoused the virtues of racial segregation, delivering a failed argument that Blacks were inherently predisposed to criminality and that miscegenation was a danger to society. Whereas such comments might have swayed some local courts, the Supreme Court favored the liberal sociological theories that the NAACP put forward. As scholar Louis Ruchames pointed out, "The provincialism of the white organizations [became] a debit where it had been an advantage before." In response, the National Association of Real Estate Boards acquiesced to the new court rulings—at least for the sake of its public face. It replaced explicit language promoting racial segregation in its bylaws with vague wording prohibiting its members from "introducing into a neighborhood a character of property or use which will clearly be detrimental to property values in that neighborhood." In essence, realtors wishing to discriminate were advised to use coded language. Black realtor Edward A. Warren, who served as the Los Angeles NAACP president in 1961, asserted that white realty boards colluded in an "underground conspiracy" to maintain segregation. Indeed, the large in-migration to Southern California provided a steady stream of white customers to keep the businesses of discriminatory agents thriving. Moreover, consistent with national trends, most local realty boards barred people of color from membership, while some—including branches in Pasadena, El Monte, and Southeast Los Angeles—also expelled white realtors who sold houses to people of color. These tactics proved quite effective. In 1955, a survey of twelve brokers serving a suburban Los Angeles neighborhood of twelve thousand new homes found that none were willing to sell to Blacks. One confessed, "Eventually there will be integration, but . . . I don't have the courage to sell to a Negro."[6]

The maintenance of discriminatory lending and trading practices ensured that the new homes of the postwar suburbs, like those built during the decentralization of the 1920s, would primarily be the preserve of whites. Taking off in 1948, the postwar building boom would ultimately dwarf its interwar-era predecessor. When wartime rationing eased, the pent-up demand for housing generated a windfall of construction. The city's homeownership rate rose to a record high of nearly 50 percent by 1950 and was still ascending. Over the next decade, the region added an astonishing 2.4 million people and over 850,000 new units of housing. Despite the fact that the urban core expanded by 600,000 persons, suburban areas (including outlying sections of Los Angeles city) accounted for three-fourths of regional growth. Former rural lands were becoming more densely populated areas with identities independent of the central city. During the fifteen years following World War II, the ranks of Orange County and the San Fernando Valley swelled by a combined 1.6 million persons. The vast majority of them were whites living in single-family housing. According to the Los Angeles County Commission on Human Relations, people of color occupied only 1.5 percent of the nearly 1 million new housing units built in Los Angeles County between 1940 and 1957. "Those that have been available have usually been on a segregated basis," it further reported. Such realities forced the commission's director, John A. Buggs, to the October 1959 statement, amounting to resignation of the Commission's goals, that the prospect of large populations of color living in the suburbs was a "practical impossibility." Since the white population of inner-city areas declined, suburbs actually accounted

TABLE 10.1.
Regional growth rate, 1950–60, and single-family housing rate, 1960

	Regional growth rate, 1950–60	Rate of residency in single-family housing, 1960
Metropolitan Los Angeles	54%	
Los Angeles County		65%
Orange County		79%
Metropolitan Detroit	25%	70%
Metropolitan Chicago	22%	44%
Metropolitan Philadelphia	18%	36%
Metropolitan New York	14%	31%

Source: Leo Grebler, *Metropolitan Contrasts* (Los Angeles, 1963), 4 and 30.

for more than 100 percent of the total white population increase in metropolitan Los Angeles. Older white residents joined with new arrivals to flood new racially exclusive neighborhoods. Between 1950 and 1956, census tracts that were less than 1 percent nonwhite accounted for 83 percent of the city's total population growth. At the extreme, ninety-seven tracts with an average of one African American resident per tract added a combined 109,000 persons. Standing at the forefront of suburbanization among ethnic minorities, Jews were routinely accepted as white in the postwar housing market. Those tending to be more secular and assimilated moved away from traditional community centers like Boyle Heights and the Fairfax district to Westside areas such as Beverly Hills, Westwood, and Brentwood. Between 1959 and 1965, the Jewish population of the San Fernando Valley, an especially popular destination, soared 70 percent to reach 120,000 persons.[7]

The postwar scale of development further enhanced the real estate industry's power to discriminate. As growth provoked the vertical and horizontal integration of the building industry, a mere 10 percent of all construction firms built 70 percent of the nation's postwar houses. A small number of developers thus possessed an immense ability to shape the design and demographics of neighborhoods. The spectacular rise of Lakewood, built on the former site of Japanese American truck farms in the southeastern part of Los Angeles County, exemplified broader patterns of suburban growth. Using newer, faster, and cheaper methods to construct tract homes, builders erected seventeen thousand units of housing for seventy thousand people in Lakewood during the 1950s. At peak levels, they started more than a hundred homes per day and sold them all within one hour. But the process was political, as well as mechanical. Driven by the organized homeowners movement, Lakewood and dozens of burgeoning suburbs facilitated their incorporation by contracting otherwise cost-prohibitive public services through a special arrangement with the county. Local control empowered suburban municipalities to engage in protective zoning designed to discourage low-income rental units while attracting revenue-enhancing retail centers. Through public omission and private commission, local control also enforced racial segregation. In October 1950, the NAACP noted it was "well known, the developers of Lakewood [had] consistently refused to sell, lease, or rent any property in Lakewood to Mexicans, Negroes, or Orientals, whether veteran or non-veteran."[8]

Arguably the most visible sign of public infrastructure investment during the Cold War, freeway construction exhibited the two-sided face of postwar development, spurring the export of growth and personal wealth to white suburbs while cutting paths of destruction through inner-city neighborhoods. Between 1950 and 1955—one year before federal funding for the mammoth Interstate and Defense Highway Act was approved—the freeway system of metropolitan Los Angeles had already grown nearly fivefold. Automobile commuters became an important political base for a postwar planning process that subsidized road construction while the old railway system was being dismantled. By 1960, 77 percent of all those employed in Los Angeles commuted to work by car, while only 5.1 percent walked and 7.6 percent used public transportation. The new highways permanently altered the region's cultural landscape, which in turn echoed throughout the nation. Developers and retailers fashioned a "drive-in" culture of shopping malls, fast-food restaurants, and outdoor cinemas to cater to the desires of the suburban populace. Homeownership was not immune to the consumer ethos that historian Lizabeth Cohen has argued "became almost a national civil religion from the late 1940s into the 1970s." Less a physical anchor of stability, a house was a status symbol owners sought to "upgrade" by "trading up." While this was far from a new phenomenon in Southern California, the quest of both old-timers and the ceaseless influx of newcomers to secure newer and better modern housing in seemingly pristine suburban communities reached a grand scale. Nearly a quarter of the city's entire population changed addresses between 1949 and 1950. By 1960, only 38 percent of all residents in the Los Angeles metropolitan area were living in the same house they occupied just five years prior. The figure for Orange County was an even lower 25 percent. A portion of those who moved, however, did so not by choice but because they were dislodged by redevelopment. From the 1930s to 1970s, the California Division of Highways evicted more than 400,000 residents and 44,000 businesses. Owners of condemned property were forced to accept what the state deemed "market value" or engage in costly legal battles to challenge the state's appraisal. Renters usually received no relocation assistance whatsoever. Even worse, communities of color often believed they were the sacrificial lambs of freeway planners. In addition to the Sugar Hill struggle, a multiethnic coalition fought to mitigate the deleterious effect of the Golden State Freeway on the Eastside. "It just seems the state builds its freeways where minority residents have their homes," declared the JACL's Blanche Shiosaki in 1958. Given the discrimination Black buyers still faced in the housing market, the *Eagle* fretted that the displaced endured a "double hardship."[9]

INTEGRATING THE SUBURBS

While postwar economic growth, public investments in education, and subsidized housing laid the basis for the rise of the white middle class, a small but growing body of middle-class Black and Japanese Americans sought to follow the trail of jobs leading to predominantly white suburbs. Resulting from private action and public policy, voluntary and gradual measures to promote integration primarily benefited Black and Japanese American professionals and high-tech workers during the Cold War. They entered rapidly expanding sectors of the economy that added a combined 162,000 jobs to metropolitan Los Angeles during the 1950s (a 78 percent gain). Growing numbers of men of color worked in accounting, medicine, education, and social work. While the greatest numbers of white-collar women of color entered clerical work, professional women of color concentrated in teaching, nursing, and social work. Above all, the Cold War "military-industrial complex" boosted employment prospects in the Los Angeles area, which became the center of production for military aircraft and missiles. In the early 1960s, 43.5 percent of the region's wage earners owed their jobs directly or indirectly to defense spending. Developments in the large field of aviation and aerospace again served as a barometer of Black and Japanese Americans' changing status within the regional economy. In 1959, the industry employed 153,337 workers, whose $6,492 median annual earnings (for males) eclipsed those of all other manufacturing industries. As the military's evolving strategy generated a shift in demand from aircraft frames to nuclear weapons and missiles, assembly-line work was replaced by the research and high-tech work of scientists, engineers, and electronics workers. In response, the numbers of Black and Japanese American engineers, designers, and draftsmen expanded exponentially. With the region employing over one thousand Japanese American engineers and nearly five hundred Black engineers at the end of the 1950s, it must have been striking to recall that the number from each group in Los Angeles County on the eve of World War II could be counted on one hand. Although entering these fields was no simple task, highly motivated people of color could obtain the credentials necessary through public education. UCLA, in particular, launched its College of Engineering in the 1940s with a focus on aeronautics.[10]

Although Black and Japanese Americans alike made striking gains in professional and technical employment, this outcome of moderate civil rights reform produced a disparate impact for the two communities of color in Los Angeles. In 1949, fewer than 5 percent of those employed within each group engaged in professional or technical work. When employment levels in these sectors were measured one decade later, the ranks of African Americans had tripled to 10,497 while those of Japanese Americans had increased 552 percent to 5,515. In the case of Japanese Americans, professional and technical workers now represented an impressive 14.7 percent of wage earners. In fact, the share of Japanese American males in these sectors (16.9 percent) actually exceeded the share of all males in these sectors (14.8 percent). As sociologist Jere Takahashi has noted, Nisei college students, opting for careers in the burgeoning "technical-organizational" economy, tended "to eschew the humanities and liberal arts in favor of business administration, optometry, dentistry, and engineering." However, the absolute number of educational and occupational openings in these elite sectors was strictly limited regardless of whether racial quotas were consciously imposed. Hence, it was not feasible for the Nisei's upward mobility strategy to serve as a "model" for other minorities. Because the regional labor force included fewer than 40,000 Japanese but over 160,000 Blacks, the growing body of professionals and high-tech workers still accounted for only 6.3 percent of employed African Americans. Meanwhile, the new masses of working-class Blacks, as well as Latinos, posed social questions of a qualitatively different nature than those posed by Japanese Americans. Before World War II, Black and Japanese populations of Los Angeles had been somewhat comparable in size. Even the city's Mexican American community had not been inordinately larger than the local Japanese community before the 1924 Immigration Act. Yet, as postwar migration pushed Los Angeles County's population above 6 million by 1960, Japanese numbered fewer than 80,000, while the number of African Americans grew to 462,000 and Latinos to 577,000. A decade later the disparity was even starker. Japanese comprised only 1.5 percent of the county's residents, but Blacks and Latinos collectively numbered 2 million and accounted for nearly 30 percent of total population.[11]

Highly educated Nisei did not come close to comprising a majority of the community. But whereas most whites viewed Black professionals as exceptional, the symbolic emergence of Nisei professionals made the

TABLE 10.2.
Japanese American population changes, 1950–60

	1950	1960	% change
Los Angeles County	37,000	77,000	108.1%
City of Los Angeles	25,500	51,500	102.0%
Gardena	741	4,373	490.1%
Long Beach	1,685	2,660	57.9%
Pasadena	1,452	2,540	74.9%
Torrance	476	1,028	116.0%
Santa Monica	254	702	176.4%
Monterey Park	5	656	13,200.0%
Montebello	197	440	123.4%
San Gabriel	178	347	94.9%
Culver City	80	239	198.8%

Source: Midori Nishi and Young Il Kim, "Recent Japanese Settlement Changes in the Los Angeles Area," *Yearbook of the Association of Pacific Coast Geographers* 26 (1964): 25–33.

"model minority" image seem plausible. Although suburban whites frequently exhibited prejudice toward Japanese Americans, overt racist hostility spiked in the immediate aftermath of the war and then began to dissipate. The majority of Japanese Americans in the region remained within the city limits of Los Angeles, yet they were moving away from older areas like Little Tokyo, Boyle Heights, and West Jefferson and toward outlying parts of the city. Others continued farther outward to middle-income suburbs in the Westside, San Gabriel Valley, and South Bay. Oftentimes they inhabited places that had been completely closed off to "Orientals" in the very recent past. In the case of Gardena, which became home to the region's largest Japanese American population outside Los Angeles during the 1950s, settlement patterns changed course. Whereas prewar Issei had established truck farms in Gardena, many postwar Nisei moved into tract homes to be near South Bay aviation and aerospace plants. Nevertheless, the Nisei did not integrate the entire Southland at once. Few settled in municipalities that were very wealthy (such as Arcadia and San Marino) or predominantly white working-class (like the southeastern suburbs Bell, Huntington Park, Lynwood, and South Gate). Furthermore, new suburban construction, as the JACL's Henry Mori

Fig. 10.3. Suburban Nisei. Reflecting a common postwar image of Japanese Americans as suburban residents, a woman paints a picket fence in West Los Angeles, ca. 1950. Shades of L.A. Archives/Los Angeles Public Library.

observed in 1956, was generally offered only to whites. Houses became available to Nisei after they were ten years old and "the first signs of repair" began to show. Still, the resolution of five housing discrimination cases the JACL presented to the President's Commission on Civil Rights in January 1959 suggested that resilient Nisei could overcome initial outbreaks of suburban white prejudice. Frank Chuman, the JACL's national legal counsel, testified that white racists had refused to allow Japanese Americans to occupy homes in Bellflower, Long Beach, and Costa Mesa and had denied others mortgages in Covina and Canoga Park. All five parties contested their exclusion, although one relented when offered a cash settlement by white neighbors. The other four parties moved into the contested homes or a similar house in the same tract seemingly without provoking white panic selling.[12]

By the end of the 1950s, Japanese and other Asian American homeowners in Southern California (and probably across most of the nation) clearly enjoyed greater residential options than most other people of color. Responding to the 1948 *Shelley* decision, Nisei realtor Ty Saito argued that Japanese Americans would "now have an opportunity to spread out to other areas instead of living in small ghettos." Several factors explain why his forecast of enhanced Nisei mobility proved more prescient than the NAACP's optimistic claim that the Supreme Court ruling would "knock out" residential segregation. Because many Nisei believed prewar segregation had reinforced white prejudices and contributed to the case for internment, they embraced the dispersed settlement that white assimilationists and WRA officials had advocated. In its amicus curiae brief for *Shelley*, the JACL argued that it was neither culture nor ideology but "race restrictions" that gave rise to the community's so-called " 'clannishness' which General DeWitt found so inimical to national safety." Given the squalid condition of downtown housing, concerns about the spread of vice, and demolition caused by civic center redevelopment, the Nisei had further negative incentives to leave Little Tokyo. Interviewed shortly after World War II, veteran Johnny Fukushima maintained it was critical that Nisei "do something to get away from Little Tokyo ghettos." Japanese American realtors likewise discouraged their customers from buying in predominantly nonwhite districts. At the same time, Cold War racial ideology predisposed whites to accept the disciplined and domesticated Nisei. With Japan remade as America's junior partner, whites no longer saw industrious Nisei engineers as a threat to national security but rather as contributors to American global hegemony. Anecdotal evidence from the modernist West Coast builder Eichler Homes provided reason to believe that whites no longer viewed Nisei as the threat to property values they still perceived African Americans to be. While the Eichler company developed a reputation for embracing open occupancy, it sold to "Orientals" four years before closing its first deal with a Black buyer. Sales associates, moreover, steered African Americans toward particular properties to avoid "bunching." The contradictory impact of postwar racial ideology did not go unnoticed by Japanese American observers. A Nisei Protestant minister in the early 1960s surmised that white sellers viewed Japanese Americans as a tolerable alternative to Blacks who, they feared, would trigger a neighborhood "invasion." "A lot of us are congratulating ourselves on working for and securing wide acceptance in the community at large," he commented. "But I suspect that we have been bailed out by the Negroes. They moved in and frightened the whites, who then found that we Japanese weren't so bad after all. They could stop hating us and start hating the Negroes."[13]

While many Nisei began to inhabit white neighborhoods without controversy, this luxury generally eluded African Americans. Even the most famous Black residents of Los Angeles could not expect to be welcomed into the ritziest sections of the Westside. In 1947, Charles B. Shattuck rallied hundreds of homeowners in the Southwestern Wilshire Protective Association to fight the " 'plague' of Negro encroachment." He advised conceding some homes to Blacks and Asians in the eastern part of the district, but fighting to enforce restrictive covenants in more exclusive western

Fig. 10.4. Racial conflict in South Central Los Angeles. Whites protest the sale of a house to a Black family, 1949. Hostile actions of this nature usually accelerated white flight. Herald Examiner Collection/Los Angeles Public Library.

sections that included the Country Club Park neighborhood. The following year, the all-white Property Owners' Association of the adjacent and even pricier Hancock Park neighborhood attacked singer and television star Nat King Cole. Cole's real estate agent had employed a light-skinned Black woman passing for white to act as the buyer of an $85,000 English Tudor house at 401 Muirfield Road. Almost immediately, outraged neighbors lambasted both the seller and the seller's agent, who required police protection after receiving a death threat. Refusing to vacate his Hancock Park house, Cole defied bribes, threats, a lawsuit, coercion, and the placement of a sign on his front lawn reading "Nigger Heaven."[14]

The postwar expansion of Black residency provoked a trail of hostile organizing by white property owners in South and Southwest Los Angeles. Yet, in nearly every case except for the Crenshaw/Baldwin Hills area, whites fled and new tensions erupted in the next neighborhood over. In March 1950, realtor Ted Lokos began convening a series of meetings drawing several hundred residents from the predominantly white neighborhood surrounding the intersection of Florence and Normandie. Sharing the group's concern that an African American family had recently moved into the area, Lokos cautioned that public outcry would only promote panic selling. He instead hoped to eliminate the singular Black presence by privately purchasing the family's house. A leader from Leimert Park advised the Normandie Association to "stop this now." "If a dozen non-Caucasian families were to move in all at once," the man pronounced, "it would be practically impossible for you to do anything about it." Indeed, while failing to stop Black buyers, white residents soon attracted the very negative attention Lokos sought to avert. In 1951, vandals defaced the home of a Black resident, and a realtor and a neighbor assaulted two white women who showed their homes to African Americans. Whites sped up their departure, and the neighborhood transitioned rapidly. The story here was a microcosm of what was transpiring throughout the city. Whereas only twenty-five African Americans lived in the three census tracts covering the Florence-Normandie area in 1950, six thousand moved into the neighborhood over the next decade. Soon enough, white flight reached the southwestern edge of the city. Donald D. Rowland, a white minister and resident of that area, described the process on the basis of firsthand observation. Realtors generally showed houses only to whites until the color line was broken by a private sale beyond the purview of the realty board. Then the floodgates opened. Sellers anxiously dealt to minorities, who were willing (and forced by limited options) to pay a premium of as much as several thousand dollars above the going rates offered to white buyers. Rowland noticed that "it was not too un-common" to witness "three or four or five houses for sale in a block" at one time. Indeed, many of the white sellers were fleeing an integrated neighborhood for the second time within several years.[15]

While housing was opening up in Los Angeles, the outer suburbs proved far more restrictive. Although a handful of middle-class African Americans secured homes there during the 1950s, they often did so under extraordinary circumstances. The well-publicized struggle of Harold Bauduit, an Annapolis graduate and naval officer, became tied to Korean American Sammy Lee's fight against housing discrimination. Lee was an Olympic diving champion for the United States in both 1948 and 1952, as well as the first person of color to win the Sullivan Award for top am-ateur athlete. The federal government, naming him its inaugural sports ambassador, sent the gold medalist around the world on propaganda tours, where he proclaimed America the most free and democratic nation on earth. Coming off twelve years of army service spanning World War II and the Korean War, Lee, a graduate of USC's medical school, planned to set up practice in Orange County. But his storied accomplishments proved immaterial to two different white sellers in Garden Grove. Both rejected Lee and his Chinese American wife Rosalind on racial grounds during the summer of 1955. "I would rather have Dr. Sammy Lee myself than half the families here," said one of the realtors to the *Los Angeles Times*, "but if you have one—a nice one—then you'll have others." After his plight generated a storm of publicity in the national media and direct intervention by Vice President Richard Nixon, who considered him a personal friend, Lee settled into a home in predominantly white Anaheim. Two years later, however, the Lees again faced threats and harassment when they sought to move to nearby Santa Ana. In the interim, racist assailants had bombed the Placentia home of a Black family. "You know what happened in Placentia," an anonymous caller told Lee. "The same can happen to you." Meanwhile, Bauduit purchased the Garden Grove home of a departing white officer only to discover a racist group calling itself the "Home Owner's Association" converge on his lawn to coerce him to sell. Though nearly resigned to move, Bauduit chose to stand his ground with backing from integration supporters in the area, including the Orange County Council for Equal Opportunity and thirty white neighbors. Sammy Lee brought more attention to the cause after two Home Owner's Association members falsely accused the Olympic champion of engaging in "drunken brawls" requiring sheriffs to be called to his home. He threatened to sue his white accusers for slander and vowed to confront them at their next meeting. In the face of negative publicity, the Home Owner's Association relented, and Bauduit stayed in his house. Nevertheless, other Orange County residents remained steadfast in their opposition to integration. The following year, another Black family endured over a year of threats and vandalism after moving to Anaheim.[16]

Like Orange County, the San Fernando Valley attracted thousands of employees working for the new plants built by the aviation and aerospace industry during the Cold War. Rampant racism kept its population and workforce predominantly white, too. Following an African American family's May 1949 offer to purchase a Van Nuys house, the *Los Angeles Sentinel* was sent a postcard with a promise to "burn" any "coons" or "Black animal cross breeds" that tried to move into "our white neighborhood." In 1960, the district president of the NAACP reported that nearly all of the Valley's Black population lived at its eastern edge in a section of Pacoima. He could locate only "fifteen to eighteen Negro families, in the entire San Fernando Valley, living in so-called 'white neighborhoods' [and] only one apartment house owner . . . willing to rent to Negro persons." Seeing his house-hunting efforts in Northridge and Granada Hills thwarted by discrimination, Lockheed engineer Preston P. Morris, Jr., was relegated to Pacoima. Although Emory Holmes actually managed to purchase a Northridge house, he and members of his family were subjected to constant protests, harassment, and vandalism by white neighbors. White agitators sent a stream of servicemen to the house on false calls and disturbed their sleep with two straight weeks of crank calls. They shattered windows by hurling rocks and firing BB-gun shots. One hatemonger painted on their wall: "Black cancer here. Don't let it spread!" Throughout the outer suburbs, housing integration proceeded slowly through the voluntary steps of individuals, who counseled others not to expect government action to assist them. Robert Maxwell, an African American engineer and Valley homeowner, urged Blacks to by-pass prejudiced realtors by negotiating directly with sellers, arrange their own financing to circumvent discriminatory bank lending, and secure the advance approval of white neighbors to avoid conflict upon taking occupancy.[17]

"INCREDIBLE CRENSHAW" AND THE NEW WESTSIDE

In June 1961, Dorothy L. Sobek wrote the *Los Angeles Times* to express the "real joy" she took from taking out-of-town guests through Crenshaw. Those who equated minority communities with squalid, impoverished ghettos were introduced to a different face of upward mobility in Los Angeles. Sobek, whose text suggested she was white, showed her friends African American homes reflecting "the obvious pride of ownership" and Japanese American gardeners working in front of homes inhabited by people of all races. "The landscaping is more consistently beautiful than in many of the 'all-white' neighborhoods," she declared. One of millions who moved to California during the postwar era, Sobek had "come to feel a certain pride in many of the things distinctive about this state and its citizens." Concluding her thoughts on Crenshaw, Sobek remarked, "This is the way it should be." With living patterns in postwar Los Angeles increasingly shaped by the assimilation of Japanese Americans and the containment of Blacks, Crenshaw stood out as the distinctive spot where postwar Black and Japanese American residential patterns intersected. A peculiar creation of both white flight and multiracial activism, the district's multiethnic diversity made it a model community for postwar integrationists.[18]

Black and Japanese American settlement in Crenshaw built on the westward migration begun several decades prior in West Jefferson. Before the war African American homeowners, backed by the legal support of the NAACP and other community organizations, had generally been the first to break down race restrictions. After the war, however, Japanese and other Asian Americans were most frequently the first people of color to live in formerly white neighborhoods. Purchasing four hundred homes throughout Los Angeles during 1945/46, recently freed internees sought a sense of security and stability. An Issei merchant noted the rush to buy houses was "an indication that the people want to stay in this country. It is not like before the war, when everyone wants to make their money and go back to Japan." Home buying was a collective effort. Gardeners and other laborers frequently pooled their resources into rotating credit associations to raise down payments. In the immediate aftermath of the war, Japanese Americans coveted modest Spanish-style houses in the "Avenues" section of Crenshaw. A family moving to a home on Eighth Avenue in 1946 found that nearby residents referred to the neighborhood as "the new Little Tokyo." But the battle against racial exclusion was still heated at this time. Nisei realtor Kazuo K. Inouye played a central role in opening the neighborhood to people of color. A warrior's mentality made him particularly suited to the task of confronting hostile whites still smoldering with anti-Japanese racism. The son of a farmer who was one of the region's earliest Issei settlers, Inouye was raised in the multiethnic environment of prewar Boyle Heights. His father taught him to sumo-wrestle, and young Kazuo regularly sparred with and defeated adults as a teenager. On top of that, he earned a black belt in judo and a street reputation as a kid not to mess with. At Manzanar, Inouye deeply resented his incarceration. Resettled to the Midwest, he experienced constant problems with job discrimination in Chicago and Detroit. Near the end of the war, he was drafted and briefly served in the 442nd Regiment. Though honorably discharged, Inouye maintained a double consciousness during his tour of duty. At first, he openly resisted the concept of serving in a unit that had a reputation for being a suicide squad. "That German never called me a Jap, never put me in a concentration camp," he remarked. Indeed, he was more incensed with "red neck senators like Bilbo and Rankin."[19]

Inouye drew on these experiences of struggling against adversity as he developed a reputation as a "blockbuster." Twenty-five years of age in 1947, he began his realty company as Japanese Americans were just beginning to enter Crenshaw. Racial restrictive covenants were widespread, and few lenders would approve mortgages for minorities. One of his first customers was a Mexican American woman who had endured the wrath of white neighbors when she purchased her Crenshaw home many years back. Only her legal standing as "white" had safeguarded her occupancy. Now, she insisted that Inouye sell her house to a person of color. When the Nisei realtor obliged by securing a Japanese American buyer, a rival white realtor—whose shiny Terraplane and "Texan's hat" boasted a conspicuous presence—turned livid. According to Inouye, the "Texan" then "hired four guys to break every window in that house." Inouye notified the police and paid a direct visit to the "Texan." "You know, I was overseas, and I killed a bunch of Nazis and fought for democracy," the Nisei veteran began. His next lines, however, belied the image of the Japanese

American soldier as a model citizen. "If you try to break the window again, if you step one foot on the property," declared Inouye, "I got a German luger that I brought back. I'm going to shoot you between the eyes." "Don't you threaten me," answered the white realtor, who by now must have had at least one flashback to Fletcher Bowron's many broadcasts about the boundless treachery coursing within the veins of every member of the Japanese race. "I'm going to sleep on the porch, and I'm going to wait for you," continued Inouye. "Try it one more time and I'll put you away. Have you heard of a kamikaze? That's me. Are you afraid to die? I'm not afraid to die. Come on, try me out." The "kamikaze" routine proved strikingly effective, and Inouye never heard from the "Texan" again. Soon his business was booming, and he was busting open entire Crenshaw blocks to both Black and Japanese Americans. Inouye's Kashu Realty advertised regularly in the Negro press, and a large segment of his business came from African Americans. Making his buyers unwitting accomplices to blockbusting, the Nisei realtor convinced them that the law required they keep their "for sale" sign up for thirty days after they moved in.[20]

Despite Inouye's blockbusting, Crenshaw's integration proceeded unevenly. In October 1948, Pauline O. Roberts, an African American doctor for the city's health department, found a cross burning on her lawn after moving to the "Avenues" section of the district. "We will get even with you for moving into a white neighborhood," stated one anonymous caller. "We will burn the house down next time." A civil rights activist reporting the incident noted that the rest was "too vile and profane to be printed." While the Avenues began to transition, the more upscale Leimert Park neighborhood in the southern half of Crenshaw stayed almost exclusively white—just as its namesake developer had laid it out in the 1920s. When six African American families moved into the neighborhood, it became the site of heated confrontation. In February 1950, the all-white Neighborly Endeavors mobilized to stop Black settlement in the neighborhood. Testing the limits of *Shelley*, the white property owners' association demanded that the court impose civil damages on those violating restrictive covenants. Forty-two of sportscaster Oscar Reichow's neighbors sued him for selling his house to an African American family. Their campaign caused him to be fired by a local radio station. Countering the racists, the Catholic Women's Club hosted a Sunday tea to welcome the new family. Soon after, however, vandals flooded a second Leimert Park home recently purchased by an African American. Undeterred, the new owner, Mrs. A. J. Hunter, vowed to stand her ground. The following year, hatemongers struck at two more Black homeowners, dousing the interior of Charles L. and Bertha M. Williams's house with oil and burning a cross in front of another home down the block. In spite

of despicable incidents like these, African American professionals continued to move into Leimert Park. The threat of lawsuits dissipated when the
1953 *Barrows* decision barred the courts from awarding civil damages
for racial covenant violations. Retreating from the older Central Avenue
district, prominent Black businesses and institutions, such as the Angelus
Funeral Home, Golden State Mutual Life Insurance, and First AME
Church, would eventually follow homeowners to Crenshaw and other
parts of the Westside.[21]

By the late 1950s, Leimert Park had developed multiple reputations. To
some of its white residents, it symbolized the intrusion of unwanted minorities into formerly restricted areas. From the perspective of whites in
outer suburbs, it was a place to contain minorities. When residents of
a white Gardena neighborhood became alarmed by the arrival of an
African American engineer from Hughes Aircraft, they sent him a letter
declaring "Leimert Park would be a much more desirable area for you."
Likewise, an Inglewood apartment owner refusing to rent to a Black in-
quirer in January 1960 advised him to check out Leimert Park because it
was "not too far away and [had] Negroes and Orientals living in the area
already." For Black and Asian Americans, however, the neighborhood
represented something quite different—an opportunity to live in upscale
suburban-style housing that had been off-limits before the introduction of
postwar civil rights measures. While the pricey homes of Baldwin Hills
remained beyond their reach, upwardly mobile African and Japanese
Americans coveted housing in Leimert Park more than anywhere else in
the city. From 1950 to 1960, the population of Blacks and Asians in the
neighborhood grew from a combined 70 persons to about 4,200 of each
group. People of color, including roughly 400 Latinos, now comprised
half of the total population. Hepburn Avenue residents Ray Charles and
Ella Fitzgerald were the most prominent members of this new grouping,
but hundreds of professional and managerial employees joined them.
"Nonwhite" adults in Leimert Park were twice as likely to have a college
education than adults of all races in the city at-large. Correspondingly,
the families of color moving in generally earned more than whites who
remained.[22]

Crenshaw's storefronts of the late 1950s and early 1960s reflected its
new status as home to the region's largest Japanese American community.
Referring to the district as *Seinan* (Southwest), a name borrowed from the
prewar Westside, Japanese Americans saw Crenshaw as a new version of
Little Tokyo, featuring an array of grocers, services, supplies, and restaurants. "You didn't have to go down to Japanese town," Kazuo Inouye recounted. "You could get anything you wanted over here." The largest
concentration of Japanese American merchants and professionals resided
on Jefferson Boulevard (west of Arlington) in the Avenues section, where

the postwar community first took root. Not surprisingly, scores of Japanese American realtors were drawn to the booming neighborhood. Many from the growing ranks of Nisei doctors and dentists also set up practice in Crenshaw, while a Nisei fish peddler roamed the neighborhood delivering fresh catches straight to the doorsteps of residents. Community institutions also thrived. Gardeners pooled resources to create a credit union, and community leaders built a neighborhood center catering especially to Issei elders and postwar Japanese immigrants. Large congregations of Christians attended nearby West Adams Church, and Buddhists joined the Senshin Temple. Membership in the JACL's Southwest Los Angeles chapter exploded from fifty in 1948 to over twelve hundred in 1957, making it the largest in the nation.[23]

Running on a latitudinal axis through the Westside, Exposition Boulevard served as a line of demarcation between the "right" and "wrong" sides of the tracks. The major artery, which actually had railways running down the center of it, served as a prewar dividing line between communities of color and segregated white neighborhoods. In the postwar era, it divided nonwhite Crenshaw residents by class. Middle-class buyers preferred to live south of Exposition in and around Leimert Park. They often looked to situate their families within the boundaries of specific neighborhood schools like Coliseum Street Elementary. Anecdotal evidence suggests that whites placed slightly less of a stigma on those who sold to Nisei rather than African Americans. One house for sale in 1962 carried reported prices of $18,500 for whites, $19,500 for Asians, and $21,500 for Blacks. North of Exposition, working-class Black and Japanese Americans filled in the small houses and apartments of the Avenues section, where the median income and education levels of residents were below 1960 citywide averages and whites comprised less than 10 percent of the population. When her family moved from an aging duplex north of Exposition to a newer single-family home in Leimert Park, Evelyn Yoshimura recognized the class differences. "Most of the parents there [north of Exposition] came home from work wearing various kinds of uniforms and work clothes," she remarked. "Across Exposition, more mothers stayed home and more fathers went to work in suits." Service workers were drawn to the older section of Crenshaw because of its affordability and its proximity to the Westside homes where they toiled. Japanese gardeners established an association headquartered on Jefferson, where supplies could also be obtained from Tak's and Kay's hardware stores. Sansei (third-generation Japanese American) youth from the Avenues formed gangs. The most feared "bad cats" might have been the Ministers, organized by Dorsey High students in 1959 and growing to incorporate as many as one hundred members. Although Japanese American gangs, which sometimes included members of other ethnic and racial backgrounds, could be found throughout the city, the Ministers brought a sense of street credibility to the Westside identity. To a degree, gangs created by youth of color were a defense mechanism. The children of whites in portions of the district, such as the wealthy Baldwin Hills area, often employed violence to mark their neighborhoods off-limits to Black and Japanese Americans. But gangs were also a source of power over others. Working-class youth from the Avenues often took out their frustrations on those from middle-class Leimert Park. "We used to hang around the dairy [at the corner of Eleventh Avenue and Exposition] and wait for someone to come across the tracks," recalled a former member of the Ministers. "If anyone came, we would kick their ass."[24]

Nisei parents throughout the city feared that juvenile delinquency was rising among the Sansei. Some in Crenshaw wondered whether living among too many Blacks was negatively influencing their children. "A great many Nisei mirror the prejudices of the white majority," remarked Seinan JACL leader Kats Kunitsugu in 1958. "They harbor preconceptions about Negroes, and it takes only one case of seeing a Negro spit on the street . . . and they are convinced with thin lip certainty that all Negroes are that way." Shock waves rumbled through the community in April of that year when Richard Sumii, a sixteen-year-old youth from the Avenues, was shot to death outside a Japanese American community dance. The Dorsey High honors student was apparently an innocent bystander caught in the cross fire of rival Japanese American gangs. Even more disturbing to many was the front-page coverage of the murder by the *Los Angeles Times*, which threatened the community's upright reputation. Although most violence was intraethnic, Sansei youth styles of music, dress, dance, and speech in the Westside were heavily shaped by urban African American culture. For instance, a Japanese American belonging to the Constituents gang in the 1950s noted that its members tended to date Sansei girls who "knew how to do the Bop and the Texas Hop—the dances that blacks did." Making racial generalizations, some Nisei parents believed that protecting their children from the ravages of urban society necessitated shielding them from intimate contact with Blacks. Although interracial dating eventually grew common in Crenshaw, a "rowdy" female Sansei classmate of Evelyn Yoshimura stunned her peers and alarmed her overseers by slow-dancing with an African American at Leimert Park's Audubon Junior High. Not only was she suspended from school, she was ultimately sent to live with relatives in Japan. More liberal-minded, the JACL's Kunitsugu nonetheless worried that Black youths' "corruption of spoken English" was having a detrimental influence on her children.[25]

Whatever the extent of these fears, they did not preclude Nisei from investing a large commercial stake in Crenshaw, especially near the growing

Fig. 10.5. Crenshaw Square. Developed by Nisei, this shopping center embodied the prominent Japanese American presence in Crenshaw during the 1960s. Photo by David Stock (ca. 1995).

numbers of Japanese Americans settling in Leimert Park. In the late 1950s, Nisei developers planned a shopping center on the district's main north-south thoroughfare, Crenshaw Boulevard, as well as a subdivision of houses and apartments on the adjacent Norton and Bronson streets. Although the residential blocks had been laid out previously, the land was completely open. In fact, just a decade prior, the body of Elizabeth Short, victim of the notorious Black Dahlia murder, had been discovered right where the new homes on Norton were springing up. Not surprisingly, this fact seems to have been omitted from the marketing materials. While there was a sprinkling of other racial and ethnic groups, Japanese Americans—several in mixed marriages—comprised most of the original owners of the single-family houses. They would soon enjoy quick access to the Crenshaw Square shopping center, a $7 million project that leasing agent Yo Taka-gaki promised would "meet the demands of Southern California's rapidly increasing Oriental population heavily concentrated in the greater Cren-shaw area." Compared to the Jefferson Park subdivision planned by Togo Tanaka and others just before the war, the new developments in Crenshaw represented considerable Nisei progress in Los Angeles. First and most obviously, the projects were not only built to completion but developed at a scale unimaginable two decades prior. But second and perhaps even more significantly, the principals behind the shopping center and the subdivision consciously promoted their ethnic character. Whereas Jefferson Park's proponents had tried to make their project sound as much like a typical white-bread "American" subdivision as possible, Crenshaw Square's "Oriental" architecture and landscaping by Dike Nakano and Kaz Katayama were highlighted as central, distinguishing features. No longer solely the preserve of whiteness, the suburbs took on a Japanese American identity in Crenshaw. A Nisei veterans' organization joined with area merchants to sponsor a Japanese summer festival in Crenshaw Square that rivaled Little Tokyo's long-established Nisei Week. With ethnic food booths and *bon odori*—traditional Japanese line dancing—defining the outdoor carnival, suburban Nisei displayed a new confidence to flaunt their ethnic heritage in public view. A visitor from Japan was stunned by the seeming contradiction. "They all have Japanese faces," he commented, "and only American words coming out of his [*sic*] mouth." Teeming with activity, Crenshaw became a beacon for Japanese Americans from across the city, especially from the vast and ever expanding Westside. A March 1960 *Rafu Shimpo* advertisement for homes in the Sunkist Park subdivision of Culver City noted they were "only minutes" away from the "Crenshaw area."[26]

Crenshaw's Japanese community exhibited the Nisei's mixed feelings about the fruits of postwar integration. They willingly pursued economic and housing opportunities that brought them into contact with other races, and they also sought to remove the stigma of exclusion. But many resisted assimilationist notions of integrationism in their social lives. Undoubtedly, Crenshaw's Nisei-operated bowling alley provided the most intriguing window into the complex process of postwar Japanese American integration. It offered simultaneous evidence of Japanese American success in mainstream America, intraethnic solidarity, and cross-cultural interaction. A symbol of collective Nisei striving, Holiday Bowl was the creation of four young Japanese Americans who dreamed of building a bowling center. They had worked various jobs, mostly under the employ of ethnic small businesses, but had failed to amass any particular wealth. Despite pooling their collective life savings, the four founders raised only a fraction of their $300,000 starting requirement. To garner the remaining amount, they called on friends and members of the Japanese American community to purchase shares in the bowl for $500 each. On the boulevard site of a former hot dog stand, proprietor Harry Oshiro and his three associates erected a thirty-six-lane alley—the largest in the city at the time. Supplemented by a Japanese-themed lounge and a pool hall, it opened in 1958 and quickly drew scores of patrons twenty-four hours a day. Yet, as Nisei eagerly partook in the hallmark American pastime of postwar suburbia, they often preferred to do so among their own ethnic cohort. Representing a true cross section of the community—through teams composed of gardeners, florists, farmers, Buddhists, 442nd veterans, and "housewives," among others—Japanese Americans comprised roughly half of Holiday Bowl's league participants in the 1960s. With Blacks, Chinese Americans, and whites making up the bulk of the rest, its program was collectively integrated. Nevertheless, many individual leagues consisted entirely or almost entirely of Japanese Americans, in this way resembling most of the community's sports and cultural associations. (As time passed, the bowl hosted leagues that were predominantly African American, as well.) For Japanese Americans who had resisted the impositions of racist exclusionists and liberal assimilationists, Holiday Bowl provided a place where a sense of cultural autonomy might reign on a small scale.[27]

Nevertheless, Holiday Bowl left its lasting mark as a symbol of cultural hybridity in multiethnic Crenshaw. Architect Helen Fong put an Asian spin on its modern "Googie" design, and its social life reflected this hybrid form. "That's our hub—the Black community and the Japanese community," recalled Rex Sullivan, who patronized the bowl for over forty years. Two lifelong friends, Nisei Charlie Tajiri and African American Scoby Roberts, had played football together at Dorsey High before the war, when the surrounding area was still predominantly white. Over five decades, they met daily for breakfast in Holiday's popular coffee shop. Though it began with run-of-the-mill diner food, the coffee shop's business took off when new cook Frank Kamimura introduced Chinese food in the 1960s. Down-home Japanese and Black soul food were soon added to create a one-of-a-kind menu. Holiday Bowl was a regular hangout for Sunday brunch after church, as well as for a late meal following a night on the town or eight-plus hours on the swing shift. Lines for a table often streamed out the door. African American bowler Ronald Hatcher moved to Los Angeles from Dallas as a child in the early 1960s. "Holiday Bowl was the first place we went to," he remembered. "I learned to eat with chopsticks as a kid." Sansei Janet Yoshii recounted her "earliest memory" was coming to the bowl as a five-year-old child in the mid-1960s. Danish American Ann Saito met her future Nisei husband at the bowl. "This is where I became Japanese," she reminisced.[28]

Anchored by institutions like Holiday Bowl, Crenshaw took on the look of a critical experiment in multiracial integration. In the late 1950s, Warren Rogers, a local publisher and self-described "longtime resident" of Crenshaw, chastised the naysayers who feared the changing character of their community. He instead welcomed the dawn of this colorful new chapter in the history of "Incredible Crenshaw." "We like it here and expect to stay," declared Rogers. "No threat of deflated values is going to scare us away. Our neighbors, on both sides, came from foreign shores speaking a different language, but we like them, and they like us." But despite the grandest pronouncements, the dream of an integrated city was about to combust in flames. While Nisei were finally gaining acceptance in the Southland suburbs as both "Japanese" and "American," white efforts to contain the region's African American population intensified as the postwar era progressed. Black community leaders' great hope that the demise of state-enforced restrictive covenants would end segregation never came to fruition. Because white flight to the outer suburbs relieved competition for space inside the city, African American housing options appeared to expand rapidly in the 1950s. Yet Black/white segregation was reinventing itself through "more insidious" methods and reproducing itself on a metropolitan scale. As the migration of tens of thousands of Black workers to the city transformed previously white neighborhoods into the South Central Los Angeles ghetto, frustration would reach new heights in the 1960s.[29]

CHAPTER 11

From Integration to Multiculturalism

IN SEPTEMBER 1961, the California advisory committee to the US Commission on Civil Rights reported that most of the state's African American population lived segregated within "great urban ghettos" owing to the combined discriminatory actions of white homeowners, realtors, developers, landlords, and financiers. Reporters asked Walter Leimert, Jr., to respond to these findings. Following in his father's footsteps, young Walter had become a prominent Southland developer, especially known for building hillside homes possessing what a *Los Angeles Times* real estate editor termed "snob appeal." In the past year, Leimert had been elected president of the Los Angeles Realty Board (LARB). Denying the report's central argument, Leimert maintained that the realty industry had "no rules or regulations against selling to Negroes." In fact, he stressed that he personally resided in his father's namesake subdivision located within "an area [Crenshaw] that was integrated not long ago." Leimert concluded, "If the owner does not want to sell to Negroes, what can the realtor do about it?" LARB executive vice president Earl Anderson provided a direct answer to the question his superior had been careful to leave rhetorical. "If the owner specifies that the house can only be sold to whites," he asserted, "then we must carry out the instructions." White realty leaders argued that they were merely "go-betweens" in no position to combat societal prejudice. "This whole problem," said Anderson, "is a matter of the Negro people themselves educating the public. Essentially, it is their problem."[1]

By the early 1960s, the quest for integration had reached a roadblock. Although only a small minority of the city's white population actively supported integration, most whites did not see themselves as racists. The vast majority probably agreed that discrimination was a "Negro problem" and admitted to no complicity in the matter. In fact, leaders of organized white homeowners and realty interests argued that civil rights measures were creating a new form of reverse discrimination. Through the 1964 voter initiative known as Proposition 14, they vowed to eliminate the state's fair housing law on the grounds that it violated "individual freedom." Cruising to a landslide victory, Proposition 14 demonstrated the continued popular support for suburban racism and restrictive covenants—now linked to an ostensibly "color-blind" discourse that would provide a foundation for neoconservative politics. At the same time, the perpetuation of Black/white segregation and inequality led the most prominent African American leaders in Los Angeles to conclude that their community had achieved but "*token* integration." Tens of thousands of Blacks were now concentrated in South Central Los Angeles, where they were subjected to harsh and often brutal policing imposed by LAPD chief William H. Parker. The effectiveness of white backlash politics and the persistence of segregation undermined the leadership of the integrationists, who proved unable to direct the resentment brewing within the Black community. As the perpetuators of white supremacy became less visible, it was not surprising that African Americans began to direct their opposition toward "whitey," "the man," and "the pigs." Capturing the attention of millions throughout the city, nation, and world, the 1965 eruption of the Watts Rebellion permanently altered the city's political landscape. Afterward, Los Angeles boosters might strive for social peace or white hegemony, but it was no longer possible to achieve both.[2]

In response to the rebellion, three different groupings in Crenshaw drew on their experience in the multiethnic district to develop new models of social organization. The Crenshaw Neighbors sought to transform the concept of the homeowners' association, long used to maintain segregation, into a new vehicle for integration. Whereas civil rights activists had fought to gain access for middle-class Black and Japanese Americans in the 1950s, Crenshaw Neighbors waged an increasingly desperate effort to stop whites from fleeing in the late 1960s. What it called the "first stand for integration" soon began to look more like the last. It was ultimately overshadowed by two visions of multiculturalism that seemed more in tune with the changing face of the city. Tom Bradley's political ascension, from Leimert Park neighborhood canvasser to the mayor's office, reflected a transformation of urban political culture with roots in Crenshaw. His notion of coalition building was designed to serve as a model of governance for a diverse democracy—one that simultaneously positioned Los Angeles to prosper as a "world city" in the global economy. While Bradley redefined the mainstream, radical activists attempted to build a "Third World" movement from the marginalized populations of Crenshaw. Defying a trend toward suburbanization, children of the Nisei situated themselves at the center of this movement. In the end, the fall of integration became a source of new and in many ways unexpected beginnings.

White Revolt: Proposition 14

The 1950s had proven to be something of a standoff for opposing sides of the open housing issue. While civil rights advocates failed to secure the passage of a fair housing law, the leading realty interests' pursuit of a constitutional amendment upholding racial restrictive covenants also fell short. Each side, however, took decisive steps during the following decade, with the key conflicts occurring at the level of the state government. First came the 1963 passage of the Fair Housing Act, which became known for its author, W. Byron Rumford, an African American assemblyman from Northern California. Garnering support from civil rights advocates plus Governor Pat Brown and most other Democrats in state government, Rumford's bill passed on June 21, 1963. For the previous fifteen years, proponents of integration had viewed such a law as the most significant follow-up measure to the *Shelley* decision. They hoped that the Rumford Act would at last provide for the positive state action they considered necessary to eradicate housing discrimination. Private citizens could file complaints with the California FEPC, which was now responsible for investigating and settling cases of both housing and employment discrimination. But the Rumford Act's detractors had convinced the state senate to pass amendments limiting its coverage and reducing the penalties for violators. The immediate impact of the new law was felt mainly by educated Black professionals with above-average incomes, who filed most of the 192 complaints lodged during its first year of operation. It offered no provisions to meet the mass housing demands of working-class communities of color.[3]

Despite its moderate agenda, the fair housing movement sparked dogged white opposition. The California Real Estate Association (CREA), the parent body to most of the state's realty boards, joined forces with the California Apartment Owners' Association to create the Committee for Home Protection. This new committee's singular mission was to qualify an initiative to nullify the Rumford Act through a state constitutional amendment. It quickly tapped widespread support among white voters. By February 1964, the committee and its allies had collected six hundred thousand signatures, more than enough to place their initiative on the November 1964 ballot as Proposition 14. One of the most emotionally charged campaigns in the state's history ensued, culminating with an 85 percent election-day turnout. Despite the formation of broad, multiethnic civil rights coalitions to combat the initiative, California voters delivered a landslide victory to Prop 14 by a 65–35 margin. In raw numbers, the initiative won by over two million votes. Although defeated at the ballot box, civil rights advocates found relief in the judicial system when the California Supreme Court overturned the amendment by a 5–2 vote in May 1966. By a narrower 5–4 margin, the US Supreme Court upheld that decision the following year. With Prop 14 thus rendered void, the Rumford Act survived. Yet the courts could not adjudicate away the suburban political base that had propelled the initiative's landslide passage.[4]

Through its popularization of a putatively nonracialist discourse to defend housing segregation, the campaign for Prop 14 ultimately had a greater impact on history than the law itself. For a half century, white developers, realtors, and homeowners had asserted that they had a right to use "private action" to bar people of color from living in white neighborhoods. Proponents of Prop 14, however, recognized that the legal and political defense of racial restrictive covenants needed to be decoupled from overtly prejudiced arguments. Shying away from publicly denigrating nonwhites, they focused on positively asserting the homeowner's "individual freedom." Here lay the basic argument of the California Real Estate Association: the Rumford Act was a "forced housing" law that deprived homeowners of the fundamental right to dispense with their own property as they saw fit. Charles Shattuck, a leading Westside realtor and self-described lifelong Democrat, declared that the key concern was "FREEDOM! The 'Freedom of Choice'—the 'Freedom to Buy'—the 'Freedom to Sell'—the 'Freedom to rent'—the 'Freedom to Make One's Own Decision' as to with whom he prefers to deal." A *Los Angeles Times* editorial outlined the corollary argument that discrimination, while "morally wrong," could not be stopped by self-defeating "artificial laws." "The philosophical fallacy of the Rumford Act, unhappily," it declared, "lies in seeking to correct such a social evil while simultaneously destroying what we deem a basic right in a free society." Stating it had no interest in promoting integration or segregation, the CREA maintained that Prop 14 had nothing to do with race. Noting that its standard was "to offer equal service to all clients without regard to race, color, religion, or national origin," the CREA proclaimed that it stood for "equal rights and equal opportunity for all." In truth, the LARB had had no agents of color before its recent addition of a handful of Black and Asian members. The even more stubborn Southwest Los Angeles branch maintained an exclusively white membership—all the while insisting it did not discriminate. But by the perverse assessment of the CREA and other Prop 14 backers, it was the fair housing law that violated the equal protection clause of the Fourteenth Amendment. Assemblyman E. Richard Barnes charged that "efforts to appease vocal minorities [were] actually violating the human and property rights of the majority of our citizens." Through these appeals, the campaign was introducing the concept of reverse discrimination to a mass audience, reinforcing a sense of victimization that unified whites across class lines. "When you say 'Civil Rights' today," the Committee for Home Protection declared, "it seems to be a slogan only for the Negro; how about the rest of us having some 'Civil Rights?' Why doesn't 'Civil Rights' apply to *all of us*?" In working-class suburbs like South Gate, as historian Becky Nicolaides has noted, southern white migrants who overwhelmingly favored Prop 14 developed a political language defined by "veiled racism" and "protecting white rights." These ideas stirred emotions considerably. Visiting Los Angeles to link fair housing to the southern civil rights struggle, Martin Luther King, Jr., found his speech picketed by a large gathering of the Rumford Act's white opponents.[5]

Prop 14 supporters also deployed nonwhite spokespersons to denounce civil rights measures. This was a further effort to appropriate rather than repudiate the discourse of "color blindness" that had previously been defined by liberals. Often the goal was to reassure whites that they were fair-minded citizens of an egalitarian nation. The invocation of Japanese Americans as a "model minority," for instance, was a crucial element of the move toward a "color-blind" defense of inequality. But that language was relatively sophisticated compared to crude efforts by the Yes on 14 campaign to put words in the mouths of "legislators and members of minority races." An apartment owners' association publication cited Joseph Vargas as being strongly opposed to the Rumford Act, for he believed that Mexican Americans needed to "earn the respect" of whites rather than "forcing their way into areas where they [were] not accepted." Under the headline "A Negro Point of View," Cora Walker stressed that African Americans were "as much to blame for the present conditions as the white majority," for they "still possess[ed] the slave mentality." Likewise, Henry Kato assured readers, "We Japanese have enjoyed a certain amount of segregation. . . . I am wondering if the Negroes don't enjoy their exclusiveness to some degree." These would-be ethnic representatives were far from chosen by random. For instance, Kato, the owner of a resort in Gilroy, had been sued in 1956 for denying service to African Americans.[6]

Fair housing advocates resolved to protect the Rumford Act by campaigning aggressively against Prop 14. Lacking the resources of the initiative's wealthy sponsors, they faced an uphill battle to sway the state's still majority white electorate. The "official" statewide No on Prop 14 campaign—involving nearly every established civil rights organization but heavily managed by political consultants and Democratic Party operatives—focused on winning over white moderates. It emphasized the modest nature of civil rights laws and warned that the initiative would jeopardize federally funded programs. Above all, opponents of Prop 14 attempted to link the initiative to right-wing extremists. Rather than fight for the moral high ground, liberals presumed they already held it. The majority of white voters, however, resented characterizations of the typical Prop 14 supporter as a racist who was full of "hate." In an unheeded directive, Governor Pat Brown's press secretary remarked, "Most of the people we are now talking to don't regard themselves as bigots, even if they do discriminate against Negroes." Antiracist arguments thus held no appeal to voters loath to acknowledging they were beneficiaries of white privilege. The more white voters heard arguments for and against Prop 14, the more strongly they backed it. Opinion polls revealed that support for the initiative actually increased over the course of the campaign. Proving crucial to the initiative's passage, Los Angeles County voters accounted for nearly half of its margin of victory. On a broader scale, the Yes on 14 campaign gave momentum to a national upsurge of "color-blind" neo-conservatism rooted in this post-*Shelley*, post-*Brown* logic of structural inequality without bigotry. While Lisa McGirr's research has traced the postwar roots of the "new Right" to grassroots organizing in Southern California suburbs, what must be stressed further is the centrality of the "new" racism to its appeal. The same election that witnessed Barry Goldwater framed as an extremist and handily defeated saw the landslide victory of Prop 14. While conservative Republicans provided a starting base of support for the initiative, LBJ voters put it over the top. Race and geography frequently outweighed party affiliation as a determinant of voting. For instance, three assembly districts in the San Fernando Valley, which would spearhead opposition to busing the following decade, were 60 percent Democratic but voted 70 percent in favor of Prop 14. Launched to political stardom from the Southland, Ronald Reagan and Richard Nixon became virtuosos at capturing this white suburban Democratic vote through their appeals to the "silent majority."[7]

Not surprisingly, the No on 14 campaign fared best among communities of color, who voted down the initiative by wide margins. The new, subtle brand of racism was still an easily detectable form of the disease. "In the South," said a Black resident of the city, "the question is 'Do you want your sister to marry a Negro?' In Los Angeles, it's 'Do you want to live next door to a Negro?' " Election returns revealed that 80 percent of African American assemblyman Mervyn Dymally's Fifty-third District and nearly 70 percent of the predominantly Mexican American Forty-eighth Assembly District voted against Prop 14. Black leaders denounced the measure as racist in print and in speeches. Likewise, Japanese American organizations embraced fair housing and publicly voiced nearly unanimous opposition to Prop 14. The Japanese American Citizens League resolved to fight the initiative at its July 1964 national convention in Detroit, while the organization's local members and other Nisei active in the Democratic Party spearheaded a statewide Japanese American coalition against 14. Both Japanese American Christian and Buddhist churches endorsed the coalition, as did the Japanese Chamber of Commerce. A large campaign poster featuring the infamous picture of the cute girl wearing a dog tag focused on the community's bitter memories of the internment. "She can't remember 1942," it read. "But you can. You know what it means to be deprived of your civil rights. You remember how it felt to be unfairly and illegally segregated from other Americans because of your Japanese ancestry." Warning the initiative would revive "legalized racism," the poster concluded with a call to "Fight now against Proposition 14."

Given the unevenness of Japanese American polling data, it is difficult to assess how closely the Japanese American community answered its leaders' call to vote the initiative down. A statewide survey in October 1964 reported that three out of five Asians opposed Prop 14. But the *Rafu Shimpo*'s Henry Mori accused some Nisei leaders of "great hypocrisy" for publicly protesting discrimination against all communities of color while privately stating "we don't like certain groups."[8]

Although working-class African Americans strongly opposed Prop 14 at the polls, many probably did so in spite of the "official" No on 14 campaign. In their efforts to attract moderate voters, mainstream Democrats and No on 14 leaders consciously marginalized working-class African Americans and stifled Black political activism. Continuing the narrowed integrationist discourse of the Cold War, they believed that middle-class whites would tolerate integration only if it meant accepting into their workplaces and neighborhoods a relatively small number of distinguished minority professionals—people who were just like them except in skin tone. Ralph M. Lewis, a prominent developer appointed by Governor Brown to the statewide No on 14 committee, asked voters "not to think of the Negro as a Mississippi field hand picking cotton" but rather "a husband and wife raised in Los Angeles who are college graduates. They have well-behaved children, are leaders in their church, and the wife may be a nurse and the husband a scientist at a local plant." At the other end of the spectrum, the campaign bore reminders of the push for "slum removal" as it deployed scare tactics to court white voters who found integration problematic. Some No on 14 manuals stressed that whites could be persuaded to accept "open housing" as a strategy to prevent the "inundation" of their neighborhood by spreading nonwhites around. Perhaps most significantly, the mainstream No on 14 campaign's strategy prioritized tightly scripted mass media outreach revolving around white fears of Black "extremism." Its leaflets charged that overturning the fair housing law would heighten social tensions by spurring "Black racism" and diminishing the influence of "responsible, non-violent Negro leaders." Without a fair housing law to resolve disputes through investigation and conciliation, the public could expect more disruptive sit-ins and "direct action." At the same time, mainstream leaders of No on 14 urged their followers to distance the campaign from these militant forms of activism. One often-expressed concern was that the public connected "direct action" protest, especially by African Americans, to communism. But integrationists were also intent on enforcing cordiality in order to maintain good standing with leading politicians. In the summer of 1964, most national civil rights leaders, including Martin Luther King, Jr., supported the call for a moratorium on demonstrations advanced by the NAACP's Roy Wilkins. Having endorsed Lyndon Johnson, the NAACP

Fig. 11.1. Protest against Proposition 14. Activists from the Congress of Racial Equality practiced civil disobedience while denouncing the Southwest Realty Board's opposition to fair housing in 1964. Herald Examiner Collection/Los Angeles Public Library.

feared that demonstrations would prompt a backlash vote for Goldwater. Despite the intense emotions generated during the Prop 14 campaign, there was only one significant day of public demonstrations against it in metropolitan Los Angeles, and that occurred nearly ten months before the election. Mainstream leaders were particularly irked by the militant agitation of the Congress of Racial Equality (CORE), which had launched a sit-in within the capitol rotunda during deliberations on the Rumford bill and now rejected the moratorium on demonstrations. An unsigned internal No on 14 directive declared it *"must not* appear" that CORE had anything to do with the No on 14 campaign. It then went much further to assert, "It is *imperative* that Negroes be heard but not seen." Some operatives thus perceived African American participation of any kind to be a political liability.[9]

Although Prop 14 was struck down in court, the integrationists' sound defeat in the campaign exposed their political weakness. On the one hand, their efforts to work within the system had stalled. Moderate whites signaled their belief that civil rights activism had already gone too far, and mainstream Democrats refused to be connected to confrontational protests designed to accelerate the pace of social change. On the other hand, integrationists were ill-positioned to lead the isolated and alienated residents of the ghetto. Even while narrowing their program to emphasize the concerns of relatively privileged people of color, they had always stressed that every fair housing or employment law would benefit all members of their communities—be it directly or indirectly, immediately or gradually. But if civil rights leaders could not adequately defend moderate reforms like the Rumford Act, there was little hope that they could remedy deep structural problems they had consciously pushed to the back burner. The integrationists' prediction that a Prop 14 victory would inflame racial tensions and damage their legitimacy within inner-city communities would prove tragically correct the following year in Watts.

BLACK REVOLT: THE WATTS REBELLION

On July 10, 1960, in Los Angeles's Shrine Auditorium, Martin Luther King, Jr., addressed the issue of "moderation in the civil rights struggle" at the "Mass Rally for Civil Rights." While embracing moderation as "wise restraint and calm reasonableness" in the course of struggle, he called on the audience to reject any definition that delayed "the move toward justice" or entailed "capitulating to the undemocratic practices of the guardian of a deadening status quo." For Los Angeles and the urban North, the influence that King and the southern civil rights movement projected was anything but moderating. Nonviolent resistance exposed not only the brutal nature of white supremacy but also what the great orator called the "conspiracy of apathy and hypocrisy" in Washington, DC. As King urged his Los Angeles supporters to escalate the assault on racism and segregation, their own experience was teaching them that the movement would need to bring about more dramatic changes. National civil rights coalitions were pushing for equality in public accommodations and voting rights, which they accomplished through the historic passage of acts in 1964 and 1965. But these rights, already secure in California, had done little to interrupt postwar patterns of residential segregation, economic inequality, and police abuse. "To say we're better off than Birmingham isn't to say anything at all," declared First AME Church's H. H. Brookins in June 1963. "We're not well off enough to live in Los Angeles County." Witnessing a growing ideological chasm along generational lines, Loren Miller wrote that "young Negro militants . . . profoundly influenced by the overthrow of white colonialism in Asia and

Africa" afforded no respect to white liberal leadership. "Their message is plain," he remarked, "To liberals a fond farewell . . . until you are ready to re-enlist in a Negro-led, Negro officered army." While established integrationists, sometimes competing among themselves, sought to guide this new upsurge, faith in the system was rapidly eroding. With communities of color having just been overwhelmed by opponents of fair housing, the ballot had proven impotent. Rebellion was just around the corner.[10]

Although pockets of Blacks resided in niches established before World War II, the vast postwar majority were confined to a ghetto whose rapid expansion burst the boundaries of the old Central Avenue district at the seams. During the fifties, the second wave of the Great Migration doubled the city's African American population yet again to reach 335,000 persons—about 250,000 more than Oakland, the next-largest Black community on the West Coast. Extending within and beyond its Eastside origins, the new ghetto reached south toward Watts but also blazed a path through the old Westside. As the Los Angeles NAACP remarked in July 1957, segregation produced a "great 'L' shaped Black Belt" that stretched "across the heart of the city." The merger of "the [prewar] West Side, Central Avenue and Watts areas" created a single bloc known as South Central Los Angeles, a ubiquitous symbol of Black life and identity. Contemporary observers noticed that, nationwide, previously all-white communities entered a period of swift racial transition once the in-migration of Blacks reached a "tipping point." While these points varied by location, evidence suggests the Los Angeles threshold was particularly low because of the expanded options postwar white homeowners enjoyed. Prewar lines of racial demarcation evaporated almost instantly. In just three short years between 1950 and 1953, the African American population of fourteen census tracts covering formerly white areas south of Exposition and west of Broadway jumped 554 percent. Fifteen thousand fleeing whites outnumbered the 13,700 Black additions. Adjacent areas transitioned rapidly, as well. By 1960, 69 of the county's 448 census tracts were at least 50 percent African American. A decade earlier, only 22 census tracts had been majority Black, and scarcely half as many had existed in 1940. Meanwhile, a parallel process created a dense concentration of Mexican Americans in East Los Angeles, where the barrio grew further into unincorporated areas of the county.[11]

If the outlook of postwar Black Los Angeles seemed a paradoxical mix of hope and discouragement, this was in large measure due to the contradictory effects of the ghetto's rapid expansion. Initially, the postwar flight of whites from neighborhoods only one generation old—most having been built during the decentralization of the 1920s—produced relatively favorable living conditions. In 1950, 73 percent of "nonwhite" renters and 93 percent of "nonwhite" homeowners in Los Angeles lived in "standard" dwellings. While three times more likely to live in substandard housing than whites, people of color in Los Angeles were far less likely to face poor housing conditions than their counterparts in New York, Philadelphia, Washington, DC, Chicago, Detroit, and most of the urban South. The African American population of Los Angeles was the nation's fourth largest, but only New York had more Black homeowners. Nevertheless, there were more ominous signs of limited opportunity. The comparatively high 36 percent rate of homeownership in the Black community was right where it stood at the outset of the twentieth century. Moreover, one in five persons of color lived in overcrowded housing, nearly triple the rate of whites and close to the nonwhite rate in New York, Philadelphia, Washington, DC, and Detroit. Finally, the persistence of racial inequality in employment combined with the flight of Black professionals out of older neighborhoods to produce a particular concentration of impoverished African Americans in South Los Angeles. By 1965, Blacks comprised over four-fifths of the 320,000 persons in the area, and Latinos made up the majority of the rest. Only two out of three residents lived in sound housing, and the percentage in extremely substandard homes deemed dilapidated and deteriorating had doubled over the past five years. Furthermore, unemployment in South Los Angeles stood at double the rate for metropolitan Los Angeles, and still more persons (not officially counted as "unemployed") had ceased actively searching for paid work. As bleak as things seemed, they were getting worse in a time of phenomenal prosperity for Southern California and the nation. Between 1960 and 1965, median family income fell 7.5 percent in South Los Angeles, while the poverty rate rose from 24 to 27 percent. Poverty and unemployment rates were even sharper among younger adults. They were also noticeably higher in Watts, where the rate of labor force participation fell to only 58 percent and the poverty rate reached 42 percent.[12]

Racial tensions had erupted in South Los Angeles and the adjacent municipality of Compton during the early postwar era when these areas underwent racial transition. Black veterans at the Allied Gardens subdivision endured repeated acts of vandalism and racist threats. As schools became integrated, race-based fights broke out in the area as well. The county's human relations director, Dale Gardner, worried in March 1953 that the school yard brawls at Fremont High "could expand into riots among adults." As Black settlement spread further, it became clear that South Los Angeles held no monopoly on conflicts of this nature. The Urban League responded to three cross burnings, ten cases of vandalism, six bombings, twelve threats of violence, four arsons or attempted arsons, and three neighborhood protests citywide during the 1950s.[13]

In the aftermath of white flight, the LAPD took on the role of policing urban space, presenting one face of guardian to the white suburbs and another of occupier to the inner city. "Police officers enforce the code of the community," said one of the city's Black residents in 1962, "and here it includes segregation." As historian Edward Escobar has noted, the LAPD was consumed with maintaining the manufacturers' "open shop" before World War II. At midcentury, however, subduing crime and delinquency among communities of color became its primary rationale for asserting power. Repressive policing heightened racial consciousness and conflict, as law enforcement promoted racialized stereotypes of gang members and criminals to justify subjecting their communities to exceptional levels of brutality. For Blacks and Latinos raised in the midst of expansive postwar ghettos, the LAPD under Chief William Parker became the preeminent symbol of white power. Although civil rights leaders were well aware of the rage building within their communities, they made little headway in the effort to stop police abuse. In 1956, the NAACP filed six brutality cases with the grand jury that it claimed had been "blocked and stymied by officials in the Police Department." The organization switched tactics the following year by filing ten civil cases seeking $500,000 in damages from Parker and other police officers. Mayor Poulson, however, did little to press the chief or threaten his job security. Unfazed, Parker always maintained that his department gave no consideration to race but merely directed its greatest force toward communities that consistently violated the law. For instance, he testified in 1960 that African Americans in the city were eleven times more likely than whites to commit crimes. Latinos, he charged, were five times but Asians only one-third as likely. Civil rights leaders countered that Parker's figures were padded by racially biased false arrests. The LAPD's widely publicized 1962 shootout at the local mosque of the Nation of Islam (NOI) exacerbated tensions still further. The NAACP attempted to stay on top of the issue while distancing itself from the NOI. Condemning police abuse, the NAACP simultaneously directed its organizers to "*avoid*, if at all possible, having Muslim speakers at your rally." But with one dead and others injured at the hands of the LAPD, the "Black Muslims" became martyrs in the eyes of a population whose own experience had led them to disdain the police. A visit by Malcolm X, whose message of self-determination and self-assertiveness appealed to the increasingly segregated Black population, drew further attention to the NOI. A *California Eagle* editorial cited "irresistible" evidence that the police had fired on unarmed persons in the mosque. The incident, it presciently warned, would "fester and nourish a whole new set of conflicts between Negro citizens and police that will finally build up to a riot that will make last week's incident seem like child's play." Another wave of protests led Parker to revise the "community relations" section of the department's manual to recognize "the constitutional guarantees of racial equality and religious liberty." He also agreed to hire more officers of color. But his actions fell far short of changing the entrenched culture of a department harboring organized groupings of extreme right-wingers and white supremacists. Any reform was, in fact, a cursory measure for Parker, who continued to insist in June 1963 that he ran "the most advanced department in the nation in human relations." Calling for the chief's resignation to no avail, civil rights leaders warned "the ghetto [was] a tinder box" ready to explode.[14]

Of course, segregation, poverty, and police abuse were not new phenomena for Blacks in Los Angeles. What was new, or at least more prominent, leading up to the Watts Rebellion was the perception of a significant portion of the Black population that it was falling well behind the rest of society. This was especially painful coming on the heels of an early postwar era marked by rising expectations. As the community activist Celes King III observed, "A lot of things were creating a thing called hope, and hope is the kind of thing that, when the bubble explodes, problems occur too." Despite apparent breakthroughs, municipal politics left most Blacks feeling little more than frustrated during the 1960s reign of white maverick Democrat Sam Yorty. In the 1961 mayoral election, the underdog Yorty defeated the incumbent Poulson by rallying outsiders against elite downtown interests. Although his career was marked by outbursts of demagoguery and red-baiting, Yorty received strong working-class Black support owing to a false rumor—which his campaign did nothing to stop—that he would fire the LAPD's Parker. But while he appointed a record seven African Americans to seats on city commissions, he refused to touch the police chief. Indeed, Yorty joined with conservative members of the city council to defeat the proposal of newly elected African American council members Tom Bradley and Billy Mills for establishment of the Human Relations Commission (to complement the county's established commission). The limits of Black political power had become "abundantly clear" to Celes King, who was a member of Yorty's inner circle of advisers. African American activists had convinced themselves electoral success would provide them "access to the decision tables" and thus help "strike down the barriers that possibly impeded [the community's] forward progress." Yet they discovered that the concern "white elected officials in the white power structure" exhibited for the Black community quickly dissipated after the votes were counted. While outside observers saw Los Angeles as the home of "the satisfied Blacks," King recognized that "they really weren't that satisfied."[15]

Once a magnet drawing Black migrants to Los Angeles, the local job market intensified such dissatisfaction. As was also occurring through much of the urban North, the heavy industry jobs that had once inspired hopes of elevating millions from poverty were relocating and drying up. "The automation and mechanization of the future brings about problems of absorbing new intelligence that only preparation can answer," warned

Golden State Mutual's Norman O. Houston in a mid-1960s speech. "Yesterday, a high school diploma was the answer to getting a good job, higher pay. Today, a high school diploma is a dead-end street." Automation undermined the power of activism, as well. Civil rights leader Robert Alexander commented that African Americans in many cases were "fighting [their] way into a shrinking market." New hires would put them "at the bottom of the ladder" in positions most likely to experience downsizing. Workplace racism, moreover, had found means to coexist with postwar civil rights laws. As historian Robert Self has remarked, the statewide "FEPC bogged down in what detractors called a 'band-aid' approach: assisting a few individuals while broad patterns of discrimination persisted." For instance, with unions conspiring with employers to reserve training programs for whites, African Americans comprised but 2 percent of those holding apprenticeships within the Los Angeles area in 1965. White workers, nevertheless, insisted there was nothing bigoted about the old boys' network. Admitting he would favor his son for an apprenticeship, a white union member responsible for selecting applicants stated, "It doesn't mean I don't like Negroes. It means I like my own son." A new standard developed by the FEPC in 1964 to combat such nepotism had only a moderate impact on employment, but it ultimately changed the way corporate America approached the issue of race relations. Since before World War II, civil rights activists had targeted Bank of America for refusing to hire Blacks, then restricting them to custodial work. Under added pressure of direct action protests by CORE, the company agreed to "a dynamic, comprehensive program of affirmative opportunity" recruitment and promotion of minorities for all jobs, including "higher-skilled, supervisory, and executive responsibilities." It even made a specific promise to advertise in ethnic media and use people of color in its ads. To be certain, these were concessions Bank of America and other corporations had long resisted. But the new "affirmative" action measures also demanded relatively little of management. The bank agreed to let the under-resourced FEPC review triannual reports specifying the race of all applicants hired, trained, promoted, and rejected; however, it refused to negotiate with CORE. Furthermore, the agreement did little to address a financial infrastructure that systematically discriminated against communities of color through "redlining." Above all, "affirmative" but selective hiring offered no serious alteration of the social relationship between corporations and the impoverished masses denied the riches of the free market system. Bolstering their public image, employers could handpick people of color from extraordinary backgrounds while telling the rest they were being rejected not because of their skin color but because they were unqualified.[16]

Recognizing the limits of lobbying and negotiation without the threat of mass protest, civil rights leaders organized a wave of demonstrations to put added pressure on the city's decision makers. At least one thousand people marched on June 24, 1963, under the banner of the United Civil Rights Committee (UCRC). Drawing momentum from another visit by Martin Luther King, Jr., it brought together what was in many ways an unprecedented coalition of seventy-six organizations representing Black, white, Jewish, Mexican, Japanese, and Chinese Americans. Members of the NAACP and ACLU worked with educators John and LaRee Caughey to assemble much of the coalition. While it established a broad agenda—which included issues of economic development, housing, and police brutality—education became the UCRC's main focus. Community activists pointed out that unchecked residential segregation had actually caused school segregation to increase in the decade following the *Brown* decision. Fifty elementary and secondary schools in the Los Angeles Unified School District were deemed to have student populations that were "almost totally Negro." That figure would more than double within another decade. And while Black students generally attended overcrowded inner-city schools, millions of dollars were spent on new school construction in outlying areas. Teaching opportunities were also restricted for people of color, who were usually assigned only to schools where the bulk of the student population was of their race. School district leaders claimed that student distribution was a product of housing patterns beyond their control. Activists, however, accused them not only of complicity in the face of racial inequality but also of intentionally gerrymandering boundaries to preserve segregation. With the school board resisting proposals for desegregation and enhanced funding for "compensatory education," the coalition's progress was limited. Court-ordered desegregation set off another round of struggle in the 1970s, but the UCRC had largely dissipated by then. In the first major blow to unity, the NAACP withdrew much of its support largely to disassociate itself from the confrontational tactics pushed by the militant integrationists in CORE. Under urging from CORE, whose local membership at this time was majority white, UCRC members engaged in hunger strikes, large protest marches, and sit-ins to disrupt school board meetings. Simultaneously, UCRC picketed the segregated Torrance subdivision of developer Don Wilson. Protracted acts of civil disobedience led to 249 mass arrests and physical scuffles between police and protestors. NAACP leaders and some leading members of the Black clergy asserted that high-profile conflicts like those were tarnishing the reputation of the nonviolent movement and impeding the prospects for progress through negotiation. But while the NAACP's membership had rebounded from the depths of the Cold War, it still fell below World

War II levels. Furthermore, the vast majority were inactive members, little more than names on paper. CORE leaders and the growing ranks of militant integrationists and nationalists countered that disruptive civil disobedience was necessary to end the intransigence of those in power. They also maintained that the police were waging unprovoked assaults to deny free speech rights to nonviolent protestors.[17]

These were the underlying conditions that led to the uprising on the evening of August 11, 1965. After a confrontation between a white highway patrol officer and a Black motorist sparked the disturbance, the broader unrest that ensued lasted six days. Authorities called in 13,900 national guardsmen and imposed a curfew over a 46.5-square-mile area. When the dust settled, thirty-four people had been killed, over one thousand injured, and nearly four thousand arrested. Declaring she had received "expert training in war time survival," *Los Angeles Sentinel* reporter Betty Pleasant wrote, "I watched while renegade Negroes stoned Caucasians, burned cars, shot at policemen, looted stores and pillaged the city." The duration and scale of the rebellion demonstrated deep feelings of resentment against poverty and racism transcending the particular incident that had touched it off. LAPD chief Parker exclaimed that disorderly populations had acted like "monkeys in a zoo," which only served to aggravate African Americans' outrage at police misconduct. Although the McCone Commission acknowledged that "many Negroes here felt and were encouraged to feel that they had been affronted by the passage of Proposition 14," its official determination that "riff-raff" were the source of the "riot" was a distortion of the reality that as many as eighty thousand persons may have participated. This new and highly race-conscious street force refused to play by the rules of any established order and had seemed at the time to have turned the world upside down. The raging fires of Watts overwhelmed the smoke and shattered the mirrors that moderate civil rights advocates had used to sustain the notion that progress toward integration was being made. While the struggle against racial segregation and the construction of interracial coalitions would continue in Los Angeles, they would do so far less frequently under the banner of integrationism. In the aftermath of the rebellion, integationists' assumptions seemed too naive and their prescriptions inadequate.[18]

Already in motion, white and middle-class flight accelerated post-Watts. Although 240,000 African Americans were residing in suburban municipalities outside the city limits of Los Angeles by 1970, Black/white segregation developed on a broader metropolitan scale. More African Americans had relocated to the suburbs from Los Angeles than from any other major metropolis during the 1960s; however, nearly half were living in areas adjacent to the ghetto. Black migration to Compton, for instance, had spawned a rapid racial transition. The city fell from 95 percent white

in 1950 to less than 60 percent in 1960. By 1970, Compton was 72 percent Black, and its residents were facing many of same social issues—
overcrowded schools, high crime rates, and inadequate public services—
confronting South Central Los Angeles. Writing in 1975, researcher
Francine Rabinovitz remarked that this was a "familiar" story. Migration
of "high-income Blacks" into suburbs provoked white flight, subsequently resulting in neighborhoods composed of "large numbers of
lower-income Blacks migrating from the City of Los Angeles." A similar
fate awaited Inglewood, the formerly white middle-class municipality that
became the suburb of choice for Black professionals during the 1960s. In
1970, Inglewood's African American residents were living in homes with
a $30,000 median value and earning a median income 14 percent higher
than that of whites. In reality, however, the city was scarcely more a
model of integration than Compton; the development of white flight was
simply at a less advanced stage. Surveyed in the early 1970s, the majority
of white residents from suburban Compton, Inglewood, Carson, and
Pomona professed a desire to move from their current neighborhood.[19]

While the Watts Rebellion unleashed pent-up animosity toward whites,
it also took aim at the pillars of integrationism. The unrest spread all the
way to Crenshaw, where Japanese American retailers in the Avenues reported looting and burning. As some Black storefronts were also hit, there
was no evidence that Japanese American merchants were singled out—one
in Compton even reported that local youths stood guard to protect his
market. Still, the political fallout from the rebellion was severe. The longtime liberal county supervisor Kenneth Hahn was stoned as he toured the
streets, and even the fair-skinned Augustus Hawkins, now a member of
Congress, feared attack. Leaders of the NAACP and prominent Black
churches like First AME and Second Baptist shared many of the frustrations of the rebels as they blasted Chief Parker and the city's leaders. Their
attempts to draw Black militants into what they saw as a constructive dialogue and political relationship, however, met with at best mixed success.
John Buggs, an African American sociologist who directed the county
Commission on Human Relations, completely reversed the tactics of what
had been the leading public institution for integrationism. He provided
staff positions to Black gang leaders in a desperate attempt to stay in touch
with this rapidly growing population, and he gave a platform to cultural nationalists, such as Maulana Karenga and the US organization. An agenda
promoting interracial harmony was thus replaced by one highlighting programs to promote Black pride and Watts secession. With the notable
exception of the heated battle over school busing, integration failed to characterize the future direction of the fight against racism.[20]

The organization Crenshaw Neighbors was an exception that proved
the rule. As Gerald Home has noted, the rebellion reflected a tidal wave

of Black nationalist sentiment, assertions of masculinity, and the explosive agency of working-class Blacks no longer willing to wait patiently for change. The integrationist, women-led, and unmistakably bourgeois Crenshaw Neighbors sought to buck the tide. While the origins of housing associations were bound to the drive for segregation, this one consciously viewed integration "as the hope and the only answer for America's racial problem." Growing out of a discussion group formed by white and Black women in 1961, Crenshaw Neighbors incorporated in July 1964 with one hundred charter members growing to six hundred over the next year. Upholding a collective "dream" that Americans would someday "live together side by side and take no notice of our neighbor's race, creed or color," they strove to make Crenshaw "a place where people of good will [would] learn to share a beautiful community and its wonderful resources with others of many different backgrounds." Backed by an assertion that "the middle-class neighborhood was where the battle must be fought for integration," Crenshaw Neighbors heralded the formation of about ten community-based organizations comprising the countywide Council of Integrated Neighborhoods in the 1960s. It also launched a national publication called *The Integrator*. But whereas Crenshaw had once stood at the cutting edge of the fight to expand housing opportunities for people of color, the integrationists were now waging an essentially rearguard battle to keep whites from leaving. A newsletter released shortly after the Watts Rebellion noted the organization's fear that "such a beautiful community" was destined to the "sad and utterly unreasonable fate" of becoming "ghettoized" if it could not maintain its appeal to "Caucasians." Members crafted neighborhood tours to show off the most attractive homes of diverse residents, organized committees to promote cordial relations, and disseminated philosophical and academic arguments to make their case to the public. They helped generate something of a paradigm shift in the approach to integration, as well. The *Los Angeles Times* dubbed Crenshaw Neighbors "the first group on the West Coast to rally homeowners in the name of neighborhood stabilization."[21]

Despite the innovative tactics, the task remained daunting. Crenshaw Neighbors executive director Jean Gregg declared that she felt "almost overwhelmed by the problem of accurately depicting what we are up against in our self-appointed task of keeping Crenshaw integrated." She viewed the situation at Dorsey High as a central problem. The school had roughly equal enrollments of Asians, Blacks, and whites from the mid-1950s to the early 1960s, but the character of multiracial relations changed noticeably over this time. When Sheila Gardette, the daughter of an African American postal worker, entered Dorsey as a sophomore in 1956, she found that "the three groups coexisted quite peacefully." Not only did Gardette see little evidence of interethnic competition; she also witnessed "a sense of camaraderie among many (although not a majority of) Black and Japanese students." But the turbulent sixties, noted Crenshaw Neighbors' Gregg, gave rise to frequent outbreaks of racial conflict "involving real injury, even hospitalization." With whites fleeing, people of color had already become 85 percent of the enrollment at Dorsey by 1965. "We are now at the point where Caucasians in the school are in such a minority," remarked Gregg, "that even the most liberal Caucasian family with high school age children would be reluctant to move into the area." Indeed, Crenshaw Neighbors drew its strongest support from the wealthier and predominantly white neighborhoods located in the uplands west of La Brea. When the school district opened Crenshaw High for these residents after the rebellion, it created short-lived hopes of slowing white flight. In 1967, the integrationists prematurely cheered that they had reduced the rate of racial transition among Crenshaw homes to "1% or less." Surveys by UCLA sociologists, however, revealed that urban fears and anti-Black sentiments were strong even in the seemingly protected hillside neighborhoods. The vast majority of white residents in Baldwin Hills spoke of the Watts "riot" disparagingly and praised the work of the LAPD. More than one out of every three whites in Baldwin Hills stated that they held negative opinions of the civil rights movement, felt uncomfortable about the idea of attending parties with Blacks, and had considered using a gun during the rebellion. Demonstrating the grip that racialized images held on Los Angeles homeowners, the hills above Crenshaw were set to become the rare instance of whites conceding luxurious highland homes to people of color. As the literal and figurative upward mobility of elite Black homeowners reached an apotheosis, so correspondingly did white flight. Ideas about race had so powerfully shaped white conceptions of what constituted a "good" or "bad" neighborhood that homeowners were now fleeing nearly mint houses that would not have looked out of place in Bel Air. Even Jean Gregg embraced the idea that civil rights advocates had pushed too fast when she remarked that she had come to view the Rumford Act as "a bad approach to achieving integration." Although it still had an active core of whites, Blacks, and Asians in the early 1970s, Crenshaw Neighbors was forced to question: "Has this dream [of integration] been realized or has it become a nightmare?"[22]

MULTICULTURAL SYNTHESES: TOM BRADLEY AND "THIRD WORLD" UNITY

Although integrationism met its demise in Crenshaw, it did not simply give way to separatism and polarization. While a full analysis of 1960s social movements is beyond the scope of this book, I close with a discussion of how two unique visions of multiculturalism emerged from the new contradictions brought to the forefront of society during that eventful decade. In both cases, political actors in Los Angeles sought to reconcile their place-based identities from Crenshaw with the transformation wrought by global developments. The first was represented by Tom Bradley's quest to build a "world city." The political career of Los Angeles's first African American mayor traced its roots to Crenshaw during the high period of integrationism. Born into a family of Texas sharecroppers, Bradley had resettled to the Central Avenue district as a small child during the 1920s. Excelling in both athletics and academics, he had strived to rise above poverty and escape the ghetto. As a student at UCLA and subsequently as an LAPD officer, Bradley had long operated within white society and resisted the pull of Black nationalism. Through its focus on Black/white cooperation, middle-class homeownership, and the use of nonconfrontational tactics, his move to Crenshaw symbolized the moderate struggle for integration. In 1950, after years of saving money, Bradley coveted a Welland Avenue home in Leimert Park. Well aware of the racist conflicts that had besieged the area, he sought to avert rather than challenge them outright. When browsing for a home, he dressed in overalls and pretended to be a maintenance worker so as not to arouse white fears of a "Negro invasion." Since he "realized that a black man's money wasn't good enough in those days," he arranged for a white couple to acquire his home in their names before transferring it to him. And though Bradley's seven-year-old daughter Lorraine was beaten up by white bullies, who yelled "Nigger, get out of my neighborhood!" he helped his family develop harmonious relations with their neighbors and make their home in Leimert Park.[23]

Young and eager, Bradley raised his level of involvement in the Democratic Party, starting at the neighborhood level and increasingly widening his scope of activity. To be certain, Bradley established roots in the Black community and saw fit to develop ties to African American leaders. He was a member of the First AME Church and an active participant in the Democratic Minority Conference, which had been started by Black activists seeking to increase African American representation in government and grew to involve some Mexican and Japanese Americans, as well. But Bradley also prioritized making connections with experienced white political operators, especially the Democratic Club movement organizers who were determined to promote the liberal wing of the Democratic Party. He became immersed in the Crenshaw Democratic Club and its Leimert Park affiliate. During the 1950s, he engaged in committee work, recruited new members, and walked precincts on behalf of Democratic candidates. Through these activities, he developed new relationships with white and Jewish liberal activists, who helped mold the newly promoted

LAPD lieutenant into a viable candidate for office. With a multiracial staff and coalition, Bradley was elected to the city council seat for the then majority white Tenth District in 1963. Reelected four years later, he next challenged mayoral incumbent Sam Yorty in 1969. A white maverick Democrat, Yorty had received scathing criticism for his caustic and bombastic reaction to the Black community in the aftermath of Watts. Even members of the establishment began to view his style as alienating and counterproductive. But though he trailed by 16 percentage points exiting the primary, Yorty made up ground in the runoff campaign with sharp negative attacks that pulled no punches. Casting Bradley as the "extremist" candidate of "Communists" and "black militants," the incumbent chastised his opponent for running a "racist campaign among Negro voters" that was further stained by "anti-Semitism." Highlighting his race-baiting and red-baiting "law and order" theme, he even characterized the LAPD veteran as "anti-police." In public discourse, Yorty championed himself the "Mayor for all the citizens of Los Angeles." In direct mailings targeting white voters, he more bluntly proclaimed, "*We* need a mayor for *our* city!" Although Yorty's antics succeeded the first time around, his old brand of racial conservatism failed thereafter. Bradley not only won the 1973 rematch; he proceeded to reign as mayor for two decades.[24]

During the Bradley era, from the early 1970s to early 1990s, Los Angeles emerged as one of the most economically and culturally influential cities in the world. As Raphael Sonnenshein has noted, the ties Bradley built with white liberal Democrats, especially Jewish Americans, in Crenshaw were unquestionably a pillar of his political ascension. Lacking the larger Black voter base and support of the Democratic Party machinery that propelled African American politicians representing inner-city districts, Bradley was forced to transcend "minority" candidate status. The Tenth District, by Sonnenshein's characterization, was a biracial meeting ground between South Central Los Angeles and the wealthier and whiter Westside. Blacks and whites who assisted him in Crenshaw "became Bradley's most enduring loyalists and comprised the inner circle of his campaign organization." By this measure, Bradley was a product of a traditional interracial notion of integrationism. Consciously inclusive of whites and recognizing that Blacks were a minority among other minorities, he maintained the image of a racial "moderate" by comparison with "Black mayors" whose careers rose in tandem with the ascension of the Black Power movement.[25]

While biracial relationships may have launched his career, multiculturalism defined Bradley's reign as mayor. The year 1965 provided another paradigmatic event as Congress liberalized immigration through the Hart-Celler Act. While the privileging of high-tech and educated workers would spawn new forms of inequality that made the new act less than the ideal of democracy its proponents had championed, the withdrawal of discriminatory "national origins" quotas opened America's door to a new wave of Asian immigrants. The post-1965 immigration of Asians, Latinos, and smaller groupings of other ethnicities would remake Los Angeles over the next generation. Bradley paid conscious attention to the increasing diversity of his local constituency, which he posited as a microcosm of a world marked by rising cultural and economic integration. Although he personally espoused a belief in the ideal of a color-blind society, the mayor's policies emblematized the new effort by civic leaders to celebrate ethnicity and reverse the postwar tendency toward assimilation. Moreover, believing that effective governance necessitated diverse representation, Bradley employed a multicultural approach to affirmative action in hiring and employment. He kept an open line of communication with local Japanese community leaders and always maintained a significant Japanese American presence in his office. Masamori Kojima, a board member of Crenshaw Neighbors, was one of Bradley's longest-standing aides. Following the cancellation of *Star Trek*, the mayor also tabbed George Takei to serve on the board of the Rapid Transit District. A diligent student of politics, the actor had helped to organize the first Asian American rally against the Vietnam War. Bradley's close friend, Takei chaired the Asian American outreach committee for his campaigns and even managed to run second in the special election to complete his unfinished third term in city council. These moves were not only critical to the maintenance of Bradley's electoral coalition; they went hand in hand with his effort to reposition Los Angeles as "world city" in a globalized economy. Multicultural diversity figured most prominently as a dominant theme of the new boosterism celebrating Los Angeles as a nexus of international trade and commerce. "Think of Los Angeles as a mosaic, with every color distinct, vibrant and essential to the whole," declared a blue-ribbon panel commissioned by the mayor in the 1980s. Though it offered recommendations to ameliorate poverty and expand opportunity for working-class residents, the commission's guiding purpose was highlighting the potential for Los Angeles to distinguish itself as a "crossroads city"—"a leading financial center and a communications axis where major business enterprises from all over the world will want to have a headquarters, a branch office or a manufacturing facility." The authors further predicted the city would become "a leading hub of world trade, especially as the United States gateway to the Pacific Rim nations." Bradley's office prioritized trade with Japan to such a degree that during the eighties he was reportedly the third most recognized American politician in Japan, trailing only Ronald Reagan and Ted Kennedy.[26]

But Japanese American assessments of Los Angeles during the Bradley era were decidedly mixed. Undoubtedly, the mayor himself provided the

Fig. 11.2. Tom Bradley. Posing here with members of the Asian Commission, ca. early 1970s, Bradley served as Los Angeles mayor from 1973 to 1993. His administration emblematized the era of multiculturalism. Shades of L.A. Archives/Los Angeles Public Library.

first meaningful opportunity for Japanese Americans to participate in municipal administration. At the grassroots level, however, many Nisei homeowners felt less inclination to remain in urban neighborhoods undergoing notable changes in racial and class composition. After the Watts Rebellion, they followed the trail of jobs and housing leading to many of the suburbs where whites had already fled. A rise in violent crime during the 1970s especially propelled Japanese American out-migration from Crenshaw. In the assessment of local Japanese community activists, some "underprivileged" African American youths were deliberately assaulting Issei elders not simply to rob them of material possessions but to take out their frustrations by "overwhelming and persecuting a physically weaker group of people."[27]

Although roughly half of the local Japanese population moved to the suburbs between the 1950s and 1970s, the central city's multiethnic politics and culture became an organic component of those who remained in

Los Angeles. Most notably, an influential body of Japanese Americans re-constructed their identity within the context of Black struggle. For example, as a Nisei youth in a concentration camp, Fred Kawano developed a consciousness of racial oppression by reading works by Richard Wright and Gunnar Myrdal. Building on two decades of continuous study of the topic, Kawano reportedly in 1965 became the first teacher in the Los Angeles school system to offer a full-fledged Black history course. He also served as adviser to the Black Students' Union at Carver Junior High in the heart of the old Central Avenue district. Likewise, Crenshaw resident John Saito drew inspiration rather than fear from the notion of Black Power. Chastising peers who saw the civil rights movement "as a struggle between white and black Americans" with no bearing on their lives, he dismissed as an "illusion" the idea that "Orientals [had] truly assimilated into the greater American society." Japanese and other Asian Americans achieving material success and receiving the "praise" of whites, Saito argued in 1968, found it all too "convenient" to ignore rising social protest because of apprehension that "rocking the boat" might jeopardize their "comfortable position." But he asserted that the younger generation, more in tune with the culture and politics of Blacks and Chicanos, would break this pattern of passivity. "The faint voice in the background will become stronger and we will hear more and more of 'Yellow Power,'" he concluded. Saito's words would ultimately prove prophetic.[28]

Although working-class Japanese American youth in Crenshaw intrinsically understood the fallacy of the "model minority" myth, they like most of their generation had been cut off from a history of resistance. Many of the Nisei who had channeled their rage at wartime injustices into postwar civil rights activism had been part of the "progressive" group who resettled to points east. Kiyoshi Patrick Okura, the civil servant who had touched off Fletcher Bowron's fear of sabotage within municipal government, moved to Nebraska and Washington, DC, as he dedicated his life to uplifting communities of color. As national JACL president in 1963, Okura provided the principal force that pushed the organization to endorse and attend the March on Washington. Dislodged from her home in San Pedro during World War II, Mary Nakahara passed the loyalty screening administered during internment and followed the government's directive to reside away from other ethnic Japanese. But the community she and her family immersed themselves in was Harlem. She became a close political associate of Malcolm X and an internationally recognized human rights activist. Known to most people today as Yuri Kochiyama, she more than any other Nisei turned the "model minority" concept on its head. Separated from the Japanese community, she became not a passive model of assimilation but instead a "Third World" revolutionary who inspired scores of younger activists. Okura and Kochiyama, however, were exceptional figures. Hoping to put the past behind them, the typical Nisei parents rarely, if ever, conveyed to their children significant knowledge of the decades of oppression the community had endured. Psychologist Donna Nagata's nationwide survey revealed that Sansei children had discussed the wartime internment with their parents a total of fifteen to thirty minutes, on average, over the entire course of their upbringing.[29]

Reared within the chilling aftermath of the internment, Japanese American youths coming of age during the 1960s and 1970s often looked to other communities of color in their search for an oppositional identity. Sansei from the Eastside of Los Angeles veered in the direction of the Chicano movement, while Westside Sansei connected with African American radicalism. "Black Power, identity, what it means being black, reflected on us Asians as well," recalled Victor Shibata, a founder of the Ministers. The gang had disbanded in the early 1960s after rivalries escalated to the point of shoot-outs. Some key members spent the mid-decade in prison, while others used military service to bring a semblance of order to life. When they returned to the Westside several years later with a broader perspective, they were troubled by what they discovered. Stung by oppression but resisting the whitewash of assimilation, Sansei youth were developing serious cases of alienation. New generations of Ministers were engaging in particularly self-destructive behavior as drug abuse took over a swath of the community. Thirty-one local Sansei died from overdoses during a single calendar year. In response, former members of the original Ministers launched the Yellow Brotherhood (YB) in 1969. Drawing on the Black Panthers' urban survival programs, they fostered political consciousness and cultural awareness in an effort to reach Japanese American youth. Focusing initially on Sansei from the working-class Avenues section of Crenshaw, YB organized a tutoring program with the assistance of the Seinan JACL and developed community involvement projects that also raised funds to maintain the group's self-sufficiency. It opened a house on Crenshaw Boulevard where youth could conduct rap sessions, engage in physical fitness activities, and peruse bookshelves stocked with contemporary classics like Mao's *Red Book* and *The Autobiography of Malcolm X*.[30]

As discourses of whiteness demonized Crenshaw as a place subsumed by the "ghetto," they simultaneously heightened the district's appeal to rebellious Japanese Americans. Raised amid the contradictions of postwar Nisei assimilation, youth from diverse backgrounds struggling with identity formation viewed Crenshaw as a marker of authenticity. As poet Amy Uyematsu would later recount, "It didn't matter where we lived / within a hundred miles of LA— / if you were Japanese growing up here / in the sixties, you weren't really buddhahead / unless you knew about the Westside." What Sansei activists sought was not simply a new way to act ethnically Japanese but a political identity that would connect their personal struggles to global and domestic movements for self-determination. As such, they helped give rise during the late 1960s and early 1970s to the panethnic and race-based construction of an "Asian American" movement that paralleled the movements for Black and Chicano Power. Working in coalition with Chinese, Filipino, and Korean Americans, the Sansei activist community in Los Angeles was a key progenitor of the Asian American movement. Many of this movement's central institutions were based in Crenshaw. Founded by five UCLA students, the radical newspaper *Gidra* kept a Crenshaw address on its masthead as it made a special appeal to suburban Sansei consciously seeking to reject the "model minority" construct. In one of the publication's most widely read articles, Uyematsu, who was then a UCLA student from Pasadena, asserted that by following the contours of white flight, Asian Americans had brought on themselves "the critical mental crises of having 'integrated' into American society." Although she may have been writing primarily from her experience as a Japanese American, Uyematsu's piece resonated with Asians of other ethnicities to become a sort of manifesto for the emerging movement. Whereas McCarthyism had constrained the domestic influence of the international Bandung Conference on Afro-Asian unity a decade prior, the radical climate of the sixties belatedly unleashed its spirit. "Yellow power" had been "set into motion by the black power movement," declared Uyematsu. Asian Americans must now link arms with "black power" in "the Third World struggle to liberate all colored people." The creation of the Storefront organization was a noteworthy attempt to actualize this revolutionary doctrine. In 1971, a group of Japanese American adherents of Marxism-Leninism began recruiting cadres of all races to conduct grassroots organizing in Crenshaw from a "storefront" on Jefferson Boulevard in the Avenues. Storefront proclaimed that "the common bond [of] geography provide[d] a basis for unity" between diverse races. Bruce Iwasaki of *Gidra* recognized its formation as "the first attempt to combine black and Asian (Japanese) elements of the Left literally under one political roof."[31]

Despite flourishes of activity, the impact of Sansei radicals was far less visible in Los Angeles than the legacy of Tom Bradley in the end. The sparkling new skyscrapers and institutions of high culture that arose downtown were hallmarks of the mayor's vision of a "crossroads city" situated at the center of globalization. Casual observers acknowledging the Asian influence on the city scarcely knew anything of short-lived anti-imperialist collectives and projects, most of which had collapsed by the end of the 1970s. What was most visible instead was evidence of transnational Asian capital investment. While the beginnings of a dramatic expansion were building in Koreatown and Chinatown, Little Tokyo was almost completely remade by redevelopment financed mainly by overseas investment from Japan. Transnational capitalist agendas again clashed with local Japanese American community interests. With its high-rise New Otani Hotel under construction in 1974, a representative of Japan's Kajima Corporation characterized the new project as a gesture of "international goodwill between the United States and Japan." However, seeing the historic remnants of the neighborhood destroyed and many of its last inhabitants displaced, community activists countered that redevelopment was turning Little Tokyo into a "Japan-oriented plastic commercial tourist and trade center." Bradley's skewed emphasis on corporate development also translated into negligence toward the Black ghetto. Under his watch, urban neighborhoods surrounding the glitzy downtown additions were consumed by poverty and the drug economy. The demise of the Central Avenue business district, which began during the postwar era, was all but complete. Increasingly, the most prominent African American community businesses and institutions had relocated to the Westside. With the Japanese American presence fading from the Crenshaw scene, Leimert Park became the new cultural center of Black Los Angeles. Given what transpired, it should not surprise that the vast majority of Los Angeles residents know next to nothing about the rich and varied intersections of Black and Japanese American history in the city.[32]

Historians, however, seek to raise consciousness of that which is not so readily apparent. This book (and the education I received while writing it) was made possible by the legacy of multiracial relations and visions of multiracial solidarity embedded in sites throughout Los Angeles. While there are fewer and fewer remaining traces of the postwar community standing in Crenshaw, its spirit lives on through the work of community organizations, activist groupings, arts projects, and ethnic studies programs that trace their political ancestry to the Black Power/Yellow Power generation. Although the concrete struggles, organizations, and social movements I have recounted in these pages have come and largely gone, the multiethnic city continues to give rise to a range of possibilities.

Conclusion

AT THE APEX OF POSTWAR integrationism, the phrase "beyond black and white" signaled an interracial commitment to the ideal of color blindness. My study, by contrast, has taken it as a call to acknowledge the nation's increasingly multiracial character. Just as Los Angeles transformed from majority white to majority "minority" during the past century, the United States is projected to do the same over the next half century. Urban America especially reflects the new demography. With the exception of some parts of the South and the formerly industrial "Rust Belt," multiethnic cities, including many with no racial majority, are fast becoming the norm. If we wish to comprehend this rapidly changing reality, we need histories that transcend conventional notions of "majority" and "minority." As we still have but a fragmented understanding of America's multiethnic past, reconstructing a multiethnic narrative from the ground up will entail the steadfast labor of a generation of scholars. I hope that my book provides insight toward the construction of a more general framework for studying multiracial relations of the past, present, and future.[1]

Interestingly, today's national population makeup is nearly a mirror image of the racial composition of Los Angeles during the transitional postwar era. It was this multiracial order that led Carey McWilliams to tell his West Coast audiences they had "a ringside seat in the great theatre of the future." At the time, he was brimming with optimism that the progressive social movements of the 1940s would transform society. McWilliams went so far as to assert, "California will lead the nation in the direction of a more liberal and tolerant attitude toward minorities just

TABLE 12.1.
Population of Los Angeles, 1960, and United States, 2000

Los Angeles, 1960		United States, 2000	
African American	13.5%	African American	13.0%
Latino	10.5%	Latino	12.5%
Asian	3.0%	Asian	4.0%

Source: US Census.

as, in times past, California was always in the vanguard of aggression against these same minorities." As we have seen, his prediction did not come to fruition. Rather than evaporate in response to repeated challenges, racism changed form to remain an effective tool of division and rationale for inequality. Los Angeles residents, on the whole, refused to relinquish the "white flight" mentality entrenched in early-twentieth-century conceptions of that Southern California city as a haven for white renewal. As national and global imperatives thrust to the fore a new paradigm of racial inclusion, overt forms of violence and hostility toward Black and Japanese Americans eventually faded. But more insidious forms of discrimination emerged to reinforce patterns of segregation and structures of inequality. Even the ostensibly salutary designation of Japanese Americans as a "model minority" was part and parcel of a broader ideological construction designed to foster global American hegemony and perpetuate anti-Black stereotypes. When Watts erupted in 1965, the city in fact became the national symbol of racial conflict and crisis.[2]

In the four decades since the Watts Rebellion, Black/white inequality has steadfastly persisted in the Los Angeles area. As highlighted in a study jointly commissioned by the United Way and the Urban League, the median income of African Americans in 2000 trailed (in descending order) that of whites, Asians, and Latinos. Not only did the median white resident of Los Angeles make 69 percent more than his Black counterpart, Blacks also had the lowest average life expectancy, owing in no small part to the fact that their death rates from homicide and HIV/AIDS more than tripled those of the three other groups. Furthermore, only 38 percent of African Americans owned their homes, meaning that the housing bubble of the current decade may have driven the Black homeownership rate below where it stood one hundred years ago. Black advances in electoral politics have only made these grim socioeconomic statistics more eye-catching. "You've got all these people in office," remarked the United Way's Johnetta Cole. "But where's the change?"[3]

Given this evidence, one could surmise that the quest for integration changed nothing at all. I would argue, however, that too much of American urban politics is derived from a one-sided analysis of integration as an aborted process. Across the ideological spectrum, we see the same prescriptions recycled again and again in the belief that they were never given a fair chance to succeed—build better and stronger coalitions between whites and Blacks, revive the Popular Front, reclaim the idealistic spirit of color blindness, and complete the unfinished agendas of the New Deal and the civil rights movement. Prescriptions like these become antiquated when one fails to reconsider their meaning in light of changing realities. If McWilliams was an imperfect prognosticator, he was not completely wrong. Multiethnic Los Angeles did establish the "new pattern of race relationships" he foresaw. Moreover, he was correct to recognize that new principles of social justice would not be created by simplistic exercises in harmony. They would instead emerge from the struggle of "minority cultures . . . in the face of an intolerant dominant group"—a struggle that McWilliams asserted was "exceptionally stimulating and creative in ways that we cannot, even now, properly appreciate." We need to acknowledge that the efforts of African Americans, Japanese Americans, and their allies to establish a presence, build homes, and raise families changed the course of Los Angeles history by generating a new sense of identity for individuals, racial/ethnic groups, and the city as a whole.[4]

Historians must be able to explain the sources of both diversity and inequality. Coming to terms with the fact that both were outcomes of the postwar conflict over integration pushes us beyond dominant notions of the crisis in urban race relations. We need to recapture McWilliams's sense that new sources of conflict and oppression also stimulate new modes of creative thought and action. "Los Angeles School" theorists Edward W. Soja and Allen J. Scott contend that the key to generating "new kinds of local social democracy," "a new vision of citizenship," and a heightened "concern for quality of life" lies in mobilizing "the new urban majority of Latino, Asian, and African-American communities." This multiracial notion of the "new urban majority" is enriched by possibilities that the concept of "ghettoization," which has been at the center of discourse on urban race relations, lacks. Instead of continually lamenting the population loss created by white flight, it focuses attention on the residents who remain tied to the central cities. Instead of embracing an integrationist ideal of white majority neighborhoods that hold minority populations below a "tipping point," it forces us to come to terms with political dynamics that arise when people of color become the majority.[5]

As an increasingly diverse American population seeks to trace its origins, the relevance of multiethnic narratives will only magnify. The intersecting histories of Black and Japanese American social movements in Los Angeles can teach us a great deal about how social actors defined their place in a multiracial order and help us to analyze the means by which they attempted to rearrange that order. Studies of the fight against restrictive covenants, campaigns for jobs and union representation, and the quest for political empowerment provide particular insight into the methods and tactics they used. Moreover, a focus on the creation of community in multiethnic neighborhoods such as West Jefferson, Little Tokyo/Bronzeville, and Crenshaw can illuminate a neglected history of solidarity and coalition building. In this manner, I have conceived of this book not in isolation but in conjunction with like-minded scholarship, especially the knowledge produced by Latino studies. Representing a plurality of today's residents of Los Angeles, Latinos have made an indelible imprint on the city's culture. While anti-Mexican racism lay at the core of the "white city," Latino labor, transnational migration, and social movements have proven integral to the rise of the "world city." Readers are encouraged to connect my narrative with those of Latino historians, who have established the fullest accounting of any ethnic group's history in Los Angeles. A multi-ethnic synthesis must in particular cross the Eastside/Westside boundary, which has served as the city's most critical line of social demarcation for the past century. Mexican Americans have been pivotal to the multiethnic political coalitions emanating from the Eastside, which also encompassed Little Tokyo and the Central Avenue district. The multiethnic histories of Westside communities like Crenshaw should be read alongside those of Eastside communities like Boyle Heights. While Boyle Heights became majority Mexican American, it drew Black and Japanese Americans to its pockets of unrestricted single-family housing and also was the historic center of Jewish radicalism.[6]

What deserves recognition perhaps above all is the dynamism of multi-ethnic history. My study has shown how the aspirations of Black and Japanese American community leaders shifted in response to external and internal stimuli over the course of the twentieth century. The pre–World War II drive for self-development and racial progress yielded to the quest for integration, characterized by assimilation for some and by social democracy for others. Postwar integration, in turn, was displaced by post-1965 multiculturalism taking the forms of corporate globalization and "Third World" liberation. We are now living through an era in which multiculturalism is being superseded by a new paradigm that has yet to emerge.

As we chart our course through rapidly shifting seas, there is no better site than Los Angeles to examine the contradictory pairings of unity and polarization and of tolerance and fragmentation lying at the core of the twenty-first-century American dilemma. While the roots of social polarization in the "world city" stem from the failure of postwar integration and social democratic reform, multicultural boosterism has accentuated cleavages based on class. Increasingly, these class divisions occur within communities of color. Given diminished prospects for mass minority advancement through the egalitarian redistribution of industrial growth and postwar prosperity, integrationist campaigns focused on the claims to belonging of relatively privileged persons of color. While the subsequent affirmative action strategies of the Bradley era enhanced cultural pluralism, they did little to address the structural bases of class inequality. Indeed, Southern California firms adopting what author Bennett Harrison has called the "high" and "low" roads to competitiveness in a globalized economy have intensified polarization. These post-Fordist strategies have relied on new waves of migration produced by both the intended and the unintended effects of immigration reform. At one end of the spectrum, "high road" proponents have sought to increase productivity through investment in research and technology, improvements to education, and the immigration of highly skilled technicians privileged by the 1965 Immigration Act's provisions. This highest-skilled sector of the labor force has prospered in the era of the "information economy" and the international marketing of American consumer culture. Moreover, Southern California has attracted streams of overseas capital investment, most visibly from Asia.[7]

At the opposite end, however, the "low road" approach to global competitiveness has emphasized cutting costs by focusing on the growth of labor-intensive industries and the heightened exploitation of workers. In significant measure, this has involved undermining regulations and workers' rights established or won in previous eras of reform. Movement in this direction has created a domestic "Third World" economy in which the lack of basic human rights, political representation, and equal protection under the law define the status of "cheap" immigrant labor that either arrives through nonquota categories (such as family reunification) or remains undocumented. While the new class of transnational Asian capitalists has drawn conspicuous attention within the "world city," the past three decades have also witnessed a resurgent migration of low-wage Asian (though primarily non-Japanese) immigrant workers. By 1990, 44 percent of Asians in Los Angeles earned less than $15,000 annually. The most glaring example of the absence of a "floor" for labor was the 1996 discovery of Thai immigrant garment workers who were kept behind barbed wire in an El Monte slave labor camp. The new employment patterns rooted in the global division of labor have undermined much of the leverage that working-class African Americans achieved through the civil rights movement. Alongside light manufacturing, service industries, and immigrant retailers in swap meets and minimalls, the contemporary sweatshops have replaced the steel mills, tire factories, auto plants, and other forms of industrial employment that once provided some hope for Black economic advancement.[8]

These new inequalities of the multicultural city have spawned new sources of unity and discord. Since the heyday of the Bradley era, some notable examples of multiethnic unity have been created through what could be called post-Fordist modes of organizing. Spurred especially by the mobilization of Latino immigrant workers, progressive trade unions and workers' centers have sought to reclaim the expansive vision of labor organizing during the Popular Front by emphasizing community issues and building broad alliances. They have developed innovative tactics necessary to address flexible industries and mobilize participants across racial, cultural, and linguistic boundaries. The Bus Riders Union has gone a step further. Seeking to reverse the sprawl mentality that defined twentieth-century planning and development, the multiracial transit activists have deemed public transport vehicles the new site of proletarian organizing for economic redistribution, civil rights, urban revitalization, and environmental justice. In fact, multiracial solidarity has been central to the mission of a broader range of organizations, some of which have been shaped by African American and Japanese American activists who came of age during the 1960s and 1970s.

Although these forward-looking groups have made a positive impact on the lives of thousands of the city's denizens, they have generally been overshadowed within both popular and scholarly discourse by the specter of interethnic conflict. Just as the Watts Rebellion exposed both the polarizing effects of postwar redevelopment and the limits of integrationism as an ideology to promote social harmony, so did the "bread riot" of 1992 with respect to "flexible accumulation" and multiculturalism. In that historic moment, however, the so-called "Black-Korean" conflict commanded the center of public attention, even displacing the police beating of African American motorist Rodney King and the acquittal of the four LAPD officers charged with abuse. What little national awareness there had been of a new pattern of race relations arising from Los Angeles became subsumed by this symbol of multicultural dystopia. Seemingly round-the-clock media attention highlighted the volatile Black-led protests against Korean American–owned retail establishments in the months leading up to the rebellion and the somewhat targeted looting and vandalism that occurred during the four-day uprising. But while inflamed by media distortions, these interethnic conflicts involved true-to-life sentiments and actions that could not be dismissed. Although historical narratives cannot single-handedly eradicate such tensions, they can serve to resituate the construction of racial identity within a broader social context. In this regard, they help to unlock the mental prisons that are created by narrow and static conceptions of identity politics. In particular, my study highlights the repeated themes and tactics deployed in the racialization of Asian and Black subjects within a triangular framework. Like Japanese Americans during World War II, Korean Americans were viewed by many whites and Blacks as a perpetually foreign population causing problems because it was out of place in America. At the same time, neoconservatives advanced a new "model minority" image of immigrant shopkeepers as the bearers of the Protestant work ethic and law-and-order ideology. Connecting the adjustment of post-1965 immigrants to the Japanese American quest for full citizenship opens our eyes to the deeply rooted struggle Asian historical actors have waged against racial oppression. At the same time, it draws attention to the insidious and repeated deployment of the "model minority" construct. Those concerned with multiracial justice most certainly need to foster a critical awareness of both.

While Black-Korean tensions have simmered over the past decade, rumors of impending riots in Los Angeles today most frequently invoke Black-Latino conflict. As neoliberal economic policies have uprooted peasants from Mexico, Central America, and Latin America, Southern California has continuously attracted job seekers from across the border. Meanwhile, dwindling job prospects, failing schools, gang violence, and repressive policing have pushed thousands of African Americans roughly a hundred miles away from the central city to exurbs like Riverside, Moreno Valley, and Palmdale. As a result, a Latino majority has emerged in places well beyond East Los Angeles—most notably South Central Los Angeles (which the city has officially renamed South Los Angeles for the twenty-first century). In fact, Latinos have come to comprise the predominant workforce in areas such as janitorial work, hotels, and domestic service that once defined Black employment patterns outside manufacturing. With this shift in demographic and economic balance, a potentially growing number of African Americans—within Los Angeles but also in other parts of America today—have come to suspect that the multicultural city offers nothing but diminishing economic and political prospects. African American journalist Erin Aubry has best chronicled the changing mood of Black Los Angeles, from a community that once inspired Carey McWilliams's boundless hopes to one that has grown increasingly pessimistic. "The cumulative effect of these [demographic and socioeconomic] trends, aggravated by the death of black activism," she writes, "has been a growing anxiety among black people that their window of opportunity may be closing, that the long era of a black-dominated social and civil rights agenda may be coming to an end." Worse for some than the direct material impact is the apprehension caused by a loss of presence and recognition. Remarks Aubry, "Blacks are even losing their historic and symbolic role as a mirror of the nation's conscience; another group [Latinos] now holds a mirror that is less damning and easier for the nation to gaze into."[9]

In this context, Crenshaw continues to serve as an emblematic place marked by struggles over who rightfully belongs in the neighborhood, in the city, and in the nation. During the interwar era, Walter Leimert's homeowners' associations maintained that the preservation of a healthy and secure living environment required excluding people of color from residence and hence from full citizenship within the body politic, as well. By contrast, as Aubry notes, Crenshaw now stands as "the only predominantly black area of Los Angeles left, and the strongest argument against cultural annihilation." It houses many of the Black community's most prominent social, cultural, and economic institutions. "Yet for all its activity," she argues, "Crenshaw has the feel of an island, a bunker." Although Blacks have overcome the racial covenants Leimert constructed in the 1920s, a small grouping of African Americans has invoked the narrow nationalism of that period. In April 2006, a newly formed Black organization called the Crispus Attucks Brigade invited the Minutemen— vigilantes sworn to prevent undocumented immigrants from crossing the US/Mexico border—to Crenshaw for a most curious interracial political demonstration. Gathering in the Leimert Park cultural center, whites, African Americans, and at least one Latino railed against immigration. "Black nationalism," opined Aubry, became "twisted into my-country-right-or-wrong black patriotism." These "Black Minutemen" are a fringe group today, but they may in fact symbolize a broader sense of desperation among the dispossessed—a feeling that Blacks must assert their "Americanness" against immigrant "others" to draw attention to their plight. What may be emerging is another "model minority" showdown in which Asian and Latino immigrant leaders counter that their "hard work" renders them more valuable to the nation-state.[10]

This idea that the success of other communities of color necessarily poses a threat to Black Los Angeles is something qualitatively new. Although African American leaders occasionally spoke out against immigration in the twentieth century, more often than not they stressed the benefits of the city's diversity. Black leaders often used narratives of Japanese "success" to push their community to strive harder during the interwar period, and they believed that rising ranks of multiple nonwhite groups strengthened the prospects for social justice during much of the integrationist era. The recent struggle to save the Holiday Bowl proved that collective memory of these struggles still exists in Crenshaw. Although the bowling alley's business was owned and operated by Nisei, its land and structure remained in the ownership of the Siskin family. Following a spring 2000 agreement to sell the land to a strip mall developer, the Siskins terminated the lease on Holiday Bowl and shut it down. In response, the Coalition to Save Holiday Bowl brought together Nisei survivors of World War II internment camps, working-class Blacks from the offspring of Negro bowling leagues, and young white preservation activists fitted in retro clothing to fight city hall. Because the city's preservation ordinances are ultimately toothless, they managed only to stave off demolition temporarily. But what the coalition's three-year battle bequeathed to Crenshaw and Los Angeles was a rich sense of place and community connecting the past, present, and future. Mass media trumpeted the campaign, and even the *New York Times* ran a national story referring to Holiday Bowl as a "landmark of diversity." Coalition founder Jacqueline Sowell had become emotionally attached to it while working as a waitress in its coffee shop. "It's the only place I know," she stated, "where you can go and see an African American eating *udon* [Japanese noodle soup] next to a Japanese American eating grits." Trumping stereotypical accounts of inner-city turmoil, Holiday Bowl regulars relayed stories of how Blacks and Asians stood guard together in front of it to ensure that it was not touched by the 1992 uprising. "We need places like this," declared Olivia Sanders, "especially when there's the perception that blacks and Asians don't get along." An African American resident of Crenshaw since the 1960s, she surmised that Holiday Bowl was "what makes Los Angeles, Los Angeles." "It's a close-knit place for Blacks and Asians," concurred Japanese American Ed Nakamoto. Borrowing a term from an earlier era, he surmised, "It has real integration." Narratives like these convinced city council member Mike Feuer that Holiday Bowl held priceless value for "a city that desperately needs models of how people from different racial backgrounds can coexist in a productive and constructive way." Feuer concluded, "That's what Los Angeles should be about."[11]

Both the "Black Minutemen" and the Coalition to Save Holiday Bowl are products of history and signs of possible futures. Their local struggles emanating from Crenshaw provide a window into the multiethnic conflicts and coalitions of a new political world in which people of color comprise not only a majority of the world's population but also a majority of Los Angeles, California, and eventually the United States. Racial politics will be less and less a question of "minorities" seeking the acceptance of whites; they will be shaped by interactions between communities of color and by transnational relations between "world city" residents and postcolonial entities. As this transpires, I believe the idea of a multicultural order marked by a conglomeration of ethnicities will gave way to a recognition that we inhabit a polycultural society in which all identities are formed at the intersection of diverse cultures. The shape of this polyethnic world is still in formation, but we can be certain that key elements of its root system have already taken shape in Los Angeles. Therein lies a history waiting to be written.[12]

Abbreviations

NAACP   Papers of the NAACP, Microform Edition, University Publications of America

NAACPW   Records of the National Association for the Advancement of Colored People, West Coast region, BANC MSS 78/180 c, The Bancroft Library, University of California, Berkeley

NNC   Papers of the National Negro Congress, Microform Edition of Manuscript Collections from the Schomburg Center for Research in Black Culture, The New York Public Library, University Publications of America

PCCAPFP   Pacific Coast Committee on American Principles and Fair Play records, BANC MSS C-A 171, The Bancroft Library, University of California, Berkeley

WCC   William C. Carr Papers, Japanese American Research Project Collection (Collection 2010), Department of Special Collections, Charles E. Young Research Library, University of California, Los Angeles

NEWSPAPERS

CE	*California Eagle*
LAS	*Los Angeles Sentinel*
LAT	*Los Angeles Times*
NYT	*New York Times*
PC	*Pacific Citizen*
RS	*Rafu Shimpo* (*Los Angeles Japanese Daily News*)

Notes

Introduction

1. Arthur F. Miley to John Anson Ford, 8 July, 10 August 1943, box 65, JAF; Los Angeles County Committee, Communist Party, "Los Angeles Needs More Housing for War Workers, Without Discrimination," 10 August 1943, box 46, ibid.; Los Angeles County Committee for Interracial Progress, "Minutes of the Eleventh Monthly Committee Meeting," 8 January 1945, folder "Housing," box 246, JRH; *CE*, 29 July 1943; *LAT*, 26 May 1944.

2. For an analysis of "triangulation" in the "Black-Korean conflict," see Claire Jean Kim, *Bitter Fruit: The Politics of Black-Korean Conflict in New York City* (New Haven, 2000).

3. Thomas Sugrue, *The Origins of the Urban Crisis: Race and Inequality in Postwar Detroit* (Princeton, 1996); Robert Korstad and Nelson Lichtenstein, "Opportunities Found and Lost: Labor, Radicals, and the Early Civil Rights Movement," *The Journal of American History* 75: 3 (December 1988): 786–811; Martha Biondi, *To Stand and Fight: The Struggle for Civil Rights in Postwar New York* (Cambridge, 2003). On suburbanization and racial segregation, see also Kenneth Jackson, *Crabgrass Frontier: The Suburbanization of the United States* (Oxford, 1985); Robert Self, *American Babylon: Race and the Struggle for Postwar Oakland* (Princeton, 2004); Arnold Hirsch, *Making the Second Ghetto: Race and Housing in Chicago, 1940–1960* (New York, 1983).

4. Gunnar Myrdal, *An American Dilemma: The Negro Problem and Modern Democracy* (New York, 1944), lxix–lxxi; *Report of the National Advisory Commission on Civil Disorders* (New York, 1968), 1.

5. Sugrue, *Origins of the Urban Crisis*, 13.

6. Huntington quoted in Carey McWilliams, *Southern California: An Island on the Land* (Salt Lake City, 1973), 133–34; Bradley quoted in Steven P. Erie, *Globalizing L.A.: Trade, Infrastructure, and Regional Development* (Stanford, 2004), 91–92.

7. Mike Davis, *City of Quartz: Excavating the Future in Los Angeles* (New York, 1992).

8. Douglas S. Massey and Nancy A. Denton, *American Apartheid: Segregation and the Making of the Underclass* (Cambridge, MA, 1993), 74–78.

9. See Christina Klein, *Cold War Orientalism: Asia in the Middlebrow Imagination* (Berkeley, 2003).

10. On the Eastside, see Richard Griswold del Castillo, *The Los Angeles Barrio, 1850–1890: A Social History* (Berkeley, 1979); Ricardo Romo, *East Los Angeles: History of a Barrio* (Austin, 1983); George J. Sánchez, *Becoming Mexican American: Ethnicity, Culture and Identity in Chicano Los Angeles, 1900–1945* (New York, 1993); Douglas Monroy, *Rebirth: Mexican Los Angeles From the Great Migration to the Great Depression* (Berkeley, 1999); Edward J. Escobar,

Race, Police and the Making of a Political Identity: Mexican Americans and the Los Angeles Police Department, 1900–1945 (Berkeley, 1999); Douglas Flamming, *Bound for Freedom: Black Los Angeles in Jim Crow America* (Berkeley, 2005); Mark Wild, *Street Meeting: Multiethnic Neighborhoods in Early Twentieth-Century Los Angeles* (Berkeley, 2005).

11. Carey McWilliams, Speech to the Annual Meeting of the California Library Association, 20 October 1944, clipping from *California Library Association (CLA) Bulletin*, December 1944, folder 42, carton 4, CMW; Carey McWilliams, "The West Coast: Our Racial Frontier," September 1945, folder 29, ibid.

CHAPTER 1: CONSTRUCTING THE SEGREGATED CITY

1. *LAT*, 4 August 1909, 1 and 15 December 1912, 1 January 1913; Natalia Molina, *Fit To Be Citizens? Public Health and Race in Los Angeles, 1879–1939* (Berkeley, 2006), 19.

2. Quoted in Clark Davis, *Company Men: White-Collar Life and Corporate Cultures in Los Angeles, 1892–1941* (Baltimore, 2000), 73–74. On the rise of Los Angeles as a metropolis, see Robert M. Fogeleson, *The Fragmented Metropolis: Los Angeles, 1850–1930* (Berkeley, 1993); Frank L. Kidner and Philip Neff, *An Economic Survey of the Los Angeles Area* (Los Angeles, 1945); Jacqueline Rorabeck Kasun, *Some Social Aspects of Business Cycles in the Los Angeles Area 1920–1950* (Los Angeles, 1954); Remi Nadeau, *Los Angeles: From Mission to Modern City* (New York, 1960).

3. R. M. Widney, "An Account of the Great Chinese Riot and Massacre in Los Angeles," November 1917, handwritten and typed manuscripts, box 1, Widney Family Papers, The Huntington Library, San Marino, CA; Remi Nadeau, *City-Makers: The Story of Southern California's First Boom, 1868–76* (Costa Mesa, CA, 1965), 63–68.

4. Joseph P. Widney, *Race Life of the Aryan Peoples*, vol. 2 (New York, 1907), 65–66, 126–34, 169–75, 180–201, 306–11. On post-1848 California, see Carey McWilliams, *North From Mexico: The Spanish Speaking People of the United States* (New York, 1990); Leonard Pitt, *The Decline of the Californios: A Social History of Spanish-Speaking Californians* (Berkeley, 1971); Griswold del Castillo, *Los Angeles Barrio*; Monroy, *Thrown Among Strangers*; Tomás Almaguer, *Racial Fault Lines: The Historical Origins of White Supremacy in California* (Berkeley, 1994); Kevin Starr, *Inventing the Dream: Southern California Through the Progressive Era* (New York, 1985).

5. Erie, *Globalizing L.A.*, 47–63; Fogeleson, *Fragmented Metropolis*, 21–134.

6. Grace Heilman Stimson, *Rise of the Labor Movement in Los Angeles* (Berkeley, 1955), 104, 366–408; Robert Gottlieb and Irene Wolt, *Thinking Big: The Story of the Los Angeles Times, Its Publishers, and Their Influence on Southern California* (New York, 1977), 35–52; Edgar Lloyd Hampton, *How the Open Shop Promotes General Prosperity in Los Angeles*, 4, 19, folder " 'Labor–Los Angeles,' 2–24," box 91, JRH.

7. David Clark, *Los Angeles: A City Apart* (Woodland Hills, CA, 1981), 20; William Mason and James Anderson, *America's Black Heritage* (Los Angeles,

1969), 44; Stimson, *Labor Movement in Los Angeles*, 267–337; *Kashu Mainichi*, 11 April 1937. According to Stimson, during 1910 and 1911, a brief effort was made to draw Mexicans, African Americans, and European immigrants into the AFL. The local AFL leaders maintained an exclusionary posture toward Asians.

8. W.E.B. DuBois, "Colored Californians," *The Crisis* 6 (August 1913): 194; "School Board Not Bothered by Japanese, Sees No Necessity for Segregation," *Los Angeles Herald*, 3 February 1907, folder 24, "Japanese," box 87, JRH; Chotoku Toyama, "The Japanese Community in Los Angeles" (MA thesis, Columbia University, 1926), 8.

9. Delilah L. Beasley, *The Negro Trail Blazers of California* (New York, 1997), 254; J. Alexander Somerville, *Man of Color* (Los Angeles, 1949), 74; DuBois, "Colored Californians," 192–95; Lonnie Bunch III, *Black Angelenos: The Afro-American in Los Angeles, 1850–1950* (Los Angeles, 1988), 18–21; Mason and Anderson, *America's Black Heritage*, 45; Rydall quoted in Quintard Taylor, *In Search of the Racial Frontier: African Americans in the American West, 1528–1990* (New York, 1998), 207.

10. William M. Mason and John A. McKinstry, *The Japanese of Los Angeles* (Los Angeles, 1969), 5–17; Koyoshi Uono, "The Factors Affecting the Geographical Aggregation and Dispersion of the Japanese Residences in the City of Los Angeles" (MA thesis, University of Southern California, 1927), 18–19. On Japanese immigrant history, see Yuji Ichioka, *The Issei: The World of the First Generation Japanese Immigrants* (New York, 1988); Eiichiro Azuma, *Between Two Empires: Race, History, and Transnationalism in Japanese America* (New York, 2005).

11. *LAT*, 31 October 1901, 28 January 1906, 12 February 1909.

12. Charles S. Johnson, *Industrial Survey of the Negro Population of Los Angeles, California* (The Department of Research and Investigations of the National Urban League, 1926), 10; Arna Bontemps and Jack Conroy, *Anyplace But Here* (New York, 1966), 266–67; Flamming, *Bound for Freedom*, 133; Ichioka, *The Issei*, 191–92.

13. Nadeau, *Los Angeles*, 211; Bunch, *Black Angelenos*, 26; *LAT*, 9 February 1915; *CE*, 6 February 1915.

14. Richard Schickel, *D. W. Griffith: An American Life* (New York, 1984), 225–30, 281; Michael Rogin, "'The Sword Became a Flashing Vision': D. W. Griffith's *The Birth of a Nation*," *Representations* 9 (Winter 1985): 150, 176; Starr, *Inventing the Dream*, 303.

15. Robert G. Lee, *Orientals: Asian Americans in Popular Culture* (Philadelphia, 1999), 117–26; *Los Angeles Examiner*, 18 May 1923; Emory S. Bogardus, *The New Social Research* (Los Angeles, 1926), 259; *RS*, 22 May 1923.

16. Mayor John Porter's 1929 election was sponsored by fundamentalist Rev. Robert Schuler, an overtly racist, anti-Semitic, and anti-Catholic Klan apologist. See Tom Sitton, *John Randolph Haynes: California Progressive* (Stanford, 1992), 219–20.

17. *LAT*, 28 June 1906, 1 July, 2 and 6 November, 1 December 1920, 24 June 1923.

18. Erie, *Globalizing L.A.*, 50; Jackson, *Crabgrass Frontier*, 179, 288; W. W. Robinson, "The Southern California Real Estate Boom of the Twenties," *Southern*

California Quarterly (March 1942): 25–30; Allan H. Spear, *Black Chicago: The Making of a Negro Ghetto, 1890–1920* (Chicago, 1967), 11–27; Scott Bottles, *Los Angeles and the Automobile: The Making of the Modern City* (Berkeley, 1987), 187–90; James R. Grossman, *Land of Hope: Chicago, Black Southerners, and the Great Migration* (Chicago, 1989), 161–80; *LAT*, 26 May, 2 June, 15 October 1925 (emphases in originals).

19. McWilliams, *Southern California*, 136–37, 161–64; Fogelson, *Fragmented Metropolis*, 67–72, 142–45, 191–98; Sánchez, *Becoming Mexican American*, 87–96; *LAT*, 12 February, 21 April 1913, 24 March, 15 September 1919, 5 March 1940.

20. *Los Angeles Examiner*, 11 March 1923; Mark Weiss, *The Rise of the Community Builders: The American Real Estate Industry and Urban Land Planning* (New York, 1987), 10, 80–99; Fogelson, *Fragmented Metropolis*, 247–72; Mark Foster, "The Decentralization of Los Angeles During the 1920s" (PhD diss., University of Southern California, 1971), 216–51; Loren Miller, *Petitioners: The Story of the Supreme Court of the United States and the Negro* (Cleveland, 1967), 244–52; Clement E. Vose, *Caucasians Only: The Supreme Court, the NAACP, and the Restrictive Covenant Cases* (Berkeley, 1959), 3–6. My understanding of "northern" racism has been shaped by Joel Kovel, *White Racism: A Psychohistory* (New York, 1970).

21. *LAT*, 1 April 1906; "invisible walls of steel" quoted in Taylor, *In Search of the Racial Frontier*, 235; Robert E. Park, "Behind our Masks," *Survey Graphic* 9: 2 (May 1926): 135. After the Great Migration, extensive campaigns emerged in Chicago to keep Blacks hemmed into their corner of the South Side, and fierce struggles ensued as white property owners sought to bind entire neighborhoods to contractual obligations prohibiting nonwhite residency. See Michael Jones-Correa, "The Origins and Diffusion of Racial Restrictive Covenants," *Political Science Quarterly* 115: 4 (Winter 2000/2001): 543–61.

22. *Title Guarantee & Trust Co. v. Garrott*, 42 Cal. App. 152 (1919); *LAT*, 20 April, 30 May 1916; Flamming, *Bound for Freedom*, 153–55. Flamming incorrectly states that the *Garrott* case was decided by the California Supreme Court, which in fact denied hearing the plaintiff's appeal on 8 September 1919.

23. *Los Angeles Investment Company v. Gary*, 181 Cal. 680 (1919); Miller, *Petitioners*, 323.

24. *Janss Investment Company v. Walden*, 196 Cal. 753 (1925); Miller, *Petitioners*, 251–55; Vose, *Caucasians Only*, 17–19.

25. *LAT*, 8 January 1928; Foster, "Decentralization of Los Angeles," 91–99, 197–203, 248–51; J. Max Bond, "The Negro in Los Angeles" (PhD diss., University of Southern California, 1936), 47; US Bureau of the Census, *1930 Census of Population* (Washington, DC, 1933).

26. *LAT*, 8 April 1927, 8 January 1928, 5 March 1939; Weiss, *Rise of the Community Builders*, 53–78.

27. *LAT*, 10 April, 27 November 1927, 24 March, 8 April, 1 September 1928, 12 January 1929.

28. Weiss, *Rise of the Community Builders*, 32–38, 68–72; *LAT*, 8 and 10 April 1927; Greg Hise, *Magnetic Los Angeles: Planning the Twentieth-Century Metropolis* (Baltimore, 1997), 22.

29. John Modell, *The Economics and Politics of Racial Accommodation: The Japanese of Los Angeles, 1900–1942* (Urbana, 1977), 65–66; Mason and Anderson, *America's Black Heritage*, 45; Lawrence de Graaf, "City of Black Angels: The Evolution of the Los Angeles Ghetto, 1890–1930," *Pacific Historical Review* 39: 3 (August 1970): 345; *LAT*, 12 February, 23 July 1922, 16 December 1923, 16 March, 14 June 1924, 10 April 1927, 4 August 1929, 16 April 1939 (emphasis in original).

30. "Achievement Report," *California Real Estate Magazine*, November 1938, as cited in Leonard D. Cain, Jr., "Absolute Discretion? Selected Documents on 'Property Rights' and 'Equal Protection of the Laws,'" April 1964, folder 16, box 2, MM; Serena B. Preusser, "Color Question in California Reveals Many Problems," *California Real Estate Magazine*, July 1927, 35, 61.

31. Bessie Averne McClenahan, *The Changing Urban Neighborhood: A Sociological Study* (University of Southern California Studies, 1929), 38; Gottlieb and Wolt, *Thinking Big*, 146; *LAT*, 22 April 1927, 30 June 1929 (emphasis in original).

32. Warren S. Rogers, *Mesa to Metropolis: The Crenshaw Area, Los Angeles* (Los Angeles, 1959), 13–16; *LAT*, 15 May, 27 November 1927, 21 October 1928, 23 April 1933.

CHAPTER 2: HOME IMPROVEMENT

1. *CE*, 4 December 1925, 15 January, 12 and 26 March 1926.

2. *LAT*, 2 August 1895, 11 October 1927, 8 February 1929, 1 September 1932, 19 May 1940; *CE*, 14 May 1926; John Anson Ford, *Thirty Explosive Years in Los Angeles County* (San Marino, CA, 1961), 150–52; Flamming, *Bound for Freedom*, 239–42.

3. Albert Camarillo, *Chicanos in a Changing Society: From Mexican Pueblos to American Barrios in Santa Barbara and Southern California, 1848–1930* (Cambridge, MA, 1979), 202–3; Bunch, *Black Angelenos*, 30; "Marshal Royal," in *Central Avenue Sounds: Jazz in Los Angeles*, ed. Clora Bryant (Berkeley, 1998), 33. See maps of Central Avenue district ca. 1920 in Flamming, *Bound for Freedom*, 93–94.

4. Wild, *Street Meeting*, 24–25; Mason and McKinstry, *The Japanese of Los Angeles*, 5–10, 29; *LAT*, 26 February 1907, 8 December 1911; Uono, "Japanese Residences," 42–46. Non-Japanese used the name "Little Tokyo" as early as 1904 or 1905.

5. Mason and McKinstry, *The Japanese of Los Angeles*, 5–9, 29; Uono, "Japanese Residences," 12–46, 72; Leonard Bloom and Ruth Riemer, *Removal and Return: The Socio-Economic Effects of the War on Japanese Americans* (Berkeley, 1949). 25.

6. *LAT*, 9 April 1923; Daniel Widener, "'Perhaps the Japanese Are to Be Thanked': Asia, Asian Americans, and the Construction of Black California," *positions* 11 : 1 (Spring 2003): 150. Black and Japanese American residential patterns commonly overlapped in West Coast cities before World War II. For a discussion of relations between African Americans and Asian Americans in Seattle's Central District, see Quintard Taylor, *The Forging of a Black Community: Seattle's*

Central District From 1870 Through the Civil Rights Era (Seattle, 1994), 106–34.

7. Romo, *East Los Angeles*, 81; Monroy, *Rebirth*, 28–29; Sánchez, *Becoming Mexican American*, 195–200; Bloom and Riemer, *Removal and Return*, 25, 91; Uono, "Japanese Residences," 48–53, 125–39.

8. *LAT*, 23 December 1921, 27 May 1923; *Los Angeles Record*, 9 and 13 January 1922 (emphasis in original); Fred Viehe, "Black Gold Suburbs: The Influence of the Extractive Industry on the Suburbanization of Los Angeles, 1890–1930," *Journal of Urban History* (November 1981): 1–26; Becky M. Nicolaides, "The Quest for Independence: Workers in the Suburbs," in *Metropolis in the Making: Los Angeles in the 1920s*, ed. Tom Sitton and William Deverell (Berkeley, 2001), 83–87; Becky M. Nicolaides, *My Blue Heaven: Life and Politics in the Working-Class Suburbs of Los Angeles, 1920–1965* (Chicago, 2002), 26–40.

9. *LAT*, 20 September 1922 (emphasis in original); Lloyd H. Fisher, *The Problem of Violence: Observations on race conflict in Los Angeles*, pamphlet by the American Council on Race Relations, undated (ca. 1945–46), 18–19, folder "American Council on Race Relations," box 230, JRH.

10. *LAT*, 7 February 1920; *CE*, 12 February 1926; Edward A. Burch, "Civil Rights and the Negro," 1936, folder 4, box 1, LAUL.

11. Charles M. Wollenberg, *All Deliberate Speed: Segregation and Exclusion in California Schools, 1855–1975* (Berkeley, 1976), 72; Irving G. Hendrick, *The Education of Non-Whites in California, 1849–1970* (San Francisco, 1977), 87–95; Toyotomi Morimoto, *Japanese Americans and Cultural Continuity: Maintaining Language and Heritage* (New York, 1997), 37–38; *CE*, 10 December 1926; Charlotta A. Bass, *Forty Years* (Los Angeles, 1960), 162; "A Fremont Poster," folder "Race Relations—And Black History," additions box 1, CAB.

12. Eshref Shevky and Marilyn Williams, *The Social Areas of Los Angeles* (Berkeley, 1949), 50–51; US Bureau of the Census, *1940 Statistics for Census Tracts, Los Angeles–Long Beach, Calif.* (Washington, DC, 1942); Bond, "The Negro in Los Angeles," 117; George Parrish and M. S. Siegel to Elmer E. Lore, 9 December 1937, box 77, JAF; quoted in Flamming, *Bound for Freedom*, 352.

13. Bond, "The Negro in Los Angeles," 68, 119–28; Council of Social Agencies of Los Angeles, Memorandum from Division of Family Welfare and Adult Services Subcommittee on the Negro Community to The Executive Committee, 13 May 1940, folder 13, box 1, LAUL; Karl Holton, "Notes on the Negro Districts in Los Angeles," Deteriorating Zone Committee, January 1940, folder 14, ibid.; Floyd Covington, "Racial Attitudes Schedule," Response to Carnegie-Myrdal Study, 25 May 1940, folder 15, box 2, ibid.

14. *LAT*, 12 February 1909; Ernest Frederick Anderson, "The Development of Leadership and Organization Building in the Black Community of Los Angeles From 1900 Through World War II" (PhD diss., University of Southern California, 1976), 94–164; Azuma, *Between Two Empires*, 17–60; Morimoto, *Japanese Americans and Cultural Continuity*, 64–65.

15. Karen Brodkin, *How Jews Became White Folks & What That Says About Race in America* (New Brunswick, 1998), 25–52; Max Vorspan and Lloyd P. Gartner, *History of the Jews of Los Angeles* (San Marino, CA, 1970), 117–18,

203–5; Lynn C. Kronzek, *Fairfax: A Home, A Community, A Way of Life* (Los Angeles, 1990), 13, 36; Sánchez, *Becoming Mexican American*, 75–77; Romo, *East Los Angeles*, 85.

16. *CE*, 5 March 1926; Bass, *Forty Years*, 98; Kevin K. Gaines, *Uplifting the Race: Black Leadership, Politics, and Culture in the Twentieth Century* (Chapel Hill, 1996), 2.

17. Bond, "The Negro in Los Angeles," 108–17; de Graaf, "City of Black Angels," 351; US Bureau of the Census, *1930 Census of Population: Special Report on Foreign-born White Families by Country of Birth of Head* (Washington, DC, 1933); Charles B. Spaulding, "Housing Problems of Minority Groups in Los Angeles County," *The Annals of the American Academy of Political and Social Science* 248 (November 1946): 220–21; *CE*, 21 May, 4 June 1926.

18. Bass, *Forty Years*, 12–13, 27–33.

19. *CE*, 21 December 1928; Fisher, *The Problem of Violence*, 9–10.

20. Fisher, *The Problem of Violence*, 9–10; *Letteau et al. v. Ellis*, 122 Cal. App. 584 (1932); Flamming, *Bound for Freedom*, 221–25; Sally Trainor to Dear Sir (received by NAACP national office), 23 February 1930, reel 2, part 5, NAACP; Leland J. Allen to National Association of the Advancement of Colored People, 28 January 1930, ibid.; H. C. Hudson to William T. Andrews, 18 March 1930, ibid.; *Du Ross v. Trainor*, 122 Cal. App. 732 (1932).

21. Azuma, *Between Two Empires*, 44; Ichioka, *The Issei*, 210–43; Naoko Shimazu, *Japan, Race and Equality: The Racial Equality Proposal of 1919* (London, 1998), 174–76.

22. Mitsuhiko Shimizu, interviewed by Mariko Yamashita and Paul F. Clark (California State University, Fullerton Oral History Program, 30 October 1978), http://content.cdlib.org:8088/xtf/view?docId=ft5r29n8rs&query= <last viewed 26 October 2006>; *RS*, 24 February, 1 and 7 March 1923; Governor C. C. Young's Mexican Fact-Finding Committee, *Mexicans in California* (California State Printing Office, 1930), 177–78; Sánchez, *Becoming Mexican American*, 75–80; Toyama, "Japanese Community in Los Angeles," 48; Uono, "Japanese Residences," 136–38. Eiichiro Azuma generously shared with me his insights about Tanigoshi based on his own research.

23. *RS*, 27 February 1923.

24. *RS*, 1–3 March 1923.

25. *RS*, 4, 16, 18, and 29 March 1923; *LAT*, 29 June 1919.

26. *LAT*, 20 June, 3 July 1924; *RS*, 21, 24, and 27–29 June 1924; Toyama, "Japanese Community in Los Angeles," 48; Uono, "Japanese Residences," 136–38.

27. Azuma, *Between Two Empires*, 61–85; Ichioka, *The Issei*, 244–54; Masayo Umezawa Duus, *The Japanese Conspiracy: The Oahu Sugar Strike of 1920* (Berkeley, 1999), 309–16; *LAT*, 1–2 July 1924; *Beikoku ni okeru hainichi mondai zakken* [Reports of the Japanese consul in Los Angeles], 24 July 1924, *Archives of the Japanese Ministry of Foreign Affairs, 1868–1945* (Tokyo, 1949–51).

28. Anderson, "The Development of Leadership and Organization," 156; *CE*, 25 June, 6 August 1926, 7 February 1930; *LAT*, 5 August 1926. On the Sweet case, see Kevin Boyle, *Arc of Justice: A Saga of Race, Civil Rights, and Murder in the Jazz Age* (New York, 2004).

29. Bond, "The Negro in Los Angeles," 94–95, 102–3, 137; Holton, "Negro Districts in Los Angeles"; Patricia Adler, *History of the Normandie Program Area* (Community Redevelopment Agency of the City of Los Angeles, 1 September 1969), 10–17; McClenahan, *Changing Urban Neighborhood*, 28; Uono, "Japanese Residences," 104–24; James M. Ervin, "The Participation of the Negro in the Community Life of Los Angeles" (MA thesis, University of Southern California, 1931, reprint, San Francisco, 1973), 12; US Census, *1940 Los Angeles–Long Beach Tracts*.

30. US Census, *1940 Los Angeles–Long Beach Tracts*; Earl Hanson and Paul Beckett, *Los Angeles: Its People and Its Homes* (Los Angeles, 1944), 22–28; Bogardus, *New Social Research*, 235–36; McClenahan, *Changing Urban Neighborhood*, 23, 38–47, 84–85; Fisher, *The Problem of Violence*, 8–9.

31. Bond, "The Negro in Los Angeles," 99–103.

32. Chester B. Himes, *If He Hollers Let Him Go* (London, 1967), 48–49; Bond, "The Negro in Los Angeles," 90–91, 102; "NAACP Membership Campaign: November 28–December 15, 1938," box 76, JAF; US Census, *1940 Los Angeles–Long Beach Tracts*.

33. *CE*, 20 November 1925, 4 and 11 June, 10 December 1926; Burch, "Civil Rights and the Negro."

34. *Wayt v. Patee*, 205 Cal. 46 (1928); *Shiedler v. Roberts*, 69 Cal. App. 2nd 549 (1945); *RS*, 4 October, 26 November 1933, 1 and 10 July, 18 August 1940.

35. McClenahan, *Changing Urban Neighborhood*, 242–45; Uono, "Japanese Residences," 108–23.

CHAPTER 3: RACIAL PROGRESS AND CLASS FORMATION

1. *CE*, 29 January, 26 February 1926.

2. See Azuma, *Between Two Empires*, esp. introduction.

3. Ralph Bunche, "Across the Generation Gap," in John and LaRee Caughey, *Los Angeles: Biography of a City* (Berkeley, 1976), 284; *CE*, Xmas Edition 1927, 12 October 1928.

4. Beasley, *Negro Trail Blazers of California*, 185, 288; *CE*, 19 June, 18 September, 6 November 1925; Ichioka, *The Issei*, 146–50; Mason and McKinstry, *The Japanese of Los Angeles*, 13, 30–31; Bloom and Riemer, *Removal and Return*, 69–73; Modell, *The Economics and Politics of Racial Accommodation*, 8.

5. Johnson, *Industrial Survey of the Negro Population of Los Angeles*, 17–73.

6. Ibid., 67–83; Octavia Vivian, *The Story of the Negro in Los Angeles County* (Federal Writers Project of the Works Progress Administration, 1936, reprint, San Francisco, 1970), 31.

7. De Graaf, "City of Black Angels," 342; Vivian, *The Story of the Negro in Los Angeles County*, 32; William T. Smith, "The Negro in Hollywood," folder 32, box 1, LAUL; Alice Burger, "The Vocational Guidance and Training of Negro Youth in Los Angeles," 1938, folder 8, ibid.

8. *Terrace v. Thompson*, 263 U.S. 197 (1923); Kidner and Neff, *Economic Survey of the Los Angeles Area*, 7; Nobuya Tsuchida, "Japanese Gardeners in Southern California, 1900–1941," in *Labor Immigration Under Capitalism: Asian*

Workers in the United States Before World War II, ed. Lucie Cheng and Edna Bonacich (Berkeley, 1984), 437–43; Isamu Nodera, "A Survey of the Vocational Activities of the Japanese of in the City of Los Angeles" (MA thesis, University of Southern California, 1936), 30–34.

9. War Agency Liquidation Unit, *People in Motion: The Postwar Adjustment of the Evacuated Japanese Americans* (Washington, DC, 1947), 60, 84; Nodera, "Vocational Activities of the Japanese," 100–15; Modell, *The Economics and Politics of Racial Accommodation*, 116–17; Bloom and Riemer, *Removal and Return*, 30, 94–95; Uono, "Japanese Residences," 54; Haru Matsui [pen name of Ayako Ishigaki], *Restless Wave: An Autobiography* (New York, 1940), 227; Tsuyoshi Matsumoto, "History of Resident Japanese in Southern California," draft manuscript in Togo Tanaka, diary, reel 11, JERS.

10. Uono, "Japanese Residences," 57.

11. Anderson, "The Development of Leadership and Organization," 94–164; Emory J. Tolbert, *The UNIA and Black Los Angeles: Ideology and Community in the American Garvey Movement* (Los Angeles, 1980), 42–63, 90–92.

12. "First Office," 23 July 1945, folder "History Of The Golden State Mutual Life Insurance Co.," box 1, GSM; "Life Story of William Nickerson, Jr., Founder of Golden State Mutual Life," folder 4, ibid.; N. P. Greggs, "Opportunity," 17 May 1925, folder 3, ibid.; William Nickerson, Jr., "A Brief Story of the Foundation, History and Objectives of the Now 'Golden State Mutual Life Insurance Company,'" ibid. Until 1931, Golden State Mutual was officially known as the Golden State Guarantee Fund Insurance Company.

13. John Lamar Hill II, *Black Leadership in Los Angeles*, 1, 16–17, 99–102, transcript of oral history conducted in 1984 by Ranford B. Hawkins, collection 300/248, BLLA; Kidner and Neff, *Economic Survey of the Los Angeles Area*, 7; Beasley, *Negro Trail Blazers of California*, 139; CE, 22 October 1942; quoted in Anderson, "The Development of Leadership and Organization," 138.

14. CE, 7 January 1921, 13 July 1934; Norman O. Houston, "Survey of Negro Business and Businessmen," 1944, folder 19, box 1, LAUL; Gunnar Myrdal to Floyd C. Covington, 4 April 1940, box 2, folder 4, ibid.

15. US Census, *1940 Los Angeles–Long Beach Tracts*; Bloom and Riemer, *Removal and Return*, 2, 26; Vivian, *The Story of the Negro in Los Angeles County*, 35; John E. Hargroves, "Survey of the Negro Wage Earner in Los Angeles, California," 1 June 1940, folder 9, box 2, LAUL; Helen E. Bruce, "Occupations for Negro Women in Los Angeles," 1933, folder 2, box 1, ibid.

16. CE, 29 January 1916; Reginald Kearney, *African American Views of the Japanese: Solidarity or Sedition* (Albany, 1998), 23, 65; Charlotta Bass, radio broadcast, November 1939, folder "BASS, C. A.—speeches, 1930s," additions box 1, CAB.

17. Masao Suzuki, "Success Story? Japanese Immigrant Economic Achievement and Return Migration," *The Journal of Economic History* 55: 4 (December 1995): 889–901.

18. Marc S. Gallicchio, *The African American Encounter with Japan and China: Black Internationalism in Asia, 1895–1945* (Chapel Hill, 2000), 47; Kearney, *African American Views of the Japanese*, 57; Shimazu, *Japan, Race and Equality*, 78–116.

19. *CE*, 28 October 1927.

20. Kearney, *African American Views of the Japanese*, 49–53; Langston Hughes, *I Wonder as I Wander* (New York, 1956), 265; *LAT*, 28 September 1920; *CE*, 30 May 1924.

21. Bloom and Riemer, *Removal and Return*, 2, 18–20; *Kashu Mainichi*, 23 April 1937; Nodera, "Vocational Activities of the Japanese," 59.

22. *Daily Worker*, 11 July 1932, 4; R. J. Smith, *The Great Black Way: LA in the 1940s and the Lost African American Renaissance* (New York, 2006), 242–43.

23. William Z. Foster, *History of the Communist Party of the United States* (New York, 1952), 257–66; Dorothy Ray Healey and Maurice Isserman, *California Red: A Life in the American Communist Party* (Urbana, 1993), 40–41.

24. Robert A. Scalapino, *The Japanese Communist Movement, 1920–1966* (Berkeley, 1967), 34–45; Karl Yoneda, *Ganbatte: Sixty-Year Struggle of a Kibei Worker* (Los Angeles, 1982), 16–19; Karl G. Yoneda, "U.S. Japanese Socialists-Communists In The 1930s And 1940s," 11 January 1977, folder 1, box 13, KGY; "Miyagi Yotoku's Notes," folder 4, ibid.; Foster, *History of the Communist Party*, 261, 292, 307, 380; Kenden Yabe, "Okinawans in America," in *History of the Okinawans in North America*, ed. The Okinawa Club of America, trans. Ben Kobashigawa (Los Angeles, 1988), 28–30.

25. Arnold Rampersad, *The Life of Langston Hughes, Volume I: 1902–1941, I, Too, Sing America* (New York, 1986), 236; *Daily Worker*, 8 September 1932, 3; "Langston Hughes at Japan Nite" (3 March 1934), folder 5, box 1, KGY.

26. International Labor Defense, "Scottsboro Boys Must Be Freed," folder 2, box 1, KGY; Vivian McGuckin Raineri, *The Red Angel: The Life and Times of Elaine Black Yoneda* (New York, 1991), 21–34.

27. Monroy, *Rebirth*, 226; *Western Worker*, clippings dated 16 April, 1 May 1933, folder 10, box 2, KGY; Almaguer, *Racial Fault Lines*, 183–204; Miscellaneous handbills from TUUL, AWIU work in 1933, folder 2, box 1, KGY; Yoneda, "U.S. Japanese Socialists-Communists In The 1930s And 1940s"; Program of Inaugural Meeting of California Japanese Agricultural Workers Union, Union Church, Los Angeles, 8 June 1935, folder 3, box 1, KGY; "JAWU-Venice strike," 2 May 1936, ibid.; "ILD-defend arrested workers," June 1936, ibid.; Tsuchida, "Japanese Gardeners in Southern California," 458–66.

28. "Pettis Perry: The Story of a Working Class Leader" (final printing and manuscript draft), folder "Personal Papers—Biographical Information, 1950–1967, 1/1," box 1, Pettis Perry Collection, Schomburg Library, New York; Pettis Perry, "How a Negro Came to Marxism" (notes from unfinished manuscript), folder "Personal Papers—notes for autobiography, n.d. 1/8," ibid.; "Pettis Perry, Communist leader, dies," *People's World*, 31 July 1965; *NYT*, 28 July 1965.

29. Pierce quoted in Gottlieb and Wolt, *Thinking Big*, 187–203; Perry quoted in Gerald Horne, *Fire This Time: The Watts Uprising and the 1960s* (Charlottesville, 1995), 6.

30. Rodolfo Acuña, *Occupied America: A History of Chicanos*, 3rd ed. (New York, 1983), 200–6; Sánchez, *Becoming Mexican American*, 210–25; Ronald Takaki, *Strangers From a Different Shore: A History of Asian Americans* (Boston, 1998), 331–35.

31. "Miyagi Yotoku's Notes"; Sadaichi Kenmotsu to Frank Specter, 16 December 1931, folder 9, box 2, KGY; Karl Yoneda to Elizabeth Gurley Flynn, 27 July 1964, folder 2, box 13, ibid.; International Labor Defense, "Mass Meeting—April 14 [1931]," ibid.; Karl G. Yoneda to Dmitry Muravyev, 9 November 1964, ibid.; Raymond F. Farrell to George E. Brown, Jr., 26 March 1973, ibid.; "Workers to be Deported, $300 Needed by End of November 1932," 15 January 1932, ibid.

32. Togo Tanaka, "The Vernacular Newspapers," 8, reel 106, JERS. My awareness of the five Issei known to have been executed under Stalin stems from fall 1991 conversations with Yuji Ichioka about Japanese media reports.

33. Foster, *History of the Communist Party*, 320–24.

34. Louis B. Perry and Richard S. Perry, *A History of the Los Angeles Labor Movement, 1911–1941* (Berkeley, 1963), 198–99, 442–91; Robert Zieger, *The CIO, 1935–1955* (Chapel Hill, 1995), 70–73; Sánchez, *Becoming Mexican American*, 239. See also Chris Friday, *Organizing Asian American Labor: The Pacific Coast Canned-Salmon Industry, 1870–1942* (Philadelphia, 1994).

35. Beth Tompkins Bates, *Pullman Porters and the Rise of Protest Politics in Black America, 1925–1945* (Chapel Hill, 2001); Alice Burger, "Negro Labor Unions in the Transportation Industry in Los Angeles," 1938, folder 7, box 1, LAUL; Flamming, *Bound for Freedom*, 358–59.

36. S. Fujii, "Japanese Workers Urged to Join Union," *The Market Worker*, 13 February 1937, folder 6, box 14, KGY; Sánchez, *Becoming Mexican American*, 239–45.

37. "Japanese Urged to Join Union," *The Market Worker*, 1 April 1937, folder 2, box 5, KGY; "Official Election Ballot—I, April 10, 1937, Wholesale Produce Market Workers Union, Local 20284, A F Of L," folder 6, box 14, ibid.; *RS*, 15 May 1937; Henry Shire, "Market Workers' Union Making Great Progress," *Los Angeles Citizen*, 28 May 1937; *Kashu Mainichi*, 15 May 1937; "Stop These Unjust Suspensions!" folder 2, box 5, KGY.

38. Larry Tajiri, "Village Vagaries: Nisei and Unions . . . ," *SF Nichibei*, 16 September 1936, clipping in folder 10, box 2, KGY; Bloom and Riemer, *Removal and Return*, 2, 91–99; *RS*, 12 April 1934; Thomas Sasaki's Daily Reports From Los Angeles, 18 October 1946, Reel 107, JERS.

39. Minutes of the Central Labor Council, 6 January 1939, box 6, LACFL; Minutes of the Executive Board, 13 and 20 January 1939, 10 February 1939, ibid.; "Cabbages, Nuts, Canned Goods, Food Clerks 770," *Los Angeles Citizen*, 24 February 1939; *Doho*, 15 April 1941.

40. Bass, *Forty Years*, 76–78; Ruth Washington, *Black Leadership in Los Angeles*, 73–74, transcript of oral history conducted in 1984 by Ranford B. Hopkins, collection 300/249, BLLA; Bruce, "Occupations for Negro Women in Los Angeles"; *CE*, 13 July 1934; Houston, "Survey on Negro Business and Businessmen."

41. Anderson, "The Development of Leadership and Organization," 101–2; Perry, "How a Negro Came to Marxism"; Loren Miller [Survey Results], folder 22, box 1, LAUL; Floyd Covington, "Negro Business and Businessmen," Response to Carnegie-Myrdal Study, 25 May 1940, folder 10, box 2, ibid.; Manning Marable, *How Capitalism Underdeveloped Black America* (Boston, 1983), 149–50.

CHAPTER 4: IN THE SHADOW OF WAR

1. *Los Angeles Daily News*, 17 July, 13 August 1940

2. *RS*, 28 July, 16 August 1940.

3. "Forward to a National Negro Congress!" reel 4, part I, NNC; Loren Miller to John P. Davis, 8 February 1936, reel 6, ibid.; Loren Miller, "How 'Left' is the N.A.A.C.P.?" *New Masses* 16: 3 (16 July 1935): 12–13.

4. Alonzo Nelson Smith, "Black Employment in the Los Angeles Area, 1938–1948" (PhD diss., University of California, Los Angeles, 1978), 116; Juanita Ellsworth-Miller, "Relief and Housing," 25 May 1940, box 2, folder 11, LAUL; Floyd Covington, "Relief and Housing," 25 May 1940, ibid.; Hargroves, "Survey of the Negro Wage Earner in Los Angeles"; Loren Miller [Survey Results]; Alice Burger, "Vocational Guidance and Training of Negro Youth in Los Angeles"; McWilliams, *Southern California*, 297; Miller to Davis, 8 February 1936.

5. Blank Letterhead, National Negro Congress Los Angeles Council, reel 4, part I, NNC; Lillian Jones to John P. Davis, 3 May 1938, reel 3, ibid.; Los Angeles Council of the National Negro Congress, "Housing in the Central Avenue District: What It Is and How You Can Help to Make It Better," [1938], ibid.

6. John P. Davis to Lillian Jones, 19 April, 3 and 23 May 1938, reel 3, part I, NNC; Lillian Jones to John P. Davis, 26 January, 17 May 1938, ibid.; Floyd C. Covington to John P. Davis, 26 May 1936, reel 4, ibid.; Loren Miller, transcript of interview with Lawrence B. de Graaf (California State University, Fullerton Oral History Program, 1967), 7–10. On El Congreso del Pueblo de Habla Española, see Mario T. García, *Mexican Americans: Leadership, Ideology, and Identity* (New Haven, 1989), 146–65.

7. Bill Hosokawa, *JACL in Quest of Justice* (New York, 1982), 57–63, 98; Sánchez, *Becoming Mexican American*, 255–64; Yuji Ichioka, "A Study in Dualism: James Yoshinori Sakamoto and the Japanese American Courier, 1928–1942," *Amerasia Journal* 13: 2 (1986–87): 49–81; Togo Tanaka, "History of the JACL, Chapter II, Emergence of National Organization (1930–1937)," 6–11, reel 106, JERS.

8. Tanaka, "Emergence of National Organization," 6–11; Togo Tanaka, "Political Organizations," 1–15, reel 106, JERS; Togo Tanaka, "History of the JACL, Chapter III, Period of Adjustment (1937–Sept. 1941)," draft 2, 18–19, ibid.; Brian Hayashi, *Democratizing the Enemy: The Japanese American Internment* (Princeton, 2004), 68; Hosokawa, *JACL in Quest of Justice*, 43–44.

9. Janet Hutchison, "Shaping Housing and Enhancing Consumption: Hoover's Interwar Housing Policy," in *From Tenements to Taylor Homes: In Search of Urban Housing Policy in Twentieth-Century America*, ed. John F. Bauman, Roger Biles, and Kristin M. Szylvian (University Park, PA, 2000), 122; Jefferson Park Tract Map (tentative), subject file 1337, box A-731, Los Angeles City Archives; *RS*, 18 and 21 April, 5 and 12 May, 21 July 1940.

10. Mr. and Mrs. Maurice L. Young to Gentlemen, date missing or illegible, subject file 1337, box A-731, Los Angeles City Archives; *RS*, 14, 24–25, and 28–29 July, 1–2 and 18 August 1940; Togo Tanaka, personal interview, 21 October 1999, Los Angeles; Togo Tanaka, diary, 15 January 1942, reel 11, JERS.

11. Tanaka, "Political Organizations," 1–15; Tanaka, "Period of Adjustment," 8–19.

12. Tanaka, "Period of Adjustment," 20–21; *RS*, 28 July 1940; Shigemori Tamaki, "Gongoro Nakamura: A Man Who Served the Japanese Community," in The Okinawa Club of America, *History of the Okinawans*, 418–20. Olson's speech is reprinted in the *Doho*, 25 September 1941.

13. *CE*, 25 December 1941; Herbert Garfinkel, *When Negroes March: The March on Washington Movement in the Organizational Politics for FEPC* (New York, 1973), 38–65.

14. Herbert Hill, *Black Labor and the American Legal System I: Race, Work, and the Law* (Washington, DC, 1977), 173–74; Statements drawn from multiple versions of "Charge Before the Committee on Fair Employment Practice of the President of the United States," 15–20 October 1941, roll 105FR, FEPC; "Statement from Mr. Jesse Battey," 5 September 1941, ibid. See also Louis Ruchames, *Race, Jobs, & Politics: The Story of FEPC* (New York, 1953).

15. *CE*, 5 February 1942.

16. *CE*, 11 December 1941; *Doho*, 7 December 1941.

17. Robert A. Hill, ed., *The FBI's RACON: Racial Conditions in America During World War II* (Boston, 1995), 15, 373–76; Kearney, *African American Views of the Japanese*, 87–127; Myrdal, *An American Dilemma*, 1006; Langston Hughes, "White Folks Do the Funniest Things," *Common Ground*, Winter 1944, 45–46.

18. *CE*, 18 December 1941, 19 February, 23 April 1942; Kearney, *African American Views of the Japanese*, 110–12; Floyd C. Covington to Charles S. Johnson, 31 December 1942, folder 28, box 1, LAUL; Cheryl Greenberg, "Black and Jewish Responses to Japanese Internment," *Journal of American Ethnic History* 14: 2 (Winter 1995): 3–37.

19. Thomas W. Robinson, personal interview, 30 December 2003, Los Angeles.

20. Tanaka, diary, 12 January 1942; *CE*, 1 January 1942.

CHAPTER 5: JAPANESE AMERICAN INTERNMENT

1. Mary Oyama, "After Pearl Harbor—Los Angeles," *Common Ground*, Spring 1942, 12–13; Minutes of the Anti-Axis Committee (AAC) Meeting, Southern District Council, Japanese American Citizens League, 8 December 1941, Union Church, box 74, JAF; Morton Grodzins, *Americans Betrayed: Politics and the Japanese Evacuation* (Chicago, 1949), 232.

2. *RS*, 15–16, 21–22, and 26 December 1941.

3. Resolution by Supervisor John Anson Ford, 9 December 1941, box 74, JAF.

4. Tanaka, personal interview; Togo Tanaka, "How to Survive Racism in America's Free Society," in *Voices Long Silent: An Oral Inquiry Into the Japanese American Evacuation*, ed. Arthur A. Hansen and Betty E. Miston (Fullerton, 1974), 88–90; AAC Minutes, 8 December 1941; *LAT*, 9 December 1941; *NYT*, 9 December 1941; *RS*, 9–10 December 1941; "Anti-Axis Committee, Japanese American Citizens League of the Southern District Council," box 74, JAF.

5. Tanaka, "Political Organizations," 37–38; Tanaka, "Period of Adjustment," 2; Togo Tanaka, "History of the JACL, Chapter IV, Period of Recurring Crises, Sept. 1941–April 1942," draft 3, 2–3, reel 106, JERS; AAC Minutes, 8 December 1941; "Anti-Axis Committee"; "Report from Minutes of the Anti-Axis Committee Meetings Held During the week of December 22," box 74, JAF; Fred Tayama to J. Anson Ford, 15 January 1942, ibid.

6. *RS*, 7 December 1941; Togo Tanaka, diary, December 1941 passim and 9 January 1942, reel 11, JERS; Hosokawa, *JACL in Quest of Justice*, 136–37; Tanaka, "Period of Recurring Crises," 21–35.

7. Tanaka, "Period of Recurring Crises," 27–29, 40–41; Sasaki's Daily Reports, 1 and 4 August 1946.

8. "Anti-Axis Committee Meeting, Southern District Council, Japanese American Citizens League," 17 January 1942, box 74, JAF; Bill Hosokawa, *Nisei: The Quiet Americans* (New York, 1969), 42–43; "Tokutaro Nishimura Slocum," in *Encyclopedia of Japanese American History: An A-to-Z Reference From 1868 to the Present*, updated ed., ed. Brian Niiya (New York, 2001), 367–68; Tanaka, "Period of Adjustment," 8–10; Tanaka, "Period of Recurring Crises," 32–35; quoted in Tanaka, diary, 11 and 23 January 1942.

9. Tanaka, "Political Organizations," 37–38; Tanaka, "Period of Recurring Crises," 32; Tanaka, diary, 11 January 1942.

10. "Statement by Mayor Fletcher Bowron," 8 December 1941, folder "Remarks at Public Events, Addresses By The Mayor, 1940," box 33, FB; "Remarks of Mayor Fletcher Bowron," 8 June 1940, ibid.; "Remarks by Mayor Fletcher Bowron on Americanism Program," KFWB, 20 August 1940, ibid.; AAC Minutes, 8 December 1941; Grodzins, *Americans Betrayed*, 100–101.

11. "Excerpt from Radio Broadcast by Mayor Fletcher Bowron, Station KECA," 9 December 1942, folder "Japanese," box 52, FB; *Korematsu v. United States*, 323 U.S. 214 (1944).

12. Roger Daniels, *Concentration Camps, North America: Japanese in the United States and Canada During World War II* (Malabar, FL, 1993), 14, 40, 52; Peter Irons, *Justice at War: The Story of the Japanese American Internment Cases* (New York, 1983), 8.

13. Grodzins, *Americans Betrayed*, 35, 59; Emily S. Rosenberg, *A Date Which Will Live: Pearl Harbor in American Memory* (Durham, 2003), 32–33.

14. Alfred Cohn to Mayor Bowron, 10 and 21 January 1942, folder "Japanese," box 52, FB; Fletcher Bowron to A. B. Chandler, 24 April 1943, ibid.

15. Bowron to Chandler; Untitled report on the Los Angeles Civil Service Department, folder "Japanese Americans," box 52, FB; "Statement by Mayor Fletcher Bowron, January 27, 1942," ibid.; Fletcher Bowron to Francis Biddle, 22 January 1942, folder "Japanese," ibid.; "Statement by Clifford N. Amsden, Secretary, County Civil Service Commission, Relative to Status of Japanese Employees in the County," 28 January 1942, box 74, JAF; J. F. Moroney to Wayne Allen, 29 January 1942, ibid.; Clifford N. Amsden to Board of Supervisors, 4 February 1942, ibid.; Mrs. Frank M. Ono to John Anson Ford, 15 February 1940, ibid.; L.Y. Arikawa to John Anson Ford, 15 February 1940, ibid.; Hosokawa, *JACL in Quest of Justice*, 135–36; Lon Kurashige, *Japanese American Celebration and Conflict: A History of Ethnic Identity and Festival, 1934–1990* (Berkeley, 2002), 32.

16. Fletcher Bowron to John M. Costello, 22 January 1942, folder "Japanese," box 52, FB; Fletcher Bowron to Edward A. Hayes, 22 January 1942, ibid.; Tanaka, diary, 12 January 1945; Roger Daniels, *The Decision to Relocate the Japanese Americans* (Philadelphia, 1975), 25–26; "Radio Broadcast by Mayor Fletcher Bowron, KECA," 29 January 1942, folder "Japanese," box 52, FB; "Excerpt from KECA—Radio Broadcast by Mayor Fletcher Bowron," 12 February 1942," ibid.; Fletcher Bowron to Tom C. Clark, 20 February 1942, ibid.; "Statement by Mayor Fletcher Bowron," 6 February 1942, folder "Japanese Americans," ibid.

17. "Excerpt from Radio Broadcast by Mayor Fletcher Bowron, Station KECA," 5 February 1942, folder "Japanese," box 52, FB; "Excerpt from KECA—Radio Broadcast by Mayor Fletcher Bowron," 12 February 1942, ibid.; "Excerpt from Radio Broadcast by Mayor Fletcher Bowron, Station KECA," 19 February 1942, ibid.; Nisei quoted in Tanaka, diary, 22 February 1942.

18. Warren quoted in Michi Weglyn, *Years of Infamy: The Untold Story of America's Concentration Camps* (New York, 1976), 37–38; Ed Cray, *Chief Justice: A Biography of Earl Warren* (New York, 1997), 118–22; *LAT*, 4 March 1942; "Excerpt from Radio Broadcast by Mayor Fletcher Bowron, KECA," 13 August 1942, folder "Japanese," box 52, FB.

19. Fletcher Bowron to Archibald MacLeish, 3 February 1942, folder "Japanese," box 52, FB; Fletcher Bowron to John M. Costello, 14 February 1942, ibid.; John M. Costello to Fletcher Bowron, 18 February 1942, ibid.; Grodzins, *Americans Betrayed*, 209. See also Daniels, *The Decision to Relocate the Japanese Americans*.

20. Quoted in Tanaka, diary, 1 January 1942; Weglyn, *Years of Infamy*, 45.

21. "Excerpt from Radio Broadcast by Mayor Fletcher Bowron, Station KECA," 5 February 1942; "Statement by Mayor Fletcher Bowron," 6 February 1942; Tanaka, "Period of Recurring Crises," 17; Tanaka, diary, 6 February 1942; *RS*, 8 February 1942.

22. Foster, *History of the Communist Party*, 409; Yoneda, *Ganbatte*, 123; *Doho*, 11 and 13 December 1941, 30 January, 6 February 1942.

23. Nisei Writers' and Artists' Mobilization for Democracy, "General Survey of the Occupational and Financial Problems of the Citizens and Alien Japanese Residing in Metropolitan Los Angeles, These Problems Resulting from the Present Conflict Between Japan and the United States, and Some Suggestions for Their Solution," stamped 6 February 1942, box 74, JAF; *Doho*, 20 February 1942; Masayo Duus, *The Life of Isamu Noguchi: Journey Without Borders* (Princeton, 2004), 111–66.

24. Thomas quoted in Weglyn, *Years of Infamy*, 111; John Anson Ford to Francis Biddle, 4 May 1942, folder "Japanese," box 52, FB; John Anson Ford to William R. Burke, 19 January 1948, box 74, JAF.

25. *RS*, 1 February 1942; *LAT*, 24–26 February 1942; Carey McWilliams, "Japanese Evacuation: Policy and Perspectives," *Common Ground*, Summer 1942, 65–72.

26. *RS*, 17–20 February 1942; Grodzins, *Americans Betrayed*, 187–96.

27. Tanaka, diary, 11 January 1942; *Doho*, 27 February, 6 March 1942

28. Tanaka, diary, 22 February 1942; Tanaka, "Period of Recurring Crises," 57–59; *NYT*, 21 February 1942.

29. *RS*, 28 February, 1 March 1942; *Manzanar Free Press*, 20 March 1943, reprinted by the National Park Service at http://www.nps.gov/manz/MFP/mfp-v3 n23n.htm <last viewed 12 July 2006>; Sasaki's Daily Reports, 31 July 1946.

30. Tanaka, "Period of Recurring Crises," 36–37, 57; Weglyn, *Years of Infamy*, 38.

31. *RS*, 20 and 22 March 1942; *Doho*, 1 and 10 April 1942; *Manzanar Free Press*, 11 April 1942, reprinted by the National Park Service at http://www .nps.gov/manz/MFP/mfp-v1-n1.htm <last viewed 12 July 2006>.

32. Mary Oyama, "This Isn't Japan," *Common Ground*, Autumn 1942, 32–34; Tanaka, diary, 22 February 1942; Weglyn, *Years of Infamy*, 111–33; Hayashi, *Democratizing the Enemy*, 100, 134–35.

CHAPTER 6: THE "NEGRO VICTORY" MOVEMENT

1. Thomas Madison Doram, "In and Before the Committee on Fair Employment Practices," 18 November 1943, roll 106FR, FEPC; *CE*, 5 February 1942; Hill, *Black Labor*, 185–92; Josh Sides, *L.A. City Limits: African American Los Angeles from the Great Depression to the Present* (Berkeley, 2003), 64–68; Taylor, *In Search of the Racial Frontier*, 259.

2. Doram, "In and Before the Committee"; *CE*, 24 March, 1 April 1943; Hill, *Black Labor*, 199–202; Smith, "Black Employment in the Los Angeles Area," 23–68.

3. Hill, *Black Labor*, 176–83; *CE*, 18 December 1941, 8 and 15 January, 12 March 1942 (emphasis in original).

4. *CE*, 12 March 1942; Kidner and Neff, *Economic Survey of the Los Angeles Area*, 9–23, 68, 100–11; Charles W. Eliot and Cecil L. Dunn, *Jobs and Security* (Los Angeles, 1944), 11; Roger W. Lotchin, *Fortress California 1910–1961: From Warfare to Welfare* (New York, 1992), 65–68, 133–34; Martin J. Schiesel, "Airplanes to Aerospace: Defense Spending and Economic Growth in the Los Angeles Region, 1945–1960," in *The Martial Metropolis: U.S. Cities in War and Peace, 1900–1970*, ed. Roger W. Lotchin (New York, 1984), 135–36; "General Outline for Presentation of CIO and UAW Position in Testimony Before Murray Comm.," box 33, record group 1, LACFL; Nelson Lichtenstein, *Labor's War at Home: The CIO in World War II* (Cambridge, 1982), 110–11.

5. Williams quoted in Anderson, "The Development of Leadership and Organization," 166–80; "Souvenir Programme and History of People's Independent Church of Christ, 20th Anniversary Celebration, October 6–13, 1935," folder 4, box 37, GSM.

6. Smith, *Great Black Way*, 67–83; *CE*, 10 February, 4 November 1943; Smith, "Black Employment in the Los Angeles Area," 117; Miller, transcript of interview, 6. According to Smith's *Great Black Way*, Clayton Russell maintained a connection to the Left through Lou Rosser, his close aide and a Black Communist. Rosser was gay, and though in public Russell appeared a dashing ladies' man, several of Smith's sources claim that he had private affairs with men. On the basis of oral histories, Smith also states that John Kinloch ghostwrote many of the words attributed to Charlotta Bass during World War II. Yet he does not clarify the

extent of Kinloch's ghostwriting, nor does he provide a specific citation to document this claim.

7. *CE*, 16 and 23 April, 25 June, 16 July 1942 (emphasis in original).

8. Anderson, "The Development of Leadership and Organization," 175; *CE*, 23 April 1942.

9. *CE*, 15 and 29 January 1942, 10 February 1943, 14 June 1945 (emphasis in original).

10. Lawrence Brooks de Graaf, "Negro Migration to Los Angeles, 1930 to 1950" (PhD diss., University of California, Los Angeles, 1962), 254–68; Smith, "Black Employment in the Los Angeles Area," 49; Spaulding, "Housing Problems of Minority Groups in Los Angeles," 222; US Bureau of the Census, *Special Census of Los Angeles, California, Population by Age, Race, and Sex, By Census Tracts: January 28, 1946*, series P-SC, no. 188 (Washington, DC, 29 October 1946).

11. Carey McWilliams, "Report on Importation of Negro Labor to California," folder 23, box 1, LAUL; *CE*, 9 July 1942.

12. Anderson, "The Development of Leadership and Organization," 180–90, 237; *CE*, 16 July 1942.

13. Citizens Defense Committee to Vierling Kersey, 29 July 1942, box 76, JAF; Anderson, "The Development of Leadership and Organization," 191–92; *CE*, 6 August 1942.

14. *CE*, 21 and 27 August, 24 September 1942 (emphases in originals).

15. Zieger, *The CIO*, 152; *CE*, 24 February, 1 April 1943; Smith, "Black Employment in the Los Angeles Area," 239; Floyd C. Covington to Charles S. Johnson, 31 December 1942, folder 28, box 1, LAUL.

16. *CE*, 12 November 1942, 8, 15, and 22 January 1943; Smith, "Black Employment in the Los Angeles Area," 201–2.

17. Zieger, *The CIO*, 71–82, 128; Perry and Perry, *History of Los Angeles Labor Movement*, 420–24, 495–97; Lichtenstein, *Labor's War*, 56–63; Hill, *The FBI's RACON*, 373–75; Richard S. Hobbs, *The Cayton Legacy: An African American Family* (Pullman, WA, 2002), 89, 157; *CE*, 15 October, 5 November 1942, 28 January 1943.

18. *CE*, 3 June 1943, 9 December 1943; Bass, *Forty Years*, 16–20.

19. Covington to Johnson; Lichtenstein, *Labor's War*, 79–81; Zieger, *The CIO*, 145–46.

20. Hill, *Black Labor*, 209–11; Perry and Perry, *History of the Los Angeles Labor Movement*, 450–51; *CE*, 6 August, 22 October 1942, 10 February, 3 June 1943; Smith, "Black Employment in the Los Angeles Area," 341.

21. *CE*, 10 June 1943; Zieger, *The CIO*, 152–59.

22. *CE*, 18 December 1942 (emphasis in original).

23. Sugrue, *Origins of the Urban Crisis*, 29; McWilliams, *North From Mexico*, 206.

24. McWilliams, *North From Mexico*, 206–16; Acuña, *Occupied America*, 254–56; *CE*, 5 November 1942, 24 February, 9 September 1943.

25. *CE*, 27 May, 3 June, 1 July 1943 (emphasis in original).

26. Acuña, *Occupied America*, 257–58; *CE*, 10 and 17 June 1943.

27. Miller, transcript of interview, 46; *CE*, 10, 17, and 24 June, 1 July 1943 (emphasis in original); Smith, *Great Black Way*, 75.

28. Penny M. Von Eschen, *Race Against Empire: Black Americans and Anti-colonialism, 1937–1957* (Ithaca, 1997), 17–95; *CE*, 24 September 1942, 24 February, 1 April, 1 July, 19 August 1943; Garfinkel, *When Negroes March*, 49–50, 131–32.

29. Richard Griswold del Castillo, "The Los Angeles 'Zoot Suit Riots' Revisited: Mexican and Latin American Perspectives," *Mexican Studies/Estudios Mexicanos* 16 (Summer 2000): 367–91; Harvard Sitkoff, "Racial Militancy and Interracial Violence in the Second World War," *Journal of American History* 58: 3 (December 1971): 678; *CE*, 23 September 1943, 3 February 1944; *LAT*, 11 January 1944; Kevin Allen Leonard, *The Battle for Los Angeles: Racial Ideology and World War II* (Albuquerque, 2006), 191; Carey McWilliams, "Los Angeles: An Emerging Pattern," *Common Ground*, Spring 1949, 4.

30. *CE*, 3 and 18 December 1942, 8 and 28 January 1943.

31. Hill, *Black Labor*, 312–15; George Lipsitz, *Rainbow at Midnight: Labor and Culture in the 1940s* (Urbana, 1994), 69–95; Zieger, *The CIO*, 152–54; *LAT*, 1 and 9 August 1944; P. B. Harris to Clarence R. Johnson, 14 April 1943, roll 21, FEPC (emphasis in original); President's Committee on Fair Employment Practice, "Alfonso Edwards, James H. Herod, Jr., Charles M. Robinson, Sidney L. Robinson, James K. Savoy, Nona Slayden, and others vs. Los Angeles Railway Corporation: Findings and Directives," 8 August 1944, 96, ibid.; Charles M. Robinson to L.A. Railway Company, 5 July [1944], ibid.

32. George W. Crockett, Jr., to Malcolm G. Ross, 17 April 1944, roll 21, FEPC; "A Plan Designed by the Mayor's Committee of Six to Aid in the Solution of the LARY Transportation Problems," 11 April 1944, ibid.; Jack B. Burke to Robt. E. Brown, Jr., 29 April 1944, ibid.; Harry L. Kingman to George M. Johnson, 25 March 1944, ibid.; Paul Tillett to Malcolm Ross, 13 September 1944, ibid.; John Edgar Hoover, "Memorandum for the Attorney General," 17 August 1943, roll 75, ibid.; *LAT*, 9 and 14 August 1944.

33. Hill, *Black Labor*, 274–316; Smith, "Black Employment in the Los Angeles Area," 69; Leon H. Washington, Jr., to Malcolm Ross and George Johnson, 22 August 1944, roll 21, FEPC.

34. *CE*, 8 February 1945; McWilliams, "The West Coast: Our Racial Frontier"; *LAT*, 20–21 November 1943; Thomas Campbell, "Investigation by Area Office Concerning Discrimination by Northrop Aircraft, Inc.," 9 August 1944, roll 106FR, FEPC; R. E. Brown, Jr., to Charles Bratt, 19 March 1945, ibid.

CHAPTER 7: BRONZEVILLE AND LITTLE TOKYO

1. *Los Angeles Tribune*, 1 June 1946.

2. "Chamber Set Up By Negro Group in Little Tokyo," clipping from *Eastside Journal*, 3 November 1943, box 76, JAF; *NYT*, 9 August 1942; "The Race War That Flopped," *Ebony*, July 1946, 5; *CE*, 9 April, 27 August 1942, 23 September 1943, 3 August 1944; Henri O'Bryant, Jr., "Some Observations of Little 'Tokio,'" folder 17, box 1, Charles Bratt Papers, Southern California Library for Social Studies and Research, Los Angeles; Smith, *Great Black Way*, 143; *LAT*, 17 January 1945.

3. Miley to Ford, 8 July 1943; "Comments—Negroes in Little Tokyo," folder 17, box 1, CAB.

4. *CE*, 29 July 1943; *LAT*, 26 May 1944; US Census, *Special Census of Los Angeles* (1946); Miley to Ford, 8 July 1943.

5. *CE*, 3 June 1943.

6. Roger W. Lotchin, *The Bad City in the Good War: San Francisco, Los Angeles, Oakland, and San Diego* (Bloomington, 2003), 215; Hise, *Magnetic Los Angeles*, 130–85; US Bureau of the Census, *1950 Census Tract Statistics, Los Angeles, California and Adjacent Area* (Washington, DC, 1952); "Minority Report: By the Negro People of Los Angeles," in Bert S. West to John Anson Ford, 15 March 1956, box 76, JAF.

7. *CE*, 27 August 1942, 24 March, 28 October 1943, 23 November 1944, 25 January 1945, 20 May 1948; Bass, *Forty Years*, 105–11; "The 'Panel Of Americans'—A Presentation Of The University Religious Conference," box 33, record group 1, LACFL; Gus Hawkins to Earl Warren, 2 November 1943, ibid.; Malcolm Thurburn, "Restrictive Covenants: Homes Handsome Faultless," *NOW*, Second Half December 1944, folder 3, box 30, ACLU.

8. *CE*, 11 and 18 December 1942, 8 January, 2 September 1943, 20 January, 1 June, 3 August 1944; Spaulding, "Housing Problems of Minority Groups in Los Angeles," 223.

9. *LAT*, 14 and 22 April 1943; California Citizens Council, "Oust the Japs from California Forever," undated, folder 2, box 53, WCC; Fletcher Bowron to A. B. Chandler, 24 April 1943, folder "Japanese," box 52, FB; "Portion of Remarks by Mayor Fletcher Bowron, Radio Station KECA," 19 May 1943, ibid.; "Broadcast by Mayor Fletcher Bowron, Station KECA," 2 June 1943, ibid.; Harry Braverman, Harry F. Henderson, and Harry Wurtzel, Statement to Grand Jury, County of Los Angeles, 8 December 1942, box 74, JAF; Charles P. Bayer to Wm. C. Carr, 26 May 1943, folder 8, box 53, WCC.

10. *CE*, 11 November 1943, 1 June, 6 July, 19 October 1944, 4 January 1945.

11. "Statement of Mayor Fletcher Bowron," 6 March 1945, box 65, FB; *Los Angeles Citizens Housing Council Bulletin* 1 (18 January 1947), box 24, record group I, LACFL; George Gleason, "The Housing Crisis in Los Angeles County," 1 April 1945, folder "Housing," box 246, JRH; Spaulding, "Housing Problems of Minority Groups in Los Angeles," 224–25; *RS*, 21 June 1946; Himes quoted in Smith, *Great Black Way*, 104.

12. War Relocation Authority (WRA), "Semi-Annual Report," 1 January to 30 June and 1 July to 31 December 1945, folder 1, box 58, MWRC; War Relocation Authority, "Terminal Departures From Centers—Cumulative Summary," *WRA Monthly Report* 3 (31 December 1944 to 30 June 1945), box 14, Japanese American Collection, Special Collections, Oviatt Library, California State University at Northridge.

13. John C. McClendon to Arthur J. Will, box 74, JAF; Arthur F. Miley to John Anson Ford, 25 September 1945, 19 April 1946, ibid.; Gracia D. Booth and Maynard Force Thayer to Homer D. Crotty, 11 December 1945, ibid.; D. S. Myer to Board of Supervisors, 29 May 1946, ibid.; Wayne Allen to Board of Supervisors, 22 January 1946, ibid.; Melvin. H. Harter to Dillon Meyer [*sic*], 4 April 1946, ibid.; Margaret Gleason to Arthur F. Miley, 8 December 1947, ibid.; Dillon

S. Myer to Carey McWilliams, 7 March 1946, folder 34, carton 20, CMW; K. Arako, T. Koyama, S. Gozawa, S. Saito, and K. Ito to Committee Members Lomita Air Strip FPHA, undated, folder 35, ibid.; *RS*, 22–23 and 29 March, 26 April, 26 June 1946; WRA, "Semi-Annual Report," 1 January to 30 June 1945; War Agency Liquidation Unit, *People in Motion*, 181.

14. George Takei, *To the Stars: The Autobiography of George Takei, Star Trek's Mr. Sulu* (New York, 1994), 71; Spaulding, "Housing Problems of Minority Groups in Los Angeles," 224–25; *RS*, 2 April, 27 June 1946; War Agency Liquidation Unit, *People in Motion*, 181–82; American Friends Service Committee and The Presbyterian Church in U.S.A., "Evergreen Hostel," folder 2, box 53, WCC; WRA, "Semi-Annual Report," 1 January to 30 June 1945.

15. Sasaki's Daily Reports, 24 July, 11 and 22 September, 21 October 1946.

16. *NYT*, 19 December 1944; *Los Angeles Examiner*, 20 January 1945; *CE*, 4 October 1945; Coordinating Committee for Resettlement, "Minutes of the Third Meeting, August 22, 1945 at 7:30 pm, YMCA," box 75, JAF; Samuel Ishikawa, "Common Ground," 10 September 1945, ibid.

17. *Los Angeles Daily News*, 4 March 1947; *LAT*, 31 December 1944, 3 January, 4 May 1945, 4 March 1947; Sasaki's Daily Reports, 25 July, 2, 4, 7, and 9 August, 19 and 26 September 1946.

18. US Census, *Special Census of Los Angeles* (1946); Sasaki's Daily Reports, 24 and 29 July, 17–18 September 1946; Smith, *Great Black Way*, 152.

19. "Pilgrim House: Los Angeles' Plymouth Rock in a Drifting Community," folder "Pilgrim House," box 258, JRH; Ishikawa, "Common Ground"; Sasaki's Daily Reports, 16 September 1946; Welfare Council of Metropolitan Los Angeles, "Report on Pilgrim House" (ca. 1947), box 76, JAF.

20. "Race War That Flopped," 3–9 (emphasis in original).

21. Sasaki's Daily Reports, 16 and 18 September 1946; Interracial Planning for Community Organization, "Racial Problems in Housing," Bulletin No. 2, National Urban League, Fall 1944, 10, folder "Race Problems," box 258, JRH.

22. *CE*, 21 October 1943, 3 August 1944, 2 August 1945; "Don't Fence Me In," folder "BASS—City Council Campaign, 1945," additions box 1, CAB.

23. *CE*, 18 January, 1 February, 22 March 1945.

24. *CE*, 12 and 26 April, 3 May 1945; *LAT*, 3 May 1945.

25. *CE*, 4 January, 2 August 1945; Bass, *Forty Years*, 107; *Los Angeles Tribune*, 14 September 1946.

26. *Los Angeles Tribune*, 27 July 1946.

27. Myrdal, *An American Dilemma*; Carey McWilliams, *Prejudice, Japanese-Americans: Symbol of Racial Intolerance* (Boston, 1944). 174–75.

28. Los Angeles Coordinating Committee for Resettlement, "Minutes of Last Meeting," 22 September 1945, folder 1, carton 3, PCCAPFP.

29. David Unoura, personal interview, 31 December 2003, Culver City, CA; Dan Genung, *A Street Called Love: The Story of All People's Christian Church and Center, Los Angeles, California* (Pasadena, 2000), 73–83, 103–6; Sasaki's Daily Reports, 22 August 1946.

30. Sasaki's Daily Reports, 22 and 24 August, 12–13 September, 19 November 1946; Art Takemoto, interviewed by James Gatewood, 19 May 1998, *REgenerations Oral History Project: Rebuilding Japanese American Families,*

Communities, and Civil Rights in the Resettlement Era, vol. 2 (Los Angeles, 2000), 411.

31. "Race War That Flopped," 7; Sasaki's Daily Reports, 9 and 23 August, 15 September, 7 November 1946; *Los Angeles Tribune*, 16 March 1946; *LAT*, 5 January 1963.

32. Richard Drinnon, *Keeper of Concentration Camps: Dillon S. Myer and American Racism* (Berkeley, 1987), 59; The Committee on Resettlement of Japanese Americans, "Planning Resettlement of Japanese Americans," July 1943, folder 2, box 53, WCC.

33. Eddie Shimano, "Democracy Begins at Home—II: Blueprint For a Slum," *Common Ground*, Summer 1943, 78; Larry Tajiri, "Farewell to Little Tokyo," *Common Ground*, Winter 1944, 92; Joe Grant Masaoka, "Working Principles for Today: Intergroup Pattens," California Conference of Social Work, Sacramento, 7–11 April 1946, folder 40, carton 20, CMW.

34. D. S. Myer to Board of Supervisors, 29 May 1946, box 74, JAF. On the relationship between Myer's administration of the WRA and Bureau of Indian Affairs, see Drinnon, *Keeper of Concentration Camps*.

35. Sasaki's Daily Reports, 11–12 September 1946.

36. Pilgrim House to Friend, 23 January 1948, box 76, JAF; Unsigned to S. B. Cortelyou, 25 April 1949, ibid.; Harold M. Kingsley to Paul W. Axe, 6 May 1949, ibid.; Mrs. Thomas G. Wight to Friend, 7 October 1950, ibid.; *LAT*, 2 February 1950.

37. *CE*, 27 January, 1 March, 7 April, 3 May 1949; "Proposed Platform of the Nisei Progressives," 18 January 1949, folder 2, box 19, Civil Rights Congress Papers, Southern California Library for Social Studies Research, Los Angeles.

CHAPTER 8: TOWARD A MODEL MINORITY

1. William Petersen, "Success Story, Japanese-American Style," *The New York Times Magazine*, 9 Janurary 1966, 21.

2. *LAT*, 9 December 1945; Rev. Sumio Koga, " 'The Cross That Opened a Community': John 3: 16," in *Nanka Nikkei Voices: Resettlement Years, 1945–1955* (Japanese American Historical Society of Southern CA, 1998), 55–56; WRA, "Semi-Annual Report," 1 July to 31 December 1945.

3. Dorothy Swaine Thomas and Richard S. Nishimoto, *The Spoilage* (Berkeley, 1946), esp. v–xiii.

4. Allan W. Austin, *From Concentration Camps to Campus: Japanese American Students and World War II* (Urbana, IL, 2004), 9–61, 83–84; Hayashi, *Democratizing the Enemy*, 138–39.

5. Albert Edward Day, "God's Design for Living or Americanism and Christianity Begin at Home," Pasadena, CA, First Methodist Church, 7 November 1943, folder 2, box 53, WCC; Letter to Evacuees from Margaret S. Moritz for Friends of the American Way, 15 September 1944, ibid.; Friends of the American Way, "Some Evacuee Families Needing Our Help To Return to the Pasadena Area," undated, ibid.

6. Hayashi, *Democratizing the Enemy*, 104, 139–40; *NYT*, 17 February 1945; Masayo Umezawa Duus, *Unlikely Liberators: The Men of the 100th and 442nd* (Honolulu, 1987), 217–19.

7. Takaki, *Strangers From a Different Shore*, 397–403; Press Release of the American Veterans Committee, 9 October 1945, box 74, JAF; Gracia D. Booth, "Church Women Ask: How Can We Help Japanese American Evacuees?" New York City, Committee on Resettlement of Japanese Americans, November 1944, folder 2, box 53, WCC.

8. "Remarks by Mayor Fletcher Bowron at Testimonial Banquet for Japanese American Veterans," 3 November 1946, folder "Addresses—Remarks 1946," box 35, FB; War Agency Liquidation Unit, *People in Motion*, 27, 41–46; Mike Masaoka with Bill Hosokawa, *They Call Me Moses Masaoka: An American Saga* (New York, 1987), 201–16.

9. Reagan quoted in Masaoka, *They Call Me Moses*, 178; Dillon S. Myer, "Japanese American Relocation: Final Chapter," *Common Ground*, Autumn 1945, 66; Dillon S. Myer, *Uprooted Americans: The Japanese Americans and the War Relocation Authority During World War II* (Tusson, 1971), 286–98, 342–43; Dillon S. Myer to Carey McWilliams, 7 March 1946, folder 34, carton 20, CMW; D. S. Myer to Board of Supervisors, 29 May 1946, box 74, JAF; Los Angeles County Committee for Interracial Progress, Minutes of the Twenty-Fifth Monthly Committee Meeting, 8 April 1946, folder 2, carton 3, PCCAPFP.

10. Americanism Educational League, "Do You Want to Take This Chance On the Pacific Coast By Having the Japanese Returned to This Area?" folder 12, box 53, WCC (emphasis in original).

11. *Los Angeles Tribune*, 24 August, 14, September 1946; Hisaye Yamamoto, "A Fire in Fontana," *Rafu Shimpo Magazine*, 21 December 1985, 8; Sasaki's Daily Reports, 1 August, 21 and 23 September, 12 November 1946.

12. Duus, *Unlikely Liberators*, 218; Takaki, *Strangers From a Different Shore*, 397–403; Alan Brinkley, *The Unfinished Nation*, vol. 2, *From 1865*, 2nd ed. (New York, 1997), 755, 772; Hosokawa, *Nisei*, 414–15; Ikuko Amatatsu Watanabe, interviewed by Arthur A. Hansen (California State University, Fullerton Oral History Program, 24 July 1974), http://content.cdlib.org:8088/xtf/view?docId =ft8x0nb520&query= <last viewed 26 October 2006>; *LAT*, 11 January 1945; *Los Angeles Daily News*, 11 January 1945; Harley M. Oka to William F. Schneider, 18 April 1945, box 74, JAF; *PC*, 15 May 1953.

13. "Case of Discrimination as reported by Miss Dorothy Takechi, YMCA," 25 September 1945, box 74, JAF; Hiro Nakamura to Citizens, 16 May 1945, ibid.

14. Coordinating Committee for Resettlement, "Minutes of the Third Meeting"; WRA, "Semi-Annual Report," 1 January to 30 June and 1 July to 31 December 1945; War Agency Liquidation Unit, *People in Motion*, 29, 90–91; Sasaki's Daily Reports, 15 and 17 October 1946.

15. Bloom and Riemer, *Removal and Return*, 124–204.

16. War Agency Liquidation Unit, *People in Motion*, 61–67, 89, 121–23; Bloom and Riemer, *Removal and Return*, 101–13; Shuji Fujii to Carey McWilliams, 7 March 1946, folder 34, carton 20, CMW; Yoneda, *Ganbatte*, 169–75; Sasaki's Daily Reports, 9 November 1946.

17. Tanaka, personal interview; Togo Tanaka, interviewed by James Gatewood, 13 December 1997, *REgenerations Oral History Project*, vol. 2, 419–64; *Who's Going to Pay for These Donuts Anyway?* directed by Janice Tanaka (1992).

18. Quoted in McWilliams, *Prejudice*, 272–73; Pearl S. Buck, "Equality," in *What America Means to Me* (New York, 1942), 37.

19. McWilliams, *Prejudice*, 272–73; *Town Hall* 5: 44 (3 November 1943).

20. John W. Dower, *Embracing Defeat: Japan in the Wake of World War II* (New York, 1999), 219–20; Hayashi, *Democratizing the Enemy*, 204–6. I also thank Nisei scholar Iwao Ishino for sharing his personal recollections of working with Leighton and fellow Nisei researchers.

21. Klein, *Cold War Orientalism*, 1–18.

22. *LAT*, 28 October 1951; Erie, *Globalizing L.A.*, 81; *RS*, 20 December 1956; Masaoka, *They Call Me Moses*, 272–80.

23. Dower, *Embracing Defeat*, 23–27, 69–81.

24. *Sayonara*, directed by Joshua Logan (1957); James A. Michener, *Sayonara* (New York, 1954); *LAT*, 26 December 1957.

25. Bill Ong Hing, *Making and Remaking Asian America Through Immigration Policy, 1850–1990* (Stanford, 1993), 54–56; Dulles and US ambassador quoted in Yukiko Koshiro, *Trans-Pacific Racisms and the U.S. Occupation of Japan* (New York, 1999), 35–41, 147; Judd quoted in Izumi Hirobe, *Japanese Pride, American Prejudice: Modifying the Exclusion Clause of the 1924 Immigration Act* (Stanford, 2001), 240; McCarran quoted in Gary Gerstle, *American Crucible: Race and Nation in the Twentieth Century* (Princeton, 2001), 260–63; Los Angeles Committee for the Protection of the Foreign Born, "For a People's Lobby to Fight the Walter-McCarran Law!" 19 March 1955, folder 68, box 9, Robert W. Kenny Papers, Southern California Library for Social Studies and Research, Los Angeles.

26. *PC*, 7 September 1956, 30 August 1957; Hosokawa, *JACL in Quest of Justice*, 293–99.

CHAPTER 9: BLACK CONTAINMENT

1. Roy Wilkins to Thomas L. Griffith, Jr., 19 May 1947, roll 7, part 18, NAACP; "Resolution on Communism adopted at the 41st Annual Convention of the National Association for the Advancement of Colored People," Boston, 23 June 1950, ibid.; "Report of Election of Officers—1946," folder "O.A.—Reports—Branch, Los Angeles, 1946–57," carton 26, NAACPW; Sides, *L.A. City Limits*, 146–47; Von Eschen, *Race Against Empire*, 96–166.

2. Robert Brenner, "The Economics of Global Turbulence," *New Left Review* 229 (May/June 1998): 39–63; Lipsitz, *Rainbow at Midnight*, 99; Kidner and Neff, *Economic Survey of the Los Angeles Area*, 106, 150; Randolph Van Nostrand, "The Industrial Outlook," Presentation to Conference on Utilization of Minority Group Workers, 20 April 1945, folder 9, carton 20, CMW; "General Outline for Presentation of CIO and UAW Position in Testimony Before Murray Comm."; California CIO Council Research Department, *The First Stage of the Depression is Here: Part III—The Employment Outlook of CIO Unions in Cali-*

fornia (28 May 1947), box 3, ibid.; Kasun, *Social Aspects of Business Cycles in the Los Angeles Area*, 23–24.

3. *CE*, 16 August 1945; Sanford Goldner, "Problem of Minority Groups in Private and Public Employment," 26 August 1945, box 9, record group I, LACFL; Schiesel, "Airplanes to Aerospace," 136–42; Scott A. Greer, *Last Man In: Racial Access to Union Power* (Glencoe, IL, 1959), 29; US Bureau of the Census, *1950 Census of Population: Characteristics of the Population* (Washington, DC, 1952); Fair Employment Practices Committee (FEPC), "Speaking About the Right of Every Person To Earn A Living. . . . For an Ordinance to Abolish Job Discrimination in Los Angeles," folder 1, box 9, GSM.

4. US Bureau of the Census, *Special Census of Los Angeles, California, September 26, 1953*, series P-28, no. 603 (Washington, DC, 11 March 1954); US Census, *1950 Census: Characteristics of the Population*; FEPC, "For an Ordinance to Abolish Job Discrimination"; Smith, "Black Employment in the Los Angeles Area," 64; California CIO, *First Stage of Depression*; "Questionnaire: Hiring and Upgrading of Minority Groups in Industry Organized by the CIO" with response from Ed Pace, box 9, record group I, LACFL; Los Angeles Committee for Equal Employment Opportunity, "Remove the Barriers: The CASE for fair employment practices legislation . . . in the city of Los Angeles . . . in the county of Los Angeles," folder 16, box 1, MM; Smith, "Black Employment in the Los Angeles Area," 51. Between 1950 and 1960, Japanese Americans comprised a little less than two-thirds of "other nonwhites" in the Los Angeles area, and other Asians, especially Chinese and Filipinos, comprised most of the rest of the category. While American Indians are also factored into the "other nonwhite" category, their numbers were small in 1950. The sharp rise of the American Indian population of the Los Angeles area to over 8,000 by 1960 means that there may be small discrepancies between the "other nonwhite" figures and the actual statistics for Asian Americans. Mexican Americans are not included in "other nonwhite" because the census categorized them as white in both 1950 and 1960.

5. US Census, *1950 Census: Characteristics of the Population*; US Bureau of the Census, *1960 Census of Populations: Characteristics of the Population* (Washington, DC, 1963); Los Angeles Community Relations Conference, "Employment Discrimination in Southern California," 25 January 1960, folder 9, box 6, MM.

6. Zieger, *The CIO*, 120, 212, 246–90; Lichtenstein, *Labor's War*, 26–43, 157–202; Nelson Lichtenstein, "From Corporatism to Collective Bargaining: Organized Labor and the Eclipse of Social Democracy in the Postwar Era," in *The Rise and Fall of the New Deal Order, 1930–1980*, ed. Steve Fraser and Gary Gerstle (Princeton, 1989), 122–35; Alan Brinkley, *The End of Reform: New Deal Liberalism in Recession and War* (New York, 1995), 201–26; Steve Rosswurm, "Introduction," in *The CIO's Left-Led Unions*, ed. Steve Rosswurm (New Brunswick, NJ, 1992), 1–17; Lipsitz, *Rainbow at Midnight*, 99–179; Walter LaFeber, *The American Age: U.S. Foreign Policy at Home and Abroad, 1750 to the Present*, 2nd ed. (New York, 1994), 476–79; Patrick Renshaw, *American Labor and Consensus Capitalism, 1935–1990* (Jackson, MI, 1991), 115.

7. Gene Tipton, "The Labor Movement in the Los Angeles Area During the Nineteen-Forties" (PhD diss., University of California, Los Angeles, 1953), 342–52;

Los Angeles CIO Council, Press Release, 2 March 1948, record group I, box 4, LACFL; Los Angeles CIO Council, "CIO Minutes Digest," 18 March 1949, ibid.; "Minutes of Meeting of Greater Los Angeles CIO Council," 3 May 1949, ibid.; "Collective Bargaining Memo: Truman's Speech and Your Third Round Wage Negotiations," 31 March 1948, box 3, ibid.; "Rump Group Crawls Into Politicians' Vest Pocket," *Los Angeles CIO Council Report* 1: 2 (17 May 1948), folder 13, box 3, Philip Marshall Connelly Collection of Los Angeles CIO Industrial Union Council Records, 1942–1957 (Collection 2015), Department of Special Collections, Charles E. Young Research Library, University of California, Los Angeles; *CE*, 24 March 1949; Healey and Isserman, *California Red*, 96–171.

8. Walter E. Williams interview, 10 November 1988 and 4 October 1990, 84–85, International Longshoremen's and Warehousemen's Union, Local 13 Oral History Project, Urban Archives, California State University, Northridge; Kenneth C. Beight and Philip M. Connelly, "Call," 12 September 1945, box 9, record group I, LACFL; Philip M. Connelly to All Local Unions and Regional or District Offices, 11 February 1948, ibid.; William S. Lawrence et al. to Fletcher Bowron, 31 August 1948, ibid.; Los Angeles CIO Council, "Resolution on the Slaying of Augustino Salcido and Police Terrorism Against Mexican-Americans," 19 March 1948, ibid.; Los Angeles CIO Council, Resolution on National Association for the Advancement of Colored People, 18 April 1947, box 25, ibid.; "Petition for a Federal Anti-Lynching Law," May 1947, ibid.; Los Angeles CIO Council, Resolution, 21 May 1948, box 4, ibid.; Los Angeles CIO Council, "Resolution Submitted by I.L.W.U. Local #13 Delegation," 18 May 1945, ibid.; Renshaw, *American Labor and Consensus Capitalism*, 157–59.

9. Greer, *Last Man In*, 142–49.

10. *CE*, 15 March 1945, 11 April, 9, 23, and 30 May, 13 June 1946, 15 and 29 October 1953; Anderson, "The Development of Leadership and Organization," 211–14; *NYT*, 15 June 1948, 9 April 1952; *Los Angeles Tribune*, 24 August 1946.

11. *CE*, 4 October 1945; Charlotta Bass, "What Socialism Means to Me," ca. late 1950s, folder "Bass, C. A.—Speeches, 1950s (Excluding 1952 Progressive Campaign)," additions box 1, CAB; Revels [Cayton] to Matt Crawford, 3 January 1946, box 9, record group I, LACFL; Hobbs, *Cayton Legacy*, 161–74; *Los Angeles Tribune*, 6 April 1946; Charlotta Bass, "N.A.A.C.P." (ca. 1955), folder "BASS, C. A.—Articles and Speeches, undated," additions box 1, CAB; Marion H. Jackson to Charlotta Bass, 14 August 1956, folder "BASS, C. A.—Letters To, 1950s," ibid.

12. *CE*, 26 April 1951; Horne, *Fire This Time*, 7; Flamming, *Bound for Freedom*, 380–81.

13. Miller, transcript of interview, 7; *CE*, 26 April 1951; Loren Miller to To Whom It May Concern, 29 July 1952, box 76, JAF; Unaddressed letter from S. Wendell Green, 12 August 1952, ibid.

14. Sides, *L.A. City Limits*, 146–47; Southern California Area Council, "Resolution, Communist Infiltration," folder "conferences, Southern California Area Conference—correspondence, Feb–April 1953," carton 34, NAACPW; Charlotta Bass, "N.A.A.C.P." ca. 1955, folder "BASS, C. A.—Articles and Speeches, undated," additions box 1, CAB.

15. Sides, *L.A. City Limits*, 141; Dale Gardner, untitled memorandum, 1 March 1952, box 76, JAF; *CE*, 9 December 1954; Thomas G. Neusom, "Annual Report of President," 18 December 1955, folder "O.A.—Reports—Branch, Los Angeles, 1946–57," carton 26, NAACPW; Tarea Hall Pittman, "Summary Report of Activity in Los Angeles Branch Membership Drive," ibid.; "Minutes of the Southern Area Conference NAACP meeting," 26 May 1956, folder "conferences, Southern California Area Conference—correspondence, 1956," carton 34, ibid.

16. Mary L. Dudziak, "Brown as a Cold War Case," *The Journal of American History* 91: 1 (June 2004): 41; *NYT*, 17 February 1947, 30 November 1948; Donald R. McCoy and Richard T. Ruetten, *Quest and Response: Minority Rights and the Truman Administration* (Lawrence, KS, 1973), 65, 134; *CE*, 30 December 1954.

17. Carol Anderson, "Bleached Souls and Red Negroes: The NAACP and Black Communists in the Early Cold War, 1948–1952," in *Window on Freedom: Race, Civil Rights, and Foreign Affairs, 1945–1988*, ed. Brenda Gayle Plummer (Chapel Hill, 2003), 106; *LAS*, 25 July 1957.

18. Hill, *Black Labor*, 373–81; *LAT*, 7–8 November 1946.

19. "United States Employment Service," box 8, record group I, LACFL; Arthur Kearns et al. to Raymond Krah, 18 July 1946, ibid.; Alvin E. Hewitt to Fay Hunter et al., 6 and 11 July 1946, ibid.; Philip M. Connelly et al. to Robert C. Goodwin, 28 May 1946, ibid.; Raymond Krah to Fay W. Hunter, 16 April 1946, ibid.; Raymond Krah to Arthur Kearns, 12 July 1946, ibid.; "Monthly Statistical Report, Industrial Relations Department of the Los Angeles Urban League," July–August 1948, box 24, ibid.; Los Angeles Committee for Equal Employment Opportunity, "Remove the Barriers"; Los Angeles Community Relations Conference, "Employment Discrimination in Southern California."

20. Gordon G. Hair to the Board of Supervisors, 12 March 1958, box 31, JAF; Howard V. Fulton to John Anson Ford, 8 June 1956, ibid.; Courtlandt S. Gross to the Honorable Board of Supervisors, 3 January 1958, ibid.; Randolph Van Nostrand, "Statement Before the Commission on Civil Rights," January 1960, ibid.

21. Los Angeles Committee for Equal Employment Opportunity, "Remove the Barriers"; Council for Equality in Employment, "Answer the Critics of Fair Employment Practices Ordinance for Los Angeles," folder 4, box 13, GSM (emphasis in original); Loren Miller and Gilbert C. Anaya to Friend, 2 July 1957, 9 January 1958, folder 16, box 1, MM.

22. *NYT*, 16 July 1967; Thomas W. Casstevens, *Politics, Housing and Race Relations: California's Rumford Act and Proposition 14* (Berkeley, 1967), 8–10; *LAT*, 24 September 1959, 7 January 1965; Dwight R. Zook, "Statement to the United States Commission on Civil Rights for the Los Angeles, California, Hearings," 25–26 January 1960, folder 9, box 6, MM.

23. *LAT*, 17 October, 15–16 November 1945.

24. "Appendix V—Human Relations: Report Submitted for Human Relations Study Group," box 72, JAF.

25. Los Angeles County Joint Committee for Interracial Progress, meeting minutes, 2 March 1944, box 72, JAF; Los Angeles County Committee for Interracial Progress, "Report of the Sub-Committee on Organization and Program," 17 April 1944, ibid.; Los Angeles County Board of Supervisors, "Minute Book No.

292, page 339," 11 January 1944, ibid.; Los Angeles County Committee on Human Relations, "Notice of Fifty-Fifth Monthly Meeting," 13 December 1948, ibid.; Los Angeles County Committee for Interracial Progress, meeting minutes, 8 January 1945, folder 2, carton 3, PCCAPFP.

26. "Project Number 3A, Alice Bordman interview of George Gleason," folder "Race Problems" 17, box 259, JRH; Lester Granger, "No Short-Cut to Democracy," *Common Ground*, Winter 1944, 15–16.

27. "Biographical Report—Beavers, George Allen Jr." folder 1, box 21, GSM; clippings from *Los Angeles Tribune*, 13 February 1957 and *LAS*, 7 March 1957, folder 5, ibid.; Norman Houston, "Big 'M'—or little 'm'—Man," transcript of speech to First A.M.E. Church, Oakland, CA, 9 July 1961, folder 6, ibid.

28. Fisher, *The Problem of Violence*, 18–19.

29. *LAT*, 24 January 1961.

30. Davis McEntire, *Race and Residence: Report to the Commission on Race and Housing* (Berkeley, 1960), 315–16; "Chronology of Events Relating to Public Housing in Los Angeles," 3 February 1953, folder "F. Marion Banks 2/2/53," box 50, FB; Thomas J. O'Dwyer et al. to Fletcher Bowron, 7 December 1951, folder "Housing Authority," box 49, ibid.; Nicola Giulii et al. to Council of the City of Los Angeles, 7 December 1951, ibid.; Housing Authority of the City of Los Angeles, "Summary of General Information of All Housing Projects," 13 June 1952, folder "Reports from Hous Authority," box 50, ibid.; Don Parson, " 'This Modern Marvel': Bunker Hill, Chavez Ravine, and the Politics of Modernism in Los Angeles," *Southern California Quarterly* 75: 3–4 (Fall/Winter 1993): 333–50.

31. Spaulding, "Housing Problems of Minority Groups in Los Angeles," 223–24; Committee Against Socialist Housing, "Don't Pay Somebody Else's Rent," folder "Election June 3, 1952," box 50, FB (emphasis in original); Letter from Geo. M. Eason, 31 January 1952, ibid.; Los Angeles Citizens Housing Council Conference on Housing, Summary Booklet, 24 January 1947, box 24, record group I, LACFL. See also Greg Mitchell, *Tricky Dick and the Pink Lady: Richard Nixon vs. Helen Gahagan Douglas, Sexual Politics and the Red Scare, 1950* (New York, 1998).

32. Daryl Michael Scott, *Contempt and Pity: Social Policy and the Image of the Damaged Black Psyche, 1880–1996* (Chapel Hill, 1997), 71–136; Walter C. Peterson to the Housing Authority of the City of Los Angeles, 26 December 1951, box 65, JAF; Los Angeles Committee for Home Front Unity, "This is Your Fault, Diseases Breed in Los Angeles Slums," folder "Housing—Los Angeles," box 246, JRH; Housing Department of the NAACP, "Housing Manual," [1959], 12–13, folder "L.A. Field Office, 250, Housing, undated, folder 1," carton 52, NAACPW.

33. Gwendolyn Wright, *Building the Dream: A Social History of Housing in America* (Cambridge, MA, 1983), 232–34; Frank G. Mittelbach, *The Changing Housing Inventory: 1950–1959* (Los Angeles: UCLA Real Estate Research Program, 1963), 5, 21–23; *LAT*, 6 July 1962.

34. Kenneth C. Burt, "Latino Empowerment in Los Angeles: Postwar Dreams and Cold War Fears, 1948–1952," *Labor's Heritage* 8: 1 (Summer 1996): 4–25; Katherine Underwood, "Process and Politics: Multiracial Electoral Coalition Building and Representation in Los Angeles' Ninth District, 1949–1962" (PhD diss., University of California, San Diego, 1992), 163.

35. Carey McWilliams, "Los Angeles: An Emerging Pattern," 8; George J. Sánchez, "'What's Good for Boyle Heights Is Good for the Jews': Creating Multiracialism on the Eastside during the 1950s," *American Quarterly* 56: 3 September 2004): 633–61; Eric Avila, *Popular Culture in the Age of White Flight: Fear and Fantasy in Suburban Los Angeles* (Berkeley, 2004), 145–84; *LAS*, 31 October 1957.

CHAPTER 10: THE FIGHT FOR HOUSING INTEGRATION

1. Carlton Jackson, *Hattie: The Life of Hattie McDaniel* (Lanham, MD, 1990), 91; *Pittsburgh Courier*, 15 December 1945; *LAT*, 7 December 1945.

2. *CE*, 27 May, 3 June 1954.

3. *PC*, 18 January 1957; *CE*, 6 May 1948; *LAT*, 24 January 1961.

4. Jackson, *Crabgrass Frontier*, 195–203; Miller, *Petitioners*, 331; McEntire, *Race and Residence*, 299–307; Arnold Hirsch, "Choosing Segregation: Federal Housing Policy Between Shelley and Brown," in *From Tenements to Taylor Homes*, 212–13; Brinkley, *End of Reform*, 259; Loren Miller, "Residential Segregation and Civil Rights," transcript of speech to Lawyers Guild Conference, Hollywood Athletic Club, Hollywood, CA, 12 May 1956, folder 1, box 30, ACLU.

5. Milton A. Senn, "Report on Efforts in the Los Angeles Area to Circumvent the United States Supreme Court Decisions on Restrictive Covenants," 31 December 1948, folder "Race Problems" 17, box 259, JRH.

6. *LAT*, 7 August 1952, 24 January 1961; Miller, *Petitioners*, 323–31; Ruchames, *Race, Jobs, & Politics*, 245–51; McEntire, *Race and Residence*, 239–50; Wm. C. Carr to Mr. Mont, 10 January 1960, folder 4, box 3, MM; Senn, "Report on Efforts in the Los Angeles Area to Circumvent the United States Supreme Court Decisions on Restrictive Covenants."

7. Kasun, *Social Aspects of Business Cycles in the Los Angeles Area*, 55–58; Mittelbach, *Changing Housing Inventory*, 6–9; Leo Grebler, *Metropolitan Contrasts* (Los Angeles, 1963), 9; Nadeau, *Los Angeles*, 276–78; County of Los Angeles Commission on Human Relations, "Minority Groups in Los Angeles County," 19 January 1959, Southern Regional Library Facility (SRLF), University of California, Los Angeles; John A. Buggs, "A Report on the State of Human Relations in Los Angeles County," 14 October 1959, SRLF; Vorspan and Gartner, *History of the Jews of Los Angeles*, 276–77; McEntire, *Race and Residence*, 42–43, 368; Health and Welfare Department, Los Angeles Urban League, "Minority Housing in Metropolitan Los Angeles," July 1959, folder 10, box 6, MM.

8. Jackson, *Crabgrass Frontier*, 233; Nadeau, *Los Angeles*, 276; Edward C. Maddox and Loren Miller to the Board of Supervisors, 11 October 1950, box 72, JAF; Davis, *City of Quartz*, 165–69. See also Gary Miller, *Cities by Contract: The Politics of Municipal Incorporation* (Cambridge, MA, 1981).

9. H. Marshall Goodwin, Jr., "Right-of-way Controversies in Recent California Highway-Freeway Construction," *Southern California Quarterly* 56: 1 (Spring 1974): 26, 61–105; Lizabeth Cohen, *Consumers' Republic: The Politics of Mass Consumption in Postwar America* (New York, 2004), 127, 202; US Census, *1950 Census Tract Statistics, Los Angeles and Adjacent Area*; Grebler,

Metropolitan Contrasts, 6; Eric Avila, *Popular Culture in the Age of White Flight*, 185–223; *PC*, 5 December 1958; *CE*, 27 May 1954.

10. US Census, *1950 Census: Characteristics of the Population*; US Census, *1960 Census: Characteristics of the Population*; US Bureau of the Census, *1960 Census of Populations, Report PC(2)-IC: Nonwhite Population By Race* (Washington, DC, 1963); Midori Nishi, "Changing Occupance of the Japanese in Los Angeles County" (PhD diss., University of Washington, 1955), 58; US Bureau of the Census, *1940 Census of Population: The Labor Force* (Washington, DC, 1943); Allen J. Scott, *Technopolis: High-Technology Industry and Regional Development in Southern California* (Berkeley, 1993), 64–69.

11. US Census, *1950 Census: Characteristics of the Population*; US Census, *1960 Census: Characteristics of the Population*; US Census, *1960 Census: Nonwhite Population By Race*; Schiesel, "Airplanes to Aerospace," 138–43; Midori Nishi and Young Il Kim, "Recent Japanese Settlement Changes in the Los Angeles Area," *Yearbook of the Association of Pacific Coast Geographers* 26 (1964): 34–35; Jere Takahashi, *Nisei/Sansei: Shifting Japanese American Identities and Politics* (Philadelphia, 1997), 125; Los Angeles County Commission on Human Relations, *Human Relations Research-Gram: Population by Major Ethnic Groupings, Los Angeles County, 1950, 1960, 1970* (Los Angeles, 1972).

12. *PC*, 18 May 1956; Frank F. Chuman, "President's Commission on Civil Rights Subcommittee on Housing," 26 January 1959, folder 10, box 6, MM; Nishi and Kim, "Recent Japanese Settlement Changes in the Los Angeles Area," 25–33.

13. *RS*, 4 May 1948; Vose, *Caucasians Only*, 194–95; Sasaki's Daily Reports, 15 October 1946; "How Eichler Sells Open Occupancy with No Fuss," *Church and Race*, September 1964, 9–13; Milton G. Gordon, "What are the Obligations of Government to Resolve Such Conflicts as Exist in This Area (Property Rights and Civil Rights)," 22 November 1963, folder 16, box 2, MM.

14. Evelyn R. Matthews to American Civil Liberties Union, 18 September 1947, folder 1, box 32, ACLU; James Hasking with Kathleen Benson, *Nat King Cole* (New York, 1984), 77–82; Senn, "Report on Efforts in the Los Angeles Area to Circumvent the United States Supreme Court Decisions on Restrictive Covenants."

15. "Community Activity by Normandie Avenue Protective Association," box 76, JAF; "Report on Meeting of Normandie Avenue Protective Association Held at Southwest Arena," 17 March 1950, ibid.; Los Angeles County Committee on Human Relations, "Semi-Annual Summary, July 1, 1951 to December 31, 1951," box 72, ibid.; Dale Gardner to Theresa Pasternak, 22 March 1951, ibid.; Dale Gardner to Arthur Miley, 10 January 1952, ibid.; US Census, *1950 Census Tract Statistics, Los Angeles and Adjacent Area*; US Bureau of the Census, *1960 Census Tracts, Los Angeles–Long Beach, California* (Washington, DC, 1962); Rev. Donald D. Rowland, "Statement," folder 10, box 3, MM.

16. *LAT*, 20–21 August, 7 September, 1 December 1955, 16 January 1957; *PC*, 18 and 25 January, 1 February 1957; "City of Anaheim, Orange County," folder 10, box 3, MM.

17. Senn, "Report on Efforts in the Los Angeles Area to Circumvent the United States Supreme Court Decisions on Restrictive Covenants"; John J. Mance to Frank H. Barnes, 12 January 1950 [actual year is 1960], folder 10, box 3, MM; *LAT*, 27 January 1960.

18. *LAT*, 5 June 1961.

19. War Agency Liquidation Unit, *People in Motion*, 179–80; Sasaki's Daily Reports, 12 September, 14, 21, and 29 October 1946; Kazuo K. Inouye, interviewed by Leslie Ito, 13 December 1997, *REgenerations Oral History Project*, vol. 2, 173–88.

20. Inouye, *REgenerations*, 190–97.

21. Senn, "Report on Efforts in the Los Angeles Area to Circumvent the United States Supreme Court Decisions on Restrictive Covenants"; Public Affairs Committee, Inc., *Discrimination in Housing in These 10 Cities* (New York, March 1951), 7–9, folder "Race Problems," box 258, JRH; clipping, "Water floods home sold to Negroes," folder 1, box 32, ACLU; A. A. Heist to John W. Heek, 11 July 1950, ibid.; A. A. Heist to A. J. Hunter, 11 July 1950, ibid.; Los Angeles County Committee on Human Relations, "Memorandum to Supervisor Raymond V. Darby on Community tensions in Leimert Park," 30 June 1950, box 72, JAF; Los Angeles County Committee on Human Relations, "Semi-Annual Summary, July 1, 1951 to December 31, 1951."

22. *LAT*, 3 July 1962; Committee of Racial Equality, "Report on Survey Testing of Rental Units," folder 10, box 3, MM; US Census, *1950 Census Tract Statistics, Los Angeles and Adjacent Area*; US Census, *1960 Census Tracts, Los Angeles–Long Beach*; Evelyn Yoshimura, "Sansei L.A.," in *Nanka Nikkei Voices*, vol. II, *Turning Points* (Japanese American Historical Society of Southern California, 2002), 104–5.

23. Inouye, *REgenerations*, vol. 2, 197; Ryo Munekata, personal interview, 23 September 2002, Los Angeles; *PC*, 19 December 1958.

24. *LAT*, 4 July 1962; Yoshimura, "Sansei L.A.," 103; Roy Nakano, "Them Bad Cats, Part II," *Gidra*, June 1973, 1; Sheila Gardette, e-mail correspondence with author, 23 June 2005.

25. *PC*, 25 April, 14 November 1958; *LAT*, 19 April 1958; Roy Nakano, "Them Bad Cats: Past Images of Asian American Street Gangs," *Gidra*, January 1973; Yoshimura, "Sansei L.A.," 103.

26. Munekata, personal interview; *RS*, 26 February 1959, 25 and 30 March 1960; Inouye, *REgenerations*, vol. 2, 200.

27. *RS*, 11 and 14 February 1959.

28. *LAT*, 3 May 2000; *RS*, 12 May, 22 June, 7 July, 4 December 2000.

29. Rogers, *Mesa to Metropolis*, 19–20.

CHAPTER 11: FROM INTEGRATION TO MULTICULTURALISM

1. *LAT*, 24 and 29 January, 10 September 1961.

2. Christopher Taylor et al., "To Men of Good Will: A Statement of Major Grievances and Immediate Requirements of the Negro Community," 6 June 1963, folder 27, box 16, California Democratic Council Papers, Southern California Library for Social Studies and Research, Los Angeles.

3. Casstevens, *Politics, Housing and Race Relations*, 18–47.

4. Ibid., 48–84.

5. Chas. B. Shattuck, "Freedom Is Ours—Lest We Forget," 20 February 1964, folder 3, box 6, MM (emphasis in original); *LAT*, 24 January, 10 September 1961, 4 July 1962, 2 February, 30 April 1964, 21 July 1967; Leonard D. Cain, Jr., "Absolute Discretion? Selected Documents on 'Property Rights' and 'Equal Protection of the Laws,'" Sacramento Committee for Fair Housing Research Bulletin No. 7, April 1964, folder 16, box 2, MM; *LAS*, 20 February, 9 April 1964; The Statewide Committee for Home Protection, "Speakers Resource Manual in Support of The Initiative Constitutional Amendment, Re: Sales and Rentals of Real Property," folder 3, box 6, MM; "Flashes," Weekly bulletin of Committee for Home Protection, 31 July 1964, ibid. (emphasis in original); Nicolaides, *My Blue Heaven*, 308–15.

6. *The Apartment Journal* 46 (August 1964), 18–19, folder 1, box 5, MM; *PC*, 2 November 1956.

7. Casstevens, *Politics, Housing and Race Relations*, 48–80; Raymond E. Wolfinger and Fred I. Greenstein, "The Repeal of Fair Housing in California: An Analysis of Referendum Voting," *The American Political Science Review* 62: 3 (September 1968): 753–69; Ethan Rarick, *California Rising: The Life and Times of Pat Brown* (Berkeley, 2005), 288; Lisa McGirr, *Suburban Warriors: The Origins of the New American Right* (Princeton, 2001); "Prop 14—The minority myth," *Los Angeles Newsletter*, 2 January 1965.

8. *LAT*, 4 July 1962; "Prop 14—The minority myth"; *RS*, 24 June, 7 July, 1 August, 26 and 29 September, 14 October 1964; "Vote No on 14," folder 19, box 5, MM; Wolfinger and Greenstein, "Repeal of Fair Housing in California," 759.

9. "'No on 14'—TV Spot Schedule," folder 10, box 5, MM; California Committee for Fair Practices, "A Manual for the 'Constitutional Amendment—No! Campaign," 5 February 1964, folder 8, box 4, ibid.; Californians for Fair Housing, "'Campaign Manual' So. Cal.," folder 20, ibid.; "Ideas for Fair Housing Speaking," folder 12, ibid.; "Speakers Handbook for Opposition to the Segregation Amendment," ibid.; clipping from "BCA Residential Builders Council," *Building Contractor, BCA Magazine*, April 1964, folder 17, box 3, ibid.; John Lewis with Michael D'Orso, *Walking with the Wind: A Memoir of the Movement* (New York, 1998), 275–76; *LAS*, 16 January, 12 November 1964; California Committee for Fair Practices, "Some Notes on How," 13 December 1963, folder 18, box 3, MM.

10. "Remarks of the Reverend Martin Luther King at NAACP Sponsored Mass Rally for Civil Rights," 10 July 1960, Shrine Auditorium, Los Angeles, reel 17, part 21, NAACP; *LAT*, 24 June 1963.

11. Taylor, *In Search of the Racial Frontier*, 286; "Black Ghetto," *NAACP Newsletter* (Los Angeles) 2:11 (July 1957), reel 2, part 25, NAACP; McEntire, *Race and Residence*, 83–86; US Census, *1950 Census Tract Statistics, Los Angeles and Adjacent Area*; US Census, *Special Census of Los Angeles* (1954); John Mark McQuiston, *Negro Residential Invasion in Los Angeles* (Los Angeles, 1969), 114.

12. McEntire, *Race and Residence*, 37–38, 120–38; *LAT*, 5 July 1962; Fair Employment Practice Commission, *Negroes and Mexican Americans in South and East Los Angeles: Changes Between 1960 and 1965 in Population, Employment, Income, and Family Status* (San Francisco, 1966), 12–21.

13. Dale Gardner to John A. Ford, March 17, 1953, box 72, JAF; Senn, "Report on Efforts in the Los Angeles Area to Circumvent the United States Supreme Court Decisions on Restrictive Covenants"; Los Angeles Urban League, "Minority Housing in Metropolitan Los Angeles."

14. *LAT*, 27 January 1960, 2 and 5 July 1962, 25 June 1963, 22 May 1964; Escobar, *Race, Police and the Making of a Political Identity*, 10–14; "Policemen, Chief Parker Sued for Half Million," *NAACP Newsletter* (Los Angeles) 2: 12 (August 1957), reel 2, part 25, NAACP; *CE*, 3 May 1962; "NAACP and the Muslims," reel 7, part 24, NAACP; Los Angeles County Commission on Human Relations, "Report and Recommendations of the Special Citizens' Law Enforcement Committee," 6 January 1964, SRLF; Taylor et al., "To Men of Good Will."

15. J. Gregory Payne and Scott Ratzan, *Tom Bradley: The Impossible Dream* (Toronto, 1987), 72–78; Celes King III, *Black Leadership in Los Angeles*, 370–401, 453–58, transcript of oral history conducted in 1985 by Bruce M. Tyler and 1987 by Robin D. G. Kelley, Collection 300/293, BLLA.

16. Norman O. Houston, "Yesterday, Today and Tomorrow," 1966, folder 6, box 21, GSM; *LAT*, 4–5 July 1965; Self, *American Babylon*, 187–89; "Memorandum of Understanding Between California State Fair Employment Practice Commission and Bank of America National Trust and Savings Association," 1 June 1964, folder 8, box 1, MM.

17. *LAT*, 2 July 1962, 25–26 June, 14, 23, and 26 July, 4 and 17 August 1963, 30 May, 12 and 19 June 1964, 12 March 1965; John Caughey with LaRee Caughey, *To Kill a Child's Spirit: The Tragedy of School Segregation in Los Angeles* (Itasca, IL, 1973), 2–25; Taylor et al., "To Men of Good Will"; Horne, *Fire This Time*, 123–24; *Fair Housing* (newsletter of the American Friends Service Committee) 10 (May 1963), folder 1, box 30, ACLU.

18. *LAS*, 19 August 1965; Payne and Ratzan, *Tom Bradley*, 73; Governor's Commission on the Los Angeles Riot, *A Report by the Governor's Commission on the Los Angeles Riot* (Los Angeles, 1965), 6A; Horne, *Fire This Time*, 339–54.

19. Francine Rabinovitz, *Minorities in Suburbs: The Los Angeles Experience* (Cambridge, MA, 1975), 8–30, 50–51.

20. Rogers, *Mesa to Metropolis*, 19–20; *RS*, 14 August 1965; Horne, *Fire This Time*, 60–63, 105, 293; *LAS*, 19 August 1965; Bruce Michael Tyler, "Black Radicalism in Southern California, 1950–1982" (PhD diss., University of California, Los Angeles, 1983), 207–310.

21. *The Integrator*, Winter 1967–1968; Jean Gregg, "Statement to the Governor's Commission on the Los Angeles Riots" with *Crenshaw Notes* 9 (October 1965) attached to testimony from 21 October 1965, Governor's Commission on the Los Angeles Riots, *Transcripts, Depositions, Consultants' Reports, and Selected Documents* (Los Angeles, 1965), microform edition; *Crenshaw Notes* 73 (January 1972), folder 10, box 22, MM; *LAT*, 2 November 1967.

22. Gregg, "Statement to the Governor's Commission," 2–4, 9–14; Gardette, correspondence with author; Richard T. Morris and Vincent Jeffries, *The White Reaction Study* (Los Angeles, 1967).

23. Raphael J. Sonnenshein, *Politics in Black and White: Race and Power in Los Angeles* (Princeton, 1993) 58–60; Payne and Ratzan, *Tom Bradley*, 49–52.

24. Sonnenshein, *Politics in Black and White*, 55–66; Payne and Ratzan, *Tom Bradley*, 31–98; James Q. Wilson, *Negro Politics: The Search for Leadership* (New York, 1980), 36–37.

25. Sonnenshein, *Politics in Black and White*, 55–66; Payne and Ratzan, *Tom Bradley*, 69, 197.

26. Mae M. Ngai, *Impossible Subjects: Illegal Aliens and the Making of Modern America* (Princeton, 2004), 227–64; Heather Parker, "Tom Bradley and the Politics of Race," in *African-American Mayors: Race, Politics, and the American City*, ed. David R. Colburn and Jeffrey S. Adler (Urbana, 2001), 153–77; *Crenshaw Notes* 73 (January 1972); Takei, *To the Stars*, 281–310; Los Angeles 2000 Committee, *LA 2000: A City for the Future* (Los Angeles, 1988), 51, 59.

27. David Monkawa, "The Westside Community: 'Getting it Together' Against Crime," *Gidra*, December 1973, 4.

28. Dwight Chuman and Dean Toji, "Fred Kawano Interview, Part 2," *Gidra*, February 1974, 6–8; John Saito, "Yellow Power," *The Integrator*, Summer 1968.

29. *LAT*, 13 February 2005; Yuri Kochiyama, *Passing It On: A Memoir* (Los Angeles, 2004), 39–77; Donna K. Nagata, *Legacy of Injustice: Exploring the Cross-Generational Impact of the Japanese American Internment* (New York, 1993), 98–99.

30. Nakano, "Them Bad Cats, Part II," 7; Sheri Miyashiro, "Yellow Brotherhood," *Gidra*, Twentieth Anniversary Issue, 122–23; Nick Nagatani, " 'Action Talks and Bullshit Walks': From the Founders of Yellow Brotherhood to the Present," in *Asian Americans: The Movement and the Moment*, ed. Steve Louie and Glenn Omatsu (Los Angeles, 2001), 148–55.

31. Amy Uyematsu, "To All Us Sansei Who Wanted To Be Westside," *30 Miles From J-Town* (Brownsville, OR, 1992), 3; Amy Uyematsu, "The Emergence of Yellow Power in America," *Roots: An Asian American Reader*, ed. Amy Tachiki et al. (Los Angeles, 1971), 9–13; "Storefront: Cooperation Over Competition," *Gidra*, January 1972, 3; Bruce Iwasaki, "Dissolving: The Storefront. It's A Long Story," *Gidra*, April 1973, 7, 18–19.

32. *LAT*, 12 November 1967, 30 September 1974.

CONCLUSION

1. See US Bureau of the Census, table 1a, http://www.census.gov/ipc/www/usinterimproj/ <last viewed 20 October 2006>.

2. McWilliams, Speech to the Annual Meeting of the California Library Association.

3. Los Angeles Urban League and United Way of Los Angeles, *The State of Black Los Angeles* (Los Angeles, 2005), 25–42; quoted in Erin Aubry Kaplan, "Cloud Over the Promised Land," *LA Weekly*, 22–28 July 2005.

4. McWilliams, Speech to the Annual Meeting of the California Library Association.

5. Edward W. Soja and Allen J. Scott, "Introduction to Los Angeles: City and Region," in *The City: Los Angeles and Urban Theory at the End of the Twentieth Century*, ed. Scott and Soja (Berkeley, 1996), 17.

6. Sánchez, " 'What's Good for Boyle Heights Is Good for the Jews,' " 633–61.

7. See Bennett Harrison, *Lean and Mean: The Changing Landscape of Corporate Power in the Age of Flexibility* (New York, 1994).

8. Paul Ong et al., *Beyond Asian American Poverty: Community Economic Development Policies and Strategies* (Los Angeles, 1993), 13–56.

9. Erin J. Aubry, "Lost Soul," *LA Weekly*, 4–10 December 1998; *LAT*, 3 and 24 May 2006.

10. Aubry, "Lost Soul"; *LAT*, 26 April 2006.

11. *NYT*, 8 May 2000; Sowell quoted in *RS*, 22 June 2000; Sanders quoted in *RS*, 12 May 2000; Nakamoto quoted in Erin Aubry, "Bowl Over," *LA Weekly*, 5–11 May 2000; Feuer quoted in *RS*, 4 December 2000.

12. On "polyculturalism," see Vijay Prashad, *Everybody Was Kung Fu Fighting: Afro-Asian Connections and the Myth of Cultural Purity* (Boston, 2001).

Acknowledgments

The great folksinger Phil Ochs once said that the world began in Eden and ended in Los Angeles. While this book engages the history of that dying world, it is more a product of the new one rising. The University of California at Los Angeles was an especially stimulating center of activity in the 1990s. I will always reserve a special place in my heart for Eric Monkkonen. As my dissertation chair, he helped me wrestle with an endless series of questions, problems, and dilemmas. Every student should be blessed with a mentor so wise, patient, flexible, and supportive. Yuji Ichioka developed the language, archives, and institutions that made it possible for scholars to conceive of Japanese American history as a field of research. I was especially fortunate to receive his personal guidance from my first day of grad school. As scholars and friends, Eric and Yuji are irreplaceable figures who are deeply missed.

I could not have made it through UCLA without the constant support of staff, faculty, and students from the Asian American Studies Center and the History Department, especially Robert Brenner, Robert Hill, Don Nakanishi, and Kyeyoung Park. I was among the last group to receive race-based affirmative action fellowships from the Graduate Division at UCLA. Funding for graduate study and research also came from the Institute of American Cultures, the George and Sakaye Aratani Graduate Fellowship, and the Civil Liberties Public Education Fund.

For the past seven years, colleagues from the University of Michigan's Asian/Pacific Islander American Studies Program, Department of History, and Program in American Culture have enriched my scholarly life in countless ways. I thank the following persons, who commented on this project through review committees, manuscript workshops, and informal discussions: Charlie Bright, John Carson, Matthew Countryman, Greg Dowd, Geoff Eley, Julie Ellison, Kevin Gaines, Kristen Haas, Howard Kimeldorf, Matt Lassiter, Maria Montoya, Rudolf Mrázek, Nadine Naber, Jim Reische, Maris Vinovskis, Stephen Ward, and Magdalena Zaborowska. Fred Cooper, Mary Kelley, Lester Monts, Sonya Rose, Richard Cándida Smith, Amy Stillman, and Alan Wald ensured a supportive institutional environment, while Phil Deloria extended himself far beyond the call of duty. Financial support was provided by the William T. Ludolph, Jr. Junior Faculty Development Award, the Humanities Block Fund Initiative, and the Office of the Vice President for Research.

I was blessed to find a home for this book at Princeton University Press. Brigitta van Rheinberg believed in this project from the outset and saw it to completion. Julian Zelizer first drew me to the Politics and Society in Twentieth-Century America series. As editor, Gary Gerstle lent his critical eye to three distinct drafts, reinforcing their strongest aspects and identifying places needing improvement. I also thank series editors William Chafe and Linda Gordon, Will Hively, Dimitri Karetnikov, Brigitte Pelner, Clara Platter, Heath Renfroe, and Lys Ann Weiss.

As I have ventured to cross disciplinary boundaries, I have been graced by connections with a rich and diverse intellectual community. Special appreciation for comments on drafts, expert assistance, and invitations to speak about my work is due Eiichiro Azuma, Beth Bates, Sundiata Cha-Jua, Robert Devens, Sheila Gardette, Tom Guglielmo, Stacey Hirose, Evelyn Hu-DeHart, Ben Kobashigawa, Ted Koditschek, Lon Kurashige, Clarence Lang, Lawrence Levine, George Lipsitz, Minkah Makalani, Joanne Meyerowitz, Natalia Molina, Helen Neville, Brian Niiya, Kent Ono, Merry Ovnick, Vijay Prashad, Laura Pulido, Greg Robinson, David Roediger, George Sánchez, Robert Self, Paul Spickard, Steve Stowe, Thomas Sugrue, Masao Suzuki, Dan Widener, Anne Woo-Sam, David Yoo, and Ji-Yeon Yuh. Particular thanks to Mae Ngai for reviewing a rough and unwieldy draft. Phil Ethington generously customized four census maps, and Karl Longstreth and Malgorzata Krawczyk of the University of Michigan's Map Library helped me design a fifth. Ted Chen, Chiaki Inutake, Sharon Lee, Steve Moon, Ellen Scott, Betty Song, Soh Suzuki, and Kristina Vassil provided invaluable help with research and translation. While the dedicated staff at all the archives cited in the endnotes facilitated my research, Robert Marshall especially helped me identify primary sources in CSU Northridge's Urban Archives.

Portions of the introduction and chapter 7 appeared as "The Many Facets of Brown: Integration in a Multiracial Society," *Journal of American History*, 91: 1 (June 2004): 56–68. Copyright © Organization of American Historians. All rights reserved. Reprinted with permission.

My family made visits to Los Angeles affordable and enjoyable. Milnes and Noriko Kurashige have contributed to this book in multiple ways. Their parental love and support have nourished me through the roller coaster of life. But they also occupy their own place in the history of racial integration in the Westside. Heartfelt appreciation also goes out to all members of the Kurashige, Lawsin, and Ozaki clans.

Among many cherished friends and comrades in LA, I thank John English, Lisa Itagaki, Mary Kao, Sojin Kim, Jenny Kuida, Dean Matsubayashi, Glenn Omatsu, John Saito, David Stock, and Jacqueline Sowell for their assistance. Ryo Munekata, Thomas Robinson, Togo Tanaka, and David Unoura graciously agreed to interviews. While writing this book, I was led to a beloved community in Detroit by Grace Lee Boggs, who revolutionized my understanding of political theory and the meaning of life.

Emily Lawsin endured every step of the ten-plus years I worked on this book in LA and Detroit. Her patience, care, and love have enriched both my life and this book in ways that are impossible to quantify. My last and youngest acknowledgee is Tula Lawsin Kurashige, who provided a much-needed bundle of joy as I was scrambling to the finish line.

This is a partial list of those whose support and encouragement made this book possible. I am truly grateful to you all. Errors and omissions are mine.

Index

POLITICS AND SOCIETY IN TWENTIETH-CENTURY AMERICA